U.S. ARMY
PSYOP

BOOK 2
IMPLEMENTING
PSYCHOLOGICAL
OPERATIONS

TACTICS, TECHNIQUES AND
PROCEDURES

FULL-SIZE 8.5"X11" EDITION

FM 3-05.301
(MCRP 3-40.6A)

Headquarters, Department of the Army

U.S. Army PSYOP Book 2 - Implementing Psychological Operations

Tactics, Techniques and Procedures - Full-Size 8.5"x11" Edition - FM 3-05.301 (MCRP 3-40.6A)

U.S. Army

This edition first published 2019 by Carlile Military Library. "Carlile Military Library" and its associated logos and devices are trademarks. Carlile Military Library is an imprint of Carlile Media. The appearance of U.S. Department of Defense (DoD) visual information does not imply or constitute DoD endorsement.

New material copyright © 2019 Carlile Media. **All rights reserved.**

Published in the United States of America.

ISBN-13: 978-1-949117-09-7
ISBN-10: 194911709X

CARLILE
MILITARY LIBRARY

WWW.CARLILE.MEDIA

PUBLISHER'S NOTE

This is book 2 of 3 in the C.M.L. U.S. Army PSYOP series (ISBN: 978-1-949117-09-7, FM 3-05.301) which builds on the previous publication to provide PSYOP commanders and planners with the information required to implement PSYOP activities at the operational level.

• PSYOP Book 1: Psychological Operations Handbook (ISBN: 978-1-949117-08-0, FM 3-05.30) covers the fundamentals of military psychological operations in support of the national interest and is the Army's keystone publication for PSYOP principles and activities. It is written not exclusively for PSYOP personnel but for a wide military audience in order to provide a general understanding of and appreciation for PSYOP potential and value.

• PSYOP Book 3: Executing Psychological Operations - Tactical Psychological Operations Tactics, Techniques and Procedures (ISBN: 978-1-949117-10-3, FM 3-05.302) is written for an audience of PSYOP personnel, providing guidance on executing effective PSYOP activities at the tactical level.

*FM 3-05.301(FM 33-1-1)
MCRP 3-40.6A

Field Manual
No. 3-05.301

HEADQUATERS
DEPARTMENT OF THE ARMY
Washington, DC, 31 December 2003

Psychological Operations Tactics, Techniques, and Procedures

Contents

Page

Marine Corps distribution: PCN 14400013500

_____

*This publication supersedes FM 33-1-1, 5 May 1994.

i

Preface

Field Manual (FM) 3-05.301 presents tactics, techniques, and procedures for implementing United States (U.S.) Army Psychological Operations (PSYOP) doctrine in FM 3-05.30, *Psychological Operations*. FM 3-05.301 provides general guidance for commanders, planners, and PSYOP personnel who must plan and conduct effective PSYOP across the full spectrum of operations. This manual also provides guidance for PSYOP personnel to accomplish a broad range of missions successfully, using the latest organizational structure, terminology, and capabilities.

FM 3-05.301 is a guide, not a regulation. As such, the tactics, techniques, and procedures it presents should not limit creativity or imagination, provided that they adhere to Army doctrine, U.S. national policy, and the commander's intent. The targeted user of this manual is primarily the PSYOP community. Written to give PSYOP officers, noncommissioned officers (NCOs), enlisted Soldiers, and civilians standardized PSYOP doctrine, FM 3-05.301 is a comprehensive how-to manual, focusing on critical PSYOP tasks, duties, and responsibilities.

This manual describes procedures and provides templates for conducting the five PSYOP missions and seven PSYOP functions in a systematic, chronological fashion. Its organization generally follows the PSYOP development process, from planning through execution.

This manual contains numerous acronyms, abbreviations, and terms. Users should refer to the Glossary at the back of this manual for their meanings or definitions.

The proponent of this manual is the United States Army John F. Kennedy Special Warfare Center and School (USAJFKSWCS). Submit comments and recommended changes to Commander, USAJFKSWCS, ATTN: AOJK-DT-PO, Fort Bragg, NC 28310-5000.

Unless this publication states otherwise, masculine nouns and pronouns do not refer exclusively to men.

This manual does not implement any international standardization agreements (STANAGs).

Chapter 1

Overview

All military action is intertwined with psychological forces and effects.

Carl von Clausewitz
On War, 1827

PSYOP are planned operations that convey selected information and indicators to foreign target audiences (TAs) to influence their emotions, motives, objective reasoning, and ultimately, the behavior of foreign governments, organizations, groups, and individuals. The purpose of all PSYOP is to create in neutral, friendly, or hostile foreign groups the emotions, attitudes, or desired behavior that support the achievement of U.S. national objectives and the military mission. In doing so, PSYOP influence not only policy and decisions, but also the ability to govern, the ability to command, the will to fight, the will to obey, and the will to support. The combination of PSYOP products and actions create in the selected TAs a behavior that supports U.S. national policy objectives and the theater commander's intentions at the strategic, operational, and tactical levels.

The nature of PSYOP is varied and ever changing. PSYOP personnel must support a broad range of missions and force structures in environments ranging from austere to highly sophisticated. PSYOP are planned, coordinated, and executed before, during, and after conflicts, and must be integrated at all echelons to achieve its full force-multiplier potential.

A force multiplier of special operations forces (SOF), PSYOP forces are assigned to the United States Special Operations Command (USSOCOM), based on the 1986 Goldwater-Nichols Department of Defense (DOD) Reorganization Act. PSYOP units deploy to conduct missions in support of geographic combatant commanders and their subordinate joint task force (JTF) and component commanders. PSYOP forces may also support U.S. Ambassadors, allies, alliance and coalition partners, and other government agencies (OGAs).

FULL-SPECTRUM OPERATIONS

1-1. PSYOP are conducted in military operations other than war (MOOTW) and war (Figure 1-1, page 1-2), and are key contributors to shaping the international security environment and reacting to events. PSYOP are inherently joint and frequently combined operations. They support joint, interagency, multinational, conventional, and special operations (SO) forces. Army PSYOP forces are organized, equipped, and trained to provide strategic, operational, and tactical support to the theater combatant commanders. PSYOP support all missions across the full spectrum of operations.

Military Operations		General U.S. Goals	PSYOP/PSYACT Examples
COMBAT	War	Fight and Win War	Loudspeakers Leaflet Drops Radio Programming Face-to-Face Communications
	NONCOMBAT Military Operations Other Than War	Deter War and Resolve Conflict	Training Host Nation Forces Information Pamphlets Television Spots
		Promote Peace	Comic Books Novelty Items Newspapers Magazines Handbills Posters

Figure 1-1. Full-Spectrum Operations

1-2. Proven in combat and peacetime, PSYOP are one of the oldest weapons in the arsenal of man, as well as an important force protector, combat multiplier, and nonlethal weapons system. Effective use and employment of PSYOP forces provides many capabilities that facilitate successful mission accomplishment. The following are examples:

- Project a favorable image of U.S. and allied forces.
- Inform TAs in new or denied areas.
- Amplify the effects of a show-of-force.
- Give TAs alternative courses of action (COAs).
- Overcome censorship, illiteracy, or interrupted communications.
- Exploit ethnic, cultural, religious, or economic differences.

PSYOP MISSIONS

1-3. PSYOP are conducted at the strategic, operational, and tactical levels of war to influence foreign audiences. PSYOP forces provide a nonlethal capability in conveying information to selected TAs and governments to influence their emotions, motives, objective reasoning, and behavior. PSYOP Soldiers perform the following five principal missions to meet the intent of the supported commander:

- *Advise the commander* on Psychological Operations actions (PSYACTs), PSYOP enabling actions, and targeting restrictions that the military force will execute. These actions and restrictions minimize adverse impacts and unintended consequences, attack the enemy's will to resist, and enhance successful mission accomplishment.

- *Influence foreign populations* by expressing information subjectively to influence attitudes and behavior, and to obtain compliance or noninterference. These actions facilitate military operations, minimize needless loss of life and collateral damage, and further the objectives of the United States and its allies.

- *Provide public information* to foreign populations to support humanitarian activities, restore or reinforce legitimacy, ease suffering, and maintain or restore civil order.

- *Serve as the supported commander's voice* to foreign populations to convey intent and establish credibility.

- *Counter enemy propaganda, misinformation, disinformation, and opposing information* to portray friendly intent and actions correctly and positively, thus denying others the ability to polarize public opinion and political will against the United States and its allies.

PSYOP FUNCTIONS

1-4. To conduct the five PSYOP missions effectively and efficiently, PSYOP units perform seven functions. These functions include the following:

- *Perform command, control, communications, computers, and intelligence (C4I) functions.* C4I is the exercise of authority and direction over assigned PSYOP forces when accomplishing their missions. A PSYOP commander performs this function by arranging personnel, equipment, communications, supplies, facilities, and procedures when planning, directing, coordinating, and controlling PSYOP. PSYOP forces play a unique role in the intelligence function. They are both a producer and a consumer. PSYOP forces have the ability to collect, process, integrate, analyze, and evaluate relevant information for their own use and for use by the supported commander, OGAs, and other intelligence organizations.

- *Develop PSYOP plans, programs, supporting programs, series, and products.* Development involves the selection of Psychological Operations objectives (POs) and supporting Psychological Operations objectives (SPOs), the conceptualization of multiple series, the construction of specific product prototypes, as well as the recommendation of actions to influence the beliefs of selected TAs to modify their behavior. This function consists of detailed coordination between various PSYOP elements involving target audience analysis (TAA), series development, product prototype development, approval process review, and evaluation before and after dissemination to measure PSYOP effectiveness.

- *Produce PSYOP media.* Production is the transformation of approved PSYOP product prototypes into various media forms that are compatible with the way foreign populations are accustomed to receiving information. Some production requirements may be contracted to private industry, while other requirements may be performed by units attached or under the tactical control (TACON) or operational control (OPCON) of the PSYOP forces.

- *Distribute PSYOP products.* Distribution is the movement of completed products from the production source to the point where disseminators are located. This function may include the temporary storage of PSYOP products at an intermediate location. Depending on the type of product, this can be done either physically or electronically. PSYOP forces must make full use of organic equipment, commercial assets, and resources of other Services to facilitate the distribution process. PSYOP planners should attempt to simplify distribution and ensure alternative and contingency techniques whenever possible.

- *Disseminate PSYOP products.* Dissemination involves the delivery of PSYOP products directly to the desired TA. PSYOP forces must leverage as many different media and dissemination means as possible to ensure access to the targeted foreign population.

- *Employ tactical PSYOP.* Tactical PSYOP forces provide PSYOP functions on a reduced and limited scale to a supported tactical commander within a designated area of operations (AO). These forces are sometimes the supported tactical commander's only link with indigenous populations. Tactical PSYOP forces also collect relevant information for use by developers and the supported commander.

- *Conduct internment/resettlement (I/R) operations.* In virtually all situations where military forces are used, the management of internees becomes an integral part of the operation. PSYOP forces dispel rumors, create dialogue, and pacify or indoctrinate internees to minimize violence, facilitate efficient camp operations, and ensure safe and humanitarian conditions persist. This function also complements other PSYOP tasks through testing of materials, assessing the culture of potential audiences, collecting information and processing intelligence, and recruiting key communicators, informants, and collaborators.

PSYOP AND INFORMATION OPERATIONS

1-5. Information operations (IO) are actions taken to influence adversary information and information systems while defending one's own information and information systems. IO are conducted at all levels of war, across all phases of an operation, and across the conflict spectrum. PSYOP function not only as an integral capability of IO but also as a leverage for IO activities and capabilities. PSYOP are, therefore, a user of IO capabilities and technologies and a contributor to the overall IO effort of the supported command.

INFORMATION OPERATIONS SUPPORT TO PSYOP

1-6. Joint and Service-specific IO support elements and organizations offer the following capabilities and technologies that enhance and facilitate PSYOP in support of a commander:

- Databases and links to other Services and to OGAs that can provide alternate distribution or dissemination means and intelligence support to PSYOP forces.

- Access to organizations that conduct media, propagation, and spectrum analysis, as well as modeling.

- Systems and links to facilitate the collection of PSYOP impact indicators.
- Access to organizations that provide critical personality profiling and human factor analysis.

FM 3-05.30 provides a detailed discussion of joint and Service-specific IO organizations and their capabilities.

PSYOP AS A CONTRIBUTOR TO INFORMATION OPERATIONS

1-7. Just as IO can enhance and facilitate PSYOP, PSYOP can contribute to the achievement of a supported commander's IO objectives. PSYOP personnel assigned or attached to a supported command—working in the J-3 (joint), G-3/G-7 (Army corps/division), or S-3 (brigade/battalion)—coordinate, synchronize, and deconflict PSYOP with IO. They participate through continuous coordination and liaison as staff members at all levels on the staff of supported commands; such as an IO cell, plans group, and targeting meetings. PSYOP personnel advise the supported commander on all aspects of PSYOP and recommend PSYACTs and PSYOP enabling actions. PSYOP support IO by—

- Influencing foreign populations by expressing information subjectively to change attitudes and behavior and to obtain compliance or noninterference.
- Providing feedback on the effectiveness of IO activities. PSYOP personnel can collect information in the performance of assigned duties that, although not specifically related to PSYOP, may indicate effectiveness in another aspect of a supported command's IO plan. For example, an IO objective may be to gain the confidence and trust of the local populace. PSYOP personnel might observe civilians within a joint operations area (JOA) or an area of responsibility (AOR) using U.S. or coalition medical facilities, rather than those provided by an adversary or competing force. This preference may indicate that the civilians trust U.S. or coalition forces for medical care, rather than trust the adversary for that care.
- Conducting PSYOP to support the commander's IO objectives. For example, an IO objective may include denying certain frequencies to adversaries. PSYOP platforms can broadcast on these frequencies and effectively deny their use to adversaries amplifying the effect of IO efforts. For example, PSYOP can publicize the efforts of CA activities, such as medical programs, engineering projects, and facilities restoration.

1-8. Usually the combatant commander, the commander of the joint task force (CJTF), or the Service component commanders establish a cell to facilitate the IO process. This cell usually has representatives for every capability and related activity of IO. PSYOP representatives to the IO cell may come from assigned PSYOP officers to the unified command headquarters (HQ) or as liaison officers from the Psychological Operations support element (PSE) or POTF. The PSYOP representative in the IO cell performs the following functions:

- Integrates PSYOP with IO plans.
- Coordinates PSYOP support from the POTF.
- Deconflicts PSYOP plans and missions with IO plans and missions.
- Serves as liaison for information flow from the POTF to the supported IO cell.
- Provides feedback on PSYOP missions to the IO cell.

IO cell support to the POTF—

- Provides fused, tailored intelligence data and support.
- Ensures the joint targeting coordination board (JTCB) supports PSYOP targeting considerations and requirements.
- Augments dissemination of PSYOP products through nonstandard dissemination platforms.
- Facilitates PSYOP planning by coordinating resources to support PSYOP.

Figure 1-2, page 1-7, is an example of an IO cell.

1-9. PSYOP and IO are mutually supportive and beneficial. Each enhances the other's capability and mission effectiveness. Full integration and synergy of PSYOP and IO activities must occur to maximize their effect. This synergy of activities ensures consistency of message and optimizes credibility. Because of its complexity and inherent risks, PSYOP must be planned, conducted, and represented on staffs by PSYOP personnel. Additionally, because PSYOP are the commander's voice to approved TAs in the JOA, PSYOP require routine and direct access to the commander. Ideas, thoughts, and messages disseminated by PSYOP forces include nuances whose impacts know no borders and know no end. Direct access to the supported commander ensures that his intent for PSYOP is not diluted in translation by coordinating staff officers or staff members, and that he is aware of the impact of such ideas, thoughts, and messages within his JOA or AOR on planned operations.

SUMMARY

1-10. PSYOP increase the relative combat power of friendly forces and adversely affect the combat power of the adversary. PSYOP accomplish this result by targeting the identified vulnerabilities of foreign audiences through the employment of the PSYOP development process. Within the DOD, the Army has the primary military role to conduct PSYOP. Army PSYOP units perform this role by supporting U.S. national policy, by conducting PSYOP in support of military operations and United States Government (USG) agencies, and by providing PSYOP training, advice, and assistance to U.S. forces and to friendly nations.

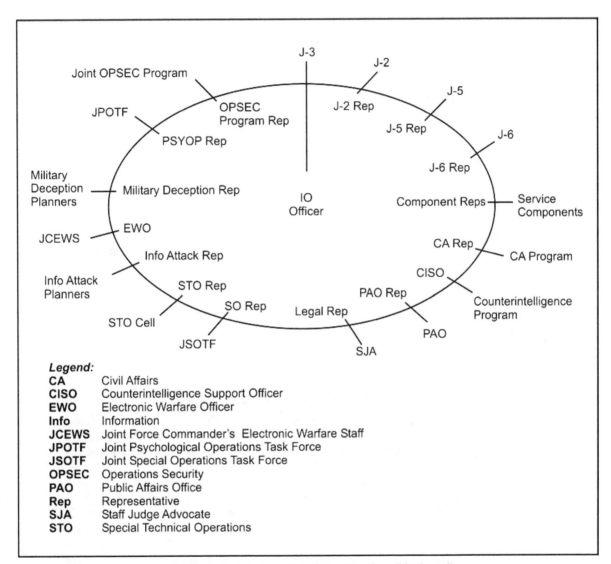

Figure 1-2. Joint IO Cell Organization (Notional)

Chapter 2

Command and Control of PSYOP Forces

The bravest are surely those who have the clearest vision of what is before them, glory and danger alike, and yet notwithstanding, go out to meet it.

Thucydides
Greek Historian, 401 B.C.

This chapter discusses command relations between PSYOP forces and supported commanders. It covers the duties, functions, and responsibilities of PSYOP elements providing support to commanders, as well as the general duties of liaison personnel. PSYOP forces at all levels use digital tools to exercise command and control (C2) of subordinate units. Digital systems are the information exchange and decision support subsystems within the C2 support system of the total force.

PSYOP STAFF OFFICER OR NONCOMMISSIONED OFFICER

2-1. The PSYOP staff officer or NCO provides expertise within the appropriate staff element at the component command or unified command. At the Army corps and division level, the Deputy Chief of Staff (DCS), G-7 IO, is responsible for coordinating and synchronizing the element of IO. At the unified command level and other than Army Service component level, IO and its elements are coordinated in the IO cell within the J-3 or G-3. The PSYOP staff officer or NCO plans, coordinates, validates, and reports PSYOP force deployments theaterwide in response to the Secretary of Defense (SecDef), the joint staff, and other operational and contingency requirements. The staff officer or NCO performs duties in the respective unified command's joint operations center (JOC), when required. He reviews and prepares detailed messages, special reports, and briefings as required by the J-3 director and the combatant commander, and provides functional expertise in joint PSYOP capabilities and doctrine. The staff officer or NCO integrates directly with the J-3 or G-3/G-7 staff and ensures PSYOP inclusion and integration. His principal duties include the following:

- Applies SO imperatives in PSYOP mission planning and execution.
- Assists and makes recommendations to the commander and staff on PSYOP matters and requirements for staff augmentation.
- Conducts mission analysis and the PSYOP portion of the intelligence preparation of the battlespace (IPB).
- Prepares the appropriate PSYOP portions of the operation plan (OPLAN) and operation order (OPORD).
- Coordinates with supporting PSYOP units.
- Identifies PSYOP information requirements (IRs).

- Nominates targets for lethal and nonlethal fires (Appendix A discusses PSYOP and the targeting process).
- Integrates PSYOP with other elements of the effects coordination cell (ECC) to achieve a synergistic effect.
- Promulgates PSYOP themes to stress and avoid throughout the command.
- Refines and updates POs and SPOs during planning.
- Integrates directly with the J-3 or G-3 staff and ensures PSYOP inclusion and integration.
- Maintains communication with the Psychological Operations task force (POTF) HQ.
- Reviews PSYOP standing OPLANs and participates in deliberate and crisis-action planning.
- Reviews and comments on joint publications and documents.

2-2. The U.S. Army established a G-7 IO coordinating staff officer at the division and corps levels in FM 6-0, *Mission Command: Command and Control of Army Forces*. The PSYOP staff officer located in the division or corps G-3 moved from the staff supervision of the G-3 to the G-7 with this change in doctrine. The PSYOP officer in G-7 performs functions similar to those of a liaison officer (LNO) in that he does not plan PSYOP but coordinates and integrates PSYOP with IO. In the absence of a Psychological Operations assessment team (POAT), PSE, or POTF, the PSYOP officer may be required to write the PSYOP appendix to the IO annex to plans and orders. The attached tactical Psychological Operations company (TPC) supporting the division (or Service equivalent) or tactical Psychological Operations battalion (TPB) supporting the corps (or Service equivalent) plans and executes PSYOP for the supported commander under the staff supervision of the G-3. The PSYOP staff officer in the supported division or corps G-3 must maintain a close relationship with the supporting TPC or TPB to coordinate planned PSYOP with IO.

PSYOP ASSESSMENT TEAM

2-3. A POAT is a small, tailored team (approximately 4 to 12 personnel) that consists of PSYOP planners and product distribution/dissemination and logistics specialists. The team is deployed to the theater at the request of the combatant commander to assess the situation, develop POs, and recommend the appropriate level of support to accomplish the mission. A POAT serves many purposes. POATs are deployed for minor crises through major conflicts to determine the feasibility of PSYOP application and the supporting requirements. POATs can augment a unified command or a JTF staff and provide a full range of PSYOP planning support. The size and composition of a POAT are mission-based and situation-dependent. A POAT may consist of as few as one regional or operational planner to as many as twelve or more personnel, including tactical, print, broadcast, communications, logistics, and strategic studies detachment (SSD) representatives.

2-4. An ideal POAT consists of the following representation:

- *Regional battalion*: C2, administration, logistical, intelligence, and PSYOP planners, and SSD analyst.

- *Tactical battalion*: Tactical planners.

- *Dissemination battalion*: Communications, print, and broadcast planner.

2-5. A POAT focuses its assessment of the operational area on eight primary areas: TAs, production facilities, communications infrastructure, competing media, available indigenous commercial and government information holders, logistics support, dissemination capabilities, and tactical considerations. A POAT assesses host nation (HN) capabilities and availability of production media (print, radio, and television [TV]), means of distribution, and broadcast equipment. The S-6 or communications representative determines the availability and practicality of electronic distribution methods for PSYOP products within the AO, both intertheater and intratheater. During the assessment, the S-4 or logistics representative identifies and coordinates for the necessary memorandums of agreement (MOAs) and contracts to ensure support from the HN, interagencies, and other Services. A POAT has the following capabilities:

- Assesses the friendly and enemy PSYOP situation, current propaganda, and PSYOP potential.

- Recommends the types and sizes of PSYOP forces to deploy and determines support requirements.

- Writes PSYOP supporting plans, PSYOP estimate of the situation, and other documents, as required.

- Evaluates the mission, enemy, terrain and weather, troops and support available—time available and civil considerations (METT-TC) and the particular needs for PSYOP forces.

- Evaluates printing needs, in-country supplies, and possible printing facilities and other assets.

- Evaluates audiovisual requirements to determine broadcast needs, locations, frequency availability, ranges, and other requirements.

- Evaluates bandwidth capability and availability and communications capabilities to implement reachback.

- Determines and coordinates all communication requirements for PSYOP forces.

- Conducts initial analysis.

- Conducts rapid deployment.

- Serves, when directed, as the advanced echelon (ADVON) for follow-on PSYOP forces.

A POAT has the following limitations:

- No product development capability.

- No dissemination capability.

- Limited research and analytical capability.

- No tactical loudspeaker capability.

- Minimal size and composition in many cases.

2-6. The POAT is a planning element, not an operational unit. The POAT may become a part of the operations portion of the unit when the unit deploys; however, the primary function of the POAT is to determine the need for, and to plan for, PSYOP activity—not conduct the activity. If the POAT becomes a PSE or POTF, then the limitations listed above must be mitigated. The mission of the POAT concludes when it either transforms into a PSE or POTF or completes all requirements.

PSYOP SUPPORT ELEMENT

2-7. The PSE is a tailored element that can provide PSYOP support. PSEs do not contain organic C2 capability; therefore, command relationships must be clearly defined. The size, composition, and capability of the PSE are determined by the requirements of the supported commander. A PSE is not normally designed to provide full-spectrum PSYOP capability; therefore, reachback is critical for its mission success. A PSE is often established for smaller-scale missions where the requirements do not justify a POTF with its functional component command status. A PSE differs from a POTF in that it is not a separate functional command. A PSE normally works for the supported force S-3, G-3/G-7, J-3, or in some cases, a government agency, such as a Country Team. A PSE can work independent of or subordinate to a POTF and, as such, provide PSYOP planners with a flexible option to meet mission requirements. A PSE can provide a wide range of PSYOP support options, ranging from a small C2 planning capability up to, but short of, the level of support requiring a more robust C2 structure normally provided by a POTF. A further discussion of a PSE is found in Chapter 4.

PSYOP TASK FORCE

2-8. A POTF is normally the highest-level PSYOP organization that supports a theater-level combatant commander. Although doctrinally a PSYOP task group can be established for C2 of multiple POTFs, historically this has not been the case. A POTF may include PSYOP forces from the Active Army and Reserve Component (RC). (RC mobilization is discussed in Appendix B.) A POTF becomes a joint Psychological Operations task force (JPOTF) with the inclusion of PSYOP forces from the various Services and other government agencies (OGAs).

2-9. A POTF plans and conducts PSYOP in support of a combatant commander or CJTF. A POTF plans, develops, designs, produces, and coordinates the distribution and dissemination of PSYOP products and recommends actions to support the combatant commander's overall plan. The SecDef, a combatant commander, a subordinate commander, or an existing commander of a JTF may establish a POTF. Like the POAT and PSE, the size, composition, and structure of the POTF depend on mission requirements. A POTF has the following capabilities:

- Advises the commander on PSYOP.
- Conducts PSYOP planning and execution.
- Coordinates with other components to ensure the most efficient PSYOP support to the CJTF.
- Produces PSYOP products and evaluates PSYOP effectiveness.
- Conducts liaison with HN agencies and other USG organizations.
- Provides cultural expertise and language capability.

- Nominates PSYOP targets as a member of the JTCB, identifies targets for inclusion in the Restricted Fires List, and evaluates targets for their psychological impact on TAs.
- Assesses hostile and neutral media capabilities and analyzes all propaganda.
- Provides in-depth analysis on TAs in the AOR.

A POTF has the following limitations:

- Limited organic distribution assets.
- Limited organic logistics support.
- Limited organic native speakers.

2-10. A POTF consists of regional, tactical, production, and dissemination assets augmented by I/R assets, as well as multipurpose assets, such as COMMANDO SOLO. A POTF also consists of representatives from other Services and joint information agencies, such as the Joint Information Operations Center (JIOC) and the 1st IO Command (Land). A POTF organization (Figure 2-1, page 2-6) is mission-dependent.

2-11. The POTF organization example summarizes the overall organization and C2 relationships within the POTF, including the multitude of LNOs from the POTF to other components, units, and agencies. Primarily, the POTF consists of two major subgroups—the special staff of the Psychological Operations development center (PDC) (discussed in detail in Chapter 6) and the command group.

2-12. The appropriate regional battalion normally forms the nucleus of a POTF. This regional battalion provides the POTF coordinating staff, the special staffs that make up the PDC, and SSD analysts. Tactical PSYOP forces are normally attached to maneuver units. The POTF retains coordinating authority with these tactical units. Multipurpose assets that are primarily PSYOP platforms, such as COMMANDO SOLO, usually remain OPCON to their Service or functional component and are TACON to the POTF. Maintaining coordinating authority of tactical PSYOP forces (discussed in detail in Chapter 8) and TACON of multipurpose assets allow the POTF to direct and coordinate theater-level PSYOP programs and activities and to delineate approval authority for disseminating products.

PSYOP TASK FORCE COMMAND GROUP RESPONSIBILITIES

2-13. The command group includes the POTF commander, deputy commander, chief of staff, assistant chief of staff, command sergeant major (CSM), and staff. The command group also exercises control over the LNOs for planning, reporting, and coordinating purposes. Table 2-1, page 2-7, depicts the command and support relationships and their inherent responsibilities (per FM 3-0, *Operations*).

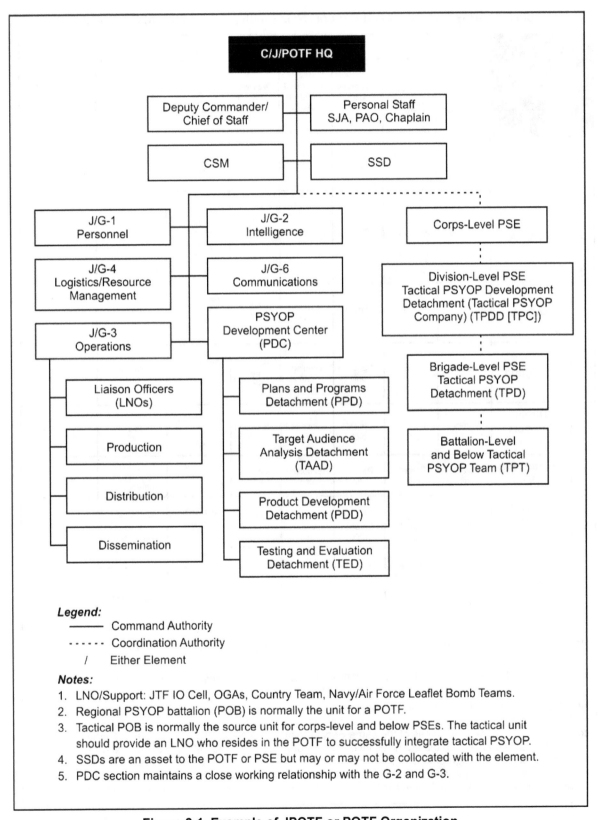

Legend:
——— Command Authority
- - - - - Coordination Authority
/ Either Element

Notes:
1. LNO/Support: JTF IO Cell, OGAs, Country Team, Navy/Air Force Leaflet Bomb Teams.
2. Regional PSYOP battalion (POB) is normally the unit for a POTF.
3. Tactical POB is normally the source unit for corps-level and below PSEs. The tactical unit should provide an LNO who resides in the POTF to successfully integrate tactical PSYOP.
4. SSDs are an asset to the POTF or PSE but may or may not be collocated with the element.
5. PDC section maintains a close working relationship with the G-2 and G-3.

Figure 2-1. Example of JPOTF or POTF Organization

Table 2-1. Army Command and Support Relationships and Inherent Responsibilities

IF RELATIONSHIP IS:		INHERENT RESPONSIBILITIES ARE:						
		Has Command Relation-ship With:	May Be Task-Organized By:	Receives CSS From:	Assigned Position or AO By:	Provides Liaison To:	Establishes/ Maintains Communica-tions With:	Has Priorities Established By:	Gaining Unit Can Impose Further Command or Support Relationship Of:
COMMAND	Attached	Gaining unit	Gaining unit	Gaining unit	Gaining unit	As required by gaining unit	Unit to which attached	Gaining unit	Attached; OPCON; TACON; GS; GSR; R; DS
COMMAND	OPCON	Gaining unit	Parent unit and gain-ing unit; gaining unit may pass OPCON to lower HQ. NOTE 1	Parent unit	Gaining unit	As required by gaining unit	As required by gaining unit and parent unit	Gaining unit	OPCON; TACON; GS; GSR; R; DS
COMMAND	TACON	Gaining unit	Parent unit	Parent unit	Gaining unit	As required by gaining unit	As required by gaining unit and parent unit	Gaining unit	GS; GSR; R; DS
COMMAND	Assigned	Parent unit	Parent unit	Parent unit	Gaining unit	As required by parent unit	As required by parent unit	Parent unit	Not applicable
SUPPORT	Direct Support (DS)	Parent unit	Parent unit	Parent unit	Supported unit	Supported unit	Parent unit; Supported unit	Supported unit	NOTE 2
SUPPORT	Reinforcing (R)	Parent unit	Parent unit	Parent unit	Reinforced unit	Reinforced unit	Parent unit; Reinforced unit	Reinforced unit; then parent unit	Not applicable
SUPPORT	General Support Reinforcing (GSR)	Parent unit	Parent unit	Parent unit	Parent unit	Reinforced unit and as required by parent unit	Reinforced unit and as required by parent unit	Parent unit; then reinforced unit	Not applicable
SUPPORT	General Support (GS)	Parent unit	Parent unit	Parent unit	Parent unit	As required by parent unit	As required by parent unit	Parent unit	Not applicable

NOTE 1. In North Atlantic Treaty Organization (NATO), the gaining unit may not task-organize a multinational unit (see TACON).

NOTE 2. Commanders of units in DS may further assign support relationships between their subordinate units and elements of the supported unit after coordination with the supported commander.

NOTE 3. Coordinating Authority – A commander or individual assigned responsibility for coordinating specific functions or activities involving forces of two or more military departments, two or more joint force components, or two or more forces of the same Service. The commander or individual has the authority to require consultation between the agencies involved, but does not have the authority to compel agreement. In the event that essential agreement cannot be obtained, the matter shall be referred to the appointing authority. Coordinating authority is a consultation relationship, not an authority through which command may be exercised. Coordinating authority is more applicable to planning and similar activities than to operations.

Commander and Deputy Commander

2-14. The POTF commander directs POTF strategy while developing and conducting the phased PSYOP supporting plan to support strategic, operational, and tactical objectives. He also exercises approval authority within the POTF for all PSYACTs and products. Finally, the POTF commander serves as the primary intermediary between the POTF and the supported commander, through the G-3 or J-3, in all component and unified commands. Although the Army corps and division PSYOP staff officer or NCO works within the DCS, G-7 IO, the POTF commander, as a functional component commander, coordinates with the supported commander through the G-3 and any attached PSYOP LNOs. The deputy commander may perform any or all of these duties at the discretion of the POTF commander or in his absence.

Chief of Staff and Assistant Chief of Staff

2-15. The chief of staff is the agent of the commander responsible for providing guidance and direction to the staff and for coordinating efforts of the staff.

Command Sergeant Major

2-16. As the senior enlisted member of the command group, the command sergeant major serves as advisor on troop issues, including quality of life, discipline, and training. He also provides input to all aspects of the PSYOP process, as necessary.

Staff

2-17. The POTF staff consists of the coordinating staff G-1, G-2, G-3, G-4, G-6, and the special staff PDC. The following paragraphs discuss the functions of each staff section.

2-18. **POTF G-1.** The G-1 primarily manages personnel and the administration of the POTF. Therefore, the G-1 monitors and furnishes applicable reports on the personnel strength of the POTF—for example, attachments and detachments, personnel missing in action (MIA) and killed in action (KIA), replacements, and leaves and passes (Figure 2-2, page 2-9). Also, the G-1 oversees other routine administrative functions of the POTF, including promotion and reduction actions, awards, officer and noncommissioned officer evaluation reports (NCOERs), and other personnel actions. Finally, the G-1 is the office of primary responsibility (OPR) for unit postal operations. The POTF G-1 staff performs the following functions:

- Prepares and issues individual assignment orders assigning Soldiers to the POTF.
- Prepares assumption of command orders for the POTF commander and the rear detachment commander.
- Publishes rating schemes for officers and NCOs.
- Coordinates and conducts preparation for overseas movement (POM).
- Maintains an accurate deployment roster.
- Maintains personnel strength on all POTF units.

- Maintains a current list of POTF personnel shortages.

- Determines future personnel requirements, formulates a priority of fill, and projects replacements.

- Reports status of enemy prisoners of war (EPWs) and civilian internees (CIs).

- Provides mail service and performs administrative functions.

- Coordinates with the combatant commander or CJTF J-1 for linguist

Line 1: Report Number

Line 2: Date-Time Group (DTG) Prepared

Line 3: Unit

Line 4: Commissioned Officers:

    a.   Authorized

    b.   Assigned

    c.   Field strength

    d.   Rear detachment strength

    e.   KIA

    f.   Wounded in action (WIA)

    g.   MIA

    h.   Nonbattle losses

    i.   Total losses

    j.   Gains

    k.   Remarks

    l.   Attachments

    m.   Detachments

Line 5: Warrant Officers *(Same as Line 4)*

Line 6: Enlisted *(Same as Line 4)*

Line 7: Department of the Army (DA) Civilians *(Same as Line 4)*

Line 8: Other *(Same as Line 4)*

Line 9: Total *(Same as Line 4)*

support and allocation.

Figure 2-2. Personnel Status Format

2-19. **POTF G-2.** The G-2 provides PSYOP-relevant intelligence on weather conditions, enemy actions, current locations, and most likely COAs (Figure 2-3, page 2-10). To facilitate this effort, the POTF G-2 must integrate POTF priority intelligence requirements (PIR) into the G-2's integrated collection plan. Additionally, the G-2 maintains oversight on POTF requests for information (RFIs) submitted to echelons above and below the POTF, ensuring that the requests are answered in a timely manner and that the information received reaches appropriate users.

Issuing Unit: XXX
For the Period: DD, MMM – DD, MMM

1. Summary of Activity.
   a. Belligerent forces (hostile, friendly, and neutral).
      (1) Political.
      (2) Military.
   b. Nonbelligerent forces.
   c. Currently targeted audiences.
   d. Other forces or groups.
2. Summary of Belligerent PSYOP: Audiences, media, and effects.
3. Significant Changes to Infrastructure: Those that affect POTF functioning and TA attitudes.
4. Weather and Terrain.
   a. Weather: Effects on friendly, enemy, and neutral COAs, and on TA attitudes.
   b. Terrain: Effects on friendly, enemy, and neutral COAs, and on TA attitudes.
5. Conclusion: Assess changes to factors that affect current and projected planning. The assessment should make planners aware of developments that may change or invalidate the assumptions and factors in mission analysis and cause the planners to alter their plans.

Figure 2-3. PSYOP Intelligence Summary Format

2-20. To monitor and counter enemy PSYOP effectively, the G-2 must coordinate closely with the TED and the SSD—using the source, content, audience, media, and effects (SCAME) approach explained in Chapter 11. Before deployment, the regional battalion G-2 determines the security clearances of personnel and compares them to clearance requirements of work locations. Certain duty positions involve work in a sensitive compartmented information facility (SCIF), which requires a Top Secret clearance and read-on. Once the determinations have been made, the G-2 must coordinate with the appropriate agencies to ensure access is granted to key individuals. The POTF G-2 staff performs the following functions:

- Identifies security clearance requirements and processes requests for security clearances, as required.
- Verifies and forwards security clearances to appropriate agencies.
- Determines official passport status and processes passport applications, as required.
- Conducts IPB of the operational area.
- Prepares and implements the intelligence collection plan; determines supporting intelligence assets that best support the gathering of IRs, PIR, and PSYOP-relevant information.
- Establishes and administers the force-protection plan.
- Reports enemy PSYOP activities and actions.
- Determines and identifies enemy dissemination structure, types of media used, and location and range of key communications nodes.

2-21. **POTF G-3.** The G-3 plans operations and tracks the current situation in relation to the POTF. To accomplish this effort, the G-3 is task-organized into three principal elements: future operations, current operations, and the message center. The future operations element is engaged in the long-term (more than 48 hours in the future) planning and coordination of POTF activities conducted at all echelons (Figure 2-4). The current operations element tracks the operational situation as it pertains to the POTF and reports PSYOP-relevant information of combined JTFs from the last 24 hours to the next 48 hours (Figure 2-5). The message center element monitors and controls information flow in and out of the POTF HQ, logging and distributing incoming messages to the appropriate user. Finally, the message center briefs the status of communication assets, as required. Specifically, the message center uses a combination of the following devices to transfer information to and from other elements of the POTF or JTF or other external agencies as directed:

- Secret Internet Protocol Router Network (SIPRNET).
- Nonsecure Internet Protocol Router Network (NIPRNET).
- Global Command and Control System (GCCS).
- Classified and unclassified facsimile (FAX) machines.
- Secure telephone unit III (STU-III).

Subject	Briefer
Enemy situation up to 72 hours out	Combined (C)/J-2/G-2
Friendly situation up to 72 hours out	C/J-3/G-3
Target identification	
Target analysis	PDC Commander/Officer in Charge (OIC)
Product development	
Asset update and new requirements	LNOs
Commander's comments	Commander

Figure 2-4. Future Operations Briefing Format

Subject	Briefer
Friendly situation	C/J-3/G-3
Enemy situation	
Enemy reactions to friendly PSYACTs and dissemination in the last 24 hours	C/J-3/G-3
Enemy PSYACTs in the last 24 hours	
Personnel	C/J-1/G-1
Logistics and changes in equipment status	C/J-4/G-4
Print	Print LNO
Broadcast	Broadcast LNO
Tactical operations	Tactical LNO
COMMANDO SOLO	193d Special Operations Wing (SOW) LNO
Product development	PDC Commander/ OIC
Friendly PSYACTs and dissemination for the next 48 hours	C/J-3/S-3
Dissemination targeting, air mission, and planning	
Commander's comments	Commander

Figure 2-5. Current Operations Briefing Format

2-22. Although LNOs are representatives of the POTF commander, they are under the J-3 or G-3 of the supported command for purposes of C2 and parallel planning. PSYOP LNOs coordinate with the PSYOP staff officer within the DCS, G-7 IO (at corps and division levels) to ensure plans of the supported command reflect POTF support and capabilities. Consequently, an obligation exists for the G-3 to provide planning guidance in the POTF commander's daily guidance letter. The POTF G-3 staff performs the following functions:

- Oversees and conducts predeployment activities.
- Identifies and schedules required individual and unit training.
- Publishes rules of engagement (ROE) and ensures all members of the POTF understand the rules.
- Oversees and coordinates all PSYOP production, distribution, and dissemination activities.
- Determines types and quantities of production assets required and establishes priority of production.
- Manages and maintains operational status of production assets.
- Coordinates movement and distribution of products to dissemination points.
- Maintains operational status of dissemination assets.
- Manages, tracks, and implements the PSYOP plan and the PSYOP program.
- Issues PSYOP program development guidance.
- Maintains current and future operations map boards. (Appendix C provides PSYOP mapping symbols.)
- Maintains communications and provides daily POTF guidance and priorities to LNOs.
- Establishes message center.
- Assists in developing time-phased force and deployment data (TPFDD).

2-23. **POTF G-4.** The G-4 oversees logistics within the POTF. Its major emphasis is on monitoring and procuring all classes of supplies and contracting for necessary services. Emphasis is also on maintaining and storing POTF equipment and individually assigned weapons and ammunition. The G-4 also manages the POTF property book in conjunction with the special operations theater support element (SOTSE) or the theater Army, as appropriate. The POTF G-4 staff performs the following functions:

- Prepares logistics estimate and identifies key shortages and requirements for additional equipment (Figure 2-6, pages 2-13 and 2-14).
- Compiles and submits statement of requirement (SOR).
- Coordinates for ammunition issue.
- Supervises supply and maintenance system.
- Establishes property accountability procedures.
- Establishes procedures for and supervises acquisition of PSYOP-peculiar equipment and supplies.

- Reports and tracks status of logistics, budget, and procurements.
- Reports status of property accountability.
- Establishes, oversees, and monitors HN support contract agreements.
- Assists in developing TPFDD.

(CLASSIFICATION)

Logistics Status

FROM: _____
TO: _____

SUBJECT: Logistics Status as of _____

1. Personnel by Location (Officer, Warrant Officer, Enlisted, Civilian):
   Location   Number
                Total:

	On Hand (O/H)	Needed Next 24 Hours	Needed Next 48 Hours	Needed Next 72 Hours
2. Class I				
a. Meals, ready to eat (MREs) (Cases)	_____	_____	_____	_____
b. Water (Gallons)	_____	_____	_____	_____
3. Class II, III, IV (Critical)				
a. _____	_____	_____	_____	_____
b. _____	_____	_____	_____	_____
c. _____	_____	_____	_____	_____
4. Class III				
a. Motor Gasoline (Gallons)	_____	_____	_____	_____
b. Diesel (Gallons)	_____	_____	_____	_____
5. Class V (Critical Ammunition)				
a. M16/M4	_____	_____	_____	_____
b. M60/M240	_____	_____	_____	_____
c. M203	_____	_____	_____	_____
d. M2	_____	_____	_____	_____
e. M19	_____	_____	_____	_____
f. M249	_____	_____	_____	_____

6. Equipment and Vehicles (Authorized or O/H)

Item	Authorized or O/H	Nonmission Capable (NMC) #	Reason	Fully Mission Capable (FMC) Date
Sensitive Items	Authorized or O/H			
a. M16/M4	_____			
b. M60/M240	_____			
c. M203	_____			
d. M2	_____			
e. M19	_____			
f. M9	_____			

(CLASSIFICATION)

Figure 2-6. Logistics Status Format

```
                          (CLASSIFICATION)

Sensitive Items       Authorized or O/H
  g. M249                _____
  h. Radios:  SABRE ____; -89A ____; -90A ____; -91A ____; -92A ____;
      PRC-119 ____; -127 ____; -150 ____; -312 ____; -838 ____; TACSAT ____; MBITR ____
  i. Night Vision Goggles:    PVS-5 ____; PVS-4 ____; PVS-7 ____; PVS-7D ____; PVS-14 ____
  j. Communications Security (COMSEC):  ANCD ____; STU-III ____; KYK-13 ____;
      KYK-15 ____; Signal Operating Instructions (SOI) ____; KY57 ____

7. NMC Equipment
        Item          Authorized          NMC #            Reason          FMC Date
                       or O/H
    a. _____     _____         _____        _____       _____
    b. _____     _____         _____        _____       _____
    c. _____     _____         _____        _____       _____

8. Class IX (Critical)
    National Stock    Nomenclature     Quantity          Status
    Number (NSN)                       Document #
    a. _____     _____       _____        _____
    b. _____     _____       _____        _____
    c. _____     _____       _____        _____

9. Transportation Requirements
        Cargo           DTG Required       Location          Destination
    a. _____   _____      _____     _____
    b. _____   _____      _____     _____
    c. _____   _____      _____     _____

10. Commander's Narrative


                          (CLASSIFICATION)
```

Figure 2-6. Logistics Status Format (Continued)

2-24. **POTF G-6**. The G-6 is the primary communications planner for the POTF. The G-6 attends initial planning conferences and determines communications and data transfer requirements based on input from the affected units. In all cases, the G-6 will coordinate closely with the POTF commander and include a communications planner throughout all stages of the planning process. Upon receipt of a mission, units should coordinate with the G-6 for communications and information systems support. During execution, the G-6 will work closely with the sustaining base and deployed communications elements to ensure communications needs are met and to coordinate with the POTF commanders as requirements change. The POTF G-6 staff performs the following functions:

- Prepares a communications estimate (Figure 2-7, pages 2-15 through 2-17).

- Establishes communications architecture.

- Determines and requests frequency allocation (Figure 2-8, page 2-18).

- Establishes secure communications.

- Provides secure and nonsecure tactical telephone support.

- Determines and coordinates for reachback requirements.

1. Deployment Information.

   a. Location.

   b. Coordinates.

   c. Contacts (for example, base communications officer, JOC commander, JTF J-6, corps G-6, Marine expeditionary force G-6, including phone numbers and message addresses).

   d. Operation dates: From _____ to _____.

   e. Scale drawings of the site.

2. Communications Facilities.

   a. Are facilities currently operational?

     (1) List by type and function.

     (2) Will they accommodate needs of the unit?

     (3) Will interface be required, possible?

     (4) Any local procedures affecting unit operations?

     (5) If foreign owned and operated, what problems are anticipated?

   b. Unit facilities and services required.

     (1) List by type and function.

     (2) Hours of operation.

     (3) Services to be provided.

     (4) Units to be served.

     (5) Associated costs.

3. Facility Sites (General).

   a. Accessibility.

     (1) Road conditions and limitations.

     (2) Anticipated adverse effects of weather.

     (3) Special safety hazards (for example, treacherous driving).

     (4) Special access requirements (for example, helicopters).

   b. Site preparation required.

     (1) Leveling.

     (2) Clearing.

     (3) Draining.

     (4) Revetments.

     (5) Availability of materials, labor, equipment, and civil engineers.

     (6) Equipment resistance to ground. Has suitable ground been tested and is it available?

   c. Is suitable commercial or base power available? Is it reliable?

   d. Antennas.

     (1) Type to be used or recommended.

     (2) Orientation.

     (3) Is clear space of suitable size available?

     (4) RFI problems (for example, power lines, transformers, and power units).

     (5) Obstruction and limiting factors (for example, buildings, mountains, and trees).

     (6) Requirement for airfield waivers.

     (7) Terrain and soil peculiarities.

Figure 2-7. Signal Site Survey Format

e. What is the proximity to fuel and ammunition storage areas?

f. Interconnections to base and other facilities.

   (1) What lines and cables are available and required?

   (2) What sizes and lengths of cable are required?

   (3) Special problems, such as cable crossing roads, runways, or taxiways?

   (4) Any special requirements (such as filters) for equipment not HN-approved? What equipment must be HN-approved? Is it?

g. Is it the best possible location from which to provide the service required?

h. Is there sufficient real estate to disperse tactically?

4. Telephone Operations.

   a. Base switchboard.

      (1) Lines available for unit use.

      (2) Is telephone service available to all facility and work administration sites?

      (3) Is telephone service available to quarters?

      (4) Is Defense Switched Network (DSN) available?

      (5) Obtain telephone directory.

      (6) Are leased circuits used?

      (7) Hours of operation.

      (8) Can it directly interface with PSYOP unit equipment?

   b. Switchboard.

      (1) Interface capability and requirements.

      (2) Interconnect requirements.

         (a) What lines and cables are available and required?

         (b) What size, type, and length of cables are required?

         (c) Special problems, such as cable crossing roads, runways, or taxiways?

         (d) Inside wire.

         (e) Number of instruments required.

         (f) Terminals, junction boxes, and similar requirements, by type and size.

         (g) What special-purpose vehicles are required and available (for example, cherry picker and pole setter)?

      (3) Prepare outside plant layout diagrams showing—

         (a) Buildings served.

         (b) Unit in each building.

         (c) Lines and instruments by each building. Diagram to scale.

         (d) Poles, terminals, and junction boxes. D-mark location.

         (e) Road, runway, taxiway crossing locations.

      (4) Ensure the following equipment is positioned within the maximum range from the AN/TTC-39 (telephone switch):

         (a) TA-938 — 2.5 miles

         (b) TA-838 — 2.5 miles (two-wire mode)

         (c) Alternating current (AC) supervisor — 4 miles (TA-838 and TA-341/TT)

         (d) Direct current (DC) supervisor — 2 miles (with TA-838 and TA-341/TT)

         (e) TA-312/pt — Wet, 14 miles; Dry, 22 miles

Figure 2-7. Signal Site Survey Format (Continued)

(f) TA-954	2.5 miles
(g) KY-68	2.5 miles

5. Communications and Cryptographic Center Operations.
   a. Units to be served.
   b. Circuits required.
      (1) Routing indicators.
      (2) Distant terminals.
         (a) Location.
         (b) Equipment.
         (c) Unit.
         (d) Routing indicator.
      (3) Interface or interconnect requirements and problems.
      (4) Cable or line requirements for interconnections.
   c. Will transportation be available for geographically separated sites?
   d. COMSEC.
      (1) COMSEC materials required (type and quantity, equipment, and key tape).
      (2) Procedures for continuing supply.
      (3) Initial source.
      (4) Physical security for the facility.
      (5) Tempest problems.
      (6) Classified destruction facility.
      (7) Storage facilities.
   e. Procedures (determine or develop).
      (1) Message delivery and pickup.
      (2) Obtain letters authorizing pickup and receipt from customer.

6. Radio Operations.
   a. Services required.
      (1) Point-to-point.
         (a) Type of circuits (voice or teletype).
         (b) Interface or interconnect problems and requirements.
      (2) Phone patch requirements (such as nets).
   b. Frequencies.
   c. Call signs.
   d. Authentication systems.
   e. Initial contact procedures.
   f. Shelter availability if bench mount equipment is used.
   g. Site selection considerations.
      (1) A sufficient amount of land must be available for antenna construction. In maintaining antenna separation, at least 100 feet between antenna terminators is required if more than one antenna is erected (250 feet is the desired distance).
      (2) Wide open spaces free of obstructions (such as trees, power lines, roads, and fences) must be used for the antenna farm. Slightly sloping land is acceptable but is not desired. Cleared farmland or pasture is preferred.
      (3) Soil conditions (for example, sand, rock, marsh, and coral) must be identified to determine the type of anchors required and whether additional equipment (jackhammer) will be required to drive the earth anchors and grounding.

Figure 2-7. Signal Site Survey Format (Continued)

```
1. Have joint communications-electronics operating instructions (JCEOI) or SOI been produced? If so, is
   a copy available?

2. Has a COMSEC callout been produced? If so, is a copy available?

3. Has a copy of all Annex K communications diagrams been requested?

4. Names and telephone numbers of primary communications planners at corps, division, and brigade
   level.

5. Is a copy of the joint or combined task force (J/CTF) J-6 and joint combat camera center (JCCC)
   organizational chart available?

6. Has a deployment telephone directory been developed and is a copy available?

7. Has a communications maintenance support unit been designated to support J/CTF? If so, is there a
   point of contact (POC)?

8. Will KY-68 digital subscriber voice terminals (DSVTs) be available at the J/CTF location? The 4th
   Psychological Operations Group (Airborne) (POG[A]) has no organic mobile subscriber equipment
   (MSE) and would have to acquire terminals if there are none available.

9. Have plain language addresses (PLAs) and routing indicators (RIs) been established for the J/CTF
   and other deployed locations? Is a copy available?

10. Will the J/CTF forward communications center be automated or semiautomated?
    Will DD-173 forms be required? What message software will be used? Is a copy available?

11. Will analog common user circuits be available at the J/CTF for use with unit STU-IIIs?

12. Will central site power be available at the J/CTF?

13. Are any site layout diagrams available?
```

Figure 2-8. Signal RFI Format

PSYOP LIAISON OFFICERS

2-25. LNOs are special staff officers or NCOs who represent the commander at the HQ of another unit to effect coordination, integration, and cooperation between the two units. Liaison, with its accompanying responsibilities of coordination and integration, is an important part of command, control, and communications (C3). Liaison is the most commonly employed technique for establishing and maintaining close, continuous physical communication between commands and for reducing the uncertainty of war through direct communication.

Liaison Officer Functions

2-26. LNOs perform several critical functions that are consistent across the full range of military operations. The extent that these functions are performed is dependent upon the mission, as well as the charter established by the commander of the sending organization. LNOs have four basic functions, as discussed in the following paragraphs.

2-27. **Monitor.** LNOs must monitor the operations of both the receiving organization and the sending organization and must understand how each affects the other. As a minimum, LNOs must know the current situation and planned operations, understand pertinent staff issues, and be sensitive to parent commanders and the receiving commander's desires. Additionally, to lend insight to the sending commander, LNOs must monitor the operating styles of the receiving commander and staff. These observations help LNOs maintain a smooth working relationship between the sending organization and the receiving HQ.

2-28. LNOs must possess the training and experience to understand the receiving staff process. They must routinely assess where they need to be during the daily operations cycle to stay abreast of the current situation and to keep the sending organization HQ fully informed.

2-29. **Coordinate.** LNOs facilitate synchronization of current operations and future plans between the sending organization and the receiving organization by coordinating with other LNOs, members of the receiving staff, and the parent command. LNOs should routinely meet with staff officers and commanders in the receiving HQ and readily know how to contact them.

2-30. To enhance the communication process, LNOs gather copies of receiving standing operating procedures (SOPs), organizational charts, and report formats, then send these to the LNOs' parent commands. Likewise, LNOs provide parent command SOPs, organizational charts, intelligence products, and other useful information to the receiving organization. Coordination between staffs alleviates problems before they become elevated to command channels. LNOs must anticipate receiving information requirements.

2-31. LNOs provide advanced warning of receiving information requirements to allow for maximum lead-time available to prepare products. In some cases, LNOs provide the required information from sources already available, thus reducing the demands and tasks communicated to their parent commands. To further assist the information flow between commands, LNOs should review message addressees and distribution lists to ensure the proper routing of official correspondence between commands.

2-32. LNOs are important catalysts, facilitating effective coordination between staffs; however, an LNO's work is not a substitute for proper interaction among staff components. Staff-to-staff coordination is essential at all levels to ensure unity of effort. Similarly, established C2 procedures (such as fragmentary orders [FRAGORDs], warning orders [WARNORDs], and alert orders) are the proper method for communicating specific orders and taskings.

2-33. **Advise.** LNOs are the receiving units' experts on the capabilities and limitations of the sending organizations. LNOs must be available to answer questions from the receiving staff and other units. As such, LNOs advise the receiving commander and staff on the optimum employment of the capabilities of the sending organizations. Simultaneously, LNOs advise the sending commander on issues of the receiving HQ. LNOs must remember that they have authority only to make decisions the commander of the sending organization authorizes. LNOs must exercise caution to ensure that they do not obligate the sending organization to taskings beyond the specified charter or taskings that should be forwarded through normal C2 channels.

2-34. **Assist.** LNOs must assist on two levels. First, they must act as the conduit between their command and the receiving organization. Second, by integrating themselves into the receiving unit as participants in the daily operations cycle of the unit (daily briefings and meetings, sometimes referred to as the "battle rhythm"), LNOs answer questions from various groups to ensure that the groups make informed decisions. LNOs facilitate the submission of required reports from their unit to the receiving organization.

2-35. LNOs must keep current of all significant problems experienced by the sending organization that could affect operations of other commands and vice versa. They make sure the information is conveyed to the appropriate staff personnel and provide recommendations to optimize the employment of the sending organization. LNOs offer clear, concise, and accurate information and recommendations in a timely manner to the receiving unit and the sending organization. LNOs should ask the following questions:

- Does my unit know?
- Will we have a need for it?
- Is it important to my commander?
- Who else needs to know?
- Is this an appropriate mission for my unit?
- Does it support the overall plan?
- Is it operationally feasible for my unit?
- Are the required resources available to execute?

Liaison Organization

2-36. The liaison element or team is the direct representative of the POTF or PSE commander and, as such, must be competent and confident in its role. Soldiers tasked with LNO missions should have significant PSYOP experience and be among the best personnel in the unit. As a minimum, the liaison team must be manned for 24-hour operations. This requirement must be taken into consideration when planning the following manning roster:

- Day shift: OIC, PSYOP specialist.
- Night shift: Noncommissioned officer in charge (NCOIC), PSYOP specialist.

Duties and Responsibilities

2-37. LNOs, to ensure all levels of command remain aware of the operational situation, provide urgent, priority, or routine information; verification of information; and clarification of operational questions. Liaison activities augment the commander's ability to synchronize and focus critical assets, ensuring precise understanding of the implied or inferred coordination measures needed to achieve desired results. LNOs must—

- Be familiar with all listed references before linkup.
- Establish primary, alternate, and contingency communications plans before linkup and report the means to contact the main POTF or PSE.
- Integrate directly into the G-3 or S-3 staff of the supported unit and ensure PSYOP inclusion.
- Report any problems with the supported unit to the main POTF or PSE immediately.

Reporting and Handling of Message Traffic

2-38. Proper information distribution and message handling are essential duties of an LNO. LNOs keep the supported unit and the POTF or PSE updated on all PSYOP activities in their AOs. The following procedures outline the proper format for conducting this task:

- Maintain a daily staff journal or log (DA Form 1594).
- Log all message traffic.
- Log all actions taken.
- Log all reports submitted to higher HQ and maintain a paper or digital file copy.
- Submit situation reports (SITREPs) to the POTF or PSE G-3 twice daily at the times directed by the G-3.
- Report action complete on all urgent and priority traffic to the message center immediately and battle damage assessment (BDA) if available.

2-39. **Priorities of Message Traffic.** The POTF or PSE chief of staff or deputy chief of staff classifies message traffic as follows:

- *Urgent*: Requires immediate action by one or more staff sections—for example, short-suspense PSYACTs or PSYOP product requests.
- *Priority*: Requires action by the staff within a given time—for example, PSYOP product folder for the combatant commander's approval.
- *Routine*: Requires awareness but no immediate action by any staff section—for example, PSYOP intelligence summary (INTSUM) distribution.

2-40. **Distribution of Message Traffic.** The POTF or PSE chief of staff or the deputy chief of staff determines distribution of message traffic. He may delegate handling of routine messages to the message center personnel. The standard distribution codes are as follows:

- *Distribution A*: Distributed to all. Message center personnel send the traffic through every staff section internally (paper copy translated) to every command post and every LNO.
- *Distribution B*: Distributed to staff and command posts only.
- *Distribution C*: Distributed to LNOs.
- *Distribution D*: Distributed to a specific individual, staff element, or LNO.

2-41. **Information Management During Shift-Change Operations.** The POTF or PSE chief of staff or deputy chief of staff, all POTF or PSE staff sections, LNOs, and the message center staff accomplish the following actions during shift change:

- Brief all urgent and priority actions completed during the last 12 hours.
- Brief all urgent and priority actions ongoing, including action required and suspense.

- Circulate a routine message using Distribution A immediately following shift change, listing all outstanding urgent and priority actions, responsible agencies, and suspenses.

2-42. **Message Numbering Procedures.** A standard message-numbering format is necessary to ensure a smooth flow of information between elements. Information shown in Figure 2-9 goes in the upper left corner of all messages distributed.

(1) Priority and Distribution:			From:		
Received by:			Message Identification:		
(2) Message Identification Format:					
In or Out	Date	Hour	Time	Month	Year
I	17	0714	Z	Jun	02
Example:	(Incoming message)		I170714ZJun02		
	(Outgoing message)		O170716ZJun02		

Figure 2-9. Standard Message Format

Reference Materials

2-43. The following is a list of materials essential in accomplishing the mission of being a competent LNO. The list is not a complete library of needed references, but it should be considered the minimum to support a wide variety of missions:

- Unclassified references:
  - Joint Publication (JP) 3-53, *Doctrine for Joint Psychological Operations.*
  - FM 3-05.30, *Psychological Operations.*
  - JP 0-2, *Unified Action Armed Forces (UNAAF).*
  - Joint Forces Staff College (JFSC) Pub 1, *The Joint Staff Officer's Guide 2000.*
  - JP 5-0, *Doctrine for Planning Joint Operations.*
  - JP 5-00.1, *Joint Doctrine for Campaign Planning.*
  - FM 3-13, *Information Operations: Doctrine, Tactics, Techniques, and Procedures.*
  - FM 101-5, *Staff Organization and Operations* (FM 5-0, *Army Planning and Orders Production,* upon revision).
  - FM 6-0, *Mission Command: Command and Control of Army Forces.*
  - USAJFKSWCS Publication (Pub) 525-5-16, *Psychological Operations: Equipment Types, Specifications, and Capabilities.*
  - Unit SOPs.
- Classified references:
  - Theater-specific OPLANs and PSYOP annexes.
  - Theater-specific concept plans (CONPLANs).

Support Requirements

2-44. In most instances, LNO elements are away from their commands and all the support their commands provide; therefore, they must take their own equipment to accomplish the mission. The minimum support requirements are as follows:

- At least one cellular telephone.
- One laptop computer with Internet access, classified if possible.
- Classes I, III, IV, VIII, and IX supplies from the supporting unit.
- Shortfalls or repair or replacement of SOF-peculiar equipment from the POTF or PSE.
- Reference materials and minimum requirements from the POTF or PSE before linkup with supported units.

NOTE: LNO elements should identify local sources of support for all classes of supplies immediately upon linkup.

Administrative Planning Procedures

2-45. The following timeline is an example of how to plan for a typical mission. Because of media operations complex (MOC) and final planning conference (FPC) timelines, the times may need adjusting. The J-3, G-3, or S-3 may already be coordinating some of these; however, LNOs must assume they are not and must double-check all coordination. The check will facilitate starting the mission immediately, rather than having to conduct coordination. The timeline for a typical mission includes the following duties for LNOs:

- *90 days out*: Contact the supporting unit; obtain the names, the telephone numbers, and the office or room numbers of the supporting personnel; give WARNORD and request office or desk space, telephone and local area network (LAN), and billeting; and if necessary, request linguists.
- *60 days out*: Call back to confirm or adjust, immediately upon linkup.
- *30 days out*: Adjust any last-minute details.
- *1 week, 2 days out*: Move to location, set up office or desk space, make communications checks with adjacent or higher units (POTF), arrange billeting, determine exact location of the unit or element liaising with.

Wartime Planning Procedures

2-46. Soldiers identified as LNOs during wartime must be prepared to adjust quickly to the flow of the battle. LNOs must remember that the elements of METT-TC are the greatest influence on their mission and that maintaining good communications with the POTF or PSE significantly improves the success of the mission. The following is a basic outline of what LNOs must do in that situation:

- Deploy from their home units to the AOR. (**NOTE:** LNOs must contact the POTF or PSE as soon as possible, if the POTF or PSE has not already contacted them.)

- Process through the point of entry. (**NOTE:** The objective is the main POTF or PSE.)
- Link up with the main POTF or PSE.
- Receive in-briefs, task organization, assessments, and equipment issue. (**NOTE:** LNOs conduct precombat inspections before moving to their supporting unit.)
- Deploy to and link up with the supporting unit.
- Establish primary, alternate, contingency, and emergency (PACE) communication and conduct communication check with the POTF or PSE to report linkup.
- Identify local sources of services and support.
- Conduct the mission.

Liaison Officer Situation Report Format

2-47. So that information is conveyed from one location to another without misinterpretation, the LNO SITREP is a standardized form. When LNOs report to the POTF or PSE, LNOs must use the SITREP format outlined in Figure 2-10.

A. Unit or Task Organization.

B. Time Period Covered (in DTG form).

C. General Situation. (A general overview of the operational environment.)

   1. Summary of last 24 hours. (Operations conducted in the last day.)

   2. Planned operations for next 24 hours. (Operations to be conducted in the next day.)

   3. Dissemination operations in AO (chart/attachment); product numbers disseminated per city or location, by product name.

   4. Impact indicators in AO. (Recurring events or observations or major events that seem to be part of a trend or something out of the ordinary. Evidence that a particular PSYACT, product, series, or program is or is not having an effect on the intended TA or an unintended audience.)

   5. Survey results from AO. (Summary of survey results, surveys being conducted [attachment].)

D. Operational Issues. (Directives from the supported unit that affect the mission.)

   1. Urgent and priority actions completed during reporting period.

   2. Urgent and priority actions ongoing as of report submission.

E. Personnel Issues. (Personnel status.)

F. Logistics Issues. (Any logistics issues and requests for equipment and supplies, in red, yellow, or green form.)

G. Sensitive Items Report. (Initial report is a complete inventory by serial number; subsequent reports give status only.)

H. Other Issues.

Figure 2-10. LNO SITREP Format

2-48. When reporting SITREPs verbally, personnel should use the phonetic alphabet. SITREPs transmitted through nonsecure means must not contain classified information and must be limited to personnel status, sensitive items status, and a plan for transmitting a full SITREP through secure channels. Figure 2-11, page 2-25, provides an example of an LNO SITREP.

A. FROKA LNO.

B. 121730ZJUL02 THROUGH 130545ZJUL02.

C. ROK/US FORCES HAVE ADVANCED FROM xxxxxx TO xxxxxx AND HAVE DISPLACED xxx CIVILIANS. xxx EPW HAS BEEN TASKED WITH ASSISTING THE REMOVAL OF THESE DISLOCATED CIVILIANS (DC'S). PSYOP SITUATION HAS IMPROVED. 2 COMPANIES HAVE SURRENDERED VIC GRID xxxx.

1. SPOKE TO CA REP ABOUT EPW SITUATION. SENT MINI SITREP TO C3 TO NOTIFY TAAD/TED.

2. KEEP IN TOUCH WITH CA REP. CONTACT FROKA S-6 REP TO TROUBLESHOOT LAN CONNECTION.

3. EPW'S STAYING OFF MSR, 2 COMPANIES SURRENDERED.

4. SEE ATTACHED CHART.

5. SEE ATTACHED CHART.

D. FROKA WILL CONDUCT JUMPTOC OPERATION 20JUL02. WILL MOVE WITH S-2 ELEMENT.

1. REPLY TO URGENT MESSAGE: GCCS-K SENT 130218ZJUL02.

2. PIR STILL NOT READY DUE TO FROKA S-2.

E. NONE.

F. NEED PENS, BLACK, BALLPOINT TYPE, 14 EACH, 2 REAMS OF COPIER PAPER NLT 15JUL02.

G. ALL ACCOUNTED FOR.

H. NONE.

Figure 2-11. LNO SITREP Example

USE OF DIGITAL SYSTEMS BY PSYOP FORCES

2-49. Digital systems are a commander's principal tool in collecting, transporting, processing, disseminating, and protecting data. Digital systems are the information exchange and decision support subsystems within the C2 support system of the total force. The continuous need for information to support PSYOP is the basis for the SOF digital systems. Availability of information can make the difference between success and failure of a PSYOP mission. The data must get to the right place, on time, and in a format that is quickly usable by the intended recipients, and it must generate appropriate actions. Special military operations conducted in peace, stability operations, support operations, and war differ significantly from conventional operations. PSYOP operators must be able to communicate long-range, anywhere in the world and at any time, while remaining completely interoperable with joint and Army systems.

COMMAND AND CONTROL

2-50. PSYOP forces at all levels use digital tools to exercise C2 of subordinate units. PSYOP forces use the Maneuver Control System (MCS) and GCCS to perform the following C2 functions:

- Participate in the military decision-making process (MDMP).

- Transmit and receive PSYOP orders, annexes, overlays, FRAGORDs, CONPLANs, and other instructions to subordinate and higher units.

- Submit SITREPs to higher PSYOP HQ.

- Coordinate for higher-level PSYOP support—for example, COMMANDO SOLO.

ARMY BATTLE COMMAND SYSTEM

2-51. The Army Battle Command System (ABCS) is the integration of C2 systems in all echelons. The ABCS integrates battlespace automation systems and communications that functionally link installations and mobile networks. The ABCS is interoperable with joint and multinational C2 systems at upper echelons, across the full range of C2 functionality. At the tactical and operational levels, integration is vertical and horizontal. The ABCS consists of three major components:

- Global Command and Control System–Army (GCCS-A).
- Army Tactical Command and Control System (ATCCS).
- Force XXI Battle Command, Brigade and Below (FBCB2).

Global Command and Control System–Army

2-52. The GCCS-A is a system built from application programs of the following systems:

- Army Worldwide Military Command and Control System (WWMCS) Information System (AWIS).
- Strategic Theater Command and Control System (STCCS).
- Echelons above corps (EAC) portion of the Combat Service Support Control System (CSSCS).

The primary scope of the GCCS-A effort is to evolve the stand-alone systems into a suite of modular applications that operate within the defense information infrastructure (DII) common operating environment (COE). GCCS-A modules interface with common applications and other shared components of the ABCS and with the joint C2 mission applications provided by the GCCS.

2-53. The GCCS-A is the Army link for ABCS to the GCCS. The GCCS-A provides information and decision support to Army strategic-, operational-, and theater-level planning and operational or theater operations and sustainment. The GCCS-A supports the apportionment, allocation, logistical support, and deployment of Army forces to the combatant commands. Functionality includes force tracking, HN and CA support, theater air defense, targeting, PSYOP, C2, logistics, medical, provost marshal (PM), counterdrug (CD), and personnel status. The GCCS-A is deployed from theater EAC elements to division.

Army Tactical Command and Control System

2-54. The ATCCS consists of five major subsystems. These subsystems are explained in the following paragraphs.

2-55. **Maneuver Control System.** The MCS is the primary battle command (BC) source. The MCS provides the common operational picture (COP), decision aids, and overlay capabilities to support the tactical commander and the staff through interface with the force-level information database populated from the Battlefield Automated Systems (BASs). The MCS provides the functional common applications necessary to access and manipulate the Joint Common Database (JCDB). The MCS satisfies IRs for a specific operation. The MCS tracks resources, displays situational awareness, provides timely control of current combat operations (offense, defense, stability, and support), and effectively develops and distributes plans, orders, and estimates in support of future operations. The MCS supports the MDMP and is deployed from corps to the maneuver battalions.

2-56. **All-Source Analysis System.** The All-Source Analysis System (ASAS) is the intelligence and electronic warfare (IEW) component from EAC to battalion. The ASAS is a mobile, tactically deployable, computer-assisted IEW processing, analysis, reporting, and technical control system. The ASAS receives and rapidly processes large volumes of combat information and sensor reports from all sources to provide timely and accurate targeting information, intelligence products, and threat alerts. The ASAS consists of evolutionary modules that perform systems operations management, systems security, collection management, intelligence processing and reporting, high-value or high-payoff target processing and nominations, and communications processing and interfacing.

2-57. The ASAS remote workstation (RWS) provides automated support to the doctrinal functions of intelligence staff officers—division or higher intelligence staff officer (G-2) and battalion or brigade intelligence staff officer (S-2)—from EAC to battalion, including SOF. The ASAS RWS also operates as the technical control portion of the intelligence node of ABCS to provide current IEW and enemy situation (ENSIT) information to the JCDB for access and use by ABCS users. The ASAS produces the ENSIT portion of the COP of the battlefield disseminated by means of the ABCS network.

2-58. **Combat Service Support Control System.** The CSSCS provides critical, timely, integrated, and accurate automated combat service support (CSS) information, including all classes of supplies, field services, maintenance, medical, personnel, and movements to CSS, maneuver and theater commanders, and logistics and special staffs. Critical resource information is drawn from manual resources and the standard Army multicommand management information system (STAMMIS) at each echelon, which evolve to the GCSS-A (the unclassified logistics wholesale and resale business end connectivity). The CSSCS processes, analyzes, and integrates resource information to support evaluation of current and projected force-sustainment capabilities. The chaplaincy is an active participant in CSSCS and is included in the development of CSS services. The CSSCS provides CSS information for the commanders and staff and is deployed from EAC to battalion.

2-59. **Air and Missile Defense Planning and Control System.** The Air and Missile Defense Planning and Control System (AMDPCS) integrates air defense fire units, sensors, and C2 centers into a coherent system capable of defeating or denying the aerial threat, such as unmanned aerial vehicles, helicopters, and fixed-wing aircraft. The AMDPCS provides for automated, seamless C2, and Force XXI vertical and horizontal interoperability with joint and coalition forces for United States Army (USA) air and missile defense (AMD) units. The system provides common hardware and software modules, at all echelons of command, which provide for highly effective employment of Army AMD weapon systems as part of the joint force. AMDPCS provides the third dimension situational awareness component of the COP. Initially, the

Air and Missile Defense Workstation (AMDWS) provides elements from EAC to battalion the capability to track the air and missile defense battle (force operations [FO]).

2-60. **Advanced Field Artillery Tactical Data System.** The Advanced Field Artillery Tactical Data System (AFATDS) provides automated decision support for the fire support (FS) functional subsystem, including joint and combined fires—for example, naval gunfire and close air support. AFATDS provides a fully integrated FS C2 system, giving the fire support coordinator (FSCOORD) automated support for planning, coordinating, controlling, and executing close support, counterfire, interdiction, and air defense suppression fires. AFATDS performs all of the FS operational functions, including automated allocation and distribution of fires based on target value analysis. AFATDS is deployed from EAC to the firing platoons. AFATDS provides the FS overlay information to the ABCS common database. AFATDS interoperates with the United States Air Force (USAF) theater battle management core system (TBMCS) and the United States Navy (USN) and United States Marine Corps (USMC) joint maritime command information system (JMCIS). AFATDS also interoperates with the FS C2 systems with allied countries, including the United Kingdom, Germany, and France.

Force XXI Battle Command, Brigade and Below

2-61. FBCB2 is a suite of digitally interoperable applications and platform hardware. FBCB2 provides on-the-move, real-time, and near-real-time situational awareness and C2 information to combat, combat support (CS), and CSS leaders from brigade to the platform and Soldier levels. FBCB2 is a mission-essential subelement and a key component of the ABCS. FBCB2 feeds the ABCS common database with automated positional friendly information and current tactical battlefield geometry for friendly and known or suspected enemy forces. The goal is to field FBCB2 to the tank and Bradley fighting vehicle and other platforms with a common look-and-feel screen. Common hardware and software design facilitates training and SOP. Tactical PSYOP units (Active Army and RC), the I/R PSYOP battalion (RC), and other ABCSs use the FBCB2 extensively.

OTHER ARMY BATTLE COMMAND SYSTEMS

2-62. PSYOP forces use several other ABCSs. The following paragraphs discuss each of these systems.

Warfighter Information Network

2-63. The Warfighter Information Network (WIN) is an integrated command, control, communications, and computers (C4) network that consists of commercially based high-technology communications network systems. The WIN enables information dominance by increasing the security, capacity, and velocity (speed of service to the user) of information distribution throughout the battlespace. A common sense mix of terrestrial and satellite communications is required for a robust ABCS. The WIN supports the warfighter in the 21st century with the means to provide information services from the sustaining base to deployed units worldwide.

WIN-Terrestrial Transport

2-64. The Warfighter Information Network-Terrestrial Transport (WIN-T) portion of the WIN focuses on the terrestrial (nonsatellite) transmission and networking segment of the WIN. The WIN-T is the backbone infrastructure of the WIN architecture, as well as the LAN in support of the ABCS-capable tactical operations center (TOC). The WIN-T provides simultaneous secure-voice, data, imagery, and video-communications services.

Tactical Internet

2-65. The Tactical Internet (TI) enhances warfighter operations by providing an improved, integrated data communications network for mobile users. The TI passes C4I information, extending tactical automation to the Soldier or weapons platform. The TI focuses on brigade and below to provide the parameters in defining a tactical automated data communications network.

LOGISTICS

2-66. PSYOP personnel use CSSCS to process, analyze, and integrate PSYOP-specific resource information to support current and projected PSYOP force sustainment logistically. Supply personnel use CSSCS to track, monitor, and requisition PSYOP-specific equipment and all classes of supply needed by subordinate PSYOP units. PSYOP personnel also use CSSCS to evacuate and transfer damaged or broken equipment and to receive new or repaired PSYOP-specific items.

ANALYSIS

2-67. PSYOP personnel use the numerous intelligence databases and links within ABCS to access all-source intelligence products and services. The ABCS supplements PSYOP-specific Department of Defense (DOD) and non-DOD intelligence sources. Intelligence sources available through ABCS enhance the ability of PSYOP forces to—

- Conduct TAA.
- Counter hostile propaganda.
- Track impact indicators.
- Support I/R operations.
- Conduct pretesting and posttesting of products.
- Submit and track RFIs.
- Provide input to the commander's critical information requirements (CCIR).
- Manage frequency deconfliction.

The ASAS provides PSYOP intelligence personnel the tools to perform—

- Systems operations management.
- Systems security.
- Collection management.
- Intelligence processing and reporting.

- High-value and high-payoff PSYOP target processing and nominations.
- Communications processing and interfacing.

2-68.   The ASAS provides PSYOP personnel with current IEW and enemy situation by means of the JCDB, allowing PSYOP intelligence personnel to monitor current tactical, operational, and strategic situations.

PRODUCT DEVELOPMENT

2-69.   PSYOP personnel use the ABCS to develop, modify, edit, transmit, and receive PSYOP products, from the tactical to the strategic level. Specifically, PSYOP personnel use the ABCS to perform the following product development functions:

- Develop print product prototypes.
- Develop audio and video product prototypes.
- Submit target audience analysis work sheets (TAAWs), product/action work sheets (PAWs), and program control sheets.
- Transmit audio and video files using the File Transfer Protocol (FTP) tool. (**NOTE:** PSYOP personnel download and view or modify files by means of the Product Development Workstation [PDW].)

INFORMATION MANAGEMENT

2-70.   PSYOP personnel use the ABCS to conduct information management. Through this process, PSYOP personnel can share PSYOP information with all IO disciplines for the purpose of synchronization, coordination, and deconfliction. Specific information management functions include—

- Posting PSYOP SITREPs, PSYOP-specific intelligence reports, and PSYOP products to files or folders accessible by all ABCS users.
- Managing message traffic.
- Managing OPORDs, OPLANs, FRAGORDs, CONPLANS, and branch plans and sequels.
- Managing RFIs, CSS support requests, and administrative support requests.

SUMMARY

2-71.   To be fully effective, PSYOP forces and activities must be integrated, deconflicted, synchronized, and coordinated early at all levels. The POTF or PSE is the foundation from which effective PSYOP are planned, coordinated, and executed. Skillfully integrated PSYOP activities support the overall combatant commander's plan and enhance successful mission accom-plishment. Choosing, preparing, and properly dispatching the LNO and the LNO team are critical to their effectiveness. Commanders make a conscious tradeoff between extensive preparation of the LNO and expeditiously dispatching the LNO to begin coordination and information exchange. In all cases, the LNO and the receiving HQ should understand the limits of the LNO's authority, which is best specified in writing. The continuous need for information to support PSYOP is the basis for the SOF digital systems. Availability of information can make the difference between success and failure of a PSYOP mission.

Chapter 3

Intelligence Preparation of the Battlespace

It is your attitude, and the suspicion that you are maturing the boldest designs against him, that imposes on your enemy.

Frederick the Great
Instruction to His Generals, 1747

The IPB process supports commanders and their staffs in the decision-making process. The IPB is the commander's and each staff member's responsibility; the S-2 or G-2 does not do the entire IPB alone. All staff sections must assist the S-2 or G-2 in developing the situation template (SITTEMP) within their own areas of expertise. The IPB process is continuous. IPB is conducted prior to and during the command's initial planning for the operation, but is also performed during the conduct of the operation. The IPB process for most SOF units results in graphic and written intelligence estimates that, at the minimum, evaluate probable threat, COAs, and vulnerabilities of hostile, friendly, and neutral forces.

The relationship between IPB and TAA needs clarification to remove the confusion between the two processes. Initial IPB for PSYOP, done during planning, deals with more traditional order of battle, weather, and terrain factors. The PSYOP-specific initial IPB concerns itself with broad target sets, demographic information, and broad cultural practices.

The ongoing IPB process that occurs throughout an operation does include TAA that is performed by the TAAD. The POTF G-2 obtains traditional military IPB information, tracks down PSYOP-specific IRs and PIR, helps with research, and then feeds that information to the TAAD for TAA purposes. The integration of traditional G-2 IPB with TAA gives the POTF commander the unique PSYOP IPB information needed to make informed decisions.

The PSYOP IPB is probably the most extensive and detailed of any IPB conducted in the Army. In addition to merely identifying various hostile or friendly elements, the PSYOP IPB contains comprehensive and in-depth analyses of numerous TAs and their conditions, vulnerabilities, accessibility, and susceptibility. IPB identifies facts and assumptions about the battlefield environment and the threat, which enables staff planning and the development of friendly COAs. IPB provides the basis for intelligence direction and synchronization that supports the command's chosen COA.

FOUR-STEP PSYOP INTELLIGENCE PREPARATION OF THE BATTLESPACE PROCESS

3-1. The Army IPB process involves the execution of four steps; while PSYOP have special considerations, PSYOP personnel follow the same steps as the rest of the Army. PSYOP require extensive intelligence collection to conduct vigorous PSYOP-relevant analyses that delve into potential TAs and the PSYOP environment. The following paragraphs review each of the steps.

STEP 1: DEFINE THE BATTLEFIELD ENVIRONMENT

3-2. In Step 1 of the IPB process, the G-2 or S-2 focuses the command's initial intelligence collection efforts and the remaining steps of the IPB process. The G-2 or S-2—

- Identifies characteristics of the battlefield that will influence friendly and threat operations.
- Establishes the limits of the area of interest (AI).
- Identifies gaps in current intelligence holdings.

In focusing the remainder of the IPB process, the G-2 or S-2 identifies characteristics of the battlefield that require in-depth evaluation of their effects on friendly and threat operations, such as terrain, weather, logistical infrastructure, and demographics. Defining the significant characteristics of the battlefield environment also aids in identifying gaps in current intelligence holdings and the specific intelligence required to fill them. Similarly, the G-2 or S-2 identifies gaps in the command's knowledge of the threat and the current threat situation.

3-3. For PSYOP, the emphasis during this first step is to identify weather, terrain, infrastructure, and potential TAs within the AOR. These functions are most often completed by G-2 or S-2 in conjunction with the PSYOP planner, POAT, and PPD. Identification of these essential elements is done during initial IPB.

STEP 2: DESCRIBE THE BATTLEFIELD'S EFFECTS

3-4. Step 2 evaluates the effects of the environment with which both sides must contend. The G-2 or S-2 identifies the limitations and opportunities the environment offers on the potential operations of friendly and threat forces. This evaluation focuses on the general capabilities of each force until COAs are developed in later steps of the IPB process. This assessment of the environment always includes an examination of terrain and weather but may also include discussions of the characteristics of geography and infrastructure and their effects on friendly and threat operations. Characteristics of geography include general characteristics of the terrain and weather, as well as such factors as politics, civilian press, local population, and demographics. An area's infrastructure consists of the facilities, equipment, and framework needed for the functioning of systems, cities, or regions.

3-5. For PSYOP, Step 2 of IPB is where analysis is conducted. The G-2 or S-2 must analyze the weather and terrain and determine how these will affect the dissemination of PSYOP products by both friendly and hostile forces. Infrastructure analysis for PSYOP considers the information environment and the media outlets that disseminate information. This analysis must determine which outlets are available for use by friendly PSYOP forces and those that are being used by opponent forces. The POTF or PSE S-2 or G-2, in conjunction with the supported unit's intelligence section, is primarily responsible for this portion of Step 2. The analysis of the potential TAs that were identified in Step 1 is done by the TAAD. The TAAD takes the potential target audience list (PTAL) from Step 1 of IPB and the SPO that was written during planning and begins to analyze each target set and SPO combination to determine the vulnerabilities, lines of persuasion, susceptibilities, accessibilities, and effectiveness of each TA. This process determines each TA's ability to affect the battlefield. The TAAD will determine the ability of each TA to influence the PSYOP and supported commander's stated objectives. A complete discussion of TAA is in Chapter 5.

STEP 3: EVALUATE THE THREAT

3-6. In Step 3 of Army IPB, the G-2 or S-2 and his staff analyze the command's intelligence holdings to determine how the threat normally organizes for combat and conducts operations under similar circumstances. PSYOP specialists concern themselves with propaganda analysis and counterpropaganda during this stage of IPB. They monitor the competing agencies within the AOR who are disseminating information and determine what effect that information will have on the conduct of the operation. This analysis is largely done by the TAAD but with significant assistance from the G-2 or S-2 who will be interfacing with the various intelligence agencies to obtain PSYOP-relevant information. A technique, which facilitates propaganda analysis, is to have TAAD and G-2 or S-2 personnel located in close proximity to one another. This function of propaganda analysis is peculiar to PSYOP IPB and, when done effectively, can be of great interest and assistance to a supported commander.

STEP 4: DETERMINE THREAT COURSES OF ACTION

3-7. Step 4 integrates the results of the previous steps into a meaningful conclusion. Given what the threat normally prefers to do and the effects of the specific environment in which he is operating now, what are his likely objectives and the COAs available to him? After the first three steps, PSYOP specialists have defined the operational environment, conducted TAA, and analyzed competing information. This information taken together allows the PSYOP force to modify behavior and counter other information to achieve PSYOP and, ultimately, supported commander objectives. In short, the IPB process allows commanders to make informed decisions that ensure mission success.

AREA OF OPERATIONS AND THE BATTLESPACE: IMPLICATIONS FOR PSYOP

3-8. The AO is the geographical area where the commander is assigned the responsibility and authority to conduct military operations. A thorough knowledge of the characteristics of this area is critical to the success of the operation. The limits of the AO are normally the boundaries specified in the OPORD or CONPLAN from higher HQ that define the command's mission.

3-9. The limits of the command's battlespace are determined by the maximum capabilities of a unit to acquire targets and physically dominate the threat. A command's battlespace generally includes all or most of the AO, as well as areas outside of the AO. The evaluation of the area within the command's battlespace may be as detailed as the evaluation of the AO. The PSYOP IPB process looks at TAs within and outside the AO that can affect the supported commander's objectives. The PSYOP AI is directly tied to the target population and may comprise an entire country or include other countries.

3-10. The PSYOP analysis process is an extension of the higher HQ IPB, and yields timely and focused products that are updated routinely. The PSYOP portion is concerned mainly with the human aspects of the situation—potential TAs and their receptiveness to information programs that seek to influence them in some fashion. Once operations begin and new data becomes available, IPB products are dynamic, changing as the situation changes in the objective area.

3-11. PSYOP specialists uniquely study other characteristics of the battlespace by employing "factor analysis," which will be addressed in detail later in this chapter. Examples are—

- Density and distribution of population groups.
- Composite groups based on political behavior and the strengths of each.
- Issues motivating political, economic, social, or military behaviors of groups.
- Economic infrastructure.
- Economic programs that can cause desired changes in population behavior.
- Formal and informal political structure of the government.
- Legal and illegal political parties.
- Nonparty political organizations and special interest groups.
- Independence of the judiciary.
- Independence of the mass media.
- Administrative competence of the bureaucracy.
- Origin of the incumbent government.
- History of political violence in the country.

3-12. The commander directs the IPB process and, in general, all staff elements are active participants in this effort. The senior intelligence officer (SIO) of the POTF or PSE is responsible for conducting and managing the PSYOP IPB process. The G-3 integrates IPB products with other staff products and applies them to mission planning and execution. The G-3 promptly provides products to the appropriate staffs and detachments.

RESEARCH AND ANALYSIS DIVISION PSYOP STUDIES PROGRAM

3-13. The Research and Analysis Division of the 4th POG(A) at Fort Bragg, North Carolina, is the only source of finished PSYOP analytical intelligence products that are tailored to the needs of the entire PSYOP community, the geographic combatant commanders, and the intelligence community. The division consists of four regionally oriented SSDs. PSYOP units begin the IPB process by consulting PSYOP studies prepared by highly educated and experienced DA civilian analysts in their respective target regions. The majority of these analysts in the SSDs of the regional PSYOP battalions have doctor of philosophy (Ph.D.) degrees in the fields of social sciences, history, economics, or cultural anthropology, to name a few. The analysts produce PSYOP studies mainly to support the development of feasibility analysis, OPLANs, and contingency-related, quick-response assessments for crisis response. The following paragraphs explain the most common of these studies.

Psychological Operations Appendix to the Military Capabilities Study

3-14. The PSYOP appendix to the military capabilities study is a concise summation (15 to 20 pages) of PSYOP-relevant issues on countries around the world. Commanders should review it if U.S. operations are possible in the countries discussed. These PSYOP appendixes are tied to a DOD intelligence production and update schedule.

Special Psychological Operations Study

3-15. The special Psychological Operations study (SPS) has a relatively narrow focus and may address any of a variety of different subjects. The SPS provides more in-depth analysis on a specific topic than any other type of PSYOP study. The study may include the following:

- Analysis of long-standing issues or problems in a particular target country.
- Detailed assessment of the PSYOP environment in a specific region or "hot spot" within a country.
- In-depth analyses of key groups and sometimes individuals.
- Analysis of the social institution and its PSYOP significance.
- Local audiences' perceptions of the United States and its policies.
- Exploration of an issue of particular importance to the population of a given area and the implications for PSYOP.

Special Psychological Operations Assessment

3-16. The special Psychological Operations assessment (SPA) is a time-sensitive intelligence memorandum (usually an electronic message, as well as a posting on the intelligence link [INTELINK]), and is therefore produced more quickly than an SPS. The SPA gives readers a timely assessment of the PSYOP significance of a crisis situation, an important event, or a pressing issue. The SPA also assesses how PSYOP may affect U.S. national interests or political-military operations.

Psychological Analytical Products

3-17. The following is a list of additional products that are produced upon request by geographic combatant commanders and other agencies:

- *Assessments of the PSYOP environment*: Analysis of the basic psychological conditions in a country or region of interest.
- *PSYOP audience analyses*: Analyses of key groups of interest for PSYOP.

- *PSYOP issue analyses*: Analyses of attitudes toward a specific issue or set of issues of concern in a country or region.
- *PSYOP spot reports*: Time-sensitive analysis of discrete events and issues of immediate concern to PSYOP.

3-18. The Psychological Operations automated system (POAS) electronically archives studies and also offers analysts access to various classified and unclassified databases. Commanders can obtain most of these studies through the 4th POG(A)'s home page on the classified intelligence link-Secret (INTELINK-S) system and on USSOCOM's home page under the J-2 on the sensitive compartmented information (SCI) INTELINK system. Copies of PSYOP studies can be downloaded or printed from the computer system. In the unlikely event that an end user does not have access to INTELINK or INTELINK-S, the POAS staff can, by exception, print out a copy of a study and send it to a commander or customer. The authors usually maintain extra copies of the studies for internal consumption. Copies can be obtained and stored at the detachment level with a current courier card for classified material transportation.

3-19. These studies are augmented with additional intelligence data in preparation for the PSYOP mission. Information may be derived from a variety of sources. The DA civilian analysts have the capability to access and analyze a vast amount of classified and unclassified information from multiple sources. However, PSYOP Soldiers may provide valuable first-hand information gleaned while conducting operations during deployments. Together, the Soldiers and analysts share information to conduct the most thorough PSYOP-relevant analysis to support operational planning and execution.

PSYOP INTELLIGENCE COLLECTION PLAN

3-20. The IPB is a four-step process in which the 14 political-military factors are used as a guide for categorizing intelligence and delegating duties and functions. The IPB process is the second step of Phase II of the MDMP. (FM 3-05.30 provides more information on the IPB process.)

3-21. The commander and his SIO develop PSYOP intelligence requirements based on the 14-factor political-military analytical framework described below. Intelligence needs focus on leveraging the social, economic, political, and psychological conditions within a targeted country or area to U.S. benefit. The political-military process is basically an analytical framework representing a multidisciplinary approach to understanding the factors that provide the basis for most all of PSYOP-relevant analyses. Once fully explored, these factors affect the conduct of PSYOP and its outcome. This framework helps the SIO and the commander develop the information required to complete the mission. The commander and his SIO use a multidisciplinary approach because no single factor is sufficient to understand the psychological dimension of a mission. (FM 3-05.30 describes these factors in detail.)

3-22. Developing a thorough intelligence collection plan tailored to PSYOP is one approach to obtaining the best possible intelligence support to PSYOP. This plan also serves as a checklist of information that is helpful in ensuring effective PSYOP. The checklist is a starting point that will provide direction to analysts who have limited experience in meeting the unique needs of PSYOP intelligence. The checklist should also be useful as a reference tool. Most importantly, it should stimulate thought on new lines of inquiry (and the intelligence necessary to support it) that are tailored to the precise needs of any given operation.

14-FACTOR POLITICAL-MILITARY ANALYTICAL FRAMEWORK

3-23. The political-military factors are considered the ideal basis for determining the PSYOP intelligence requirements, and moreover, provide the best possible framework to conduct accurate and exhaustive PSYOP-relevant analyses to support planning and operations. Fundamental to all PSYOP-relevant analyses of the political-military factors is that every PSYOP analyst not only describes each of the factors, but must also provide an explanation of why they occur. Determining probable behavior is the key to developing PSYOP plans, programs, and products that will influence a TA.

3-24. The SSD analysts assess these factors as they pertain to their target countries as a matter of course and routinely update their analyses. SSD analysts address these factors in PSYOP studies in one way or another depending on the purpose of the study. In the case of the military capabilities study or PSYOP environment study, many of these factors are explored, whereas an SPA or SPS may provide a more focused analysis on several of the factors. The following paragraphs provide a review of each of the factors and how they relate to PSYOP analysis.

History

3-25. Studying the history of a country, region, or a people is useful for several key reasons. These reasons include the following:

- *Discern a pattern of behavior*. Historical accounts of TA reactions to certain events may provide a basis for predicting similar behavioral responses in similar instances. Patterns of behavior may be discerned through events in a culture's past, helping to predict how a TA will react to various actions of a force or PSYOP products. Knowledge of a group's history may assist the PSYOP Soldier to develop more precise products containing more appropriate messages, consistent with the TA's past behaviors, experiences, and attitudes.

- *Understand how a TA perceives its history*. A PSYOP specialist should be more concerned with understanding how and why the TA perceives its history than what the actual historical record shows.

- *Determine the relative importance of political, social, and economic factors*. History shows which factors were manifested in the past and their significance to the TA. From long-term behavioral patterns, the PSYOP specialist can focus on those factors in developing effective programs and products.

- *Identify historical issues that remain significant today and resonate with the population*. Many historical issues are long-term. Examples of such issues are historically based border disputes and perceived historical wrongs. Such historical issues are usually unresolved, striking an emotional chord in the minds of the TA.

Natural Environment

3-26. The natural environment, and economic, political, social, cultural, and military behavior affect many factors within a society. The natural environment is an important aspect to study. It is helpful to know how much the natural environment plays a role in the way a society is organized—its population growth, distribution, and migration; its culture and daily life; and even its security.

Culture

3-27. Culture is a critical aspect of any TAA. In studying culture, the PSYOP specialist learns how a TA perceives reality. This analysis provides the best way to determine how the TA learned and shared attitudes, values, and behavior.

Political System

3-28. The political system is a set of structures and processes by which people make authoritative collective decisions. All nations and cultures have at least one such system. The two main issues for PSYOP specialists to consider are—

- *Legitimacy.* TAs, themes, and products can be derived from knowing the degree of government legitimacy and the sources of that legitimacy. The PSYOP specialists must understand the formal political structure of the government and the sources of its power. PSYOP specialists must also determine whether a country has a pluralist democracy based on the consensus of the voters or a strongman rule supported by the military.

- *Determining the most important issues.* Every system has a set of issues that are at the forefront of either the minds of the government leaders or the populace or both. Generally, providing a solution to past issues formed the government. Understanding the issues over which an existing regime was formed is important. Also important to know is how a government perceives and reacts to changes in the importance of those issues.

Political Economy

3-29. Politics and economics together often determine the power of a state or a group. Economics have an impact on politics since almost every political decision has an economic outcome. Economic issues are important to PSYOP specialists to better understand the strength of competing groups in a society.

Military

3-30. The military plays an important role in most societies. It is crucial for PSYOP specialists to determine the military's role in a particular society, and how the government and its people view the military. In many instances, the military is a potential TA, and the subgroups within the military (senior leaders, junior officers, NCOs, and conscripts) have varying attitudes, perceptions, and behavior. Key issues for the PSYOP intelligence specialist in studying the role of the military are—

- Identifying the type of security force (regular, reserve, paramilitary, police, or other).
- Identifying the nonpolitical and political roles of a society's military force.
- The tendency of a military force to intervene in politics (and by implication the extent to which the military is controlled by civilian authorities).
- Identifying the public perception of the military's legitimacy or efficacy.

Ideology

3-31. A society's value system generates a certain ideology that most citizens are inherently aware of, but may or may not agree with. An ideology can serve to integrate communities, to advance the position of a particular group, and to strengthen group resolve to act to change the status quo. Ideology is often politicized: it consists of a view of the present and the future, it is action-oriented, it is directed at the masses, and it is usually explained in simple terms. Understanding a society's ideology and the acceptance or rejection by certain groups provides the PSYOP specialist with insights into the TA's willingness to change its attitudes or behavior.

Religion

3-32. All cultures have some form of religion that influences its political, economic, and social systems. The impact of religion on a TA is critical to analyze, since it can potentially affect aspects of a person's life. The TA's perception of any line of persuasion can be critically filtered by their religious beliefs.

Foreign Influence

3-33. Recognizing and understanding the role foreign influence plays in the political-military environment of a country is crucial in planning how PSYOP will influence another nation's TA. Foreign influence can be either direct or indirect. Direct influences are actions (for example, military force or economic sanctions) taken by a foreign government or actor with the express purpose of influencing policy or actions of a specific state. Indirect actions (for example, immigration and technological advances) are not under the direction of a specific outside agency, but can be equally as important as direct actions.

Leadership

3-34. This factor addresses the behavior of leaders and how they use motives, purposes, and resources to mobilize other people to realize goals independently or mutually held by both leaders and followers. For PSYOP planners, influencing the influential (leaders) can be a key step in affecting the behavior of a TA. Identifying key communicators and leaders, both formal and informal, is a critical task for PSYOP intelligence specialists. An understanding of the leadership's decision-making process is also essential for anyone who seeks to influence that process. The Human Factors Analysis Center (HFAC) is part of the IPB Division (TWI-2) of the Information Warfare Support Office at the Defense Intelligence Agency. The HFAC provides assessments of the influence of cultural, psychological, and other human factors on leadership operations and decision making. HFAC products focus on the decision-making processes of the national leadership in potential adversary countries to support IO planning and operations. HFAC products are valuable resources for information and analysis on national-level key communicators and their decision-making processes.

Regional Perspectives

3-35. PSYOP planners must always take into account regional perspectives since they affect the manner in which events are perceived, leading to reactions that may be unanticipated. PSYOP specialists must be able to identify and understand the general regional perspectives on a broad range of issues to judge their effect on future actions within the region. Regional perspectives focus on those issues that more immediately threaten local security and stability. Key issues for PSYOP specialists include regional organizations to which the country belongs, regional treaties and alliances, foreign policy trends, and the pattern of crisis response.

National Interests

3-36. In the international arena, self-interested behavior is the principal assumption upon which the actions of nations and TAs are interpreted. All actors will choose and pursue policies based on their own perception of their national interests. It is critical for PSYOP specialists to know another actor's national interests from the actor's perspective. National interest can most often be identified in terms of survival, sovereignty, and economic well-being.

Ethnicity

3-37. Within most nation-states, there are ethnic groups that may not belong to the politically dominant groups, maintaining their own distinct cultural or social differences. These ethnic differences may transcend all other political-military factors. The PSYOP specialist must determine whether ethnicity is a critical element in the behavior of the TA.

Role of the Media

3-38. The media, both news and literary, plays a vital role in any society. The media and other information networks' increasing availability to society's leadership, population, and infrastructure can have a profound impact on national will, political direction, and national security objectives and policy. PSYOP planners must understand the role of the media and its perception, as it affects each potential TA and actors external to the AOR (Figure 3-1, pages 3-11 through 3-13). PSYOP planners must also examine the literary media because literature itself conveys important (and exploitable) themes, symbols, and myths of that culture and society.

Radio and Television

a. Where are the key radio and TV transmitters within the country?

b. Who physically controls this site?

   (1) Who owns the station and controls the programming?

   (2) Is it possible to buy advertising time or other time segments for programs?

   (3) Who indirectly controls the viewpoints reflected in the programming? Are they progovernment or antigovernment?

c. How is the site protected (physical barriers, personnel barriers)?

d. What is the power of the transmitter?

e. What is the frequency or channel used to transmit? What is the frequency or channel capacity for transmission?

f. What is the effective broadcast range? What major terrain features affect transmission (for example, high or low ground)?

g. Are there any repeating stations for the broadcasts? What are the locations?

h. What type of antenna system is in use? What frequencies does it use? What is the configuration of the antennas?

i. What type of equipment is at the site?

   (1) What country produced the equipment?

   (2) How old is the equipment?

   (3) What is the maintenance record of the equipment?

   (4) What format and type of prerecorded messages can the station broadcast?

j. What is the on-site repair capability of technicians at the facility?

k. How long can the facility operate without outside services? Where does its energy source originate?

l. What is the listening or viewing audience of the station?

m. What type of programming does the station broadcast?

   (1) Does the station do live broadcasts or record tapes?

   (2) What type of audio and audiovisual editing equipment does the station have?

   (3) What is the station's video broadcast standard (NTSC 3.58, NTSC 4.43, PAL, or SECAM)?

   (4) What is the station's video format (BETACAM SX, BETACAM SP, VHS, S-VHS, or HI-8)?

   (5) What types of music does the station play?

   (6) What are the operating hours of the facility?

   (7) Who is the POC with whom to coordinate station and equipment usage?

   (8) What subjects for discussion are popular on the station?

   (9) What topics are taboo or avoided for broadcasting?

  (10) What are the peak viewing and listening hours for the population and for different target groups?

n. Is the station credible in the eyes of the population? Does perceived credibility differ by economic background, social group, religious group, or military unit and rank?

o. Does the populace listen to outside broadcasts from other countries or international entities? How are these received and perceived?

p. What are the locations of in-theater contractors and vendors who can provide services and supplies for audio and audiovisual equipment?

Figure 3-1. Media Analysis

Print Media

a. What are the major printed media in the country (imported or printed in-country)?

b. How influential is printed media within specific regions of the country?

c. Who controls printed media?

    (1) Does any particular group edit or censor printed media (for example, government, military, religious, political, insurgent, or ethnic)?

    (2) Can ads be purchased?

    (3) Can editorials be submitted?

d. In what language does printed media need to be printed?

e. What are the subjects most often written about? Are these subjects popular with the readers?

f. Who are the primary and secondary consumers of printed media? How credible are the media to groups within the country (for example, ethnic, religious, social, political, or military)?

g. How is printed media delivered to consumers?

h. Where are the major print plants within the country?

    (1) Who controls the sites?

    (2) What protective barriers are around the sites (physical barriers and personnel barriers)?

    (3) Where do their energy sources originate?

i. Where do the plants get their supplies (imported, in-country)? Would these sources of supply also be available to PSYOP personnel?

j. Can PSYOP personnel stop these supplies? How long can the facilities operate once PSYOP personnel cut off outside services?

k. What is the on-site repair capability of the technicians at the facilities?

l. What type of equipment is at the sites?

    (1) What country produced the equipment?

    (2) How old is the equipment?

    (3) What is the maintenance record of the equipment?

    (4) What is the output capacity of the equipment?

m. What type of paper can be used in the presses?

n. What colors can be used on the presses?

o. What is the standard for outdoor media? Are billboards, posters, handbills, or banners used? How sophisticated are these outdoor media?

p. Is there a system for mailing printed materials to particular segments of the population? Do mailing lists exist and are they available to PSYOP personnel?

q. What are the locations of in-theater companies that can provide services and supplies to HN, Psychological Operations dissemination battalion (PDB), and USG assets?

r. What are the major lines of communication (railroads, highways) located near existing print assets?

s. Is printed media credible in the eyes of the population? Does perceived credibility differ by economic background, social group, religious group, or military unit and rank?

Communications

a. What languages are spoken within the country?

b. What written languages are used throughout the country? How literate are people within the country and within different regions, states, and provinces?

Figure 3-1. Media Analysis (Continued)

c. What media do people trust most for obtaining information, and how accessible are the various groups through the different media?

   (1) What is the availability of TVs to the population and to the specific target groups?

   (2) What is the availability of radios to the population and to the specific target groups?

   (3) What is the availability of printed materials to the population and to the specific target groups?

   (4) How many people have access to printed material?

d. What are the literacy rates for all selected target groups?

e. What are the key symbols within the country? Do they differ by ethnic group, religion, social group, political group, military unit and rank, or insurgent group?

f. What are the visual or written taboos that might affect audiences when they look at print or other visual PSYOP products?

g. What are the Internet or web sites in the country or in countries friendly to the target country? Are assessments of the country's computer capabilities being collected and maintained?

h. Who are the Internet service providers?

Figure 3-1. Media Analysis (Continued)

PSYOP INTELLIGENCE PREPARATION OF THE BATTLESPACE PRODUCTS

3-39. There are several products that PSYOP Soldiers produce during IPB that are extremely valuable. During Step 1, PSYOP G-2 or S-2 personnel, with the help of SSD analysts, often complete environmental analysis and area assessments, which include an operational area evaluation, terrain analysis, and weather analysis. Step 2 yields detailed TAAWs, which are discussed in Chapter 5. Step 3 results in the completion of SCAME analysis, which is the method PSYOP Soldiers use to evaluate opponent propaganda and is discussed in Chapter 11. These products are the base intelligence documents that are used to plan and execute effective PSYOP.

ENVIRONMENTAL ANALYSIS AND AREA ASSESSMENTS

3-40. The SSD is the primary source of PSYOP environmental analysis. In this category, the analyst delves into each of the 14 political-military factors and addresses their role over time in influencing a society. This information may be very detailed; however, it is relatively enduring and is usually compiled over an extended period of time.

3-41. The IPB typically begins with an evaluation of the area. This assessment considers the overall nature of the friendly and enemy forces and the operational environment. The assessment normally entails a detailed analysis of the AO and AI. The PSYOP AO is tied to its targeted populations, and may comprise part of a country or a geographical region. The commander selects the AI based on the staff estimate of the situation, which covers future threats to the command and supports future operations.

3-42. The various PDC detachments, the SIO, S-3, and POATs (as required), with assistance from the SSD analysts, may choose to prepare a matrix identifying groups, their leaders, preferred media, and key issues that need to be developed. A collaborative effort results in the best possible analyses to—

- Select potential TAs.
- Locate mass media facilities in the AO that aid in the dissemination of PSYOP products and identify their operational characteristics.
- Evaluate studios and transmitters for amplitude modulation (AM) and frequency modulation (FM) radio and TV, and their operational characteristics (wattage, frequency, and programming).
- Evaluate heavy and light printing facilities, including locations, types, and capacities of equipment that can supplement the capabilities of PSYOP units.
- Evaluate accessibility of such facilities to PSYOP forces (for example, who controls them and whether they will cooperate with the United States).
- Identify ethnic, racial, social, economic, religious, and linguistic groups of the area, their locations, and their demographics.
- Identify key official and unofficial leaders and communicators in the area.
- Discern cohesive and divisive issues within a community.
- Gauge the literacy rates and levels of education.
- Assess the types and proportions of media consumed by the community.
- Assess any concentrations of third-country nationals in the AO, and their purposes and functions.

Operational Area Evaluation

3-43. Using the intelligence gathered, analysts may also prepare an operational area evaluation (OAE). The analysts will determine the following:

- Possible target groups.
- Key communicators within this target group.
- Preferred media to effectively reach this target group.
- Possible PSYOP themes for consideration during TAA.

Examples of products that will help perform the OAE include—

- Population overlays for the country or affected area.
- Radio station overlays with footprints, to include radio stations in nearby countries.
- TV station overlays with footprints, to include TV stations from other countries.
- Language overlays (written and spoken).
- Religion overlays displaying the religious beliefs within the target area.
- Ethnic group overlays that display the different ethnic groups within the target area.
- Terrain and weather overlays with a focus on effects on target groups and product dissemination.
- City maps or grid reference graphics for each country.

Terrain Analysis

3-44. PSYOP terrain analysis focuses on how geography affects the population of the AO and the dissemination of PSYOP products. This portion of the IPB includes preparing a line-of-sight (LOS) overlay for radio and TV stations derived from an obstacle overlay that shows elevations and other LOS information. For PSYOP, terrain analysis, for example, may focus on determining the respective ranges and audibility of signals from the most significant broadcast stations identified during OAE.

3-45. The engineer (terrain) detachment that supports divisions, corps, and EAC usually conducts the major portion of the terrain analysis, combining extensive database information with the results of reconnaissance. The engineer (terrain) detachment has access to special terrain databases compiled by the National Imagery and Mapping Agency (NIMA). TERRABASE, if available, also offers automated terrain analysis capabilities. If engineer terrain support is unavailable, analysts evaluate the terrain through a map analysis. NIMA produces specialized maps, overlays, and databases to aid in map-based evaluations. Specialized NIMA products address such factors as—

- Cross-country mobility.
- Transportation systems (road and bridge information).
- Vegetation type and distribution.
- Obstacles.

Weather Analysis

3-46. Weather and climate can play an important role in the development of a PSYOP mission. In foreign internal defense (FID) and unconventional warfare (UW) missions, particularly, weather and climate affect PSYOP media and dissemination operations. For example, wind direction and speed at specific above ground level (AGL) increments are required for leaflet operations, recruitment of locals in subzero weather is extremely difficult, periods of drought may force farmers to become bandits or insurgents, and flooding can interfere with food and medicine distribution. The effects of weather and climate can be integrated with terrain analysis.

3-47. Analysts can obtain climatology-based overlays for planning purposes from the USAF Environmental Technical Applications Center. Once deployed, the supporting USAF weather team can prepare similar but less detailed overlays depending on the availability of data. FM 34-81/AFM 105-4, *Weather Support for Army Tactical Operations*, provides information on support by USAF weather teams.

THREAT EVALUATION

3-48. An important feature of the IPB is the threat evaluation. For PSYOP, threat evaluation serves two purposes. First, it gives the POTF commander an understanding of the existing and potential opposing propaganda in the JOA. Opposing products may come from governments, political parties, labor unions, or religious groups. U.S. PSYOP forces in the AOR must anticipate and be able to counter or prevent threat products directed at U.S. and allied forces and the local populace. The Soldiers, analysts, and SIO may work in concert to compile all available intelligence to analyze the threat propaganda capability and program effectiveness, as well as their ability to counteract the threat propaganda. It is a safe assumption that U.S. PSYOP will be countered by the threat. Analysts should also focus on the ability of the threat country or target to distort or stop the dissemination of U.S. PSYOP data (electronic jamming, air defense). Second, the supported unit commander depends upon the POTF commander for advice on any PSYOP consequences of U.S. operations, and for recommended alternative measures within each COA.

3-49. To conduct threat evaluation, the PSYOP staff must determine the capabilities of hostile organizations to conduct product operations and to counteract U.S. and allied PSYOP. Specific capabilities to be evaluated include the ability to—

- Conduct offensive product operations targeting U.S. forces, allied forces, or the local populace.
- Inoculate its personnel against U.S. PSYOP efforts.
- Counteract U.S. PSYOP efforts by exploiting weaknesses in U.S. PSYOP.
- Conduct active measures campaigns.
- Conduct jamming of U.S. or allied PSYOP broadcasts.

SUMMARY

3-50. The PSYOP IPB process is cyclical and requires continuous evaluation. PSYOP personnel use this systematic and continuous process to analyze and integrate intelligence data regarding characteristics of foreign populations. The PSYOP analysis process builds on the IPB of the higher HQ, but is oriented on the human aspects of the situation and the capabilities of audiences to receive and be influenced by information.

Chapter 4

PSYOP Planning Process

The real target in war is the mind of the enemy commander, not the bodies of his troops.

Captain Sir Basil Liddell Hart
Thoughts on War, 1944

The importance of planning cannot be overstated in relation to the overall success of an operation. Military planning is a continuous process that incorporates both supported unit and operational planning. Supported unit planning includes both deliberate and crisis-action planning where the end state is the production of an OPLAN or OPORD for a supported unit, which will include a PSYOP annex or tab depending on the echelon that the planner is working. Operational planning develops a PSYOP support OPLAN or OPORD that considers all the facets of how PSYOP will achieve its stated objectives. Operational planning continues throughout the operation and incorporates all PSYOP assets and addresses external requirements. Army planning, regardless of whether it is supported unit or operational, is performed within the framework of the MDMP and the 5-paragraph format; therefore, this chapter will highlight both types of PSYOP planning within that context.

SUPPORTED UNIT PLANNING

4-1. The PSYOP planner must integrate PSYOP into the supported unit's planning process. It is extremely difficult, if not impossible, to incorporate PSYOP into a completed plan as an afterthought. It is crucial that PSYOP planners arrive at the supported unit as soon as possible to become involved in the entire planning process.

4-2. PSYOP planners integrate at many levels, from combatant command to battalions, and thus need to be familiar with both the Joint Operations Planning and Execution System (JOPES), as well as the Army's MDMP (Figure 4-1, page 4-2). Although their methodology is slightly different, the essence of what they accomplish is the same. They are both processes that military planners use to make decisions and ultimately publish OPLANs and OPORDs. Since the MDMP is the standard for Army planning, it will be discussed in detail in this chapter.

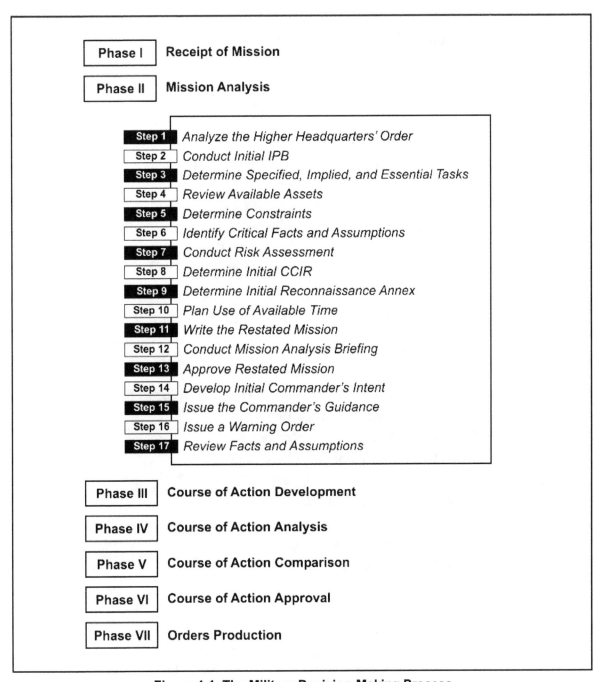

| Phase I | Receipt of Mission |
| Phase II | Mission Analysis |

Step 1 Analyze the Higher Headquarters' Order
Step 2 Conduct Initial IPB
Step 3 Determine Specified, Implied, and Essential Tasks
Step 4 Review Available Assets
Step 5 Determine Constraints
Step 6 Identify Critical Facts and Assumptions
Step 7 Conduct Risk Assessment
Step 8 Determine Initial CCIR
Step 9 Determine Initial Reconnaissance Annex
Step 10 Plan Use of Available Time
Step 11 Write the Restated Mission
Step 12 Conduct Mission Analysis Briefing
Step 13 Approve Restated Mission
Step 14 Develop Initial Commander's Intent
Step 15 Issue the Commander's Guidance
Step 16 Issue a Warning Order
Step 17 Review Facts and Assumptions

Phase III	Course of Action Development
Phase IV	Course of Action Analysis
Phase V	Course of Action Comparison
Phase VI	Course of Action Approval
Phase VII	Orders Production

Figure 4-1. The Military Decision-Making Process

PHASE I: RECEIPT OF MISSION

4-3. Upon receipt of the mission, the PSYOP planner must begin gathering the tools to begin mission analysis. This phase requires collecting all pertinent facts and data that may impact the mission. Essentially, the task is to assist the supported unit in the development of their plan from a PSYOP perspective. The PSYOP staff planner should review and be familiar with, as a matter of course, all available background information and policy guidance regarding PSYOP and the AOR, which include the following:

- U.S. laws and international treaties in the AOR that may affect PSYOP:
  - Military Committee (MC) 402, *NATO PSYOP Policy*.
  - Allied Joint Publication (AJP) 3.10, *Information Operations*.
  - Bi-Strategic Commands (Bi-SC) 80-1, *Psychological Operations*.
- Presidential Decision Directives (PDDs) that may affect PSYOP:
  - PDD 56, *Complex Contingency Operations*.
  - PDD 68, *U.S. International Public Information (IPI)*.
- Chairman of the Joint Chiefs of Staff (CJCS) and DOD instructions or directives regarding or affecting PSYOP:
  - Chairman of the Joint Chiefs of Staff Instruction (CJCSI) 3110.05C, *Joint Psychological Operations Supplement to the Joint Strategic Capabilities Plan FY 2002 (CJCSI 3110.01 Series)*.
  - CJCSI 3210.01A, *(S) Joint Information Operations Policy (U)*.
  - DOD Instruction S-3321.1, (S) *Overt Peacetime Psychological Operations Conducted by the Military Services in Contingencies Short of Declared War (U)*.
  - DOD Directive S-3600.1, (S) *Information Operations (IO) (U)*.
- The National Security Strategy.
- The National Military Strategy.
- The Unified Command Plan (UCP).
- The Joint Strategic Capabilities Plan (JSCP).
- The theater security cooperation plan.
- Country plans (if any.)
- Applicable joint doctrine.
- Applicable Army doctrine.

4-4. Deliberate planning provides more opportunity for accessing or requesting information. Planners, as a minimum, should request the PSYOP appendix to the military capability study of the targeted country, SPAs and SPSs from the SSDs of the 4th POG(A), and an electromagnetic spectrum analysis for commercial bands in the AOR or JOA from the Joint Spectrum Center (JSC), as soon as possible. Additionally, the PSYOP planner should obtain information analysis from the JIOC (formerly known as the Joint Command and Control Warfare Center [JC2WC]) and key personalities and human factors analysis information from the HFAC. Further, the planner will need to gather media analysis data from the Foreign Bureau of Information Services (FBIS) and foreign media reaction information from the Office of International Information Programs (OIIP). Planners should also start the process to obtain polling data and surveys from other governments or commercial information holders in the area (to include the Office of

Research and Media Reaction), while simultaneously studying as much about the current situation as possible.

4-5. Upon completion of Phase I, the PSYOP staff (in close coordination with the supporting PSYOP battalions) should have analyzed and answered the following questions:

- What is the U.S. national policy toward the country or region in question?
- Who are the major decision makers within the JOA or AOR?
- What is the source of the decision makers' power?
- What is the current social, political, and economic situation, in the broadest sense, within the AOR?

4-6. Mission analysis can begin once the PSYOP planner has obtained a body of pertinent data and established a broad understanding of the AOR.

PHASE II: MISSION ANALYSIS

4-7. During the second phase, the PSYOP staff planner may be augmented with a POAT depending on the level of planning. Regardless of whether or not the planner receives a POAT, he should maintain contact with the supporting regional and tactical PSYOP battalions for assistance throughout the planning process. The mission analysis phase consists of 17 steps, not necessarily sequential. The result of mission analysis is defining the problem and beginning the process of determining feasible solutions. Anticipation, prior preparation, and cooperation are the keys to timely mission analysis. Mission analysis begins with a review of the commander's intent of the next two higher echelon orders. This guidance, along with documents obtained during Phase I (Receipt of Mission) will be the primary sources of initial planning information, which will ensure that the PSYOP objectives developed will support both the national and supported commander's objectives.

Step 1: Analyze the Higher Headquarters' Order

4-8. This step is done by the supported unit with PSYOP assistance. Planners thoroughly analyze the mission and intent of the next two higher echelons. For example, when working at the theater command level, the planner must understand the intent of the combatant commander and the SecDef. Knowledge of the intent is drawn from the mission statement, the intent specifically stated in the early planning process, and the concept of the operation that the combatant commander is developing. Direct coordination between PSYOP planners at different levels allows for each level to begin planning as early as possible. Regardless of how information is shared, it is essential that PSYOP planners at the supported geographic combatant commander HQ, the designated CJTF, the major component commands, functional component commands, and the supporting regional and tactical PSYOP battalion commanders should routinely exchange information.

4-9. An example of the SecDef's intent follows: After a failed diplomatic effort, the United States will abandon all current and future mediation efforts aimed at convincing Haiti's military government to step down peacefully. Diplomatic efforts, such as the trade embargo, are failing and there is little hope of the military relinquishing power peacefully. The time for military action has arrived. With or without the cooperation of the Haitian military, a U.S.-led multinational force will establish a stable political climate so that President Aristide can be reinstated, restoring this democratically elected leader to office.

4-10. An example of the combatant commander's intent follows: Assist the Haitian people in recovering control over their government and curb systematic political repression. Support the freely elected president and assist in the process of replacing the corrupt and repressive army with a nonpartisan, competent police force.

4-11. Upon completion of Step 1, the PSYOP planner should have determined—

- The objectives of the next two higher echelons.

- The time available from mission receipt to mission execution and determined the time needed for planning, preparation, and execution.

Step 2: Conduct Initial Intelligence Preparation of the Battlespace

4-12. IPB is discussed in a broad context in the preceding chapter; however, the PSYOP estimate, which is continually updated throughout the process, is usually begun at this step and can be a valuable tool for the planner throughout the remainder of MDMP. Depending upon time available, the PSYOP estimate may not be completed and submitted as a formal estimate, particularly in crisis-action planning, but serves as a valuable checklist to remind planners of required information for continued planning. The estimate should be as detailed as possible and the PSYOP planner should request assistance in preparing this document from the regional PSYOP battalion and the SSD. The better the estimate, the better the planner will be able to integrate PSYOP into the rest of the supported commander's plan. Upon completion of Step 2, the PSYOP planner should have completed the following tasks:

- Construction of a key target sets overlay (PTAL in the broadest sense).

- Weather impact analysis upon PSYOP (may be presented as an overlay or other graphic display).

- Terrain impact analysis upon PSYOP (may be presented as an overlay or other graphic display).

- Media infrastructure analysis of the AO (listed by type, political affiliation, output or dissemination, antennas, satellite up-link sites, readership or viewership, and so on; this analysis may be a list with a graphic overlay to provide an estimate of coverage).

- Coordination for as much assistance as possible in completing the PSYOP estimate.

4-13. Figure 4-2, pages 4-6 and 4-7, is the format to use when conducting a PSYOP estimate. This document can serve as a tool for the entire MDMP and may not be able to be completed at this point, but the planner should have the regional PSYOP battalion and the SSD working on it while he is integrating into the supported unit's planning cycle. The supported unit's G-2 or S-2 may be able to assist greatly in completing portions of the estimate. The more detail it contains, the better tool it will be.

(CLASSIFICATION)

Headquarters
Place
Date, time, and zone

PSYOP ESTIMATE OF THE SITUATION NO._____

(U) REFERENCES:

a. ( ) List maps and charts.

b. ( ) Include other relevant documents (military capability study, SPSs, SPAs, and intelligence estimates).

(1) ( ) When the PSYOP estimate is distributed outside the issuing HQ, the first line of the heading is the official designation of the issuing command, and the final page of the estimate is modified to include authentication by the originating section, division, or other official, according to local policy.

(2) ( ) Normally, PSYOP estimates are numbered sequentially within a calendar year. The estimate is usually distributed as an appendix to the operations annex.

1. ( ) MISSION.

a. ( ) Supported unit's restated mission resulting from mission analysis

b. ( ) PSYOP mission statement. Describe the PSYOP mission to support the maneuver commander's mission.

2. ( ) SITUATION AND CONSIDERATION.

a. ( ) Characteristics of the AO.

(1) ( ) Weather. How will weather affect the dissemination of PSYOP products and access to TAs? (Winds – leaflet drops, precipitation – print products, etc.) End Product – PSYOP Weather Overlay.

(2) ( ) Terrain. How will terrain affect dissemination of PSYOP products and movement of tactical PSYOP elements? End Product – PSYOP Terrain Overlay.

(3) ( ) Analysis of media infrastructure. (Location and broadcast range of radio and TV broadcast facilities, retransmission towers, print facilities, distribution and dissemination nodes; identification of denied areas [not accessible by particular medium].) End Product – PSYOP Media Infrastructure Overlay.

b. ( ) Key target sets. (**Note:** These sets will be further refined into a PTAL. The TAs will then be analyzed and further refined during the TAA process.) (Reason: FM 101-5 labels this section "Enemy Forces." This is not the only target set that PSYOP personnel will have to deal with. To fully support the supported unit commander, PSYOP personnel must consider all key target sets, not solely enemy forces.) PSYOP key target sets overlays (hostile, friendly, neutral) include the following:

(1) ( ) Hostile target sets. For each hostile target set, identify strength, disposition, composition, capabilities (ability to conduct propaganda, ability to help or hinder the PSYOP effort), and probable COAs as they relate to PSYOP.

(2) ( ) Friendly target sets. For each friendly target set, identify strength, disposition, composition, capabilities (ability to conduct propaganda, ability to help or hinder the PSYOP effort), and probable COAs as they relate to PSYOP.

(3) ( ) Neutral target sets. (Include target sets whose attitudes are unknown.) For each neutral target set, identify strength, disposition, composition, capabilities (ability to conduct propaganda, ability to help or hinder the PSYOP effort), and probable COAs as they relate to PSYOP.

(CLASSIFICATION)

Figure 4-2. PSYOP Estimate of the Situation

(CLASSIFICATION)

c. ( ) Friendly forces.

(1) ( ) Supported unit COAs. State the COAs under consideration and the PSYOP-specific requirements needed to support each COA.

(2) ( ) Current status of organic personnel and resources. State availability of organic personnel and resources needed to support each COA under consideration. Consider PSYOP-specific personnel, other military occupational specialties (MOSs) and availability of PSYOP-specific equipment.

(3) ( ) Current status of nonorganic personnel and resources. State availability of nonorganic resources needed to support each COA. Consider linguistic support, COMMANDO SOLO, leaflet-dropping aircraft, and RC PSYOP forces.

(4) ( ) Comparison of requirements versus capabilities and recommended solutions. Compare PSYOP requirements for each COA with current PSYOP capabilities. List recommended solutions for any shortfall in capabilities.

(5) ( ) Key considerations (evaluation criteria) for COA supportability. List evaluation criteria to be used in COA analysis and COA comparison.

d. ( ) Assumptions. State assumptions about the PSYOP situation made for this estimate. (For example, Assumption: Enemy propaganda broadcast facilities will be destroyed by friendly forces not later than (NLT) D+2.)

3. ( ) **ANALYSIS OF COAs.**

a. ( ) Analyze each COA from the PSYOP point of view to determine its advantages and disadvantages for conducting PSYOP. The level of command, scope of contemplated operations, and urgency of need determine the detail in which the analysis is made.

b. ( ) The evaluation criteria listed in paragraph 2 (c, 5) above establish the elements to be analyzed for each COA under consideration. Examine these factors realistically and include appropriate considerations that may have an impact on the PSYOP situation as it affects the COAs. (Throughout the analysis, the staff officer must keep PSYOP considerations foremost in his mind. The analysis is not intended to produce a decision, but to ensure that all applicable PSYOP factors have been considered and are the basis of paragraphs 4 and 5.)

4. ( ) **COMPARISON OF COAs.**

a. ( ) Compare the proposed COAs to determine the one that offers the best chance of success from the PSYOP point of view. List the advantages and disadvantages of each COA affecting PSYOP. Comparison should be visually supported by a decision matrix.

b. ( ) Develop and compare methods of overcoming disadvantages, if any, in each COA.

c. ( ) State a general conclusion on the COA that offers the best chance of success from a PSYOP perspective.

5. ( ) **RECOMMENDATIONS AND CONCLUSIONS.**

a. ( ) Recommended COA based on comparison (most supportable from the PSYOP perspective). Rank COAs from best to worst.

b. ( ) Issues, deficiencies, and risks for each COA, with recommendations to reduce their impact.

(signed) _____
G-3/G-7 PSYOP Officer
ANNEXES:
DISTRIBUTION:

(CLASSIFICATION)

Figure 4-2. PSYOP Estimate of the Situation (Continued)

Step 3: Determine Specified, Implied, and Essential Tasks

4-14. This step is done by the supported unit with PSYOP assistance. Specified tasks are those specifically assigned to a unit by its higher HQ. The PSYOP planner will normally find specified tasks in paragraph 3 of the higher headquarters' order or plan and also may find them in annexes and overlays. Implied tasks are those that must be performed to accomplish a specified task, but which are not stated in the higher headquarters' order. Implied tasks are derived from a detailed analysis of the higher headquarters' order, the enemy situation, and COAs, as well as terrain. The PSYOP estimate is a tool that should be used throughout the MDMP and can be very useful during this step as the planner identifies tasks. Once a staff planner has a list of specified and implied tasks, he ensures he understands each task's specific requirements. After analyzing specified and implied tasks, the staff planner presents to the commander for his approval a tentative list of tasks that must be executed to accomplish the mission. These tasks are the essential tasks. The following are some possible PSYOP-specific examples of specified tasks (these are not written as POs, which will be done later, but simply as considerations that must be taken into account when developing POs):

- Set conditions for introduction of U.S. forces.
- Portray narcotics traffickers and narcotics corruption as a threat that affects all nations.
- Shape the global information environment to promote perception that U.S. actions are IAW international law, treaties, and United Nations (UN) Security Council resolutions.
- Limit the effectiveness of hostile propaganda, misinformation, and other forms of political warfare directed against the United States.
- Encourage regional stability and cooperation.
- Create conditions that reduce collateral damage (material, buildings).
- Provide direct information support to humanitarian operations.
- Reduce resistance to U.S. operations.
- Enhance safety of U.S. citizens.
- Facilitate civil order.
- Support civil-military operations.
- Support strategic PSYOP actions in support of flexible deterrent options (FDOs).
- Increase effectiveness of HN police and military.
- Increase support by the people for the HN government.
- Reduce concern among populace over the departure of U.S. forces.
- Facilitate transition to HN government.

The following are some possible PSYOP-specific examples of implied tasks:

- Convince key communicators to speak out against the aggressions of HN forces.
- Convince the TA that deployment of U.S. forces is temporary; forces are there only to quell aggressions.

- Publicize the redeployment of U.S. forces.
- Develop credible news outlets, thereby keeping TAs informed of the truth.
- Inform the TA of goals for transition to normalcy.
- Promote the military and technological superiority of U.S. and joint task forces.
- Convince the TA that U.S. involvement is in support of democratic governments, free from manipulation.
- Discourage the TA from committing destructive acts.
- Educate the TA on the ROE.
- Inform the TA that acts of aggression against U.S. and coalition forces will not be tolerated.
- Convince the TA to surrender or abandon its post.
- Educate the TA of available humanitarian assistance assets.

4-15. The PSYOP planner will use the list of specified and implied tasks to begin the development of POs. A PO is a statement of measurable response that reflects the desired behavior or attitudinal change of selected foreign TAs as a result of PSYOP. Another way of stating the purpose of a PO is what PSYOP is going to do to help the commander accomplish his mission. POs provide the framework around which the overall PSYOP plan is built. Planners develop this framework from several sources of information in the supported unit's OPLAN or OPORD, to include the commander's intent or end state, concept of operations (CONOPS), tasks to PSYOP units in paragraph 3, and verbal guidance from the commander. The POs will begin to be developed at this point, but will not be finalized until later in the MDMP.

4-16. The format for a PO is verb - object. The verb describes the direction of the change desired. The object is the overall behavior or attitude to be changed. Some action verbs commonly used in PSYOP are reduce, decrease, prevent, increase, gain, and maintain. For example, one task taken from the commander's intent in the OPORD is "create a safe and secure environment for the people of Pineland." This is not a statement of measurable response that reflects a desired behavior or attitude change. If it is restated as "decrease criminal activity within Pineland," it can now be used as a PO because it now can be measured and depicts a desired behavior or attitude change within a selected foreign TA.

4-17. Planners usually develop between four and ten POs depending on the size of the operation. The POs cover all aspects of the operation from introduction of forces to the exit strategy and are sometimes referred to as written "cradle to grave." Cradle to grave means that the PSYOP planner must develop objectives from force entry to the final transition of the force back to local HN authorities. Basically, POs are what PSYOP will do for the supported commander. PSYOP planners usually find POs in supported units' mission statements, commander's intent or end state paragraphs, and in the execution paragraph. The following are examples of possible POs:

- Decrease violence in the AO.
- Increase participation in national democratic institutions.

- Decrease effectiveness of insurgency or opposition force.
- Decrease local population injuries due to mines and unexploded explosive ordnance (UXO).
- Decrease opponent's will to fight.

4-18. POs are developed at the highest level of PSYOP support and do not change when subordinate units work on their plan. There are no special tactical POs. The POs that are written will be used by Soldiers at the POTF, as well as the Soldiers on a tactical Psychological Operations team (TPT). For example, the POTF during an air campaign develops, designs, and produces a leaflet that advises enemy soldiers to not turn on air defense artillery (ADA) equipment. This product falls under PO "decrease combat effectiveness of enemy forces." Two weeks later, after ground forces have entered the AO, a TPT broadcasts a loudspeaker message that tells enemy soldiers that surrendering in the following manner will ensure soldiers will not be hurt. That product is also under PO "decrease combat effectiveness of enemy forces."

4-19. A SPO is the specific behavioral or attitudinal response desired from the TA as a result of PSYOP. The SPO is what PSYOP will do to get the TA to achieve POs.

4-20. SPOs also begin to be developed during this step of the MDMP. SPOs are unique for each PO, and there are always two or more SPOs for each PO. If two or more SPOs cannot be developed for a PO, then the PO is probably too narrow in focus and needs to be rewritten. All SPOs must assist in accomplishing the PO. Figure 4-3 provides an example.

PO: Decrease Violence in the AO

SPO #1: TA refrains from committing acts of violence directed against the JTF.

SPO #2: TA refrains from committing acts of interethnic violence.

SPO #3: TA refrains from committing acts of criminal violence.

Figure 4-3. Example of PO and SPO Linkage

4-21. SPOs follow a simple noun - verb - object format. The noun is the TA. A specific TA is not written into the SPO because there are often several TAs that can be targeted to accomplish the desired behavior or attitude change. The verb - object combination describes the desired behavior or attitude change. If the PO is "decrease criminal activity," then the SPO could be "TA refrains from committing acts of violence." In this example, the SPO directly supports the PO. The following are some examples of SPOs:

- TA voluntarily eradicates coca crop.
- TA surrenders.
- TA votes in elections.
- TA refrains from committing acts of interethnic violence.
- TA reports the locations of mines and UXO.
- TA registers to vote.

4-22. Following the development of POs and SPOs, planners begin identifying potential TAs. Potential TAs are those audiences the planner initially thinks have the ability to accomplish the SPOs. Planners may group potential TAs underneath the applicable SPOs. This initial PTAL will be very broad as the planner rarely has the time to complete exhaustive research in this area. The PTAL will be refined several times later in the PSYOP process. At the end of step three of mission analysis, the PSYOP planner has done the following:

- Assisted the supported unit in discerning specified and implied tasks.

- Looked for those tasks specifically oriented toward PSYOP.

- Begun the development of POs that support the commander's objectives.

- Begun the development of SPOs that support the POs.

- Established an initial, although broad, PTAL.

Step 4: Review Available Assets

4-23. Once objectives are derived, the PSYOP planner reviews all available assets and develops a mission-tailored task organization. This includes personnel, equipment, where they will be located, and what unit they will support. It is critical to allocate the proper resources to accomplish the mission without wasting valuable and limited resources.

4-24. This review allows the staff to picture the means available with which to accomplish its preliminary restated mission. In this case, PSYOP planners are interested in the organizations peculiar to the POTF or PSE, as well as unique organizations that support PSYOP missions from within the CJTF or the combatant commander's organization, or from external agencies. When the PSYOP task organization is determined, planners consider the forces required to C2 the force, provide intelligence, develop PSYOP programs, produce series via the desired media, distribute products to media disseminators, conduct dissemination, and ensure logistics support. Locations of these forces are critical. Whether these forces should support the PSYOP mission from home station, from inside the theater, from a location with the CJTF or its tactical units, or from other locations is the PSYOP commander's decision based on the current situation and METT-TC. Assets are dedicated to the mission from the J-3 of the combatant command, the JSCP, and the CJTF.

4-25. The decisions regarding the task organization, however, must be made by the planner in close consultation with the PSYOP commander he represents. The planner should also review the HN government and commercial telecommunications capabilities, as well as the non-PSYOP military forces. These capabilities may facilitate more responsive PSYOP and reduce the equipment and personnel requirements of the force. Moreover, the planner must know in detail the components of each unit of the military force and their actual purpose. It is often possible to leverage TACON of these forces to provide PSYOP support. For example, carrier battle groups of the U.S. Navy have robust printing capabilities. It is also important to define the command relationships (OPCON, TACON) of the elements to PSYOP. Examples include the following:

- *Army forces (ARFOR)*. Tactical PSYOP forces will normally be attached. The POTF will maintain coordinating authority for PSYOP-specific direction and support. Based upon mission requirements, rotary-wing support from the ARFOR may be TACON to the POTF or PSE for aerial loudspeaker missions.

- *Air Force forces (AFFOR)*. PSYOP forces may have personnel attached to the AFFOR if leaflet bomb operations are to be conducted. The AFFOR may also have aerial electronic warfare (EW) platforms capable of disseminating PSYOP messages.

- *Marine Corps forces (MARFOR)*. Like ARFOR, the MARFOR will normally have tactical PSYOP units attached and under the coordinating authority of the POTF for PSYOP support and direction.

- *Navy forces (NAVFOR)*. PSYOP Navy dissemination and production units and facilities may be TACON to the POTF or PSE. Navy logistics systems are ideal for supporting the PSYOP mission.

- *JSOTF*. Tactical PSYOP units can be attached to the JSOTF and under the coordinating authority of the POTF or PSE. Also, Air Force Special Operations Command (AFSOC) units under OPCON to the JSOTF, such as the 193d SOW or the 16th SOW, may be under TACON to the POTF or PSE for operations.

- *POTF*. The POTF may have forces apportioned and attached from various organizations to accomplish the PSYOP mission. USSOCOM, as a supporting command, will normally task forces to support PSYOP after close consultation with the POAT and the PSYOP staff of the supported geographic combatant commander. The following forces may be attached or under OPCON to the POTF if USSOCOM validates the requirement:

  - 4th POG(A) will normally form the nucleus of the PSYOP force.

  - The 2d and 7th POGs can integrate with 4th POG(A), under the direction of the United States Army Civil Affairs and Psychological Operations Command (USACAPOC) upon mobilization. The Air Intelligence Agency (AIA) will augment the POTF G-2.

  - AFSOC may provide a weather team to the POTF G-2.

  - The fleet information warfare center (FIWC) can provide the POTF G-3 with additional staff, production, and dissemination assistance.

  - The JIOC, the 1st IO Command (Land), and the Joint Warfare Analysis Center (JWAC) may form an IO support team led by JIOC.

  - The Joint, Army, and Fleet Combat Camera Centers can augment PSYOP production efforts.

  - The 528th Special Operations Support Battalion of the Special Operations Support Command (SOSCOM) will provide the POTF G-4 liaison and assistance.

  - The United States Army Intelligence and Security Command (INSCOM), Naval Security Group (NAVSECGRU), and AIA may provide translator assistance in addition to that available in USSOCOM and those contracted by USASOC for PSYOP use.

- The 16th SOW and 193d SOW of AFSOC may provide air operations planners, as required.

- The Naval Air Warfare Center, Aircraft Division (NAWCAD) may provide organizational and direct support maintenance for some unique PSYOP equipment.

- The supported geographic combatant commander's assigned communications, intelligence, and counterintelligence staff and units often provide support as outlined and coordinated for C2, distribution, and pretest or posttest support upon request and if available. Support to a POTF is normally facilitated by the collocation of the POTF or PSE with the HQ of the supported commander.

- The 112th Signal Battalion of SOSCOM may provide communications support when available.

- Coalition allies may provide intelligence support, C2, translation, PSYOP development, production, distribution, and dissemination support within their capabilities.

4-26. A PSYOP force can consist of many elements. Whenever task-organizing a PSYOP force, three factors should be considered. The following paragraphs further explain each factor.

4-27. **Mobilization Planning.** Mobilization planning is critical to PSYOP. Two-thirds of the PSYOP forces reside in the RC. PSYOP forces are normally drawn from regional, tactical, and dissemination battalions, as well as a group HQ when supporting an operation. Without detailed mobilization planning, the PSYOP force will not be sufficiently trained and ready for operations.

4-28. **Deployment.** Deployment of PSYOP forces must be specified in the initial task-organization planning. Normally, PSYOP forces are one of the first units to receive deployment and execution orders for an operation, to deter armed conflict, or set conditions for successful military operations should deterrence fail. The organization of PSYOP forces in support of an operation is heavily influenced by the availability and timing of strategic transport. The PSYOP planner, therefore, must be capable of justifying the resources used by explaining the value added for each aircraft apportioned for deployment. The PSYOP planner should attempt to incorporate the necessary PSYOP forces with the supported unit's initial TPFDD package. Doing so will help ensure that PSYOP forces have the deployment means at the earliest time possible. The planner must also ensure each package for deployment is somewhat capable of operating independently, in case strategic deployment plans are changed or delayed.

4-29. **Rotation or Redeployment.** Rotation or redeployment of PSYOP forces must be planned in detail and reflected in the task organization. PSYOP forces are often employed throughout an entire operation, from pre-hostilities to conflict through stability and finally return to peace. These types of missions often take months or years to complete and therefore necessitate the need for a rotation plan. It is difficult for PSYOP commanders to rotate PSYOP forces without a Presidential Reserve Call-Up Authority (PRCA) and ample time to train and prepare forces regarding the JOA because each geographic combatant commander is apportioned only one regional POB and one TPC in the Active Army. Further, when operations shift from one phase to another, new and different challenges arise that can influence the PSYOP approval process and PSYOP authority. Thus, it is important to obtain early approval for these planned transitions and required force rotations.

Step 5: Determine Constraints

4-30. A higher commander normally places some constraints on subordinate commanders that restrict their freedom of action or limit the availability of assets due to specified tasks. There may also be laws or treaties that constrain the conduct of PSYOP. Constraints can take the form of a requirement to do something (for example, produce a mine awareness video) or a prohibition on action (for example, do not target corps-level commanders). Common constraints include the size of the PSYOP force allowed in-theater, strategic lift assets available (this constraint reinforces the importance of a mission-tailored task organization), themes to be stressed and avoided, and communication bandwidth available. The PSYOP planner must identify and understand how these constraints affect the conduct of PSYOP.

4-31. PSYOP planners must consider any limitations or restrictions for the operation. PSYOP staff planners must clearly articulate PSYOP requirements. This data allows USSOCOM and the Services to properly determine how best to provide the requested support. Planners should provide enough information to describe the requirement without detailing how to provide the support and perform the mission. The following is an example statement that identifies a requirement for PSYOP support: "A regionally oriented POTF with the capability to plan, develop, produce, distribute, and disseminate visual, audio, and audiovisual products from XXX locations, and provide tactical PSYOP forces to support XXX separate corps/divisions/brigades."

4-32. Constraints are normally found in the scheme of maneuver, the CONOPS, and coordinating instructions of the higher headquarters' order. PSYOP planners should consider the following areas where limitations or restrictions commonly occur:

- Themes to be stressed and avoided.
- TAs to be avoided.
- Perceived or actual violations of national sovereignty that could occur.
- Strategic transport allocations for deployment.
- Funding limitations.
- Basing rights limitations.
- Restrictions on frequency allocation for PSYOP use.
- Force caps.
- Logistics restrictions.
- Timing constraints.

- Strategic communication usage.
- Mobilization constraints.
- Rotation of forces and redeployment constraints.
- Cross-border broadcast restrictions.
- Indigenous (HN) media production assets.
- Strategic lift restrictions.
- Political constraints.

4-33. By the end of step five, the PSYOP planner, in direct consultation with the commanders of the appropriate regional and tactical PSYOP battalions and possibly USACAPOC if reserves are involved, should have a tentative mission-tailored force proposal.

Step 6: Identify Critical Facts and Assumptions

4-34. The PSYOP planner determines critical facts and assumptions that can or will directly affect successful accomplishment of the mission. Facts are statements of known information concerning the situation, including enemy and friendly dispositions, literacy rates, media usage, and dissemination assets. Assumptions are suppositions about the current or future situation that are assumed to be true in the absence of facts. They take the place of necessary but unavailable facts and fill the gaps in the commander's knowledge of the situation. Much of this information will be included in the PSYOP estimate, and that document should be consulted during this step.

4-35. In some cases, the commander may direct PSYOP personnel to consider only those facts and assumptions that he wishes. The PSYOP planner must consider the facts and assumptions as they relate to the PSYOP process. The key areas to consider include development, production, distribution, dissemination, and logistics.

4-36. **Development.** An example of facts for development would be the proposed force and their equipment. Assumptions may include the time necessary to develop certain series, supporting programs, or programs.

4-37. **Production.** Facts may include that the element deploys in a "heavy" configuration where print assets are part of the deployment package. Another option would be to deploy in a light configuration where reachback will be used. Facts may also include the space the supported unit has allocated for PSYOP assets. Also, if arrangements have been made for HN support via contracting, then HN production is one of the main facts for planning purposes. If using an HN asset is necessary but not certain, then these assets can become assumptions. If translators are required, the unit may deploy with them or have a source to acquire them in-country. Assumptions may have to be made on the quality of local area translators and perhaps energize other means to obtain this resource.

4-38. **Distribution.** When using reachback techniques for support, the means to move products becomes critical. Strategic airlift is a valuable commodity and, to be properly employed, requires careful planning. The airframe that the planner confirms for the deployment and initial distribution is a firm assumption. The air support that is planned but based on availability further into the operation may be an assumption that has a large chance of changing. An example of a fact for distribution is the availability of a storage facility for products produced at Fort Bragg. Distribution of PSYOP products is always a tremendous concern. Considerations must include ground and sea shipments and target country infrastructure. Using distribution resources from the HN may be a fact if these resources are already under U.S. control. However, if the use of HN vehicles is simply an assumption, then the planner must assume they will not be damaged during hostilities and that they will remain in good working order. Another important distribution consideration is the physical security of products being transported or stored prior to dissemination.

4-39. **Dissemination.** Dissemination includes face-to-face communication, portable or local radio stations, leaflet delivery into denied territory, or a speech through a key communicator. Assumptions are often a part of the planning process. For example, if the PSYOP force "owns" a particular dissemination asset, then the use of this asset is an actuality (fact) for planning purposes. However, PSYOP personnel must assume they can build an audience for this dissemination asset and that takes time. They must assume a time period to develop a following of listeners or obtain the use of a frequency that already has the following of the TA.

4-40. **Logistics.** PSYOP forces will typically deploy with a 14-day basic load of supplies. The first week of operations may support using prepackaged, preapproved products. Although PSYOP forces rely heavily on state-of-the-art systems, planning must take into consideration the potential for having to integrate less sophisticated systems often found in underdeveloped areas of the world. HN support is often the source for providing PSYOP-required supplies. Early identification of the HN's ability to fulfill PSYOP needs is critical. Establishment of agreements or contracts within the HN can facilitate the requisition of necessary PSYOP-related supplies, equipment, and facilities. As with production, the level of HN support (via agreements, a directive, or contracts) determines what will be certain logistically and what will become an assumption. Any logistics requirements that are not met via the organic deployment package may become assumptions. A severely degraded or nonexistent communications infrastructure in the HN or terrain and insufficient assets can adversely affect C4I. Consequently, PSYOP forces are usually dependent upon the HN support capabilities for commercial communications.

4-41. The PSYOP planner will need to distinguish between fact and assumption so that when the proposal of PSYOP forces goes to the supported commander, these considerations are known and not a surprise.

Step 7: Conduct Risk Assessment

4-42. From a PSYOP planner's perspective, a risk assessment is conducted to ensure PSYOP programs will not jeopardize the supported commander's objectives. Knowledge of the culture, experience in the region, and thorough analysis shield against unintended consequences of a product or program. Planners must make supported commanders aware of the potential of unintended consequences and what their impact may be. The planner will not know if a program or specific product will have an unintended effect at the time of planning, but should make the commander aware of the potential risks involved in PSYOP and also the measures taken that attempt to mitigate those risks. Planners must also consider the time factor. They must ensure the supported commander is aware that it takes time for PSYOP programs to achieve results. Planners must limit the risk of not allotting sufficient time to prepare PSYOP products by explaining to commanders that success is not always instantaneous. In-depth analysis and exhaustive pretesting minimize the risk of time and unintended consequences.

4-43. PSYOP planners must consider all the risks normally associated with military operations, such as airborne operations, as well as unique considerations that are outside of the norm. Examples include the following:

- It is imperative that the supported commander clearly understands that unilateral PSYOP (PSYOP without supporting actions) will not be successful and can be a very risky method to accomplish the combatant commander's objectives.

- Time is always a risk when conducting PSYOP. It takes time for PSYOP personnel to develop PSYOP series, products, and actions tailored to one particular TA. It takes time for those targeted by PSYOP personnel to understand the line of persuasion and symbols, filter them through their belief system, and act in the desired manner. Not allocating sufficient time to conduct the PSYOP development process is the single greatest risk to effective PSYOP.

- Planners should analyze the risk of using preparatory PSYOP versus surprise. All supported commanders hope to achieve some degree of surprise during military operations and may view preparatory PSYOP as an element that can compromise surprise. Therefore, PSYOP planners must weigh the advantages and disadvantages of using preparatory PSYOP. Usually, commanders at the tactical and operational levels are concerned with concealing or disguising the method and timing of military operations. PSYOP may be employed as part of a deception mission to help with disguising an operation or can be left unused to achieve maximum surprise. Should the situation occur when the commander must choose between PSYOP and surprise, the planner must weigh the loss of surprise (using PSYOP) against the loss of the legitimacy (not using PSYOP) of the operation, and advise the commander. For example, if the commander decides to attack and numerous noncombatants are killed because they were not warned to stay away from the area prior to the operation, all military success may be offset by the loss of international legitimacy for U.S. operations.

4-44. At the conclusion of step seven, the PSYOP planner has made the supported unit commander aware of the peculiar risks of PSYOP that need to be included in the commander's risk assessment.

Step 8: Determine Initial CCIR

4-45. The CCIR identify information needed by the commander to support his battlefield visualization and to make critical decisions, especially to determine or validate a COA. The CCIR can include information about enemy forces' disposition, equipment, and location, or information about the capabilities of his adjacent units. The CCIR answer the question, "What does the commander need to know in a specific situation to make a particular decision in a timely manner?" The PSYOP planner would nominate CCIR if specific information is crucial to the success of the PSYOP mission. The planner must be able to articulate to the supported unit why this piece of information is critical.

Step 9: Determine Initial Reconnaissance Annex

4-46. Based on initial IPB and CCIR, the staff, primarily the G-2 or S-2, identifies intelligence gaps and determines an initial reconnaissance and surveillance plan to acquire the necessary information. PSYOP planners do not usually have direct involvement in this plan, but may be able to use the information that is collected.

Step 10: Plan Use of Available Time

4-47. Time is critical to planning and executing successful operations and must be considered an integral part of mission analysis. Poor planning and poor timing may result in unsuccessful PSYOP. The PSYOP planner must continually conduct time analysis until mission accomplishment. He must balance detailed planning against maximizing speed and surprise by immediate action.

Step 11: Write the Restated Mission

4-48. The restated mission is based on mission analysis and contains all elements of a mission statement. These elements include—

- *Who* will execute the action?
- *What* type of action is considered?
- *When* will the action begin?
- *Where* will the action occur?
- *Why* will each force conduct its part of the operation?
- *How* will the commander employ available assets?

4-49. The "What" portion of the restated mission addresses the essential tasks. The restated mission clearly defines tasks and purpose. The Chief of Staff or G-3 (S-3) prepares a restated mission statement for the unit based on mission analysis. This is the mission statement of the supported unit and not the mission statement of PSYOP. The PSYOP planner must advise and ensure PSYOP considerations are incorporated into the restated commander's mission statement.

Step 12: Conduct Mission Analysis Briefing

4-50. The staff briefs the commander on its mission analysis using the following outline:

- Mission and commander's intent of the HQ two levels up.
- Mission, commander's intent, concept of the operation, and deception plan or objective of the HQ one level up.
- Review of commander's initial guidance.
- Initial IPB products.

- Specified, implied, and essential tasks.
- Constraints on the operation.
- Forces available.
- Hazards and their risks.
- Recommended timelines.
- Recommended restated mission.

4-51. The mission analysis briefing is given to both the commander and the staff. This is often the only time the entire staff is present and the only opportunity to ensure that all staff members are starting from a common reference point. Mission analysis is critical to ensure thorough understanding of the task and subsequent planning. The briefing focuses on relevant conclusions reached as a result of the mission analysis. This briefing helps the commander and his staff develop a shared vision of the requirements for the upcoming operation.

Step 13: Approve Restated Mission

4-52. Immediately after the mission analysis briefing, the commander approves a restated mission. This restated mission could be the staff's recommended restated mission, a modified version of the staff's recommendation, or one that the commander has developed himself. Once approved, the restated mission becomes the unit's mission.

Step 14: Develop Initial Commander's Intent

4-53. During the mission analysis, the supported commander develops his initial intent for the operation. The commander's intent is a clear, concise statement of what the force must do to succeed with respect to the adversary's environment and to the desired end state. The commander's intent provides the link between the mission and the CONOPS by stating the key tasks that, along with the mission, are the basis for subordinates to exercise initiative when unanticipated opportunities arise or when the original CONOPS no longer applies. Key tasks are those that must be performed by the force, or conditions that must be met, to achieve the stated purpose of the operation. The mission and the commander's intent must be understood two echelons down. The commander personally prepares his intent statement and, when possible, delivers it along with the order. Commanders from company level up prepare an intent statement for each OPORD or OPLAN. The intent statement at any level must support the intent of the next-higher commander.

Step 15: Issue the Commander's Guidance

4-54. After the commander approves the restated mission and states his intent, he provides the staff with enough additional guidance (preliminary decisions) to focus staff activities in planning the operation. By stating the planning options he does or does not want them to consider, he can save the staff members time and effort by allowing them to concentrate on developing COAs that meet the commander's intent. The commander's guidance may be written or oral. It must focus on the essential mission accomplishments.

Step 16: Issue a Warning Order

4-55. Immediately after the commander gives his guidance, the staff sends subordinate and supporting units a WARNORD. This WARNORD contains as a minimum—

- The restated mission.
- The commander's intent.
- The AO.
- The CCIR.
- Risk guidance.
- Reconnaissance initiated by subordinates.
- Security measures.
- Deception guidance.
- Specific priorities.
- The time plan.
- Guidance on rehearsals.

4-56. The PSYOP planner, who should be in constant contact with the PSYOP unit who will most likely execute the mission, immediately sends the WARNORD to the unit to facilitate their preparation.

Step 17: Review Facts and Assumptions

4-57. During the rest of the decision-making process, the commander and staff periodically review all available facts and assumptions. New facts may alter requirements and analysis of the mission. Assumptions may have become facts or may have become invalid. Whenever the facts or assumptions change, the commander and staff must assess the impact of these changes on the plan and make the necessary adjustments.

PHASE III: COURSE OF ACTION DEVELOPMENT

4-58. After mission analysis is complete and the commander has issued his restated mission, intent, and guidance, planners develop COAs for analysis and comparison. COA development starts off with a brainstorming session, where the components and staff throw out ideas on how to accomplish the various tasks and complete the mission. Usually, there is a facilitator who controls the discussion (most often from the S-3 or G-3, but he can be from the joint force J-5 Plans or a planner from a deployable joint task force augmentation cell [DJTFAC] augmenting the planning staff). He or she guides the planning process through all of its stages and is responsible for the completion of the planning products (commander's estimate and subsequent OPORDs). As the ideas take shape, the focus is on two or three (usually three) distinct COAs. The PSYOP planner must be aggressively involved in this process and suggest ways that PSYOP can support both the overall effort and specific component tasks. The PSYOP planner has the responsibility to advise the supported unit from a PSYOP perspective. Thus, the PSYOP planner must be involved in analyzing the specific tasks and the mission, as well as know the other component representatives' plans for executing their tasks and accomplishing their missions. If the representatives do not address PSYOP or feel they do not want PSYOP support, it is the PSYOP planner's job to bring to their attention what PSYOP could do for their mission accomplishment. PSYOP planners should not wait for the commander to ask what PSYOP can do. Another approach that invariably has disastrous results is to go to the supported commander and ask, "Sir, what is it exactly you want me to do for you?"

4-59. The commander's staff generally prepares three COAs. The PSYOP planner provides input to each COA. Each COA will usually differ for PSYOP in task organization and method of employing the force. The PSYOP planner during this phase is providing guidance to the supported unit. He will take each proposed COA and determine how best PSYOP can assist. For each COA, PSYOP planners will need to consider the amount of forces needed, whether or not they need to refine POs and SPOs that were initially developed, and consider the psychological impact on the enemy and noncombatants. Again, this phase in the process will be helped tremendously if the PSYOP planner has had help from all the PSYOP assets in writing the PSYOP estimate, which would now be consulted to help in COA development. The PSYOP planner must always remember that he is not developing PSYOP COAs here, but instead is recommending PSYOP support to the supported unit's COAs.

PHASE IV: COURSE OF ACTION ANALYSIS

4-60. Each COA is then analyzed and war-gamed to ensure that all elements are fully integrated and synchronized. Each COA must meet the following criteria:

- *Suitability*: It must accomplish the mission and comply with the commander's guidance.
- *Feasibility*: The unit must have the capability to accomplish the mission in terms of available time, space, and resources.
- *Acceptability*: The tactical or operational advantage gained by executing the COA must justify the cost in resources, especially casualties.
- *Distinguishability*: Each COA must differ significantly from others. This difference may result from the use of reserves, different task organizations, day or night operations, or a different scheme of maneuver.
- *Completeness*: The COA must result in a complete mission statement. Does it answer what, when, where, why, and how?

4-61. Each COA is analyzed to meet the above stated criteria. Again, the PSYOP planner is providing guidance to the supported unit from the PSYOP perspective and not war gaming PSYOP in a vacuum insulated from the activities of the supported unit.

PHASE V: COURSE OF ACTION COMPARISON

4-62. After each COA is war-gamed and it is determined that it meets the established criteria, it is compared to the other COAs. Each staff member will evaluate the advantages and disadvantages of the COAs from their perspective. The PSYOP planner will evaluate each COA to determine which will best utilize PSYOP assets, provide flexibility for contingencies, and has the highest probability of achieving mission success from the PSYOP viewpoint. The PSYOP evaluation of the supportability of the COAs is normally included as part of the overall IO supportability of the COAs. A tool used for this comparison is the COA matrix. A matrix is used to compare each COA based on criteria chosen by the PSYOP planner in conjunction and coordination with the IO planner. This matrix will show the commander how effectively PSYOP can support each COA. The planner will use the outcome of this matrix to give his recommendation to the supported unit for integration into their COA matrix. This matrix allows the planning staff to determine which COA will best accomplish the overall mission. Figures 4-4 and 4-5, pages 4-22 and 4-23, are examples of the two matrixes often used in COA comparison.

CRITERIA	WEIGHT (Note 1)	COA 1		COA 2		COA 3	
Psychological Impact	3	2	(6)	3	(9)	1	(3)
Flexibility	2	3	(6)	1	(2)	2	(4)
Ratio of Force	3	2	(6)	1	(3)	1	(3)
Risk	2	3	(6)	2	(4)	3	(6)
Reachback	2	1	(2)	3	(6)	2	(4)
Total (Note 2)		11	(26)	10	(24)	9	(20)

NOTES:
1. Weight can be assigned to any specific criteria if it has been directed by the supported unit or can be added by the PSYOP planner if he thinks the supported unit is more concerned with certain aspects.
2. The higher the number assigned, the better the COA is from the PSYOP perspective (1 being the least desirable and 3 being the most desirable). In the above example, the PSYOP planner would tell the supported commander that all three COAs are supportable, but COA 1 is the best from a PSYOP perspective.

Figure 4-4. PSYOP-Specific Decision Matrix

CRITERIA	WEIGHT (Note)	COA 1		COA 2		COA 3	
Maneuver	5	2	(10)	3	(15)	1	(5)
Simplicity	3	3	(9)	1	(3)	2	(6)
Fires	3	2	(6)	1	(3)	1	(3)
Intelligence	1	3	(3)	2	(2)	3	(3)

Figure 4-5. Sample Supported Unit Decision Matrix

CRITERIA	WEIGHT (Note)	COA 1		COA 2		COA 3	
Air Defense Artillery	1	1	(1)	3	(3)	2	(2)
PSYOP (Note)	1	3	(3)	2	(2)	1	(1)
Mobility/Survivability	1	2	(2)	1	(1)	3	(3)
Total		16	(34)	13	(29)	13	(23)

NOTE: PSYOP are sometimes incorporated into evaluation as part of a nonlethal fires criteria section or as a subordinate criteria element under IO. PSYOP planners should attempt to justify the need to have a distinct PSYOP criteria section, either as a separate category or as a distinct line under IO to reflect the most effective use of PSYOP in the COAs; otherwise, PSYOP supportability of each COA may not be apparent.

Figure 4-5. Sample Supported Unit Decision Matrix (Continued)

4-63. The PSYOP planner uses the matrix in Figure 4-4, page 4-22, to visualize how best the PSYOP forces would support the various COAs. This matrix will help the planner to explain to the commander how PSYOP can support each COA to a greater or lesser degree. Typically, the planner will give his matrix to the G-3 or S-3 for inclusion in the supported unit matrix that often looks similar to Figure 4-5, pages 4-22 and 4-23. The supported unit matrix may include IO and the IO components relevant to the plan as a major section of the matrix. At the Army corps and division, the DCS, G-7 may include the IO components as part of the G-3 matrix or may brief the IO components concurrently. In either case, the PSYOP planner ensures that PSYOP are considered in all COAs of the supported unit.

4-64. When the COAs are compared and weighted as in Figure 4-5, it demonstrates that for all units participating in the mission, COA 1 is the best COA. These matrixes are examples and each commander will have his own way of comparing COAs, but the essential element for the PSYOP planner is to evaluate each COA as it pertains to PSYOP and then be prepared to execute whichever COA is chosen by the supported commander.

PHASE VI: COURSE OF ACTION APPROVAL

4-65. The COAs are then briefed to the commander along with the staff's recommendation. The commander makes the final decision. Once the decision is made and the commander gives any final guidance, the staff immediately sends an updated WARNORD, refines the COA, and completes the plan.

PHASE VII: ORDERS PREPARATION

4-66. The final step of the MDMP is producing an OPLAN or an OPORD. A plan becomes an order when execution is directed. An order is a written or oral communication directing actions. An OPLAN differs from an OPORD in that an OPLAN has an unspecified execution time and typically contains assumptions. The focus of orders production is ensuring the plan is effective, integrated, and executable. PSYOP planners should build the annex or tab with as much PSYOP-specific information as possible, as this document will be the baseline PSYOP source for component or subordinate PSYOP forces and personnel. Examples of additional appendixes and enclosures are—

- Media list.
- TAA list (and any analysis as available).
- PO/SPO.
- Internal approval process procedures (within the staff).
- PSYOP SITREP procedures.
- Approval delegation guidelines.
- PSYOP support request procedures.
- Anticipated opponent themes and objectives.

TARGETING

4-67. PSYOP planners should be present at supported unit targeting meetings and boards to obtain necessary support for the execution of the PSYOP mission. The targeting cycle is critical if PSYOP forces intend to disseminate any of its products with air assets. For example, if PSYOP forces want to drop leaflets, use an EC-130 for radio broadcast, or conduct an aerial loudspeaker mission, then a PSYOP representative must attend the targeting meetings. The representative must have some familiarity with the targeting process and understand the steps that lead to the publication of the air tasking order (ATO).

4-68. At the unified command or CJTF level, the PSYOP representative will usually participate in action-officer-level targeting meetings or working groups and the JTCB. During the targeting meetings, the PSYOP planner will give input to the psychological impact of any targets that may have been nominated for destruction. This input may raise or lower a prospective target's priority. During the nonlethal fires discussion, the PSYOP representative ensures that PSYOP forces are allocated the necessary means to deliver their products. This is where, for example, he ensures that the EC-130 is scheduled for inclusion on the ATO. The JTCB provides the forum for component representatives to voice concerns with regard to the joint integrated prioritized target list (JIPTL) to the senior leadership. The JTF deputy commander or director of the joint staff normally chairs the JTCB at the joint level. The chief of staff or senior fire support officer (corps or division artillery commander) normally chairs the equivalent meeting or board at the Army corps or division level. The PSYOP staff officer, a PSE targeting representative, and/or a POTF representative must attend the JTCB to ensure PSYOP targets or considerations maintain visibility in the targeting process. The PSYOP representative should be familiar with common targeting terms, such as high-payoff targets (HPTs) (a target whose loss to the adversary will significantly contribute to the success of the friendly COA) and high-value targets (HVTs) (a target the adversary commander requires for the successful completion of his mission). Attendance at this board will allow for PSYOP forces to receive the support they need for dissemination assets, as well as ensure coordination between other fire support assets.

FREQUENCY MANAGEMENT

4-69. Frequency management is another aspect of operations of which PSYOP planners must be aware. Planners must ensure that friendly jamming assets do not jam a PSYOP signal; for example, a radio broadcast frequency, thus minimizing its effect. IO officers will also monitor this deconfliction. The joint restricted frequency list (JRFL) is a management tool designed to minimize frequency conflicts between friendly communications and noncommunications emitters and jamming equipment. More specifically, the JRFL is a time and geographical listing of prioritized frequencies essential to the conduct of the battle and restricted from targeting by friendly electronic jamming capabilities. Consisting of taboo, protected, and guarded frequencies, the JRFL assists staff members involved in spectrum management.

4-70. Taboo frequencies are any friendly functions or frequencies of such importance that they must never be deliberately jammed or interfered with by friendly forces. Protected frequencies are those friendly functions or frequencies used for a particular operation, identified and protected to prevent them from being inadvertently jammed by friendly forces while active EW operations are directed against hostile forces. Protected frequencies are time-oriented, can change with the tactical situation, and are updated periodically. The frequency on which an EC-130 is broadcasting a PSYOP radio product would be a protected frequency. Guarded frequencies are enemy functions or frequencies that are currently being exploited for combat information and intelligence. If PSYOP is conducting missions in which frequency management plays a role, then the PSYOP planner should request a copy of the JRFL for review.

MEASURES OF EFFECTIVENESS

4-71. PSYOP measures of effectiveness (MOEs) provide a systematic means of assessing and reporting the impact a PSYOP program (series of PSYOP products and actions) has on specific foreign TAs. PSYOP MOEs, as all MOEs, change from mission to mission, and encompass a wide range of factors that are fundamental to the overall effect of PSYOP. PSYOP impact indicators collectively provide an indication of the overall effectiveness of the PSYOP mission. Development of MOEs and their associated impact indicators (derived from measurable SPOs) must be done during the planning process. By determining the measures in the planning process, PSYOP planners ensure that organic assets and PSYOP enablers, such as intelligence, are identified to assist in evaluating MOEs for the execution of PSYOP. Evaluating the effectiveness of PSYOP may take weeks or longer given the inherent difficulties and complexity of determining cause and effect relationships with respect to human behavior.

OPERATIONAL PLANNING

4-72. Operational planning deals with how the PSYOP forces will execute the PSYOP support plan developed with the supported unit. Operational planning is the development of the POTF or PSE OPLAN or OPORD. The development follows the same MDMP that was described above but has some unique considerations. This section will elaborate by exception and not repeat all of the steps discussed earlier. The second phase of operational planning is the planning, coordination, and synchronization of PSYOP activities. This will be discussed in Chapter 6 in the PSYOP development process. The factors for operational planning are time, resources, and the supported unit's plan.

POTF OR PSE OPLAN OR OPORD

4-73. Operational planning for PSYOP units begins simultaneously with supported unit planning. The PSYOP annex or tab to the supported unit's OPLAN or OPORD will be incorporated as part of the supporting PSYOP OPLAN or OPORD. The level of detail contained in the supporting PSYOP OPLAN or OPORD will depend on the time allocated for its creation. Some sections of the POTF or PSE OPORD will be exactly the same as the supported unit's PSYOP annex or tab. The POs and SPOs are an example. The POTF or PSE OPORD will direct and coordinate the operations of all PSYOP forces to ensure the execution of an effective and synchronized PSYOP effort. The PSYOP OPLAN or OPORD is written from an operations perspective of the supporting PSYOP element or unit, not by the PSYOP staff planner to the supported unit staff. The supporting PSYOP planner, when working on the POTF or PSE order, has several considerations that are fundamentally important: task organization, logistics, level of reachback, and establishing approval authority and guidelines for subordinate units. These are the issues that, once resolved and promulgated to all PSYOP elements, will ensure an effective PSYOP effort.

4-74. The planner assigned or attached to the supported unit will ultimately be responsible for the supported unit's PSYOP annex or tab while the G-3 or S-3 of the POTF or PSE will be responsible for the OPLAN or OPORD. The sharing of information between the two is critical because certain decisions, constraints, and COAs of the supported unit will have enormous repercussions for the POTF or PSE OPLAN or OPORD. Likewise, the operational tempo and assets available to PSYOP units will affect the input the planner makes to the supported unit. The importance of sharing information cannot be overstated.

4-75. A consideration when matching the POTF or PSE plan to the supported unit is to ensure that POs, which are written "cradle to grave," are prioritized so that they align with the supported unit's phasing. The prioritizing of POs will give the subordinate PSYOP elements their initial focus. Phasing a mission, which is done by the supported commander, requires that PSYOP forces match those phases with emphasis on the correct objectives. For example, the establishment of democratic institutions as a PO will probably not be the POTF's emphasis in Phase I: Initial Entry of the Force. Close coordination with the supported commander and G-3 or S-3 will assist in this prioritizing. In some situations, certain parts of the AO may require different priorities than others. For example, PSYOP forces may be addressing PO "increase support for democratic institutions" in the western portion of the AOR, while at the same time be working on PO "decrease hostilities of enemy forces" in the east. This will require a careful allocation of resources based upon the commander's guidance of priorities at that time. These priorities will change based on the situation over time.

4-76. There are many considerations when developing the task organization of PSYOP forces. The complexity of the operation and the availability of forces will be the underlying considerations behind the establishment of a POTF as a stand-alone functional component command or the use of a PSE embedded within the supported unit G-3, S-3, or other element. The two main advantages of a POTF are its ability to provide full-spectrum PSYOP support and its designation as a component command with inherent C2, with resulting access to the commander. The POTF has a robust C2 element and includes all the staff sections. The PSE is a smaller tailored force that has the advantage of not needing all of the accompanying staff elements. It decreases the numbers required significantly from that of a POTF. The disadvantages of a PSE are that it cannot provide full-spectrum support, its reachback requirements are greater, and it can sometimes be buried in a supported unit's staff where it is difficult to obtain the direct access to the commander, which is necessary for effective PSYOP. Figure 4-6 gives a quick reference to the advantages and disadvantages of both the POTF and PSE models.

POTF	PSE
Advantages	
Access to commander	Minimal footprint
Greater support to task force	Less personnel impact
Priority of effort from home base	Reduced administrative/logistics concerns
Less reliance on reachback	Focused purely on PSYOP
Inherent C2	
Disadvantages	
Increased logistical trail	Less access to commander
Increased personnel	Lower priority of effort
Increased cost	Less capability to support task force
Large space requirement	More reliant on others' assets

Figure 4-6. Advantages and Disadvantages Between the POTF and the PSE

4-77. Logistics are the next consideration that will have a large impact on the PSYOP plan. A determination as to the level in which organic or HN assets will be used is critical. An operation within a denied area usually requires PSYOP forces to utilize organic equipment that requires significant space, strategic airlift, and manpower. The more organic assets used, the larger the force required and the greater the amount of logistical support needed. The benefit of organic equipment is easier quality control, timeliness, and operational security. Using indigenous or HN assets curtails the logistical problems significantly. For example, the force no longer has to concern itself with procuring paper and ink and their storage. Soldiers must also be familiar with the procedures for contracting officers and Class A agents to use operational funds. Ideally, a certified contracting officer or Class A agent should be included in the organizational structure to facilitate PSYOP logistics. The PSYOP planner has to take into account that logistical requirements will change over the course of an operation as the footprint of PSYOP assets changes. For example, when an operation begins, the emphasis will most likely be on organic assets, but as the operation continues, the emphasis switches to more indigenous assets so that force structure can be curtailed. Figure 4-7 gives examples of the advantages and disadvantages between using organic and HN assets.

Organic	HN
Advantages	
Maximum control over production	Reduced footprint
Responsiveness to POTF	More acceptable to locals
Smaller budget	Storage requirements
Secure-capable production	Quality issues
24/7 capability	
Disadvantages	
Increased footprint	No secure production capability
Increased storage requirements	Cannot dictate responsiveness
Quality issues	May not have 24/7 capability
Waste issues	Budget/payment concerns
	Potential for product manipulation

Figure 4-7. Advantages and Disadvantages Between Organic and HN Assets

4-78. Another important aspect to the POTF or PSE OPLAN or OPORD is the level of reachback that will be used. A smaller force forward deployed may be necessitated by force cap requirements, which will dictate a larger amount of reliance on reachback capabilities. Planners must remember that there are limitations when employing reachback. A smaller PSYOP footprint can be easily offset by a larger communications support footprint, in effect not reducing the overall footprint of PSYOP assets. There may be logistical problems with doing production in the continental United States (CONUS) and distribution via strategic airlift to theater. Strategic airlift to distribute printed material from CONUS into an operational theater can be extremely difficult and is based upon the theater's mission priorities.

4-79. One of the most important considerations for the PSYOP planner is to, as completely as possible, delineate the approval authority. A technique that can be used to establish the supported unit's approval chain is an enclosure to the supported unit's OPLAN or OPORD that establishes the approval process. Therefore, when the commander approves the OPLAN or OPORD, the PSYOP approval process will be approved as a matter of course. The approval chain should also be included in paragraph 5 of the supported unit's OPORD or OPLAN. At the beginning of an operation, the POTF commander, PPD planner, or PSYOP forward force planners must coordinate with the combatant commander or joint force commander (JFC) to establish the PSYOP product approval process that best balances timeliness with proper oversight. The combatant commander or JFC must also delineate what specific PSYOP approval authorities will be delegated, if any, to subordinate component commanders. In some peacetime operations, or in the case of noncombatant evacuation operations (NEOs), in which the Department of

State (DOS) is the lead organization, DOS in coordination with the Country Team may be the PSYOP product approval authority. In some cases, the POTF commander may be given approval authority for routine, noncontroversial PSYOP products, while the combatant commander or JFC will retain approval authority for other PSYOP products and actions that fall outside of established parameters. PSYOP approval authority may be retained at the combatant command or SecDef level because of the sensitivity of PSYOP combined with the need to coordinate all U.S. information efforts.

4-80. PSYOP planners should seek to minimize the participants within the approval chain. The following graphics (Figure 4-8 and Figure 4-9, page 4-30) are published in JP 3-53 and illustrate the PSYOP approval process beginning at the highest levels.

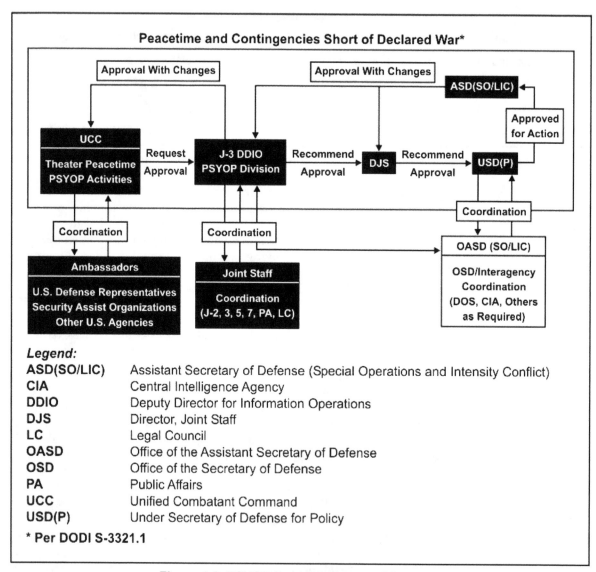

Peacetime and Contingencies Short of Declared War*

Legend:
ASD(SO/LIC)   Assistant Secretary of Defense (Special Operations and Intensity Conflict)
CIA   Central Intelligence Agency
DDIO   Deputy Director for Information Operations
DJS   Director, Joint Staff
LC   Legal Council
OASD   Office of the Assistant Secretary of Defense
OSD   Office of the Secretary of Defense
PA   Public Affairs
UCC   Unified Combatant Command
USD(P)   Under Secretary of Defense for Policy
* Per DODI S-3321.1

Figure 4-8. PSYOP Program Approval Process

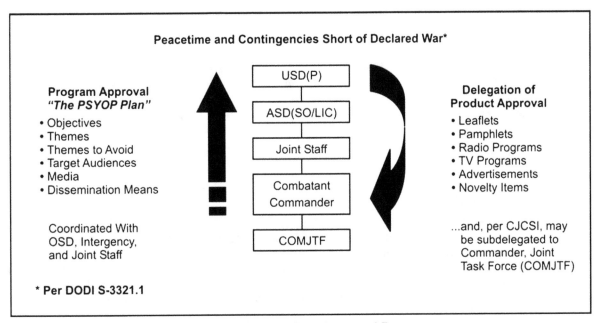

Figure 4-9. PSYOP Plan Approval Process

4-81. CJCSI 3110.05C, dated 18 July 2003, states "when a PSYOP plan is approved for execution, the SecDef normally delegates execution and approval authority for operational and tactical-level PSYOP products and actions to the supported combatant commander in the execute order. The combatant commander is authorized to subdelegate that authority to a subordinate component or JFC. Approval authority may not be subdelegated below the component or JFC level without SecDef approval. The USD(P) retains approval authority for strategic-level products and products with significant political implications unless otherwise stated in the execute order." Figure 4-10, page 4-31, demonstrates how this delegation might be done, although it must be stressed that this would need to be an enclosure in the PSYOP annex and approved at the SecDef level.

NOTE: Figure 4-10 is an example of a technique allowing approval authority to be delegated down to the tactical level, within guidelines. Doing so helps avoid the time delays in obtaining approval, but the SecDef must approve this proposal.

TACTICAL PSYOP EXECUTION GUIDELINES

1. SITUATION.

A. General. This Appendix provides guidance from COMJTF to the tactical commanders regarding the scope and limits of PSYOP activities and products, which tactical commanders can execute without gaining approval from COMJTF.

B. Friendly Forces.

2. MISSION.

3. EXECUTION.

A. Concept of the Operation.

(1) General. JTF _____ will plan and coordinate a centralized PSYOP plan throughout the AOR. Tactical commanders will support this overall plan and execute PSYOP activities within their unit AORs. To support the tactical commanders' ability to execute PSYOP activities, COMJTF will delegate PSYOP activity and product approval authority, within the following guidelines, to tactical commanders.

(2) Guidelines. The following guidelines will determine which PSYOP activities and products can be approved at the tactical commander level. Any PSYOP activities and products falling outside of these guidelines will be submitted through PSYOP channels to COMJTF for approval.

a. Tactical commander approval authority. Tactical commanders are delegated the authority to approve the following PSYOP activities and products:

- Loudspeaker operations.
- Mine awareness products.
- Checkpoint-related products.
- Vehicle or dwelling search products.
- General force protection products or activities.
- Products containing primarily command information.
- Retransmissions or use of commander's statements.
- Retransmissions of PAO releases.

b. Tactical commanders will refrain from executing PSYOP activities and products in the following specific areas without COMJTF approval:

- Elections.
- Democratic institutions/democratization products.

- Person(s) Indicted for War Crimes (PIFWC)/war criminal products.
- Counterpropaganda products (outside PAO responses).
- Organized crime-related products.

c. The JPOTF commander and S-3 will coordinate and deconflict any confusion concerning these guidelines. Tactical commanders will contact COMJTF if there is an immediate need for PSYOP activities and/or products for approval authority delegation outside of the specified parameters.

4. SERVICE SUPPORT.

5. COMMAND AND SIGNAL.

Figure 4-10. Example of Specific Delegation

4-82. The POTF or PSE OPLAN or OPORD will have the basic 5-paragraph format and can have numerous appendixes that articulate all the necessary information that will allow PSYOP elements to execute a centralized plan.

These appendixes should include the following and will be updated as the operation unfolds:

- Annex A – Task organization to include location.
- Annex B – Intelligence.
    - TAAWs.
    - SPAs/SPSs.
    - PIR/IRs.
    - Enemy disposition.
    - Anticipated opponent PSYOP and information plan.
    - Population status.
    - Media infrastructure.
    - Language analysis.
    - Religion analysis.
    - Ethnic group analysis.
    - Weather analysis.
    - Terrain impact on dissemination.
    - Reconnaissance and surveillance plan.
    - Area study.
    - Architecture of connectivity.
- Annex C – Operations.
    - PSYOP plan (matrix) including POs and SPOs.
    - Dissemination means.
    - PSYOP SITREP format.
    - Approval process.
    - Reachback process.
- Annex D – Logistics.
    - Logistical support.
    - Request for PSYOP support format.
    - POTF or PSE SOR.
    - Logistics purchase request.
    - PSYOP-specific support.
    - SOF (SOTSE) support.
- Annex E – Signal.
    - Communication security.
    - Bandwidth requirements.
    - Joint frequency management.
    - Transmission system.
    - Data network communication.
    - Information assurance.
    - Communication network management.
    - Coalition communication.

MISSION STATEMENTS

4-83. The PSYOP force (POTF, PSE) mission statement is written based upon mission analysis of the higher headquarters' OPLAN or OPORD and should not be a simple restating of the supported force's mission statement. It should reflect the essential tasks derived from mission analysis. The PSYOP mission statement is written in conjunction with the combatant command's mission statement. For example, if the combatant command's mission statement reads, "When directed by the Secretary of Defense, JTFXXX conducts operations to gain and maintain a secure environment so that UNSCR 4421 can be implemented. On order, JTFXXX will assist the United Nations in establishing a free, multiethnic, democratic, and autonomous province within the territorial integrity of Gingerale." The PSYOP mission statement should not simply restate the mission, but briefly explain how the PSYOP commander will support the mission. Often this is done by summarizing the POs into the POTF or PSE mission statement and could look similar to: "On order, POTFXXX provides operational and tactical PSYOP support to facilitate establishing a secure environment, minimizing insurgent activity, establishing the force and the UN as credible sources of information, promoting the use of democratic institutions, easing the internally displaced persons (IDP) repatriation process, and promoting the benefits of nongovernmental organization (NGO) programs until a free, multiethnic, democratic, and autonomous province exists within the territorial integrity of the country of XXXXXXXX."

4-84. Operational planning for PSYOP units begins simultaneously with supported unit planning. Figure 4-11, the Army PSYOP annex, pages 4-33 and 4-34, and Figure 4-12, the joint PSYOP tab to the IO appendix, pages 4-35 through 4-38, explain the PSYOP-related input required during planning. The PSYOP annex or tab to the supported unit's OPLAN or OPORD will be incorporated as part of the supporting OPLAN or OPORD. The level of detail contained in the supporting PSYOP OPLAN or OPORD will depend on the time allocated for its creation. Some sections of the POTF or PSE OPORD will be exactly the same as the supported unit's PSYOP annex or tab. The guide at the end of the chapter, Table 4-1, pages 4-38 through 4-44, is provided for the PSYOP planner as a quick-reference input guide to the actions associated with each step of the MDMP.

ANNEX R (PSYCHOLOGICAL OPERATIONS [PSYOP]) TO OPERATIONS ORDER NO.___

1. SITUATION.

a. Enemy. State enemy resources and capabilities, both military and civilian, to conduct PSYOP. State past enemy PSYOP efforts (who was targeted, using what means, and their effectiveness).

b. Friendly. Outline the PSYOP plan of the higher HQ as it pertains to the functional area. List nonfunctional area units capable of assisting in functional area operations (such as non-engineer units capable of emplacing scatterable mines). Indicate designation, location, and outline of the plan of higher, adjacent, and other PSYOP assets that support or would otherwise have an impact on the issuing HQ or would require coordination, and any other assets supporting the unit.

c. Attachments and Detachments. List units attached or detached only as necessary to clarify task organization. Highlight changes in PSYOP task organization that occur during the operation, including effective times or events.

Figure 4-11. Example of the PSYOP Annex to an Army Operations Order

2. MISSION. State the mission of PSYOP in support of the basic OPLAN or OPORD.

3. EXECUTION.

a. Scheme of Psychological Operations. Address how PSYOP efforts are centrally orchestrated and managed by the supporting POTF, and the commander's role in the decentralized execution of PSYOP programs of higher HQ.

b. Tasks to Subordinate Units. Ensure that tasks clearly fix responsibilities and provide feedback on effectiveness of PSYOP activities.

c. Coordinating Instructions.

(1) Identify Presidential and SecDef-approved POs, themes to stress, and themes to avoid. (These themes are the broad guidelines that come from higher HQ that establish the left and right limits of what is allowed. These themes should not be confused with lines of persuasion, which are the arguments that PSYOP personnel will use to persuade a TA to modify its behavior and are developed during TAA.)

(2) Identify TAs in the AOR; include key communicators. Identify relevant background information on TA perspectives, vulnerabilities, effectiveness, and susceptibility to friendly and enemy PSYOP.

(3) Identify military activities and actions conducted by subordinate units that support or facilitate PSYOP efforts.

(4) Provide OPSEC guidance on PSYOP sensitivity and employment, if applicable.

(5) State classification authority for PSYOP activities.

(6) Address mechanisms for coordinating with attached PSYOP detachments, assigned staff, and other informational activities operating in the commander's AO.

(7) State procedures for coordinating fixed-wing aircraft, rotary-wing aircraft, unmanned aerial vehicle (UAV), and field artillery delivery of PSYOP products.

(8) State PSYOP-specific current intelligence requirements.

4. SERVICE SUPPORT.

a. Command-Regulated Classes of Supply. Highlight subordinate allocations of command-regulated classes of supply that affect PSYOP (such as the controlled supply rate).

b. Supply Distribution Plan. Discuss provisions for control and maintenance of PSYOP-unique supplies and equipment, to include products.

5. COMMAND AND SIGNAL.

a. Command.

(1) Explain command relationships between attached PSYOP elements, POTF elements operating in the AO, the supported unit, and the POTF itself.

(2) State the PSYOP approval process and release authority that has been delegated or retained by higher HQ.

(3) State the PSYOP approval authority the commander has delegated or specifically retained to subordinate commanders for the development of proposed PSYOP products, actions, and programs.

(4) State the PSYOP release authority the commander has delegated (or specifically retained) to subordinate commanders for releasing and disseminating approved products in their respective AORs.

b. Signal. Identify and explain unique PSYOP-related acronyms and abbreviations.

Figure 4-11. Example of the PSYOP Annex to an Army Operations Order (Continued)

TAB D (PSYOP) TO APPENDIX 3 (INFORMATION OPERATIONS) TO ANNEX C (OPERATIONS) TO U.S. GEOGRAPHIC COMBATANT COMMANDER XXXX OPLAN XXXX-XX (X) PSYCHOLOGICAL OPERATIONS (X)

REFERENCES: List plans, estimates, basic Psychological Operations studies (BPSs), SPAs, media production mobilization plans, combined military PSYOP committee agreements, peacetime PSYOP programs, relevant messages, orders, and other documents that have a significant bearing on the conduct of PSYOP.

1. SITUATION. Brief general description of the political-military situation in the AOR and specific PSYOP actions and factors influencing activities.

a. Overview. (Depending on the supported command, the situation paragraph may encompass enough detail to exclude an overview paragraph.) Describe the general situation, competing goals, and the task to be accomplished. (Quite often the overview is a brief description of PSYOP support and employment with regard to the supported commander and his mission and tasks.)

b. U.S. (or U.S. and Allied) Perspective (if applicable). Briefly outline intentions (how the task will be accomplished), capabilities (resources to be used), and activities (current actions and general phasing of future actions). (Sometimes the information that is asked for here is written in paragraph 3, Execution, in the Concept of Operations.) Another heading often used in this paragraph is Friendly, which gives information on friendly forces that may directly affect the action of subordinate commanders. An example listing here might indicate a foreign government that is willing to provide support to PSYOP units. Friendly organizations might include ministries of information, defense, and foreign affairs, national-level organizations, and other combatant commanders who directly support PSYACTs.

c. Neutral Perspective (if applicable). Briefly outline estimated neutral intentions under various circumstances, the resources available to neutrals, and their activities. State neutral actions and behavior that would favor mission accomplishment. Explain how neutrality plays a part in overall geographic combatant commander or JFC objectives and how opponents may try to exploit the issue of neutrality. (Identify, if needed, all influential individuals, staff factions, groups of related planner and decision maker essential elements of friendly information [EEFI]. For each group list, identify estimates of background knowledge and desired and harmful appreciation.)

d. Enemy Perspectives. Describe the environment and negative messages that deployed geographic combatant commander or JFC forces are likely to encounter upon entering the AOR. Identify groups that can influence and interfere with plans, operations, and actions. Identify opponent psychological vulnerabilities and susceptibilities to the geographic combatant commander or JFC PSYOP. Identify opponent PSYOP strengths and weaknesses in all phases of the plan. Describe apparent goals, motivations, and characteristics of various opponent groups and the leaders who can influence them to behave in ways unfavorable to the geographic combatant commander or JFC objectives. Describe the effects of opponent PSYOP on local and regional audiences. List expected opponent themes and objectives. Identify opponent centers of gravity for all levels of war. Indicate the need for EPWs to be interviewed for PSYOP-relevant information, and for that information to be analyzed to determine vulnerabilities for exploitation. Under enemy perspectives, the following subparagraphs are listed; use them only if they apply.

(1) Decision Maker and Staff. Identify the decision makers that can direct development or allocation of resources of COA execution pertinent to the task assigned. Outline feasible, alternative actions that would favor or harm friendly operational effectiveness. Describe the characteristics of enemy decision makers, their key advisors, and staff (particularly intelligence analysts).

(2) Intelligence Systems. Identify intelligence systems that support decision makers and their staffs, and intelligence system capabilities pertinent to the situation. Describe objective and subjective factors and the characteristics of collection planners and decision makers that affect development and selection for use of information-gathering resources.

Figure 4-12. Example of the PSYOP Tab to the IO Appendix to the Operations Annex to the Joint Operations Plan

(3) TAs. Although TAs are subparagraphed under enemy perspectives, it is not wrong for TAs (themes and objectives included) to be listed separately as exhibits to the tab.

(4) Command Systems (if applicable). Describe opponent communication systems and command centers used to plan COA, and control, coordinate, and supervise execution of the planned COA. State targets for jamming or attacking. Indicate when to execute operations to demoralize and disorganize opposing commands, reduce opposing operational effectiveness, enhance the effectiveness of planned deceptions and PSYOP, and support OPSEC to maximum advantage. (Quite often the above is written for compartmented operations, and the appendixes that are written to support such operations are listed separately and not contained in the basic plan.)

2. MISSION. The PSYOP mission statement is written in conjunction with the geographic combatant commander's or JFC's mission statement. Example: If the geographic combatant commander's or JFC's mission statement reads, "When directed by the President and SecDef, U.S. geographic combatant commander-XXX/JFC-XX conducts operations in support of joint military operations in the Gingerale Islands AOR to restore Government of Terrifica's (GOT's) sovereignty, neutralize Government of Snoring's (GOS's) power projection capability, and ensure access through vital lines of communication (LOCs). Should deterrence fail, U.S. geographic combatant commander-XXX/JFC-XX conducts operations to destroy the GOS's will to fight and to achieve war termination objectives on terms favorable to the GOT/United States. U.S. geographic combatant commander-XXX/CJFC-XX will be prepared to assist in conduct of NEO of American citizens (AMCITs) and designated foreign personnel," the PSYOP mission statement should read similarly, "On order, U.S. geographic combatant commander-XXX/JFC-XX conducts operational and tactical PSYOP in support of joint military operations in the Gingerale Islands AOR to restore GOT's sovereignty, deter hostile activities, neutralize GOS's power projection capability, and ensure access through vital LOCs. Should deterrence fail, U.S. geographic combatant commander-XXX/JFC-XX conducts PSYOP to destroy the GOS's will to fight and to achieve war termination objectives on terms favorable to the GOT/United States. PSYOP supports crowd control and security operations and, on order, assists in NEOs."

3. EXECUTION.

a. Concept of Operations.

(1) Overview. (In almost all supporting plans, including geographic combatant commander campaign plans, the overview is the commander's intent. Under execution, the CONOPS is usually broken down by the operational phases. Most phase paragraphs start off with the commander's intent and go on to list all missions, tasks, and objectives per phase of the campaign plan.) Outline the overall concept for employing PSYOP in support of task accomplishment by phase. If the geographic combatant commander's campaign plan states a prehostilities phase, address strategic PSYOP actions in support of FDOs. For each phase of the plan, address the level of PSYOP support that is being provided, when and where it is arriving, and whom it is supporting. Explain what tasks and POs are being carried out in support of components per phase and what equipment is being used and by whom. Denote PSYOP locations and linkup of tactical forces with maneuver units. Explain the general actions taken to facilitate product development and dissemination in conjunction with HN assets and sister service facilities. Finally, determine which products will be used in each phase. Sometimes, the conditions to be achieved for each phase are listed, as well as descriptions for tasks executed under deep, close, and rear operations.

(2) Provide the following as general guidance to units and forces involved, by phase if applicable:

(a) Valid PSYOP themes and objectives to be promoted and themes to be avoided and discouraged. (These themes are the broad guidelines that come from higher HQ that establish the left and right limits. These themes should not be confused with lines of persuasion, which are the arguments that PSYOP personnel will use to persuade a TA to modify its behavior and are developed during TAA.) Description of the cultural and psychological characteristics of TAs to aid operational planners and personnel in selecting COAs and interacting with TA members.

Figure 4-12. Example of the PSYOP Tab to the IO Appendix to the Operations Annex to the Joint Operations Plan (Continued)

(b) Description of adversary PSYOP (including disinformation) directed at U.S. personnel and at foreign groups in the AO and guidance for countering such operations.

b. Situation Monitoring. Describe how intelligence, multidiscipline counterintelligence, security monitoring, and operational feedback will be provided. State requirement for running situation estimates; periodic estimates of target appreciations responsive to critical iformation, actions, and attitudes and behavior; and current reporting of intelligence and multidiscipline counterintelligence information, security monitoring results, and implementing actions. Identify resources required and their availability.

c. Control. (Control is the same as coordinating instructions.) Usually the last paragraph in the execution section, it contains coordinating instructions pertaining to two or more elements of the task organization. Outline coordination with adjacent commands and civilian agencies, U.S. diplomatic missions, and United States Information Agency (USIA). Address information coordinating committees (ICCs), coordination with IO teams, and designated coordinating authority, if applicable. If coordinating with personnel centers and joint interrogation and exploitation centers performing interrogation, address coordination procedures with them. Address direct liaison and coordination issues among components and subordinate and supporting commands.

d. Tasks. Assign responsibilities to implement the concept. When multiple organizations are involved, designate an executive agent to coordinate implementation, if applicable. Ensure tasks clearly fix responsibilities and provide for feedback about effectiveness. Tasks to components in support of PSYOP often call for the coordination of component aircraft, surface vessels, and submarines to distribute materials and to conduct radio and TV broadcasts. Provide for shipboard printing and photo facilities to print products as required, and call for the integration of component air delivery systems into daily-integrated tasking orders to support PSYOP missions.

4. ADMINISTRATION AND LOGISTICS. Provide a statement of the administrative and logistical arrangements applicable to PSYOP but not covered in the basic plan or another annex thereof.

a. Administration. Addresses the following issues: financial, morale, welfare, medical, dental, postal, legal, graves registration, and religious support, as necessary; identification of workspace as necessary for PSYOP personnel attached to other components and organizations; rating chain issues and clearance requirements; and coordination for the use of indigenous personnel, facilities, or materials to support PSYOP.

b. Logistics. Addresses the following: requisitions for standard and nonstandard PSYOP supplies through national service supply channels; special operating funds; coordination for logistical support for leaflet production, aerial delivery, and media dissemination teams; requests for maintenance support not available through military channels; designated component or agency responsible for providing routine common-use logistical support to the POTF in-theater; provisions for living space accommodations; contracting for special purchase of supplies, equipment, and the hiring of HN personnel to support product development; and deployment into theater with supplies for 30 days, water rations, and so on.

5. COMMAND AND CONTROL.

a. Command Relationships. Refer to Annex J of the basic plan. Joint operations can have complex command relationships. Campaign plans must be specific concerning these arrangements, including shifts that may take place as the operation progresses from one phase to the next. Clearly state all command relationships. Include command posts and alternate command posts. Command and support relationships for PSYOP personnel fall into this paragraph.

b. PSYOP Product Approval. At the beginning of an operation, the POTF commander, PPD planner, or PSYOP forward force planners must coordinate with the geographic combatant commander or JFC to establish the product approval process that maximizes proper oversight and timely dissemination. Planners should strive to delegate approval authority down to the lowest level. They must ensure it is clearly understood that product approval authority is consistent with approved objectives, themes, symbols, and the ROE. The geographic combatant commander or JFC must also delineate what specific approval authority will be delegated, if any, to subordinate component

Figure 4-12. Example of the PSYOP Tab to the IO Appendix to the Operations Annex to the Joint Operations Plan (Continued)

commanders. In some peacetime operations—or in case of NEOs in which the Department of State (DOS) is the lead organization—DOS in coordination with the Country Team may be the product approval authority. In some cases, the POTF commander should be given approval authority for routine, noncontroversial products, while the geographic combatant commander or JFC should retain approval authority for other products and actions that fall outside of established parameters. Approval authority may be retained at the Presidential, SecDef, or geographic combatant commander level, and in some situations because of the sensitivity of PSYOP, combined with the need to coordinate all U.S. information efforts.

Figure 4-12. Example of the PSYOP Tab to the IO Appendix to the Operations Annex to the Joint Operations Plan (Continued)

Table 4-1. Quick-Reference Guide to PSYOP Input to the MDMP

MDMP Task	Information Sources (Inputs)	POTF/PSE Actions	POTF/PSE Results
Receipt of Mission— Phase 1	• Higher HQ OPLAN/OPORD. • Commander's initial guidance. • Higher HQ PSYOP estimate. • SPA, SPS, and PSYOP appendix to military capability study.	• Understand higher HQ OPLAN/OPORD. • Receive the commander's initial guidance. • Perform an initial PSYOP assessment. • Prepare for planning. • Allocate time to perform POTF/PSE tasks.	• General overview of current situation. • PSYOP input to initial WARNORD. • PSYOP estimate is begun.
Mission Analysis— Analyze the Higher HQ Order— Phase 2 (Step 1)	• Higher HQ OPLAN/OPORD (particularly the PSYOP annex). • Commander's intent two echelons up. • Commander's initial PSYOP guidance.	• Understand higher commander's intent and concept of operation. • Analyze the mission from a PSYOP perspective. • Determine PSYOP-related tasks assigned to the unit by higher HQ.	• Higher HQ mission is understood. • PSYOP-related tasks assigned to the unit.
Mission Analysis— Conduct IPB— Phase 2 (Step 2)	• Higher HQ IPB. • Higher HQ staff estimates. • Higher HQ OPLAN/OPORD. • SPAs, SPSs, and SSD input. • Other PSYOP IPB sources: Internet, OGAs, HN assets.	• Perform PSYOP input to IPB. • Identify initial key target sets. • Analyze weather and terrain as it pertains to dissemination. • Analyze media infrastructure. • Initiate PSYOP estimate.	• Weather analysis. • Terrain analysis. • Media infrastructure analysis. • Target groups overlay. • Nominations to HVT list for lethal and nonlethal attack (targeting).
Mission Analysis— Determine Specified, Implied, and Essential Tasks— Phase 2 (Step 3)	• Specified and implied PSYOP-related tasks from higher HQ OPLAN/OPORD. • Higher HQ estimates. • SPAs, SPSs and SSD input. • Other PSYOP IPB sources.	• Identify specified and implied PSYOP-related tasks in the higher HQ OPLAN/OPORD. • Begin development of POs, SPOs, and PTAL. • Develop PSYOP input to the command targeting guidance.	• Initial PSYOP POs, SPOs, and PTAL. • Provide critical asset list to G-3. • PSYOP input to the command targeting guidance.

Table 4-1. Quick-Reference Guide to PSYOP Input to the MDMP (Continued)

MDMP Task	Information Sources (Inputs)	POTF/PSE Actions	POTF/PSE Results
Mission Analysis— Review Available Assets— Phase 2 (Step 4)	• Current PSYOP force structure. • PSYOP unit capabilities. • Complexity of proposed operation/mission. • Nonorganic PSYOP support assets.	• Identify organic PSYOP assets and resources. • Identify nonorganic/HN additional resources (such as print support assets) needed to execute PSYOP. • Compare available assets and resources to PSYOP-related tasks.	• List of available PSYOP assets and capabilities (PSYOP estimate). • Submission of requests for additional PSYOP resources needed.
Mission Analysis— Determine Constraints— Phase 2 (Step 5)	• Commander's initial guidance. • Higher HQ OPLAN/OPORD. • Availability of resources. • PSYOP-specific ROE (for example, State Department prohibitions/limitations).	• Identify constraints (requirements and prohibitions) on PSYOP.	• List of constraints on PSYOP. • Development of plan on how to overcome or mitigate constraint issues.
Mission Analysis— Identify Critical Facts And Assumptions— Phase 2 (Step 6)	• Higher HQ OPLAN/OPORD with assumptions. • Commander's initial guidance. • Staff estimates.	• Identify facts and assumptions concerning PSYOP elements. • Submit PSYOP IRs that will confirm or disprove facts and assumptions.	• List of facts and assumptions pertinent to PSYOP elements (PSYOP estimate).
Mission Analysis— Conduct Risk Assessment— Phase 2 (Step 7)	• Higher HQ OPLAN/OPORD. • IPB. • Commander's initial guidance.	• Identify and assess hazards associated with PSYOP. • Begin to determine PSYOP impact indicators. • Establish provisional PSYOP measures.	• List of assessed hazards to PSYOP. • PSYOP input to risk assessment. • List of provisional PSYOP measures.
Mission Analysis— Determine Initial CCIR—Phase 2 (Step 8)	• PSYOP IRs.	• Determine information needed to make critical PSYOP decisions or to assess PSYOP actions. • Identify PSYOP IRs to be recommended as CCIR.	• PSYOP IRs nominated as CCIR.
Mission Analysis— Determine Initial Reconnaissance and Surveillance Annex—Phase 2 (Step 9)	• Initial IPB. • PIR/PSYOP IR.	• Identify gaps in information needed to support PSYOP planning and to support execution and assessment of early-initiation actions. • Confirm that the initial reconnaissance and surveillance annex includes PSYOP IRs.	• Submission of any additional PSYOP IRs. • Coordination for intelligence assets that can assist in identifying PSYOP impact indicators.

Table 4-1. Quick-Reference Guide to PSYOP Input to the MDMP (Continued)

MDMP Task	Information Sources (Inputs)	POTF/PSE Actions	POTF/PSE Results
Mission Analysis— Plan Use Of Available Time— Phase 2 (Step 10)	• Revised G-3 time plan.	• Determine time required to accomplish PSYOP objectives. • Compare time available to accomplish essential PSYOP tasks within the higher HQ timeline and the adversary timeline developed during IPB. • Refine initial time allocation plan.	• PSYOP timeline (provided to G-3), with emphasis on the effect of PSYOP on long lead-time events.
Mission Analysis—Write The Restated Mission—Phase 2 (Step 11)	• Initial PSYOP mission. • Initial PSYOP objectives.	• Ensure PSYOP considerations have been included in restated mission.	• PSYOP-related essential tasks. • Restated PSYOP mission.
Mission Analysis— Conduct Mission Analysis Briefing —Phase 2 (Step 12)	• PSYOP estimate. • Unit SOP.	• Prepare to brief PSYOP portion of mission analysis, much of which is in the PSYOP estimate. • Brief PSYOP estimate.	• Updated PSYOP estimate briefed.
Mission Analysis— Approve The Restated Mission—Phase 2 (Step 13)	• Restated mission. • Mission analysis briefing.	• Receive and understand the approved mission statement.	• None.
Mission Analysis— Develop Initial Commander's Intent— Phase 2 (Step 14)	• Higher HQ commander's intent. • Results of mission analysis. • PSYOP estimate.	• Develop recommended PSYOP input to the commander's intent.	• Recommendation of PSYOP input to the commander's intent.
Mission Analysis—Issue Commander's Guidance— Phase 2 (Step 15)	• Higher HQ OPLAN/OPORD. • Mission statement. • Commander's intent.	• Receive commander's guidance and understand it as it pertains to PSYOP. • Develop recommended PSYOP input to the commander's guidance.	• Prepare to develop PSYOP input to COAs that are in line with commander's guidance. • Recommended PSYOP input to the commander's guidance. • Recommended PSYOP targeting guidance.

Table 4-1. Quick-Reference Guide to PSYOP Input to the MDMP (Continued)

MDMP Task	Information Sources (Inputs)	POTF/PSE Actions	POTF/PSE Results

Mission Analysis—Issue Warning Order — Phase 2 (Step 16)	• Commander's restated mission, guidance, and intent.	• Prepare input to the WARNORD. Input may include—
		    ▪ Develop early taskings to subordinate units.
		    ▪ Reconnaissance and surveillance taskings.
			• WARNORD sent to unit preparing for mission.

Mission Analysis—Review Facts and Assumptions— Phase 2 (Step 17)	• Commander's guidance and intent. • Approved restated mission. • PSYOP estimate.	• Review PSYOP facts and assumptions. • Write initial PSYOP mission statement for annex or tab.	• Updated facts and assumptions. • PSYOP mission statement to supported unit's plan.
COA Development— Analyze Relative Combat Power— Phase 3 (Step 1)	• IPB. • Task organization. • PSYOP estimate.	• Analyze PSYOP effects on TAs. • Analyze psychological impact of proposed supported unit actions on TAs.	• Determination of potential impact of PSYOP and supported unit actions.
COA Development— Generate Options— Phase 3 (Step 2)	• Commander's guidance and intent. • IPB. • PSYOP estimate.	• Develop different ways for PSYOP to support each COA. • Determine the appropriate PSYOP element to be used. • Determine how to focus PSYOP on the objective. • Determine PSYOP's role in the decisive and shaping operations of each COA.	• Determination of PSYOP concept of support for each COA.
COA Development— Array Initial Forces— Phase 3 (Step 3)	• Mission statement. • Commander's guidance and intent. • IPB.	• Allocate assets to each PSYOP concept of support. • Identify requirements for additional resources. • Consider if a "deception story" needs to be developed.	• Initial PSYOP asset locations. • Submission of additional PSYOP resource requirements. • Deception story proposed to commander.

Table 4-1. Quick-Reference Guide to PSYOP Input to the MDMP (Continued)

MDMP Task	Information Sources (Inputs)	POTF/PSE Actions	POTF/PSE Results
COA Development— Develop Scheme Of Maneuver— Phase 3 (Step 4)	• COAs. • IPB. • Determined PSYOP support concept. • PSYOP estimate.	For each COA— • Ensure all PSYOP element's actions are coordinated. • Nominate selected HVTs as HPTs. • Refine PSYOP risk assessment. • Develop initial PSYOP task execution timeline. • Develop impact indicators for PSYOP support to each COA. • Consider any support required for PSYOP to execute its mission. • Develop PSYOP assessment plan. • Conduct a risk assessment for each PSYOP COA.	For each COA— • PSYOP-related HPT nominations are submitted. • PSYOP execution timeline is determined. • PSYOP input to risk management plan is submitted. • Impact indicators are determined. • Support request is prepared to submit if COA is chosen.
COA Development— Assign Headquarters— Phase 3 (Step 5)	• IPB. • COA with its corresponding PSYOP support concept. • PSYOP estimate. • PSYOP tasks by element.	• Develop task organization recommendation for PSYOP units.	• Submission of task organization recommendation for PSYOP units and resources to tasks assigned.
COA Development— Prepare COA Statements and Sketches— Phase 3 (Step 6)	• COA statement. • PSYOP concepts of support for each COA.	• Prepare input for each COA statement/sketch to G-3. • Prepare PSYOP concept of support sketch for each COA, if needed.	• Submission of input for each COA statement/sketch.
COA Analysis— Phase 4	• COAs. • IPB. • PSYOP input work sheets. • PSYOP execution timeline. • PSYOP estimate.	• Develop evaluation criteria for each COA. • Synchronize PSYOP activities with supported unit activities. • Synchronize PSYOP tasks performed by different PSYOP elements. • War-game friendly PSYOP capabilities against adversary vulnerabilities.	• An evaluation of each PSYOP COA in terms of criteria established before the war game. For each COA— • Refined PSYOP CONOPS. • Refined POs. • Refined PSYOP tasks.

Table 4-1. Quick-Reference Guide to PSYOP Input to the MDMP (Continued)

MDMP Task	Information Sources (Inputs)	POTF/PSE Actions	POTF/PSE Results
COA Analysis—Phase 4 (Continued)		• War-game adversary PSYOP capabilities against friendly vulnerabilities. • Refine and synchronize PSYOP targeting guidance and HPT list. • Determine whether modifications to the COA result in additional EEFI or PSYOP vulnerabilities. If so, recommend PSYOP measures to shield them. • Determine decision points for executing PSYOP measures. • Determine whether any PSYOP measures require additional coordination.	For each COA (Continued)— • Refined PSYOP input to attack guidance matrix and target synchronization matrix. • PSYOP IRs and RFIs identified during war game. • Refined EEFI and PSYOP vulnerabilities. • Completion of paragraph 3, PSYOP estimate. • Submission of PSYOP input to G-3 synchronization matrix. • Submission of PSYOP input to HPT list.
COA Comparison—Phase 5	• COA evaluations from COA analysis. • COA evaluation criteria. • PSYOP estimate.	• Compare the COAs with each other to determine the advantages and disadvantages of each. • Determine which COA is most supportable from a PSYOP perspective.	• PSYOP advantages and disadvantages for each COA. • Determination of which COA is most supportable from a PSYOP perspective. • PSYOP COA decision matrix. • Completion of paragraph 4, PSYOP estimate.
COA Approval—Phase 6	• Results from COA comparison. • Recommended COA. • PSYOP estimate.	• Provide PSYOP input to COA recommendation. • Reevaluate PSYOP input to the commander's guidance and intent; refine PSYOP concept of support, POs, and PSYOP tasks for selected COA; and develop associated PSYOP execution matrix.	• Finalized PSYOP CONOPS to approved COA. • Finalized POs, SPOs, and PTAL. • PSYOP input to WARNORD. • PSYOP execution matrix.

Table 4-1. Quick-Reference Guide to PSYOP Input to the MDMP (Continued)

MDMP Task	Information Sources (Inputs)	POTF/PSE Actions	POTF/PSE Results
COA Approval— Phase 6 (Continued)		• Prepare PSYOP input to the WARNORD. • Participate in COA decision briefing.	
Orders Production— Phase 7	• Approved COA. • Refined commander's guidance. • Refined commander's intent. • PSYOP estimate. • PSYOP execution matrix. • Finalized PSYOP mission statement, PSYOP concept of support, POs, SPOs, and PTAL.	• Ensure PSYOP input (such as EEFI and PSYOP tasks to subordinate units) is placed in base OPLAN/OPORD. • Finalize PSYOP annex. • Conduct other staff coordination. • Refine PSYOP execution matrix.	• PSYOP synchronization matrix. • PSYOP annex, appendix, or tab to OPLAN/ OPORD is completed.

SUMMARY

4-85. The POTF or PSE OPLAN or OPORD is crucial to ensure that all PSYOP elements are working toward the same objectives. When PSYOP is centrally controlled, planned, and promulgated, the effectiveness of the PSYOP effort will be greater. There are many considerations that the PSYOP planner must consider when writing the PSYOP portion of the supported unit's OPLAN or OPORD or the POTF or PSE supporting OPLAN or OPORD. The more complete the planning products are prior to execution, the more likely the PSYOP effort will be coordinated and integrated with the supported unit's plans. PSYOP planning and support is often executed in the crisis mode making detailed planning a difficult undertaking. Templating of force package options and coordination requirements facilitates the planning effort and ensures that critical planning elements are not left out.

Chapter 5

Target Audience Analysis

Different men seek after happiness in different ways and by different means, and so make for themselves different modes of life and forms of government.

Aristotle

TAA is the transitional phase where PSYOP planning moves toward execution. When the PSYOP planner has finished writing the appropriate annex or tab, he has developed POs, SPOs, PTAL, and themes, which are broad overarching statements or ideas that establish the parameters within which PSYOP are conducted. These themes often come from U.S. policymakers. That annex or tab is then further refined by the plans and programs section of the POTF or PSE where a more specific PTAL is completed. Once these planning activities have been completed, TAA can begin.

TARGET AUDIENCE ANALYSIS PROCESS

5-1. TAA is a detailed, systematic examination of PSYOP-relevant information to select TAs that can accomplish a given SPO. The purpose of TAA is to determine how to persuade one TA to achieve one SPO. It is not an overview of a TA and will not cover all aspects of the TA. This analysis is extremely precise research designed to determine how to elicit a specific response from a specific TA.

5-2. The TA will be analyzed in relation to a given SPO. For example, the TA "student body of Sarajevo University" is selected for SPO "TA votes in democratic elections" and SPO "TA uses National Bosnia Bank," which both support the PO "increase participation in national democratic institutions." The TA will be analyzed twice because the conditions, beliefs, attitudes, and vulnerabilities will be different in relation to each SPO. Therefore, different lines of persuasion and symbols will need to be developed or selected to influence the TA to achieve each of the different SPOs.

5-3. The target audience analysis process (TAAP) seeks to answer four basic questions:

- What TAs will be most effective in accomplishing the desired behavioral or attitudinal response?
- What lines of persuasion will influence the TA to achieve the objective?
- What media will effectively carry the chosen line of persuasion?
- What events will indicate success or failure of the PSYOP effort?

5-4. The TAAP is the primary research and analysis method for developing PSYOP products and actions, which are the essential elements of series, supporting programs, and programs. There are ten steps in the TAAP, which will allow the PSYOP Soldier to answer the above-stated questions. At the end of this process, a TAAW is produced and will recommend the lines of persuasion, symbols, and media that PSYOP Soldiers can use in the development of PSYOP products and actions. The TAAW must be updated on a frequent basis until a change in objectives or achievement of the objective. Since conditions and vulnerabilities within a TA are continually changing, the PSYOP analyst continually reviews, refines, and updates the analysis. Appendix D discusses advertising and social marketing used in developing PSYOP products to influence TA behavior.

5-5. The TAA process includes ten steps. Each of these is discussed in the following paragraphs.

STEP ONE: HEADER DATA

5-6. This data helps form a frame of reference for the analyst. It includes the series number, the date the original analysis started, analyst name, date the analysis was revised, the revising analyst's name, the national objective, supported unit objective or mission, PO, and SPO. The SPO is the most important part of the header data as the entire TAAP must always be directly related to the SPO. If the analyst keeps the SPO foremost in his mind during the process, the likelihood of an effective TAAW will increase dramatically.

STEP TWO: TARGET AUDIENCE SELECTION

5-7. The TAAP begins when the PSYOP analyst is given an SPO and a TA from the PTAL. Since the TAs on this list are usually broad or vague, the TA assigned will need further refinement during the TAAP. It is not unusual to redefine the TA several times during this process. The more specifically defined the TA is, the more accurate the analysis and the more effective the PSYOP effort will be. To select an appropriate TA, it first must be broken into a homogenous group of people with similar characteristics and vulnerabilities with the ability to achieve the desired behavioral or attitudinal change. The PSYOP analyst must look for the following characteristics before defining a specific TA:

- The TA must experience similar conditions and possess similar vulnerabilities (these will be defined later).
- The TA must be related to the SPO.
- The TA must retain the ability to accomplish the SPO.

The following describes techniques of organizing people so they can be used as TAs:

- *Groups*:
  - *Primary groups.* Primary groups share many different types and a wide breadth of activities (Table 5-1, page 5-3). Social groups, families, and groups of friends are good examples of primary groups. A primary group is extremely protective of its members from outside interference. Primary groups do not always make

good TAs for PSYOP because they have no particular purpose and their bonds are strong. They prefer to receive information from other members in the group and tend to shun information from outsiders. Primary groups are usually small in size and many times lack the power to have a significant impact.

- *Secondary groups.* People form secondary groups to achieve some goal or purpose. Once the group achieves that purpose, the group disbands or moves on to another purpose. Examples of secondary groups are political or legislative bodies (congress), organizations, and associations (Table 5-1). Members of a secondary group are goal oriented and while they may make friends with other members of the group, they typically view other members as associates or coworkers. As a whole, members of a secondary group do not share a large number of activities; relationships vary in length and are often short term, lasting only as long as the need to achieve the stated goal exists. Secondary groups are the best types of TA. They have a common goal or goals that PSYOP personnel can use as vulnerabilities. Secondary groups readily receive information from outside sources. This type of TA best meets the definition of a TA because they generally have similar conditions and vulnerabilities and are usually large enough to have some power to accomplish the objective.

Table 5-1. Examples of Primary and Secondary Group Orientation

	Primary Groups	Secondary Groups
Quality of Relationship	Personal orientation.	Goal orientation.
Duration of Relationships	Usually long-term.	Variable, often short-term.
Breadth of Relationships	Broad, many activities.	Narrow, few activities.
Subjective Perception	As an end in themselves.	As a means to an end.
Example	Families, circle of friends.	Coworkers, political organizations, associations.

- *Categories.* Categories are collections of people who share specific demographic characteristics. Categories may be very broad or extremely well defined. The more specifically defined the category, the better the TA for PSYOP. The problem with categories is that even if they are specifically defined, they may not share similar conditions and vulnerabilities except in the broadest sense. Blue-collar factory workers between the ages of 21 and 35 are an example of a fairly well-defined category.

- *Aggregates.* Aggregates are collections of people identified solely by a common geographic area. Aggregates rarely if ever make a good TA since they almost never share common conditions and vulnerabilities. For example, a TA such as the population of New York City may experience similar events and issues (such as taxes) that may apply to all, but their orientation toward these conditions and their behavioral reaction will vary tremendously.

- *Centers of gravity*. Centers of gravity are individuals or small groups who have a large degree of power over others. Centers of gravity are very good TAs if they are susceptible to PSYOP products and actions; however, members who make up these groups are usually very powerful and thus their susceptibility is low. When a center of gravity can be persuaded, the impact can be tremendous. The Korean Worker's Party Central Committee Secretariat is an example of a center of gravity where the susceptibility to PSYOP is extremely low; however, if they were persuaded, could possibly end Kim Jong Il's regime.

- *Key communicators*. Key communicators are individuals to whom members of a TA turn to for information, opinion, or interpretation of information. Many times PSYOP personnel cannot send the PSYOP message directly to the TA, or the TA would be more susceptible if the message came from an intermediate TA. Identifying and communicating with key communicators, whether they are teachers, principals, religious figures, town elders, or prominent businessmen, can be very helpful. A key communicator can also be thought of as a celebrity spokesperson. The use of key communicators can add credibility to a PSYOP message.

5-8. A TA that has been well defined and researched will allow for the PSYOP process to be effective. For example, the TA "Kosovo greater Albania political party members, Kacanik municipality" is a very well-defined secondary group. "Subsistence farmers growing coca to supplement income, Chapare region, Bolivia" is a well-defined category. Defining a TA as completely as possible is essential in the TAAP.

STEP THREE: CONDITIONS

5-9. Conditions are those existing elements that affect the TA but over which they have limited control. Conditions affecting a particular TA are limitless and many may be irrelevant to the SPO. During the TAAP, only those conditions that affect the TA and are relevant to the SPO are listed or considered. Conditions have three elements: a stimulus, an orientation, and a behavior.

5-10. A stimulus can be an event, issue, or a characteristic. An event is anything that happens that affects the TA. Examples include an increase in the cost of consumer goods, enemy shelling of the TA's town, or the election of a new leader or representative. An issue is an existing factor that affects the TA. Examples include the current cost of consumer goods, laws, regulations, or policies, or the current political structure. A characteristic is any demographic feature of the TA and may also be classified as vulnerability. Examples include average age, income level, level of training, religion, or ethnicity. It is not crucial that the PSYOP analyst identify which types of stimulus exist, only that they are affecting the TA in relation to the SPO.

5-11. A TA's orientation refers to how they think or feel about a particular stimulus. To understand the TA's orientation, the PSYOP analyst must look at attitudes, beliefs, and values. An attitude is a consistent, learned predisposition to respond in a particular way to a given object, person, or situation. Beliefs are convictions about what is true or false based on experiences, public opinion, supporting evidence, authorities, or even blind faith. Values are conceptions of ultimate goods and evils. Attitudes, beliefs, and values are all shaped by the TA perceptions. Perceptions are internal representations of sensory input from seeing, hearing, smelling, tasting, or touching. The analyst may be able to determine some of these attitudes, beliefs, and values by examining how the TA reacted to situations in the past.

5-12.   Behavior is an individual's response to stimulus. This is the outward observable action or lack of action of an individual after he has been exposed to a stimulus and has filtered it through his own personal orientation.

5-13.   All three elements are interrelated in that one will affect the other two. For example, when encountered with a particular stimulus the TA will exhibit behavior, or lack of behavior, based upon their internal orientation to that stimulus. The stronger their orientation to the stimulus, the stronger the TA's behavioral reaction.

5-14.   This formula can be used to predict behavior. By understanding the TA's orientation, the PSYOP analyst can predict the TA's behavior if a particular stimulus is introduced. This method is extremely useful for predicting the psychological impact of operations, such as the introduction of U.S. military forces into a foreign country.

5-15.   Identifying and listing conditions that affect the TA in relation to the SPO is a six-step process. The first step is to identify the problem. This is already provided in the form of the SPO. For example, if the SPO is "TA votes in elections," the problem is "Why doesn't the TA vote now?"

5-16.   The second step is to select a research method. Most initial research for TAA is conducted in the rear with little or no direct access to the TA and therefore necessitates secondary research. However, once PSYOP personnel are in the country they can conduct primary research to supplement and update the TAAW.

5-17.   The third step is to conduct the research. There are an infinite number of sources for TAA research. The main sources are SPAs and SPSs published by the SSD. Intelligence reports, summaries, and estimates are excellent sources for current information about TAs. Additionally, the Internet can be used to access the sites of government agencies and NGOs for open source information. All sources must be evaluated for credibility, accuracy, and relevance.

5-18.   The fourth step is to place each identified condition obtained from the analyst's research into a category on the TAAW. The categories are typically—

- Foreign relations (treaties, alliances, border issues).
- Demographics (age, race, religion, literacy, ethnic group, gender).
- Economic (income, employment, infrastructure).
- Political (laws, elections, leaders, issues).
- Environmental (soil quality, acid rain, droughts, earthquakes).
- Social (health, crime, education).
- Military (disposition, status, relation to TA).

5-19. Some of these categories may not apply depending on the TA and SPO being analyzed. These examples are not an exhaustive list of categories that can be used on the TAAW. The only requirement is that the conditions be categorized logically so that the reader can quickly and easily understand the relationship between the TA and the SPO.

5-20. The fifth step is that each condition is numbered sequentially regardless of its category. If there is a total of 100 conditions, they should be numbered 1 through 100. This numbering allows for referencing later in the TAAW.

5-21. The sixth and final step is that each condition must have its source identified to allow the reviewer to check the credibility of each condition. Additionally, this step allows for quick and efficient updating of the TAAW at a later date. When listing conditions on the TAAW, the classification must also be noted.

5-22. There are an infinite number of conditions that affect any TA and listing them all on the TAAW would be counterproductive. Only those conditions that affect the TA in relation to the SPO should be included. All others should be filed in a TA file for future use. These conditions may be useful when the TA is analyzed in relation to a different SPO.

STEP FOUR: VULNERABILITIES

5-23. Vulnerabilities are the needs that arise from the conditions of a TA, which they will strive to satisfy or benefit from once they are satisfied. Without properly identifying vulnerabilities, PSYOP will have a difficult time influencing the TA. A vulnerability is a manifestation of an unfulfilled or perceived need in a TA. The key word in this definition is "need." It is these needs that PSYOP will use to influence the TA.

5-24. Needs, wants, and desires are all expressions of the same concept. A TA that has one of these will, at varying levels of effort, strive to satisfy them. For the purposes of PSYOP, they are all the same. If the TA strives to satisfy it, PSYOP can use it. The desire of the TA to fulfill, alleviate, or eliminate a need provides the motivation for them to change their behavior.

5-25. There are two basic types of needs identified by social scientists—biological (or physiological) and social. Biological needs are those elements necessary to sustain life: food, water, air, shelter, and procreation. These needs are common to all cultures, though different cultures will seek to satisfy these needs in different manners. Social needs are those learned from society through the enculturation process (the process by which an individual learns the traditional content of a culture and assimilates its practices and values). Every culture will have different social needs and different priorities for satisfying those needs.

5-26. Maslow's Hierarchy of Needs is the most widely known explanation of needs satisfaction. Using a pyramid (Figure 5-1, page 5-7), Maslow explained that an individual must satisfy basic needs before moving up to social needs. He also argued that each individual must satisfy the needs at each level before progressing upward.

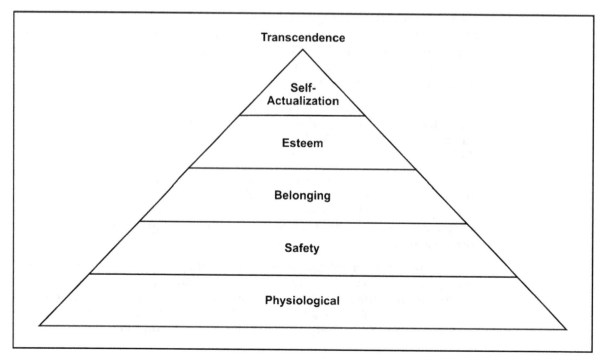

Figure 5-1. Maslow's Hierarchy of Needs

5-27.   Maslow placed all human needs into five prioritized categories:

- *Physiological needs*: Food, water, air, shelter, and procreation.
- *Safety needs*: Physical safety and security, stability, and familiar surroundings.
- *Belonging needs*: Love, friendship, affiliation, and group acceptance.
- *Esteem needs*: Status, superiority, self-respect, prestige, usefulness, and accomplishment.
- *Self-actualization needs*: Self-fulfillment and realization of individual potential.

5-28.   Maslow's hierarchy works very well with most western cultures. It is quickly seen that not all cultures, however, put the same priorities on the same needs, and Maslow's theory cannot be applied directly.

5-29.   The PSYOP analyst must categorize and prioritize the TA's needs to continue the TAAP. Maslow's theory is only one way of doing it and in some instances breaks down quite easily. Most people will operate according to his hierarchy during normal times, but may alter their behavior significantly at other times, especially if they are under large amounts of stress that can be defined as mental, emotional, or physical strain. For example, members of a military force during conflict endure high levels of stress and are trained to overcome basic needs to achieve group objectives. When evaluating these members as a TA, that training must be considered, and thus they would not fit neatly into a Maslow needs hierarchy.

5-30.   Another way of developing a needs hierarchy is to modify Maslow slightly in the following manner. Once needs are established, based on conditions, they are categorized as critical, short-term, and long-term. Different cultures will place different priorities on certain needs, and the PSYOP Soldier must apply his regional expertise to adjust the needs categories accordingly. A general example is that critical needs are usually biological or possibly safety depending on the severity of the safety situation.

5-31. Short-term needs often fall into what Maslow considered safety and belonging needs. These include needs that do not have to be satisfied immediately to sustain life. Severe economic hardship, extremely high crime, lack of any political freedom, or severe lack of medical facilities are examples of short-term needs.

5-32. Long-term needs include what Maslow considered esteem and self-actualization needs. Examples may be a stable and equitable governmental system where freedom of expression is possible, a strong economy, an equitable justice system, or the freedom to pursue a variety of endeavors.

5-33. The prioritization should reflect the desire of the TA to satisfy the need. A need that will address multiple conditions will usually be prioritized higher as it will be pursued by the TA with more effort. Once the needs have been prioritized, they must be categorized as critical, short-term, and long-term, which will help the PSYOP Soldiers determine their priority of effort.

5-34. At this point, the PSYOP analyst will disregard any need that is not related to the SPO. He must be very careful of disregarding a critical need as they typically must be satisfied prior to any short- or long-term need. Critical needs can usually be matched with almost any SPO.

5-35. Many times when a TA seeks to satisfy a need, there will exist a conflict. There are three types of need conflict:

- *Approach – Approach* needs conflict arises when there are two or more ways to satisfy one need, but the TA only has the means to choose one. Example: The TA has a need for representation in government. Out of the three candidates, two appeal to the TA, but they can only vote for one candidate.
- *Approach – Avoidance* needs conflict exists when the satisfaction of one need conflicts with the need to avoid something unpleasant or dangerous. Example: The need to eat ice cream conflicts with the need to avoid putting on extra weight.
- *Avoidance – Avoidance* needs conflict is when the TA is faced with two choices with neither of them being desirable; however, the TA must choose one or the other. Example: The TA wants to avoid a trip to the dentist because of the pain and discomfort involved. Yet, they also wish to avoid any dental problems. They must then choose between the "lesser of the two evils."

5-36. A TA's needs are determined by analyzing the conditions that affect them. While it is possible, as with a secondary group, that the TA freely publicizes their goals or needs, most often the PSYOP analyst must construct them from conditions.

5-37. Determining vulnerabilities is a five-step process. The first step is to identify needs based on the conditions affecting the TA.

5-38. The second step is categorizing and prioritizing the needs. The goal during this step is to determine what needs are most important and which PSYOP should try to use first.

5-39. The third step is to determine if there are any needs conflicts and what type of conflict exists. The PSYOP analyst then predicts how the TA will try to resolve the conflict, which may give the analyst insight into how best to address a specific need.

5-40. The fourth step is to determine the relationship between the needs and the SPO. If a need is related to the SPO, it can be kept on the TAAW. If it is not related, it should be removed from the TAAW and placed in the TA file.

5-41. Finally, each need or vulnerability is examined to determine the necessary PSYOP action. Vulnerabilities with a high priority and a strong relationship to the SPO can be exploited to influence the TA to achieve the SPO. Any vulnerability that when satisfied will prevent the accomplishment of the SPO must be minimized. Other vulnerabilities with low priority, but a strong relation to the SPO, can be enhanced and then exploited.

5-42. Each vulnerability listed on the TAAW must have a thorough explanation. The PSYOP analyst begins by providing a brief description of the vulnerability, to include the priority of the need and how much effort the TA is or will expend to satisfy the need. The PSYOP analyst includes a summary of all related conditions and lists the reference number for each related condition. He describes any needs conflict and how the TA can be expected to resolve the conflict. He describes the relationship between the vulnerability and the SPO. He also describes how direct or strong the relationship is. Finally, the PSYOP analyst explains which action must be taken to use this vulnerability to influence the TA.

STEP FIVE: LINES OF PERSUASION

5-43. A line of persuasion is an argument used to obtain a desired behavior or attitude from the TA. PSYOP lines of persuasion are used to exploit, minimize, or create vulnerabilities. A line of persuasion is a detailed, thorough, and concise argument that will persuade the TA to behave or believe in the desired manner. It is not a slogan or tagline.

5-44. PSYOP lines of persuasion resemble persuasive essays and use the same basic format. There are four steps to developing a line of persuasion:

- Articulate a main argument.
- Identify any necessary supporting arguments (what evidence must be provided for the TA to believe the PSYOP personnel's main argument).
- Determine what type of appeal will be useful toward this TA.
- Determine which technique has the greatest possibility of success (how will PSYOP personnel present their supporting arguments?).

5-45. The main argument is the central idea or conclusion that PSYOP personnel wish the TA to believe. If the TA believes the PSYOP conclusion, they should behave or believe in the desired manner. This line of persuasion is being written to address the needs of the TA, and if it is convincing they should want to follow it. In writing a traditional style essay, the main argument is commonly referred to as the thesis statement. If the proper appeal is chosen and supporting arguments are presented using effective techniques, the TA should agree with the main argument. It is only the main argument that the TA must remember after all PSYOP products within a series have been disseminated.

5-46. Supporting arguments are a series of arguments that should lead the TA to the main argument. It is the evidence presented to influence the TA. As with a persuasive essay, supporting arguments are presented in a logical easy-to-follow manner.

5-47. An appeal is the overall approach used to present the argument. It is the flavor or tone of the argument. Appeals gain the TA's attention and maintain their interest throughout the argument. Appeals are selected based upon the conditions and vulnerabilities of the TA. For example, a TA that does not believe the government of their country is legitimate will not be swayed by an appeal to legitimacy, whereas a military TA may be greatly affected by an appeal to authority.

5-48. There are an infinite number of appeals that can be used. The following is a list of appeals commonly used in PSYOP:

- Legitimacy.
- Inevitability.
- In group - out group.
- Bandwagon.
- Nostalgia.
- Self-preservation (self-interest).

5-49. Legitimacy appeals use law, tradition, historical continuity, or support of the people. The following are types of legitimacy appeals:

- *Authority*: An appeal to laws or regulations, or to people in superior positions in the social hierarchy. For example, the Uniform Code of Military Justice (UCMJ), NCOs and officers, police officers, parents, or government officials. The TA must recognize the authority for the appeal to work.

- *Reverence*: An appeal to a belief-teaching institution or individual that is revered or worshiped. For example, the Bible, the Dalai Lama, the Catholic Church, or even a sports figure like Michael Jordan.

- *Tradition*: An appeal to that which the TA is already used to. It is behavior that is repeated continually without question. Why have turkey on Thanksgiving? Because it has always been that way.

- *Loyalty*: An appeal to groups that the TA belongs to. Examples are military units, family, or friends. This appeal is usually used to reinforce behavior that already occurs.

5-50. Inevitability appeals most often rely on the emotion of fear, particularly fear of death, injury, or some other type of harm. For example, if you do not surrender, you will die, or if you do not pay your taxes, you will go to jail. It can also be an appeal to logic. Both require proof that the promised outcome will actually occur. Therefore, it is crucial that credibility be gained and maintained throughout the argument.

5-51. An in-group–out-group appeal seeks to divide a TA or separate two TAs. It creates an enemy of the out group, and it encourages the TA to rebel against or avoid the out group, thereby becoming the in group. This appeal frequently points out major differences between TAs or factions of a TA. If PSYOP cannot effectively portray the out group in a negative manner, the appeal will fail.

5-52. Bandwagon appeals play upon the TA's need to belong or conform to group standards. The two main types of bandwagon appeal are an appeal to companionship and an appeal to conformity. "Peer pressure" is an example of the conformity type of bandwagon appeal.

5-53. Nostalgia appeals refer to how things were done in the past. This appeal can be used to encourage or discourage a particular behavior. In a positive light, it refers to the "good old days" and encourages the TA to behave in a manner that will return to those times. In the negative, it points out how things were bad in the past and how a change in behavior will avoid a repeat of those times.

5-54. Self-interest appeals are those that play directly to the wants and desires of the individuals that make up a TA. This type of appeal can play upon the TA's vulnerability for acquisition, success, or status.

5-55. Techniques are the methods used to present information (supporting arguments) to the TA. Effective techniques are based on the conditions affecting the TA and the type of information being presented. The following are techniques common in PSYOP:

- *Glittering generalities.* These are intense, emotionally appealing words so closely associated with highly valued concepts and beliefs that the appeals are convincing without being supported by fact or reason. The appeals are directed toward such emotions as love of country and home, desire for peace, freedom, glory, and honor.

- *Transference.* This technique projects positive or negative qualities of a person, entity, object, or value to another. It is generally used to transfer blame from one party in a conflict to another.

- *Least of evils.* This technique acknowledges that the COA being taken is perhaps undesirable, but emphasizes that any other COA would result in a worse outcome.

- *Name-calling.* Name-calling seeks to arouse prejudices in an audience by labeling the object of the propaganda as something the TA fears, loathes, or finds undesirable.

- *Plain folks or common man.* This approach attempts to convince the audience that the position noted in the PSYOP message or line of persuasion is actually the same as that of the TA. This technique is designed to win the confidence of the audience by communicating in the usual manner and style of the audience. Communicators use ordinary language, mannerisms, and clothes in face-to-face and other audiovisual communications when they attempt to identify their point of view with that of the average person.

- *Testimonials*. Testimonials are quotations (in and out of context) that are cited to support or reject a given policy, action, program, or personality. The reputation or the role of the individual giving the statement is exploited. There can be different types of testimonial authority. Official testimonials use endorsements or the approval of people in authority or well known in a particular field. Personal sources of testimonials may include hostile leaders, fellow Soldiers, opposing leaders, and famous scholars, writers, popular heroes, and other personalities.

- *Insinuation*. Insinuation is used to create or increase TA suspicions of ideas, groups, or individuals as a means of dividing the adversary. The PSYOP Soldier hints, suggests, and implies, but lets the TA draw its own conclusions.

- *Presenting the other side*. Some people in a TA believe that neither of the belligerents is entirely virtuous. To them, propaganda messages that express concepts solely in terms of right and wrong may not be credible. Agreement with minor aspects of the enemy's point of view may overcome this cynicism.

- *Simplification*. In this technique, facts are reduced to either right or wrong or good or evil. The technique provides simple solutions for complex problems and offers simplified interpretations of events, ideas, concepts, or personalities.

- *Compare and contrast*. Two or more ideas, issues, or choices are compared and differences between them are explained. This technique is effective if the TA has a needs conflict that must be resolved.

- *Compare for similarities*. Two or more ideas, issues, or objects are compared to try and liken one to the other. This technique tries to show that the desired behavior or attitude (SPO) is similar to one that has already been accepted by the TA.

- *Illustrations and narratives*. An illustration is a detailed example of the idea that is being presented. It is an example that makes abstract or general ideas easier to comprehend. If it is in a story form, it is a narrative.

- *Specific instances*. These are a list of examples that help prove the point.

- *Statistics*. Statistics have a certain authority, but they must be clear enough to show the TA why they are relevant. In most cases, it is best to keep the statistical evidence simple and short so the TA can easily absorb it.

- *Explanations*. These are used when a term or idea is unfamiliar to the TA.

5-56. A line of persuasion that addresses more than one need will likely be more persuasive to the TA. Each need or vulnerability must have a line of persuasion developed. At this point, the analyst should not worry about how effective the line of persuasion is as this will be determined in a later step. Once the line of persuasion has been established for the TA and includes the four elements of a main argument, supporting argument, appeal, and technique, the PSYOP Soldier must identify corresponding symbols.

STEP SIX: SYMBOLS

5-57. Symbols are a visual (graphic or short textual), audio, or audiovisual means used to convey, reinforce, or enhance a line of persuasion. To be effective, symbols must be recognizable, meaningful, and relevant to the TA. Each line of persuasion will have its own list of symbols. For symbols to be useful, they must meet three criteria:

- *Symbols must be recognizable by the TA.* Marketers and advertisers spend millions of dollars and great time and effort developing, designing, and familiarizing their TAs with symbols (logos) that will help convey their messages. PSYOP personnel rarely have the time, manpower, or funding to create new symbols for their messages. Therefore, PSYOP personnel should always strive to use symbols that are already recognizable to the TA. If a new symbol is created, then it is best to use something closely related to a symbol that is already familiar to the TA.

- *Symbols must have meaning for the TA.* Without meaning, the symbol will not carry the message. Once the TA recognizes the symbol, they must easily be able to discern its meaning.

- *Symbols must convey the line of persuasion.* Even if the TA recognizes the symbols and they have meaning for them, the symbols must be appropriate for the line of persuasion. PSYOP analysts must pay particular attention to the use of state and religious symbols. If overused, they may offend or annoy the TA. Additionally, patriotic or religious symbols might offend the TA if used by "outsiders." An option may be the subtle use of symbols; for example, in the background of a poster.

STEP SEVEN: SUSCEPTIBILITY

5-58. PSYOP analysts evaluate each line of persuasion on its ability to influence the TA to achieve the desired behavior. As with any argument, different lines of persuasion will influence people to different degrees. Susceptibility ratings identify which line of persuasion will have the greatest influence on the TA and why. PSYOP analysts use susceptibility ratings to choose between the various lines of persuasion developed. Susceptibility is the degree to which the TA can be influenced to respond in a manner that will help accomplish the PSYOP mission, or simply put, how well a vulnerability can be manipulated. The stronger the vulnerability, the more susceptible the TA will be to the line of persuasion that exploits it. Using a scale of 1 to 10 works well. For example, PSYOP analysts rated susceptibilities of initial entry training (IET) Soldiers to follow all Army rules and regulations during the year 2001. The following are some possible lines of persuasion, and under usual circumstances these lines of persuasion receive the following ratings:

- 1. *It is the duty of a Soldier to follow all rules and regulations.* Rating 5: This line of persuasion is not rated very high because the TA has not yet developed a strong sense of pride in belonging to the Army yet. This is related to their belief that the rest of the Army perceives them as merely "trainees or children."

- 2. *Not following rules and regulations results in punishment under UCMJ.* Rating 6: This line of persuasion rates a little higher because they know the rules have changed from their civilian life and they are now more accountable for their actions, but they have also seen Soldiers who have violated the rules that have not been punished severely. In other words, they can be punished but it is no big deal.

- 3. *Students who follow the rules are rewarded with increased privileges.* Rating 8: Students have been separated from all those things that remind them of their life before the military, to include civilian clothes, radios, CD players, and access to TV. They are under constant supervision by cadre and have no decision-making authority. They have been promised passes and access to their personal belongings if they follow the rules, which make this line of persuasion very influential.

5-59. As conditions and vulnerabilities change, so does the TA's susceptibility to a particular line of persuasion. In the example, the above ratings were constant for many classes. However, the two classes of IET students polled immediately following 11 September 2001 rated their susceptibility to line of persuasion #1 as a 9 and line of persuasion #3 as a 5. These ratings changed due to the events of 11 September and the upsurge in patriotic feelings; therefore, TAA has to be frequently reviewed.

5-60. A general guideline is that a line of persuasion that addresses a critical need will be very effective and thus normally receive a higher rating. Lines of persuasion that address several needs are also likely to be rated higher.

STEP EIGHT: ACCESSIBILITY

5-61. PSYOP analysts study all available media to determine the best way to communicate with the TA. Accessibility is defined as the availability of an audience for targeting by PSYOP. It seeks to answer the question "what mix of media will effectively carry the developed lines of persuasion and appropriate symbols to the TA?" Media analysis is a seven-step process that allows PSYOP Soldiers to evaluate each form of media for a specific TA. The seven steps include the following:

- Evaluate how the TA currently receives their information.
- Determine their current media patterns by assessing the reach and frequency.
- Analyze the TA's use for each medium.
- Determine if the TA's contact with each medium is active or passive.
- Analyze the dynamics of the TA when accessing each particular medium.
- Determine any new media that may be effective on the TA.
- List each medium on the TAAW in the proper format, which includes the format, advantages and disadvantages, and 1 to 10 rating.

5-62. The first step in media analysis is to determine how the TA currently receives information. Specifically, what types of media does the TA access (not what media do they have access to, but what media do they actively receive) and what format is it in? Answering several questions with regard to various forms of media can accomplish this task. The following are examples of the first step:

- Does the TA access radio? Is it FM, AM, or short wave? Do they most frequently receive messages in the form of spots (ads), talk shows, or documentaries? What is the length of these spots, talk shows, or documentaries? What are the formats of the radio stations they listen to, news or entertainment?

- Are the newspapers they receive all black and white or do they have color photos and ads? Do they receive information through articles, editorials, ads, or all? What size are ads: 1/4, 1/2, or full page? Do they use inserts?

- How does the TA receive information through TV? What is the most prevalent format: ads, documentaries, comedy, or other programs? What is the normal length of each type?

5-63. The second step in media analysis is to determine current media patterns and usage. This will allow the PSYOP analyst to select the best media from those that the TA receives. The two primary methods of determining media patterns are reach and frequency.

5-64. Reach is the total number of TA members that receive the medium at least once during a given period. Most marketers and advertisers use a four-week period. Any time period can be used, however, but it must be consistent for all media and therefore the PSYOP Soldier must pick a standard and use it for all forms of media being evaluated. For printed material, such as newspapers, magazines, or newsletters, reach equals readership, which is the subscription rates plus other sales plus secondary readership. For example, a household would only be counted once for subscription rate. However, if there were three other people who read the same paper, in addition to the subscriber, this would result in a readership rate of 4. A common mistake with radio and television is to count the number of radio receivers and television sets owned. In some parts of the world there may be only one television set for every fifty people. Yet if 25 people regularly watch that one television set, that equals a reach of 50 percent. Thus, viewership for television and listenership for radio are more important than the number of radios and TVs owned.

5-65. Frequency is the number of times an individual member of the TA receives a particular medium during a given time period. If a TA member subscribes to a newspaper five days a week and the given time period is four weeks then the TA member would have a frequency rate of 20 for that medium. Most human beings are creatures of habit and thus a certain TA will see certain types of media on a routine basis. This is important information for PSYOP since repetition and reinforcement of a line of persuasion is essential to behavior modification. An example of reach and frequency for the TA is truck drivers working for a Cola company in Detroit and the medium billboards:

- *Reach*: 100 percent of the TA has exposure in a one-week time period.

- *Frequency*: 5. Each driver passes the billboard once a day when he picks up his Cola and thus is exposed 5 times during a week.

5-66. The third step in media analysis is to determine how the TA uses the medium. It must be determined if and why the TA accesses the medium. Does the TA access this medium for entertainment or for news and information? If they access it for entertainment they may not listen to serious messages. If they access the media for news and information, a longer more serious message may be well received.

5-67. The fourth step is to determine how involved in the process is the TA. Are they actively or passively engaged? If the TA actively accesses the medium for news or information, there is a greater probability it will be easier to gain and maintain their attention, and it is more likely that the TA will absorb and understand the message. If the TA passively accesses the media, such as listening to a radio while working, it will be more difficult to gain and maintain attention and the TA may not absorb the message.

5-68. Step five is to evaluate whether the TA accesses the media individually or with others. Accessing a media in the presence of others will affect their perception of the message. Some material may be seen as inappropriate for young children, and parents may not want to hear certain messages in their presence. However, accessing the media in the presence of others may lead to further discussion of the message. If the message being addressed by PSYOP is being further discussed after reception by the TA, the better the chance that the TA will be persuaded.

5-69. After analyzing all media that the TA currently receives, the PSYOP analyst then, in step six, determines what new media can be used to access the TA. A new media is anyone that the TA does not currently receive.

5-70. New media has the advantage that they may attract and hold the TA's attention, simply because of the novelty of the media. Additionally, new media may increase the overall reach and frequency by filling voids left by other media.

5-71. There are several disadvantages to new media that must be considered. A new medium may focus all attention on the media itself and detract from the actual message. A new media may also be seen as foreign propaganda, directed by "outsiders," leading to disbelief of the message.

5-72. The final step in the media analysis process is including all of the information on the TAAW. PSYOP analysts must include the following information for each medium:

- *List medium.* PSYOP analysts list the medium as specifically as possible; for example, TV spot, radio spot, newspaper insert, highway billboard, or video documentary. They do not list the medium as a major category; for example, TV, radio, print, audio, visual, or audio-visual.

- *Describe format.* As specifically as possible, PSYOP analysts describe the format. This description should include size, shape, number of pages, length (in time), color versus black and white, and so on. Also included are the names of any particular media outlets available, such as names of specific newspapers, magazines, or TV and radio stations.

- *List advantages and disadvantages.* PSYOP analysts list all advantages and disadvantages in using this medium for this TA. They include reach, frequency, literacy rate, TA involvement, and the TA's perception of the credibility of the medium.

- *Rate media.* PSYOP analysts rate each medium on a scale of 1 to 10, with 1 being the least preferred and 10 being the most preferred. This is a subjective rating based on the analyst's interpretation of the medium; however, a consistent standard should be kept throughout the TAAW. This is a critical rating as it will allow the product development team to decide how many and what types of products to design. Therefore, each medium should be rated so the appropriate mix of product types can be designed.

STEP NINE: EFFECTIVENESS

5-73. By determining effectiveness, PSYOP can accurately target those audiences who have the greatest probability of accomplishing the mission. The definition of effectiveness is "the actual ability of a TA to carry out the desired behavioral or attitudinal change." Effectiveness is a term that is used widely throughout PSYOP and the military. Its use in TAA should not be confused with the overall impact of the PSYOP effort or how well products will work. This rating (1 to 10) is how successful this particular TA will be in accomplishing the SPO assuming the line of persuasion is successful in modifying the TA's behavior. It can also be used to make choices between multiple TAs when resources are scarce. For example:

> SPO: *TA does not provide food to the enemy.*
>
> TA1: Chicken farmers - 4
>
> TA2: Vegetable farmers - 6
>
> TA3: Convenience store owners - 3
>
> TA4: Produce wholesalers - 8

5-74. In this example, if time, manpower, and other resources dictate that after examining the effectiveness block of several different TAAWs, only two TAs can be targeted, the logical choices would be TA2 and TA4 because they have the greatest likelihood of accomplishing the objective.

5-75. For a TA to be effective, they must have some type of power, control, or authority. In other words, they have some degree of control over their environment, they have the authority to act, and they have the power to accomplish a goal. No TA is all-powerful, however, and all TAs will have some restrictions on their effectiveness. The following are the most common types of restrictions, but the list is not exhaustive:

- Physical restrictions:
  - TA is physically unable.
  - TA is physically restrained.
  - TA is geographically restrained.

- Political restrictions:
  - TA lacks political power.
  - TA's alliances prevent action.
- Economic restrictions:
  - TA lacks economic power.
  - TA has conflict of needs.
  - TA must sacrifice livelihood.
- Legal restrictions: Desired behavior violates laws or regulations.
- Sociological restrictions:
  - Desired behavior violates norms or taboos.
  - Desired behavior would cause expulsion of TA from group or society.
  - Desired behavior violates religious beliefs.
- Psychological restrictions: Fears or phobias.

5-76.   PSYOP have little or no control over most restrictions on effectiveness; however, sociological and psychological restrictions can sometimes be mitigated through PSYOP. Restrictions will also change over time depending on conditions.

5-77.   Effectiveness is listed on the TAAW by first determining an effectiveness rating on a scale of 1 to 10. A concise explanation is then provided by describing what control, authority, and power the TA has to accomplish the SPO and then describing any restrictions on effectiveness that affect the TA. Below is an example of what an effectiveness rating might look like.

Effectiveness: 6. The TA has the authority to vote but voting booths are located far from their homes and many TA members have no means of traveling that distance. Additionally, within its culture voting is seen as "giving in to the oppressors."

STEP TEN: IMPACT INDICATORS

5-78.   Impact indicators are those events that aid in determining the success of the PSYOP effort. These are clues that the PSYOP specialist will look for once PSYOP products are disseminated to the TA. A detailed discussion of impact indicators is in Chapter 7.

5-79.   Figure 5-2, pages 5-19 and 5-20, and Figure 5-3, pages 5-20 through 5-24, provide a format and example of a TAAW that includes each of the TAAP steps discussed above. This TAAW is an abbreviated example that gives an insight into what this process leads to. A well-researched TAAW will often be much more detailed than the example provided, as the conditions are usually very lengthy. A TAAW will be the source document for an entire series of PSYOP products and actions.

1. Header Data:
   a. Date and analyst name.
   b. Supported unit objective.
   c. PSYOP objective.
   d. Supporting PSYOP objective.
   e. Series number.

2. Target Audience:
   Target audience is defined specifically.

3. Conditions:
   a. Conditions are facts, not opinion or analysis.
   b. Conditions have sufficient detail.
   c. Conditions affect the target audience.
   d. Conditions listed create a vulnerability.
   e. Categorized logically.
   f. Numbered sequentially.
   g. Footnoted.
   h. Sources are credible and classification is noted.

4. Vulnerabilities:
   b. Defined as need, want, or desire.
   c. Each vulnerability is linked to one or more conditions.
   d. Vulnerability can be exploited or needs to be countered to achieve the SPO.
   e. Prioritized.

5. Lines of Persuasion:
   a. A logical explanation of how to exploit a vulnerability.
   b. Detailed enough to create a series of products or actions.
   c. A line of persuasion that contains an argument, appeal, and technique.

6. Symbols (by line of persuasion):
   a. Symbols are listed for each line of persuasion.
   b. Symbols convey the line of persuasion they are linked to.
   c. Symbols are recognizable by the TA.
   d. Symbols already have significance to the TA.

7. Susceptibility (by line of persuasion):
   a. Each line of persuasion is rated from 1 to 10.
   b. Each rating has an explanation.
   c. Explanation lists favorable elements and constraints.

Accompanying each rating is a detailed explanation for that rating.
Rating scale:

   10 TA will be automatically influenced with one or two exposures to the line of persuasion.
   8–9 TA will need only minimal exposure to line of persuasion over a short time period to be convinced.
   6–7 TA will need multiple exposures over a medium time period to be convinced.
   4–5 TA will need multiple exposures over a long period of time and still may not be convinced.
   2–3 TA will probably not be persuaded regardless of number of exposures and period of time.
   1 TA will not be convinced by this line of persuasion.

8. Accessibility:
   a. Each medium is listed individually.
   b. Each medium is given its own rating from 1 to 10.
   c. Each medium rating is explained—pros and cons.

Accompanying each rating is a detailed explanation for that rating.

Figure 5-2. TAAW Checklist

Rating scale:

 10 Extremely effective medium for reaching the TA.
 9–8 Very effective medium for reaching the TA.
 7–6 Largely effective medium for reaching the TA.
 5–4 Somewhat effective medium for reaching the TA.
 3–2 Largely ineffective medium for reaching the TA.
 1 Extremely ineffective medium for reaching the TA.

9. Effectiveness:
 a. TA is rated from 1 to 10 on its ability to achieve the SPO.
 b. Explanation is given detailing what makes the TA effective followed by constraints and limitations to effectiveness.

Accompanying each rating is a detailed explanation for that rating.
Rating scale:
 10 TA has full power and ability to achieve desired objective.
 9–8 TA has much power and ability to achieve desired objective.
 7–6 TA has some power and ability to achieve desired objective.
 5–4 TA has limited power and ability to achieve desired objective.
 3–2 TA has extremely limited power and ability to achieve the desired objective.
 1 TA has neither power nor ability to achieve the desired objective

10. Impact Indicators:
 a. Impact indicators are positive or negative, direct or indirect.
 b. Impact indicators are measurable and observable.
 c. Impact indicators list a baseline figure.

Figure 5-2. TAAW Checklist (Continued)

TARGET AUDIENCE ANALYSIS WORK SHEET

SERIES # - COA02fw

Analyst name:

Date:

SUPPORTED UNIT OBJECTIVE: DETER AGGRESSION BY THE PDRA AND, IF ORDERED, DESTROY THE ENEMY FORCES IN CORTINA.

PSYOP OBJECTIVE: Gain and maintain acceptance of coalition forces.

SUPPORTING PSYOP OBJECTIVE: TA cooperates with U.S. and coalition forces.

TARGET AUDIENCE: Blue-collar factory workers.

CONDITIONS: (**NOTE:** This is extremely abbreviated. Most TAAW conditions would consist of many pages. Here are some examples to demonstrate what they might look like.)

Demographics

 1. (U) TA speaks English. (Area Study, Republic of Cortina – CH 5, Pg. 4)
 2. (U) TA has 80% literacy rate. (Request for Information received from J-2)

Foreign Relations

 3. (U) United States sent Military Training Teams (MTTs) to Cortina in 1991. TA responded positively to its perception that the Government of Cortina (GOC) was allying itself militarily with the United States. (Area Study, Republic of Cortina – CH 3, Pg. 1)

Politics

 4. (U) TA is politically liberal and they believe that government programs are necessary to ensure a minimal sense of equality. (Area Study, Republic of Cortina – CH 5, Pg. 4)

Figure 5-3. TAAW Abbreviated Example

5. (U) TA has attempted unsuccessfully to form a union in the past. Reiterates the TA's liberal political persuasion. TA is extremely concerned with protecting their jobs. (PSYOP Appendix to Military Capabilities Study)

Economics

6. (U) TA generally cannot escape from poor economic/education standards. Schools in the area are underfunded and many factory workers' families have been in the profession for generations. (Area Study, Republic of Cortina – CH 5, Pg. 4)

7. (U) Unemployment rate is rising (currently 12.6%). Instability created by the Cortina Liberation Front (CLF) has affected the economy over the last 12 months. (Area Study, Republic of Cortina – CH 5, Pg. 6)

8. (U) Skilled U.S. and European workers have taken many white-collar jobs causing discontent in the Cortinian workforce. This is a product of the poor education system and hostility toward foreigners entering the workforce is rapidly growing. (Area Study, Republic of Cortina – CH 5 Pg. 2)

9. (U) TA earns $12,000 to $22,000 per year. The TA is concerned that if the economy continues to worsen, they will make even less. One reason they attempted to form a union was to have more ability to lobby for increased wages. (Request for Information received from J-2)

Social Issues

10. (U) TA has had an increase in crime rate caused by unemployment and low wages. There has been a decrease of manufacturing jobs in urban areas, which has led to underground crime rings, bandit gangs, and organized crime. (The latter now exists in all major cities and some workers are unaware that they are working for them.) This increase in crime is directly related to a sense of desperation in the TA. Many are beginning to feel hopeless as they see the CLF grow stronger. (Area Study, Republic of Cortina – CH 5, Pg. 6 and CH 3, Pg. 3)

11. (U) TA has poor health care (74% have access but many are restricted by high cost). Few factory workers can afford to get medical treatment. There has been an increase in practicing home remedies. (Area Study, Republic of Cortina – CH 7, Pg. 3)

12. (U) The Cortinian Government views the expansion of health care as a high priority item. TA views this as positive but is concerned that the government's plan may not lower their out-of-pocket expense which is what they are truly concerned with. (Republic of Cortina, Country Plan – III-C-6)

13. (U) Tenant living is the norm in cities; multiple family apartment complexes, both private and government-owned, are the common housing available to the poor (Area Study, Republic of Cortina – CH 5, Pg. 2)

Cultural Activities

14. (U) TA members are active gamblers as betting on sporting events and playing cards are frequent activities. With the security situation deteriorating, TA seeks entertainment without having to go outside their home or factory. Gambling is seen as entertainment and stakes are typically very low. (Focus group survey on leisure activities)

Cortina Liberation Front

15. (U) TA has been targets of and been killed by CLF terrorists. This has been increasing over the past 6 months. TA perceives this as a crisis situation. TA, although somewhat supportive of the Cortinian government, feels that may be why they were targeted and thus government support is decreasing. (Area Study, Republic of Cortina – CH 8, Pg. 1)

Military

16. (U) TA views Government of Cortina military as the nation's protector and military service as an honorable profession. At least 15% of TA served in the military and percentage may be higher. (Area Study, Republic of Cortina – CH 6, Pg. 3)

17. (U) TA does not receive sufficient Government of Cortina protection from CLF (Area Study, Republic of Cortina – 6.43); for example, military police have been assigned areas of operation that are too large for effective operations. The increase in CLF activity around the factory location is extremely disconcerting for the TA. (Area Study, Republic of Cortina – CH 6, Pg. 13)

Figure 5-3. TAAW Abbreviated Example (Continued)

VULNERABILITIES: (Note: This is extremely abbreviated. Vulnerabilities would need many conditions to determine but this has been shortened for demonstration purposes.)

1. TA needs help defending itself from the Cortina Liberation Front (3, 15, 17) (critical). The needs conflict that arises here is approach-avoidance. The TA would like to support coalition forces for protection; however, they may be targeted more aggressively by the CLF if they do. Coalition forces will need to address this conflict immediately to ease their apprehension.

2. TA needs reassurance that U.S/coalition forces are there to help (3, 6, 8, 10, 11, 12, 15, 16, 17) (short term). The TA perceives that coalition forces could help their situation in many ways, but they are apprehensive about the possibility that coalition forces may be an occupying force and not really coming for their benefit.

3. TA needs job security. This is directly related to political and economic stability. Because the TA is in the lower income bracket, they will base decisions largely on this need. If they lose their jobs, they see crime as the only alternative due to their lack of education and other skills. (5, 6, 7, 8, 9, 11) (short-term)

4. TA needs a decrease in crime rate to feel safe. This need is connected to the TA's feeling of hopelessness. This need would also be addressed by an increase in stability and a real sense that a future is present. This is a short-term need but is being caused by a perception that will not be changed in the near term. (10, 15) (short-term)

5. TA needs better medical care. (6, 11, 12) (short-term) Medical care exists in Cortina, but its cost is extremely high. The TA's income is far beneath what would be necessary for health coverage, and their jobs do not provide medical care. Even a way to obtain routine preventative care would be a great benefit to this TA.

6. TA needs greater sense of economic and political enfranchisement (2, 4, 5, 6, 7, 8, 9, 10, 15, 16, 17) (long-term). TA wants greater representation and ability to shape their environment. Their desire for a union is long-standing and demonstrates the perception that no one is looking out for their interests.

LINE OF PERSUASION (LOP) 1: (NOTE: This is extremely abbreviated. Lines of persuasion should be even more elaborate than this and there should be enough LOPs that each vulnerability is addressed. Here we have provided only one example.)

Main Argument – Coalition forces will help the Cortinian military protect innocent citizens from the aggression of the CLF and return stability and safety to Cortina.

Supporting arguments:

- Coalition forces were invited by GOC because it acknowledges the fact that it does not have the resources to protect its own citizens.

- Coalition forces' exit strategy is publicized.

- Coalition forces and GOC military have worked together in the past.

- Lack of cooperation will continue instability in Cortinian society.

Appeal – Legitimacy (Tradition) Support for GOC military is something deeply inherent in TA's beliefs and values. (Self Interest) Coalition force involvement is the quickest path to stability that is the long-term solution to many of the TA's needs.

Technique – Compare and contrast – Cooperate with U.S./Cortinian forces and CLF will be overcome. Do not cooperate and CLF may take over. This technique will be helpful in addressing the TA needs conflict. Compare for similarities – TA has in the past accepted U.S./Cortinian military cooperation. Emphasize that coalition forces are military members and not coming to take jobs away.

SYMBOLS TO USE WITH LOP 1

Cortinian falcon flying with American eagle. Both these symbols are known and conjure feelings of pride and honor.

Cortinian military seal evokes pride, trust, and confidence within the TA.

Figure 5-3. TAAW Abbreviated Example (Continued)

SUSCEPTIBILITY OF LOP 1

(7) It is in their best interest to support U.S./coalition forces because if they support them then Cortina will have the opportunity to prosper. The TA will likely be convinced because this line of persuasion capitalizes on the TA's respect for military service and positive prior working relationship with U.S. military. Hurdles that must be overcome include the resentment that the TA has toward American white-collar workers. The second obstacle will be the TA's fear of reprisal from CLF if they cooperate with coalition forces.

ACCESSIBILITY: (**NOTE:** This section is also abbreviated. Each individual station should be considered individually but has been grouped here in the interest of space.)

1.   Television (8): KSRV Shreveport, WALX Alexandria, WMNR Monroe, KLEE Leesville. Reach of television is 94.5% of TA. Weekly frequency is 7. In areas within broadcast footprints of television stations, 98.7% of homes own a television. Family viewing of news over the evening meal is standard. Nighttime talk programs featuring political/economic issues have a high share in the Cortina TV ratings among the TA. The TA perceives television news as the single most credible news source. Political advertisements and government public service announcements lack credibility with the TA. TA sees short 30- second to 1-minute spots as nothing more than propaganda. Best means of using TV would be 30-minute debates or interviews. All four stations broadcast news magazine shows similar to "60 Minutes" that are very well received by the TA. High coverage is the chief advantage of television. The chief disadvantage would be a lack of credibility of short messages. (Area Study, Republic of Cortina – CH 5, Pg. 2 and CH 3, Pg. 3)

2.   AM radio (4): KSRV Shreveport, WOPF Shreveport, WALX Alexandria, KLFT Alexandria, WMNR Monroe, KLEE Leesville. Reach of AM radio is 99.6%. Weekly frequency is 11. 93.8% of TA own AM radios. The TA accesses AM radio almost universally. AM radio is played in public places, at businesses, and the TA accesses by default on busses and in privately owned cars that generally only have AM radios. The TA considers AM radio either purely as entertainment or is dogmatically committed to its credibility. The latter group is those who listen to WOPF and KLFT. These stations are rabidly antigovernment. KLFT has been charged with sedition unsuccessfully on three different occasions. Although exact figures are impossible, approximately 11.2% of TA actively pursue access to WOPF and KLFT. The primary advantage of AM radio is its reach and frequency. The disadvantage is a near-universal lack of credibility. (Area Study, Republic of Cortina – CH 5, Pg. 2 and CH 6, Pg. 4)

3.   FM radio (7): KSRV Shreveport, WOPF Shreveport, WALX Alexandria, KLFT Alexandria, WMNR Monroe, KLEE Leesville. Reach of FM radio is 73.6%. Weekly frequency is 4. FM radios are owned by 89.8% of TA. The TA will access FM in the home frequently. Many households will play FM radio stations in the mornings. TA will access FM radio on daily commute to work if possible. TA regards FM radio as generally credible with the exception of political commercials and some government public service announcements. The TA will go out of its way to hear several radio talk shows. Ken Applewhite can be considered a key communicator with his show "Defending the Republic." WOPF and KLFT are simultaneous broadcasts of their AM counterparts. Due to lack of receivers and smaller footprints, approximately 7.3% of TA deliberately access these stations. The advantages of FM radio include its superior quality in the arena of both content and technical quality of broadcast. The disadvantages of the media are the large areas uncovered by it and credibility issues with certain formats. (Area Study, Republic of Cortina – CH 5, Pg. 2 and CH 6, Pg. 4)

4.   Newspapers (5): "Shreveport Times," "The World Today." Reach of national newspapers is 63.2%. Weekly frequency is 2. Only 27.4% of TA subscribe to the daily versions of either nationwide newspaper. 77.4% of TA do subscribe to or buy the Sunday printings. Significant editorials will often be passed around workplaces. Both the "Times" and the "World" have dramatically upgraded the quality of their papers by incorporating color pictures and graphics. Both have also conducted promotions and giveaways. However, production and distribution problems continue to plague both papers. Several rural areas do not have access to either paper. The TA generally considers purchase of the daily paper as either a luxury or a frivolous use of money. Both papers have significant credibility issues as well. The "Times" was implicated in printing government-sponsored disinformation in 1985 and the "World" was successfully sued for libel in 1987 by two mayoral and one gubernatorial candidate. The TA generally perceives that the "Times" and the "World" both serve

Figure 5-3. TAAW Abbreviated Example (Continued)

the interests of the rich. In addition, the "Shreveport Times" is perceived by the TA as antimilitary due to editorials in the late 1980s and early 1990s. A decade of pro-military editorials has not eliminated this perception. The chief advantage of this media is its quality to cost ratio as both papers have low advertising costs. The chief disadvantages of this media are its lack of reach and credibility. (Area Study, Republic of Cortina – CH 5, Pg. 6 and CH 6, Pg. 3)

5.   New media (6): Text messaging on cellular phones. Reach of cellular coverage is 88.6%. Weekly frequency is 18. Cell phones are owned by 93.1% of TA. Cellular phones are more frequently used and owned by the TA than landlines. Many homes have only cellular phones. The TA utilizes text messaging very frequently. Companies in Cortina often send advertisements via text messages. The TA perceives this media as credible. The advantage of this media is its reach. The disadvantage is the fleeting impressions produced. (Area Study, Republic of Cortina – CH 5, Pg. 6 and CH 7, Pg. 4)

EFFECTIVENESS:

(8) TA wants protection from CLF terrorist attacks and wants conditions of life to improve. The TA is patriotic and predisposed to a favorable view of the military. The TA has traditionally been the target of CLF attacks rather than CLF recruitment due to early recruitment failures by CLF. The TA regards itself as the backbone of the Cortinian economy and nation. The distinct possibility that the presence of U.S./coalition forces might hurt TA's pride because of the need for assistance would have to be addressed. A balance between the simple need to improve security and physical conditions would have to be balanced with nationalistic pride.

IMPACT INDICATORS:

Positive:
1.   TA offers information to U.S./coalition forces.
2.   TA participates in organized demonstrations in support of U.S./coalition forces.
3.   TA participates in informal conversation with U.S./coalition force troops.
4.   TA displays pro-government products.

Negative:
1.   TA joins CLF.
2.   TA protests U.S./coalition force involvement.
3.   TA actively opposes U.S./coalition forces.
4.   TA participates in strikes.

Indirect:
1.   Acts of sabotage increase.
2.   Increased targeting of TA by CLF death squads.
3.   Increased targeting of TA by CLF propaganda.

Figure 5-3. TAAW Abbreviated Example (Continued)

SUMMARY

5-80.   PSYOP developers' ability to modify the behavior of a foreign TA is largely dependent upon their TAA. The more thorough and complete each TAAW is, the better chance PSYOP developers will have in producing a series of products and actions that will successfully modify the TA's behavior. This ten-step process is time consuming and resource demanding but cannot be shortcut when employing effective PSYOP. Detailed TAA will also help facilitate PSYOP product approval because it gives substantial documentation for the reasons behind a certain series of products. Once a TAAW is complete, it is sent to the PDD (TPDD) where it then becomes the base document for the rest of the PSYOP development process.

Chapter 6

PSYOP Development

Your first job is to build the credibility and the authenticity of your propaganda, and persuade the enemy to trust you, although you are his enemy.

A Psychological Warfare Casebook
Operations Research Office
Johns Hopkins University, Baltimore, Maryland, 1958

The PSYOP process is a systematic and continuous method that includes the various elements of planning, analyzing, synchronizing, developing, designing, producing, distributing, disseminating, managing, and evaluating PSYOP products and actions presented to selected TAs. The POTF or PSE HQ and each detachment or team within the PDC or TPDD have specific tasks and responsibilities to complete throughout this process. They complement each other and are mutually coordinated and supportive.

The missions of the POTF, PSE, PDC, and TPDD during PSYOP development are mutually supportive and require continuous coordination. For example, the G-1 or S-1 produces attachment orders that ensure appropriate manning of the POTF. The POTF or PSE G-2 or S-2 submits intelligence requests (IRs, PIR), monitors intelligence reports, gathers PSYOP-relevant information, and searches all available means to collect impact indicators. The G-2 or S-2 supports the TAAP and assists in the evaluation process. The POTF or PSE G-3 or S-3 coordinates and tracks aspects of production, distribution, and dissemination of products and actions. The G-3 or S-3 coordinates and synchronizes the necessary assets to ensure a cohesive PSYOP effort. The G-4 or S-4 obtains the necessary assets needed to produce products. The SSD supports the PSYOP development process by providing expert analysis and advises the commander and the PDC on TAs and the AO. The PDC and TPDD plan, develop, design, and obtain approval of programs. The PSYOP development process and PDC organization are discussed in detail below. The functions of the POTF or PSE staff, TPDD, and TAA are discussed in separate chapters. The PSYOP planning process, media production, distribution, and dissemination are also discussed separately.

PSYOP DEVELOPMENT CENTER

6-1. The PDC within a regional POB and the TPDD within a TPC are responsible for developing, evaluating, and adjusting PSYOP products and actions.

6-2. The PDC consists of four detachments: the plans and programs detachment (PPD), the target audience analysis detachment (TAAD), the product development detachment (PDD), and the test and evaluation detachment (TED). The TPDD is similarly organized with three teams: the plans and programs team (PPT), the target audience analysis team (TAAT), and the Psychological Operations development team (PDT). Two important missions of the PDC and TPDD are product development and PSYOP program management.

6-3. This chapter discusses the functions and responsibilities within a PDC. These exist regardless of the organization of the PDC. Commanders task-organize their elements to meet mission requirements dependent on available resources.

6-4. When a POTF or PSE is established, the PDC can be deployed at various echelons to best support the mission. The decision to create multiple PDCs is determined by the mission and capabilities. PDC representatives are sent where they can best facilitate coordination between PSYOP development and C2 or production.

6-5. An entire PDC is not always required to conduct small contingencies and operations. When such situations arise, Soldiers from each detachment can be deployed to form a smaller PDC. Leaders must ensure that the smaller team is capable of performing all phases of the PSYOP development process.

6-6. Each of the four detachments within the PDC has distinct responsibilities and individual tasks. The following paragraphs describe these detachments in detail.

PLANS AND PROGRAMS DETACHMENT

6-7. The PPD is the operational center of the PDC. The PPD maintains coordination authority over the other detachments in the PDC to establish production priorities and to coordinate efforts. PPD personnel coordinate product development and PSYOP planning with the POTF or PSE G-3 or S-3. PPD personnel analyze the supported commander's objectives to determine need and priority of PSYOP support. When a POTF or PSE is established, the PPD Soldiers are normally collocated with the POTF or PSE HQ. The PPD plays a vital role in PSYOP planning, and manages and executes the plan. Planning responsibilities of the PPD include the following:

- Ensure staff integration and coordination.
- Conduct mission analysis and develop the PSYOP estimate.
- Identify key target sets during the development of the PSYOP estimate.
- Conduct weather, terrain, and media infrastructure analysis.
- Analyze, compare, and prioritize PSYOP supportability of the supported commander's COAs.

- Finalize POs and SPOs for the selected COA.
- Write the PSYOP section of the supported commander's plan.
- Identify potential TAs and key communicators.

6-8. Management and execution responsibilities of the PPD include the following:

- Provide input to the J-3, G-3, or S-3 on products, media, and dissemination.
- Develop series and product concepts.
- Deconflict series dissemination.
- Initiate and track product development; create and assign product numbers.
- Provide guidance to other detachments concerning product development priorities and the production process.
- Hold periodic meetings with other detachment OICs/NCOICs to plan, coordinate, and deconflict current and future PDC operations.
- Ensure product development is supportive of the PSYOP plan and that plan "needs" are addressed.
- Recommend personnel and equipment deployment packages to the PDC commander.
- Maintain a current exercise and deployment calendar.
- Track equipment status and locations.
- Ensure exercise and mission planners are accurate and thorough in their planning and conduct proper battle handoff to mission OIC/NCOIC (such as all planning conference trip reports, CONOPS, and past after action reports [AARs] are in the planners' possession).
- Ensure classes and other material have been translated.
- Submit consolidated request for orders (RFO) to G-3 or S-3 and SORs to G-4 or S-4.
- Ensure all PDC computers have been accredited by the S-2.
- Archive trip reports, AARs, SITREPs, CONOPS, classes, and products from past missions.
- Coordinate with the S-6 to ensure all communication needs are met.
- Maintain oversight of FTP site and monitor all communications.

6-9. There are many individual tasks within the PPD. These individuals and tasks are as follows:

- PSYOP officer—
  - Conducts staff integration and coordination.
  - Conducts mission analysis.
  - Develops PSYOP portion of the supported commander's plan.
  - Is responsible for internal approval and facilitates the external approval of PSYOP products.

- Participates in the planning of all PDC operations and PSYOP activity.
- Senior PSYOP sergeant—
  - Assists PSYOP officer in staff integration, coordination, and planning.
  - Monitors the Product Book to ensure that all approved products are catalogued.
  - Responsible for the management of the PSYOP plan, including the PSYOP objective priority matrix and program control sheet.
  - Monitors product development process to include the TAAW, series concept work sheet (SCW), series dissemination work sheet (SDW), and PAW.
  - Consolidates SOR input from all detachments and submits SORs to the G-4 or S-4 for each deployment.
  - Prepares and submits RFOs to the G-3 or S-3 for each deployment.
  - Monitors the transfer of products by all available secure digital means.
- Team chief—
  - Maintains the Product Book.
  - Reviews the product tracking and program control sheets.
  - Reviews all TAAWs, SCWs, SDWs, and PAWs.
  - Monitors the assignment of all product numbers.
  - Monitors all message traffic pertaining to the mission.
  - Assists other PDC detachments in the product development process.
  - Participates in the planning of all PDC operations.
  - Supervises the transfer of products and messages by all available secure digital means.
- Human intelligence (HUMINT) collector—
  - Maintains a technical and tactical proficiency in all 97E individual tasks and performs those duties within TED.
  - Establishes and maintains a close working relationship with the S-2 and SSD, monitoring all message traffic and INTSUMs for PSYOP-relevant information.
  - Coordinates with the S-2 to ensure all PDC Soldiers have current official passports.
  - Coordinates with the S-2 to ensure all deploying PDC Soldiers have received threat briefs.
- PSYOP sergeant—
  - Convenes work group for series and product concept development.
  - Ensures each product is tracked throughout the development process using a product tracking sheet.
  - Assigns product numbers to products and annotates them on the product tracking log.

- Maintains the program control sheets.
- Transfers products and messages by all available secure digital means.
- PSYOP specialist—
  - Receives, files, and tracks the status of all products and PSYACTs.
  - Tracks status and location of all PDC equipment in coordination with other PDC detachments.
  - Maintains all PPD equipment, reporting deficiencies and shortages in a timely manner.
  - Maintains an archive containing all PSYOP classes, briefings, and mission histories.
  - Transfers products and messages by all available secure digital means.
- Administrative specialist—
  - Maintains DA Form 1594 on all PDC operations, deployments, and exercises.
  - Copies to disk and files all SITREPs, trip reports (format is in Appendix E), AARs (format is in Appendix F), and CONOPS.
  - Maintains a publications library for the PPD.
  - Tracks status and location of all PDC Soldiers in coordination with PDC HQ and other PDC detachments.
  - Transfers products and messages by all available secure digital means.

TARGET AUDIENCE ANALYSIS DETACHMENT

6-10. The TAAD identifies TAs and analyzes their attitudes, beliefs, vulnerabilities, and susceptibilities. TAAD members combine efforts with the SSD to determine the best forms of media. The members also maintain country area files while monitoring intelligence reports to detect TA attitudes and behavioral trends for possible exploitation or product or action modification.

6-11. Once the product development process is initiated, some of the Soldiers in TAAD may be sent to work in the PDD to facilitate product development, ensure priority of effort, and decrease the backlog of product prototypes in the PDD. The Soldiers will continue to work for and receive guidance from the TAAD NCOIC. The number of people sent in this situation is dependent on the workload of the TAAD. Responsibilities of the TAAD include the following:

- Conduct TAA IAW Chapter 5.
- Participate in work groups to further develop series and product or action concept development.
- Compile country area files:
  - Develop country area files for each target country in the assigned AOR.
  - Continually research countries in the assigned AOR.

- Review intelligence traffic.

- Monitor country and area media.

- Recommend personnel and equipment deployment packages to the PPD.

- Coordinate with PPD to ensure accreditation of TAAD computers.

- Ensure TAAD input is reflected on SOR.

6-12. There are many individual tasks within the TAAD. These individuals and tasks are as follows:

- PSYOP officer—

  - Assists in development of the PSYOP portion of the supported commander's plan.

  - Conducts staff integration and coordination.

  - Conducts mission analysis.

- Senior PSYOP sergeant—

  - Supervises target analysis.

  - Supervises development of country area files.

  - Advises and assists in mission analysis.

  - Assists in staff integration and coordination.

  - Participates in the planning of PDC operations and PSYOP activity.

  - Monitors all PSYOP work sheets accompanying product concepts and prototypes passing through the TAAD.

  - Monitors the transfer of messages by all available secure digital means.

- Team chief—

  - Monitors TAA.

  - Monitors country area files.

  - Coordinates with the SSD.

  - Reviews all TAAWs.

  - Monitors all message traffic received from PSYOP personnel.

  - Assists other PDC detachments in the product development process.

  - Participates in the planning of PDC operations.

  - Supervises the transfer of messages by all available secure digital means.

- HUMINT collector—

  - Maintains a technical and tactical proficiency in all 97E individual tasks and performs those duties within TED.

  - Conducts language support for TAAD.

  - Establishes and maintains a close working relationship with the S-2 and SSD, monitoring all message traffic and INTSUMs for PSYOP-relevant information.

- Coordinates with the S-2 to ensure all deploying TAAD Soldiers have received threat briefs.
- PSYOP sergeant—
  - Conducts TAA.
  - Coordinates with SSD.
  - Compiles country area files.
  - Continues product development by completing the TAAW for each product concept.
  - Transfers messages by all available secure digital means.
- PSYOP specialist—
  - Conducts TAA.
  - Coordinates with SSD.
  - Compiles country area files.
  - Assists the product development process by updating the TAAW for each TA.
  - Maintains all TAAD equipment, reporting all deficiencies and shortages in a timely manner.
  - Transfers messages by all available secure digital means.

PRODUCT DEVELOPMENT DETACHMENT

6-13. The PDD is the largest of the four detachments. The PDD designs audio, visual, and audiovisual product prototypes based on input from other PDC detachments. The PDD has the PDC's only illustration and graphics capability. Soldiers in the PDD work closely with broadcast personnel in scriptwriting, storyboarding, and audiovisual production. PDD Soldiers also work closely with print personnel to facilitate and expedite print operations and product turnaround time. Responsibilities of the PDD include the following:

- Review the TAAW, PAW, and SCW.
- Design visual product prototypes:
  - Determine best graphic representation.
  - Ensure graphics that are appropriate to the TA are selected.
  - Minimize white space to reduce opportunities for counterpropaganda.
- Design audio product prototypes:
  - Tailor scripts for radio and loudspeaker broadcasts.
  - Ensure radio broadcasts fit in standard programming hour.
  - Coordinate with broadcast specialists to ensure script quality.
- Design audiovisual product prototypes:
  - Tailor scripts for TV broadcast.
  - Develop storyboards.
  - Ensure TV broadcasts fit in standard programming hour.

- Coordinate with PPD for translation of products:
    - Incorporate translation into product prototype.
    - Modify English versions to accurately reflect cultural differences.

6-14. There are many individual tasks within the PDD. These individuals and tasks are as follows:

- PSYOP officer—
    - Reviews product development procedures and operations.
    - Assists in program planning.
    - Conducts staff integration and coordination.
    - Conducts mission analysis.
- Senior PSYOP sergeant—
    - Monitors development of product prototypes.
    - Advises and assists in mission analysis.
    - Assists in staff integration and coordination.
    - Participates in planning PDC operations.
    - Monitors TAAWs, PAWs, and SCWs.
    - Monitors the transfer of products and messages by all available secure digital means.
- Multimedia NCO—
    - Supervises product prototype development.
    - Coordinates with the PDD PSYOP sergeant.
    - Coordinates with broadcast and print personnel.
    - Supervises maintenance of all PDD computers.
    - Participates in planning of PDC operations.
    - Supervises the transfer of products and messages by all secure digital means.
- PSYOP sergeant—
    - Supervises product prototype development.
    - Coordinates with the TAAD on concept interpretation and intent.
    - Reviews all TAAWs, PAWs, and SCWs.
    - Participates in planning of PDC operations.
    - Supervises maintenance of PDD equipment.
    - Supervises the transfer of products and messages by all secure means.
- HUMINT collector—
    - Maintains a technical and tactical proficiency in all 97E individual tasks and performs those duties within TED.
    - Conducts language support for the PDD.

- Establishes and maintains a close working relationship with S-2 and the SSD, monitoring all message traffic for PSYOP-relevant information.

- Multimedia illustrator—

  - Designs product prototypes.

  - Interfaces with print personnel.

  - Maintains PDD computers.

  - Transfers product prototypes and messages by all secure digital means.

- PSYOP specialist—

  - Designs product prototypes.

  - Interfaces with TAAD personnel.

  - Maintains all PDD equipment.

  - Transfers product prototypes and messages by all secure digital means.

TESTING AND EVALUATION DETACHMENT

6-15. The TED develops pretests and posttests to evaluate the PSYOP impact on TAs. The TED also provides information essential to product development and program planning by collecting PSYOP-relevant information and analyzing hostile propaganda. The TED obtains feedback from TAs, including EPWs/CIs/DCs, through interviews, interrogations, surveys, and other means to further assess impact and to obtain feedback and determine PSYOP-relevant intelligence. TED personnel use reports and information provided by TPTs. The TED may also assist the POTF and PSEs with translation tasks. Responsibilities of the TED include the following:

- Collect PSYOP information:

  - Develop a collection matrix to focus on specific tasks.

  - Request PSYOP SITREPs from the PPD.

  - Extract PSYOP-relevant information from source documents.

- Evaluate the selected PSYOP MOEs.

- Pretest products:

  - Develop questionnaires and surveys.

  - Conduct surveys and interviews.

  - Provide results to TAAD to update country area files and TAAWs.

  - Assist and advise the PDD in product adjustments.

- Posttest products:

  - Conduct surveys and interviews using TA samples or focus groups.

  - Provide results to the PPD and brief the POTF or PSE J-3, G-3, or S-3 on all testing.

  - Provide results to the TAAD to update country area files.

- Analyze hostile propaganda using the SCAME approach:
  - Determine the source, message content, total audience reached, medium of dissemination, and the effects on the TA.
  - Attempt to build the opponent's propaganda plan.
  - Provide a summarized analysis to the PPD.
  - Provide recommendations for or against the use of counterpropaganda to the PPD.

6-16. There are many individual responsibilities within the TED. These individuals and tasks are as follows:

- PSYOP officer—
  - Reviews testing and evaluation procedures and operations.
  - Reviews PSYOP information collection plan.
  - Assists in program planning.
  - Conducts staff integration and coordination.
  - Conducts mission analysis.
- Senior PSYOP sergeant—
  - Monitors pretesting and posttesting of prototypes and products.
  - Monitors the development of questionnaires and surveys.
  - Advises and assists in mission analysis.
  - Participates in planning PDC operations.
  - Monitors information collection.
  - Monitors the transfer of products and messages by secure digital means.
- PSYOP sergeant—
  - Supervises pretesting and posttesting of prototypes and products.
  - Supervises the development of questionnaires and surveys.
  - Assists in mission analysis.
  - Monitors information collection.
- HUMINT collector NCO—
  - Maintains a technical and tactical proficiency in all 97E individual tasks and performs those duties within TED.
  - Conducts language support for TED.
  - Establishes and maintains a close working relationship with the S-2 and SSD, monitoring all message traffic for PSYOP-relevant information.
  - Supervises PDC information collection.
- PSYOP specialist—
  - Pretests and posttests prototypes and products.
  - Develops questionnaires and surveys.

- Participates in information collection.
- Transfers product prototypes and messages by all secure digital means.
- HUMINT collector—
  - Maintains a technical and tactical proficiency in all 97E individual tasks and performs those duties within TED.
  - Conducts language support for TED.
  - Establishes and maintains a close working relationship with the S-2 and SSD, monitoring all message traffic for PSYOP-relevant information.
  - Conducts PDC information collection.

PHASES OF THE PSYOP DEVELOPMENT PROCESS

6-17. The PSYOP development process is complex and has many components. The process consists of seven phases. These phases are not necessarily sequential and often occur simultaneously. For example, one potential series may still be in the TAA phase while another is in the dissemination phase. As each phase is discussed individually, it will become clear how employing the entire process is the most effective means of implementing PSYOP. The PSYOP development process requires a clear understanding of national policy, mission, and ROE.

PHASE I: PSYOP PLAN DEVELOPMENT AND MANAGEMENT

6-18. The PSYOP process begins with planning, which has two segments. The first segment begins when the planner integrates with the supported unit and begins MDMP. Chapter 4 discussed this portion in detail, and it ends, in a sense, with the publication of the OPLAN or OPORD. The second segment of PSYOP planning continues throughout the execution of the plan and is referred to as programming. PSYOP units constantly receive new and updated information concerning the situation, TAs, and impact of previous PSYOP products and actions. Each significant change requires modification of the plan.

6-19. Programming is the strategic time phasing, placement, and coordination of multiple PSYOP programs within a PSYOP plan. During programming, it is extremely important for the PSYOP Soldier to have a full understanding of the geographic combatant commander's OPLAN or OPORD, the current situation, and as much general information about the AOR as possible. Programming is a continuous cycle, updated as the situation changes and as results from evaluation reflect needed changes.

Management of the PSYOP Plan

6-20. The PSYOP plan encompasses all POs identified to support the supported unit commander's mission. Each PO and its corresponding program, within a PSYOP plan, are prioritized to ensure coordination with the supported unit's phased operation. Developed programs are the means PSYOP uses to modify foreign TA's behavior. All PSYOP programs developed for the supported unit commander's mission make up a PSYOP plan. One program is the combination of all supporting programs within a PO. A supporting program includes all the series that address a specific SPO. A series includes all the products and actions targeted at one TA to achieve one SPO. PSYOP personnel build a plan by beginning broad and then working more narrowly toward specific products and actions by developing programs, supporting programs, and series. Figure 6-1 shows a graphic depiction of the following:

- *PSYOP program*: All products and actions developed in support of a single PO.

- *Supporting PSYOP program*: All products and actions developed in support of a single SPO.

- *Series*: All products and actions developed in support of a single SPO and single TA.

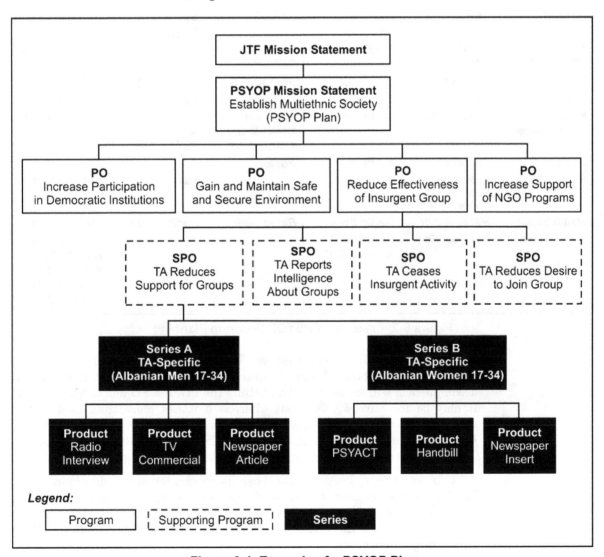

Figure 6-1. Example of a PSYOP Plan

6-21. PSYOP objectives are statements of measurable response that reflect the desired behavior or attitude change of selected foreign TAs due to PSYOP. Since each plan has multiple POs, it will have multiple programs. All the programs for the POs identified constitute a PSYOP plan. A program is all products and actions directed at all TAs to achieve all POs for the plan or all the programs developed to accomplish one plan. Each PO will have two or more SPOs and therefore will have multiple supporting programs within it. All the supporting programs under one PO constitute a program (Figure 6-2).

PSYOP PROGRAM PO A: Gain and Maintain a Safe and Secure Environment					
SUPPORTING PROGRAM SPO #04: TA decreases acts of violence.			SUPPORTING PROGRAM SPO #07: TA decreases curfew violations.		
SERIES TA ak: Adults, ages 20-29	**SERIES** TA pm: Teens, ages 13-19	**SERIES** TA ko: Parents	**SERIES** TA ak: Adults, ages 20-29	**SERIES** TA pm: Teens, ages 13-19	**SERIES** TA ko: Parents
PRODUCTS *Handbills* KSA04akHB01 KSA04akHB02	**PRODUCTS** *Handbills* KSA04pmHB01	**PRODUCTS** *Handbills* KSA04koHB01	**PRODUCTS** *Handbills* KSA07akHB01 KSA07akHB02 KSA07akHB03	**PRODUCTS** *Handbills* KSA07pmHB01 KSA07pmHB02 KSA07pmHB03	**PRODUCTS** *Handbills* KSA07koGHB01
Posters KSA04akPS01	*Posters* KSA04pmPS01 KSA04pmPS02 KSA04pmPS03	*Posters*	*Posters*	*Posters* KSA07pmPS01	*Posters* KSA07koPS01
Radio Script	*Radio Script* KSA04pmRD01	*Radio Script* KSA04koRD01 KSA04koRD02	*Radio Script*	*Radio Script*	*Radio Script* KSA07koRD01 KSA07koRD02 KSA07koRD03 KSA07koRD04 KSA07koRD05

Figure 6-2. Example of PSYOP Program Planning

6-22.   Each PO will have at least two SPOs. SPOs are the specific behavioral or attitudinal responses desired from the TA because of PSYOP. Each SPO, if accomplished, will assist in accomplishing the PO. If a PO has only two SPOs, it may be too narrowly defined, whereas if it has more than twelve it is probably too broad. There are usually two or more TAs for each SPO, as PSYOP will attempt to elicit the same behavior or attitude from multiple TAs. The TAs are selected from the PTAL and analyzed during the TAAP.

6-23.   A completed TAAW is the base document for series development. A PSYOP series consists of all products and actions directed at one TA to achieve one SPO. A SPO will have multiple TAs and consequently multiple series. All the series developed to achieve a SPO will constitute a supporting program.

Product Numbering and Tracking

6-24.   To effectively manage a PSYOP plan, there must be a numbering and tracking mechanism in place. During series development, discussed later in this chapter, each product is assigned a product number. In addition to being a tracking mechanism, product numbers describe the product (tells the PO, SPO,

TA, and media type). A PSYOP product numbering and filing system is a tool designed to allow products to be accurately and easily sorted, tracked, and filed. An established universal product numbering system greatly facilitates work when varied units are involved in an operation. The high possibility that a POTF or PSE will consist of both tactical and regional elements, as well as Active Army and RCs, necessitates an established system. A product number is designed to be "cradle to grave." Assigned during the series development phase, the product number does not change and is therefore easily tracked within a database. This system allocates eleven characters that distinguish each individual product according to the following criteria:

- *Country Code/Operation Code*: First two-character code (AA-ZZ) identifies the country or named operation. (Appendix G includes information on country codes.)
- *PSYOP Objective*: The third character code (A-Z) is designated in the PSYOP annex, appendix, or tab.
- *Supporting PSYOP Objective*: The fourth and fifth characters (01-99) are designated in the PSYOP annex, appendix, or tab.
- *Target Audience*: The sixth and seventh characters (aa-zz) are designated by the TAAD.
- *Product Type*: The eighth and ninth characters (AA-ZZ) are designated in the Product Type Information Chart, Figure 6-3.
- *Product Number*: The tenth and eleventh characters (01-99) are the actual product number in sequence for each TA.

AC—Action	FF—Face to Face	NP—Newspaper/Insert	TC—Tactical Communication
BB—Billboard	GF—Graffiti	NV—Novelties	TE—T-shirt
BU—Button/Pin	HB—Handbill	OO—Other	TF—Tri-fold
CB—Comic Book	HV—Hat/Visor	PM—Pamphlet	TH—Theater
CL—Clothing (Other)	IN—Internet	PS—Poster	TV—Television
DE—Decal/Sticker	LF—Leaflet	RD—Radio	TY—Toys
DG—Durable Goods	LS—Loudspeaker	RL—Rally/Demonstration	VD—Video/Cinema
EM—E-Mail	LT—Letter	SP—Sports Equipment	WR—Wireless Messaging
FD—Packaged Food	MS—Medical Supplies	SS—School Supplies	

Figure 6-3. Product Type Information Chart

6-25.   The example in Figure 6-4, page 6-15, product number KSA01abHB01, depicts handbill "01" for South Korean audience "alpha bravo." It corresponds to SPO "01," which falls under PO "A." Country codes (Appendix G) are standardized according to the DOS list. Use of this list ensures synergy not only between PSYOP units and DOS assets, but also establishes a single convention for organizations, such as the Department of Justice (DOJ) and Drug Enforcement Administration (DEA). The POTF or PSE commander, based on guidance from the supported unit commander or geographic combatant commander, will designate a two-letter code for a named operation.

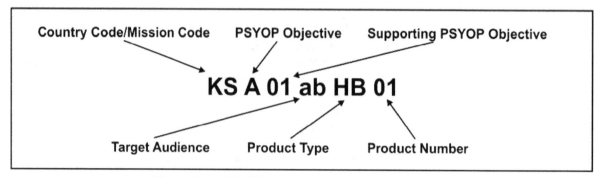

Figure 6-4. PSYOP Numbering and Filing System

6-26. The different types of products used to transmit a PSYOP product or action are limitless and new technology will no doubt create new media. The standardized list in Figure 6-3 will cover the vast majority of products and actions.

6-27. Most products will fall under the above-stated categories and PSYOP Soldiers should avoid making numerous additional designations. The product type of Novelties (NV) is a broad category that can cover several types of products, such as keychains or lighters. Durable goods (DG) is also a broad category that includes consumer goods other than clothing that will be of use in homes and offices for a long period of time. Examples include small radios or dishes or cups bearing a PSYOP message.

6-28. The category of other (OO) is designated not only for current products that may be difficult to categorize under existing categories but also to serve as a catchall for emerging media. The designation OO will be used exclusively for all products that otherwise fall outside the categories present in Figure 6-4. POs, SPOs, and TAs are normally found in the PSYOP annex, appendix, or tab. Product numbers should be assigned sequentially.

Product Number Location

6-29. Product numbers for visual media are placed in the bottom right-hand corner. Product numbers will contrast in color with the background of visual media types. The font size of product numbers on visual media will be small enough so that it does not interfere with the TA's perception of the product. Product numbers for audio and audiovisual media are placed in the top right-hand corner of the scripts and annotated on the label and cover of the compact disc (CD), digital video disc (DVD), videocassette, or audiocassette. Placing product numbers on visual media is extremely helpful with the evaluation process as feedback can easily be matched with its corresponding product.

Planning Work Sheets

6-30. After the development of a plan and a tracking mechanism, PSYOP Soldiers use three work sheets to accurately manage and track the PSYOP effort. These work sheets are called the PSYOP objective priority matrix, program control sheet, and the series dissemination matrix. Each is dependent on the other, and their proper use is essential to an effective, controlled, and coordinated PSYOP effort. These work sheets are effective tools that ensure the PSYOP plan is cohesive and not contradicting itself at any given time or giving too much or too little attention to any specific TA. These work sheets or reports are easily generated and maintained by using a database but can be done by hand if necessary.

6-31. **PSYOP Objective Priority Matrix.** This matrix uses the POs and SPOs developed during planning that allow the PSYOP commander to depict to the supported unit his priority of effort. This matrix ensures that PSYOP emphasis is in line with the supported unit and helps ensure that each objective is receiving adequate attention at the appropriate time. This matrix includes all of the POs, SPOs, and a timeline (usually in months) in conjunction with a color-coded bar graph to depict where PSYOP is focusing its effort during any given point in time. Often there is also an area at the top where significant events or OPORD phases are included that may affect a change in priority of the PSYOP effort. Figure 6-5, pages 6-16 and 6-17, displays an example.

	Month	Jan	Feb	Mar
	Weather Conditions	Snow	Snow	Thaw
	Event/Phase of OPORD			22: elections
Psychological Objectives	**Supporting PSYOP Objectives**			
A) Gain and maintain a safe and secure environment.	1) TA refrains from interethnic violence.			
	2) TA refrains from acts of violence toward KFOR.			
	3) TA avoids contact with UXO/mines.			
	4) TA abides by MTA and UCK transformation.			
	5) TA decreases participation in organized crime.			
B) Reduce effectiveness of insurgent activity in the vicinity of TF Falcon AOR.	1) TA ceases insurgent activity.			
	2) TA decreases support for insurgent activity.			
	3) TA decreases volunteering for insurgent groups.			
	4) TA provides information about insurgent activity.			
C) Gain and maintain acceptance of International Security Forces (ISF), international organization, and NGO presence.	1) TA believes that ISF, international organizations, and NGOs are beneficial.			
	2) TA accepts KFOR as a crisis intervention force.			
	3) TA reduces interference with ISF, international organization, and NGO operations.			
	4) TA increases participation in ISF, international organization, and NGO programs.			
Legend: Priority Effort ■	Continue Focus ▧	Decrease Focus ▨		

Figure 6-5. PSYOP Objective Priority Matrix

	Month	Jan	Feb	Mar
	Weather Conditions	Snow	Snow	Thaw
	Event/Phase of OPORD			22: elections
Psychological Objectives	**Supporting PSYOP Objectives**			
D) Gain and maintain KFOR as a credible source of information.	1) TA accepts KFOR messages as truthful and unbiased.	Decrease Focus	Decrease Focus	Decrease Focus
	2) TA seeks out KFOR media for news and information.	Continue Focus	Decrease Focus	Decrease Focus
	3) TA decreases amount of disinformation directed at KFOR.	Decrease Focus	Continue Focus	Continue Focus
E) Increase participation in the IDP/refugee repatriation process.	1) TA accepts the return of IDP/refugees to their homes.	Decrease Focus	Continue Focus	Priority Effort
	2) TA decreases interference with IDP/refugee repatriation process.	Decrease Focus	Continue Focus	Priority Effort
	3) TA increases participation in IDP/refugee repatriation process.	Decrease Focus	Continue Focus	Priority Effort
F) Increase participation in democratic institutions.	1) TA participates in national democratic institutions.	Decrease Focus	Continue Focus	Continue Focus
	2) TA participates in the electoral process.	Continue Focus	Continue Focus	Priority Effort
	3) TA complies with judicial decisions.	Decrease Focus	Decrease Focus	Decrease Focus
	4) TA complies with institutions of law enforcement.	Continue Focus	Continue Focus	Continue Focus

Legend: Priority Effort ■ | Continue Focus ▨ | Decrease Focus ▢

Figure 6-5. PSYOP Objective Priority Matrix (Continued)

6-32. **Program Control Sheet.** A program control sheet allows the PSYOP unit an easy means of tracking a current PSYOP program to achieve a PO. The program control sheet is a planning and management tool that allows the PSYOP commander to update the supported unit's commander easily on what actions are being taken to support his mission. This document lists the program, supporting program, series, TA, and products with their current status. Figure 6-6, page 6-18, provides an example.

6-33. **Series Dissemination Matrix.** This matrix uses the information from the series dissemination work sheet, discussed during Phase III of the PSYOP development process, to ensure that proper media mix and timing are being employed. This matrix includes series number, PO, SPO, and TA as header data and then has product, media, and date so that an easy graphic representation can be viewed. Figure 6-7, page 6-18, provides an example.

6-34. These work sheets allow for effective management of the PSYOP plan. Synchronizing the PSYOP effort is the goal of these work sheets. The danger that PSYOP must avoid is minimizing its own effectiveness by having too many different programs occurring simultaneously. PSYOP Soldiers that are managing the plan must ensure that a specific TA is not receiving too many messages at the same time and rendering the TA member to a state of confusion.

```
┌─────────────────────────────────────────────────────────────────────────┐
│                     PROGRAM CONTROL WORK SHEET                            │
│                           JTF FORTITUDE                                   │
│ PROGRAM: KSA: Decrease combat effectiveness of enemy forces.             │
│ SUPPORTING PROGRAM: KSA03: Target audience provides information to        │
│ coalition forces.                                                         │
│ SERIES: KSA03qf                                                           │
│ TA: Truck drivers transporting cargo in the Barfield area.               │
└─────────────────────────────────────────────────────────────────────────┘
```

Product Number	Name	Media	Status
KSA03qfRD01	Save Yourself	Radio Script	Waiting Approval
KSA03qfRD02	Tenuous Grip	Radio Script	Disapproved
KSA03qfPS01	Enlightened Leader	Poster	Dissemination
KSA03qfPS02	Immediately	Poster	Review Board
KSA03qfPS03	External Pressure	Poster	Pretest
KSA03qfHB01	Save Your Future	Handbill	Production
KSA03qfHB02	Extreme Effort	Handbill	Dissemination
KSA03qfTV01	Courage	TV Spot	Dissemination
KSA03qfTV02	Kindness	TV Spot	Posttest
KSA03qfTV03	Self-respect	TV Spot	Production

Figure 6-6. Example of a Program Control Sheet

Series #KSA03qf							
PO A: Decrease combat effectiveness of enemy forces.							
SPO 03: TA provides information to coalition forces.							
TA: Truck drivers transporting cargo in the Barfield area.							
Product #	Media	JAN 1-7	JAN 8-14	JAN 15-21	JAN 22-28	JAN 29-FEB 5	FEB 6-12
KSA03qfPS01	Poster	▨	▨				
KSA03qfHB01	Handbill			▨	▨		
KSA03qfTV01	TV Spot				▨	▨	▨
Legend: Dissemination Period ▨							

Figure 6-7. Example of a Series Dissemination Matrix

PHASE II: TARGET AUDIENCE ANALYSIS

6-35. TAA is the second phase in the PSYOP development process and is fundamentally important to modifying foreign audiences' behavior. TAA is the beginning of series development. A detailed discussion of the TAAP is in Chapter 5. TAA must be tied to a specific SPO, must produce a TAAW that is the base document for series development, and must be continuously reviewed and updated. The PSYOP Soldier must remember that detailed, accurate TAA is the single most important phase in the product development process.

PHASE III: CONDUCT SERIES DEVELOPMENT

6-36. A PSYOP series is all products and actions directed at one TA to achieve one SPO. PSYOP uses series in the same way a marketer or advertiser will use multiple media and multiple products to sell goods or services. Historically, there are few examples where a single advertisement has caused a dramatic change in the behavior of consumers. Marketing research has shown that a TA is best influenced by a series of multiple products and actions that incorporate a good mix of media. Additionally, those products and actions must have a consistent message and coordinated dissemination. The TAAW is the source document for series development. Each TAAW will create one series. While the TAAW recommends lines of persuasions and media, the series development process actually selects which lines of persuasion and media to use. Series development has two parts: the development of a series concept, and the determination of how (placement, frequency, location) and when (timing, duration) to disseminate the series. The series concept is developed, usually in a working group setting, using the SCW. Once that is complete, the SDW is completed.

Series Concept Work Sheet

6-37. The SCW is a tool used to begin the development of all products for a specific TA for one SPO. Members from all the different sections within PDC, usually led by the PPD, participate in series development. This group examines the TAAW and discusses the path the TA must be led down to arrive at the conclusion that is desired. The question is how does the TA proceed from their current behavior pattern to the desired one? Using the TAAW as the source document, the working group determines what types of media, products, and actions are necessary to convince the TA to modify their behavior. Developing a series concept is a creative process that takes a team effort. The working group determines if there is going to be a tagline or slogan (textual symbol) for all products in the series. Input from the members of all the various forms of media are considered to ensure that the agreed upon concepts will be usable in all proposed media forms. The exchange of ideas, the exhaustive research and analysis present in the TAAW, and creativity are the keys to successful series development. The steps discussed in the following paragraphs will assist the working group in efficiently developing a series concept.

6-38. The lines of persuasion that will be used are selected from the TAAW and should be based on the susceptibility ratings given to each line of persuasion. It is possible to use all lines of persuasion presented in a TAAW or choose only the ones that are determined to be most appropriate. If a single line of persuasion is strong enough, it may be used by itself. Attempting to put too many lines of persuasion out to the TA congruently may overwhelm the TA and make them nonreceptive to all messages. Once lines of persuasion are selected, they are prioritized and sequenced to ensure maximum impact on the TA.

6-39. Selecting media type is the second step in developing a series concept. Media are selected based upon the accessibility ratings from the TAAW, not on availability of dissemination assets. If a dissemination asset is not available for a particular product, modifications can be made later. It is critical to select types of media that ensure a good media mix and sufficient coverage. A good media mix allows the TA to see the same message through various media forms with each exposure reinforcing past exposures.

6-40. The third step is determining the number of products for each media type. The number of products developed for each media are based on several criteria: how much information the media type can convey on one product, the amount of information that needs to be conveyed, and the complexity of the information that needs to be conveyed. In addition, enough products must be developed to ensure that the TA does not lose interest over time.

6-41. The fourth and final step in series concept development is to establish a suspense date for all prototypes to be completed. This suspense date is determined by applying the backwards-planning process, allowing for pretesting, approval process, modifications, production, distribution, and dissemination. Once there has been a determination as to the lines of persuasion, the mix of each media type, the number of products necessary, and the suspense date for a series, it is possible to complete an SCW (an abbreviated example is provided in Figure 6-8, pages 6-20 and 6-21). The SCW is then used as the base document for the PDD in conducting product concept development and prototype design.

(Information taken from example TAAW in Figure 5-3, pages 5-20 through 5-24.)

Series #: COA02fw

PSYOP Objective: Gain and maintain acceptance of coalition forces.

Supporting PSYOP Objective: TA cooperates with U.S./coalition forces.

Target Audience: Blue-collar factory workers.

DATE: 10 September 2003.

LINE OF PERSUASION 1: Coalition forces will help the Cortinian military protect innocent citizens from the aggression of the CLF and return stability and safety to Cortina.

MEDIA TYPE 1: 8.5" x 5.5" inch two-sided handbill.

 # OF MEDIA TYPE 1: 4.

PRODUCTS:

COA02fwHB01 - This product must capitalize on the positive emotional response of the TA towards the GOC military. The symbols and layout must be extremely vivid to evoke that emotional response.

COA02fwHB02 - Links the GOC military with coalition forces. Use the successful cooperation of past MTTs.

COA02fwHB03 - Compares and contrasts the suffering and instability that exists with the CLF and the stability and peacefulness of GOC/coalition force presence.

COA02fwHB04 - Must emphasize the exit strategy of coalition forces to reassure the TA that they are not an occupying army.

SUSPENSE: 23 December 2003.

MEDIA TYPE 2: 30-second television spots.

 # OF MEDIA TYPE 2: 2.

PRODUCTS:

COA02fwTV01 - This product will show a series of pictures of GOC military working together with coalition forces. Use footage from present and past cooperative efforts.

COA02fwTV02 - Product graphically displays the terror and suffering caused by the CLF and contrasts it with GOC/coalition forces administering humanitarian aid.

SUSPENSE: 23 December 2003.

Figure 6-8. Series Concept Work Sheet Example

LINE OF PERSUASION 2: Repeat process for each additional line of persuasion selected
MEDIA TYPE 1:
OF MEDIA TYPE 1:
PRODUCTS:
SUSPENSE:

MEDIA TYPE 2: Repeat process for each media type selected.
OF MEDIA TYPE 2:
PRODUCTS:
SUSPENSE:

Figure 6-8. Series Concept Work Sheet Example (Continued)

Series Dissemination Work Sheet

6-42. The SDW synchronizes and deconflicts dissemination of all products within the series as reflected on the SCW. There are several considerations in completing an SDW.

6-43. PSYOP personnel begin the SDW by determining the overall series dissemination, which includes the overall duration or start and end dates. The duration can begin and end based on date, phase of OPLAN or OPORD, or events. Often it is beneficial to divide the series into stages. Doing so allows the information in the supporting arguments to be disseminated in the proper order. If a series is staged, each stage must be put in the proper order and then given a duration. Again, the start and end dates for a stage can be date or event driven.

6-44. Dissemination for each product in a stage or series must also be determined. There are six criteria for product dissemination that must be considered: duration, timing, frequency, location, placement, and quantity. This information needs to be determined for each product in the series. PSYOP Soldiers should avoid oversaturating the TA with too many products at any one time, while at the same time ensuring sufficient coverage to influence the TA. The criteria are discussed below:

- *Duration* is the start and end date for a particular product. Like series and stage duration, product duration is determined by a calendar date or a specific event. The end date should reflect the amount of time the product must be accessible by the TA to ensure sufficient exposure to the message.

- *Timing* is the time of the day, week, month, or year that the product is to be disseminated.

- *Frequency* is the number of times during any given time period that the product is to be disseminated.

- *Location* is the geographic area in which the product is to be disseminated. This area is dictated by the location of the TA.

- *Placement* is the physical placement of the product within the geographic location (for example, on telephone poles, in shop windows, in schools, or at local markets). For products going out through mass media, placement is the type of outlet (radio, television, or newspaper) and the type of programming or section of the periodical the product should be inserted into.

- *Quantity* is the number of copies that need to be actually produced.

6-45. Once all these factors have been determined, an SDW is completed. The SCW is directed to the PDD so that product concepts can be developed while the SDW stays within the PPD and is incorporated into the management of the PSYOP plan. Figure 6-9 is an example format of an SDW.

SERIES DISSEMINATION WORK SHEET

SERIES #: Input series number (found on TAAW).

PO: (found on TAAW)

SPO: (found on TAAW)

TA: (found on TAAW)

DATE: Date SDW completed.

SERIES DURATION: Start and end dates for dissemination of the entire series.

STAGE 1 DURATION: Start and end dates for the first stage.

PRODUCTS, STAGE 1:

PRODUCT #: List product number.

DURATION: Either start and end dates for dissemination, time period over which product must be disseminated, or key events.

TIMING: Time of day, week, month, or year product should be disseminated.

FREQUENCY: How often during a given time period the product should be disseminated.

LOCATION: What geographic location the product should be disseminated.

PLACEMENT: How or where the product should be placed within the geographic location.

QUANTITY: The number of copies to be produced.

PRODUCT #: Repeat process for each product.

DURATION:

TIMING:

FREQUENCY:

LOCATION:

PLACEMENT:

QUANTITY:

STAGE 2, DURATION: Repeat process for each stage.

PRODUCTS, STAGE 2:

PRODUCT #: Repeat process for each product.

DURATION:

TIMING:

FREQUENCY:

LOCATION:

PLACEMENT:

QUANTITY:

Figure 6-9. Series Dissemination Work Sheet Format

PHASE IV: PRODUCT/ACTION DEVELOPMENT AND DESIGN

6-46. There is a distinction between product development and product design. Product development is the conceptualization of the product or its general idea. The result of product development is a product concept in the form of a PAW. Product design is the process of turning a product concept into a product prototype, such as a radio script, video storyboard, or visual prototype. The design of prototypes cannot occur before the development of the product concept.

6-47. Product development is based on the information contained in the TAAW, SCW, and synchronized with the SDW. As a rule, all products within a series should be developed by one team to ensure consistency and avoid contradictions in message and style. At the minimum, PAWs within a series should be developed cooperatively within the PDD so that each product in the series is consistent and reinforces each other. A product concept is not a prototype. The product concept as listed on the PAW includes the following sections:

- A detailed description of the product to include size, color, sounds, voices, and so on. It should not "script" out the product.
- Identification of the key points of the product that must be included in the prototype.
- Explanation of what symbols should be used, how they should be used, and what their meaning is.
- Sketches for clarification (may or may not be included).

6-48. Once a product concept is developed, a PAW is completed. The PAW provides a framework for product/action design. Essentially, it is a work order telling prototype designers what the product should be. One PAW is completed for each product concept. The PAW is produced by the PDD based on the information contained in the TAAW and SCW. There is no set format for the PAW (Figure 6-10, page 6-24, provides an abbreviated example), but it is usually a WORD document and contains the following information:

- Product/action number.
- PSYOP objective.
- Supporting PSYOP objective.
- Series number/related products.
- Target audience.
- Lines of persuasion/symbols.
- Media type.
- Suspense.
- Product/action concept.

6-49. Once all PAWs for a given series are completed, they are checked for continuity of lines of persuasion and compatibility. All products in a series should reinforce each other. Once compatibility and continuity are ensured, the PAWs are given to the product designers where typically a PSYOP specialist and an illustrator work together on visual media, a PSYOP specialist and a broadcaster work together on audio media, a PSYOP specialist and cameramen work together on audiovisual media, and a PSYOP planner coordinates with the supported unit on PSYACTs.

6-50. Once a prototype is complete, the PDD organizes a PDD working group, a formal or informal group that provides expert review of a PSYOP product prototype. The PDD working group may include representatives from each PDC section, print, broadcast, and SSD personnel, to provide input to the prototype prior to being finalized and submitted to the PDC commander at the product approval board. This review ensures the product prototype reflects the proper journalistic style and format for the TA, as well as ensures the prototype is within the production capabilities of the POTF or PSE. Once the prototypes are completed, the PDD ensures the product meets all specifications as outlined on the TAAW, SCW, and PAW. Techniques on how to design visual, audio, and audiovisual products are provided in Chapter 9.

PRODUCT/ACTION WORK SHEET	DATE: 27 NOV 03

(This is an abbreviated example to show what should be included on the PAW.)

1. **Product/Action Number:** COA02fwHB01

2. **PSYOP Objective:** Gain and maintain acceptance of coalition forces.

3. **Supporting PSYOP Objective:** TA cooperates with U.S./coalition forces.

4. **Series Number/Related Products:** COA02fw: COA02fwHB02; COA02fwHB03; COA02fwHB04; COA02fwTV01; COA02fwTV02.

5. **Target Audience:** Blue-collar factory workers.

6. **Line of Persuasion and Symbols: Main Argument** - Coalition forces will help the Cortinian military protect innocent citizens from the aggression of the CLF and return stability and safety to Cortina. Appeal being used is Legitimacy (Tradition) - Support for GOC military is something deeply inherent in TA's beliefs and values and this product will amplify, reiterate, and reinforce that belief. Symbols for this LOP are the Cortinian falcon, which conjures feelings of pride and honor, and the Cortinian military seal, which evokes pride, trust, and confidence within the TA.

7. **Media Type:** 8.5" x 5.5" inch two-sided handbill with both sides depicting the same scene.

8. **Suspense:** 23 DEC 03

9. **Product/Action Concept:** High-quality HN assets will produce this product and therefore there are no constraints as to color or design. The text on the product will say "GOC Military always ready to defend our nation." A GOC soldier will be looking out over the plains from a hilltop with the Cortinian falcon perched on his shoulder. The soldier must look strong and confident. The landscape must be recognizable but idealized with peace and tranquility. The Cortinian military seal will be displayed in the corner, big enough to be easily seen but not so big that it detracts from the mood of confidence, pride, and tranquility.

Figure 6-10. Product/Action Work Sheet Example

Psychological Operations Actions

6-51. PSYACTs are operations, conducted by SOF and conventional forces or other agents of action, which are planned and conducted as part of a PSYOP supporting program. PSYACTs are considered during series concept development and are used in conjunction with other types of products to modify the behavior of a TA. Specific PSYACTs are developed in a similar manner to other products and are annotated on a PAW. The PPD or PSYOP planner submits the fully developed PSYACT concept to the supported commander for approval and initiation. The supported command's operation section coordinates PSYACTs separately, but PSYOP personnel must work closely with the section to ensure that each PSYACT is properly integrated and synchronized to ensure it has the proper effect on the TA.

Types of Psychological Operations Actions

6-52. Only the limitations of the supported unit in planning and accomplishing the action (and the imagination of PSYOP personnel) restrict the variety of operations that can be considered PSYACTs. PSYACTs include the following operations:

- Raids.
- Strikes.
- Shows of force.
- Demonstrations.
- Insurgency operations.
- Civic action programs (CAPs).

6-53. Regardless of the type of action selected, the PSYOP staff officer must maintain close coordination with other services and agencies to ensure proper timing, coherence, and economy of force.

6-54. Units conducting PSYACTs provide an extra dimension to the overall PSYOP plan. PSYACTs that are properly planned, coordinated, and included as a part of a PSYOP program allow PSYOP personnel to capitalize on the success of the actions and use that success in the conditioning or behavior modification of the TA.

Psychological Agents of Action

6-55. Psychological agents of action are those persons, units, and agencies that perform PSYACTs that enhance and amplify the overall PSYOP plan. While these agents are not PSYOP personnel, the missions they perform, when properly planned and coordinated, may have a profound psychological impact on a TA. These agents of action include, but are not limited to, the following types of units:

- Conventional combat units.
- SOF (excluding PSYOP units).
- Units of other DOD services.
- Other government agencies.

6-56. There are two types of agents of action—incidental and discretionary. All PSYACTs are conducted by discretionary agents of action. Since all military operations inherently have a psychological effect, PSYOP personnel must remain aware of operations conducted by incidental agents of action to capitalize on their successes. Incidental agents are those whose activities have a psychological effect secondary to their operations. Discretionary agents conduct their activities primarily for their psychological effect and must be briefed by the PSYOP staff officer so they do not inadvertently release sensitive information.

6-57. Although these agents are not under the control of PSYOP personnel, the responsible commander should state their mission with specific psychological objectives in mind and direct their coordination to ensure timing and mission goals coincide with other PSYACTs planned or in progress.

6-58. When properly coordinated and used, psychological agents of action provide additional manpower and force to support and accomplish psychological objectives. The best use of these forces depends greatly on the amount of mission planning and coordination between unit operations and the PSYOP staff officer.

PHASE V: APPROVAL PROCESS

6-59. PSYOP products go through both an internal and external approval process. Several techniques have proven successful in working products through this process. The PDC commander usually chairs the internal approval board and has representatives from various sections on the board. He convenes a product approval board to assess each PSYOP product prototype. An entire series should be considered at one time as this accomplishes several tasks. First, it allows for the commander to see the entire impact of the series as each product reinforces the others. Secondly, it ensures that the line of persuasion is consistent across all mediums. After considering all products within a series, the PDC commander makes a decision about the series.

6-60. If approved, the prototypes are sent to the POTF or PSE commander for his consideration. If it is not approved, the series is sent back to the PDD for further refinement. Once a series is approved by the PDC commander, it is translated into the appropriate language so that pretesting can be conducted. Ideally, pretesting is conducted at this point in the process but several factors need to be discussed in regards to pretesting, translating, and approval. The advantage to pretesting at this early stage of approval is that if results are positive, they can be sent up the approval chain with the prototypes, which gives further credibility as to why the products should be approved. If pretest results are negative and identify that the series needs further refinement, then the POTF or PSE commander and the supported unit commander's time is not wasted.

6-61. Conversely, the disadvantage to early translating and pretesting is that if the approval authority makes modifications, the translators will have to retranslate the product. If the product is disapproved, then a translation asset has been wasted. Another concern is if a product is translated and pretested prior to the POTF or PSE commander reviewing it, and it causes a disturbance that could be problematic for the PDC commander. A PDC commander will have to assess the risk involved in pretesting and then determine the timing based on that assessment. Time is always going to be a factor in the ability or timing of pretesting. Once the decision to translate and pretest has been made, the PDC coordinates for translation into the language of the TA.

6-62. Completed product prototypes are translated into the language of the TA using PDC Soldiers, HN military members, or contracted linguists. The preferred method of translation is a "double-blind" process in which one translator or translation team translates from English to the target language, and another translator or team retranslates the translation back to English.

Discrepancies between the two are then reconciled and a final version in the target language is approved.

6-63.   Checking translations is an art that relies on the appropriate approach and questions. A reviewer should not be asked a broad question, such as "What do you think of this translation?" This is not precise enough to pinpoint mistakes. It allows too much latitude for cultural reticence to modify the reply. Politeness or cultural imperatives may lead the reviewer to spare PSYOP personnel embarrassment by not telling them there are serious mistakes in the translation. The significance of mistakes may be minimized for the same reasons. When a translation is checked, whether by the original linguist or by a second one, it should be checked in detail. PSYOP personnel should ask the linguist to compare the English and the translation word for word and determine if the translation is exact and complete. Is anything missing? Has anything been added? If liberties have been taken to make a translation idiomatic, as they often are and must be, the precise nature of the liberties should be reviewed to ensure that they truly convey the desired meaning.

6-64.   The product should also be approached from a culture's perspective to ensure the product will have a cultural resonance with the TA. Culturally dictated modifications may be made automatically by a translator; questions should be asked that reveal such changes and then determined whether they convey the intended message. The opposite may also occur—the first draft of a translation may be idiomatically and culturally swayed, perhaps making it difficult for a native speaker to understand or perhaps even making it laughable. The product might also be written in a vulgar idiom or grammatically incorrect style that might appeal to some TAs and offend others. The reviewer should be asked specific questions to determine if this is the case and, wherever necessary, changes should be made to make the message appropriate to the intended TA.

6-65.   It is essential to follow up in detail on all questions to make sure that the reviewer is not simply being polite. All caveats and recommendations for change should be carefully noted. Additionally, after a product is produced, it should be carefully reviewed to ensure that no typographic errors or other changes have been inadvertently introduced during the production process. Tiny calligraphic changes can dramatically alter or even reverse the meaning of a word or phase. A product, once translated, is sent to the TED for pretesting. The TED organizes a pretest panel to review translated products. Pretesting is discussed in greater depth in Chapter 7.

6-66.   Once a series is sent to the POTF or PSE commander, he may convene an approval board consisting of the members of the PDD working group or assess the series on his own. If the POTF commander approves the series, it must be packaged and sent to the supported unit for external approval. If the POTF or PSE commander does not approve the series, it returns to the PDD for further refinement.

6-67.   External approval is sometimes difficult and time-consuming although several techniques have been used to expedite this process. PSYOP planners work during planning to ensure only required personnel are included in the approval chain. Normally, the approval authority designates several key members of the staff to provide input on PSYOP products. They may include the Chief of Staff (COS), G-3, G-7 IO, political advisor (POLAD), SJA, and possibly others. Figure 6-11, page 6-28, usually included in the PSYOP annex, is a proven method of streamlining this process.

6-68. This process has proven successful in minimizing the time it takes to staff PSYOP products. Conducting simultaneous staffing is the most efficient way of incorporating staff input in a timely fashion. Having the products come back to the POTF or PSE commander before being sent to the approval authority also allows the POTF or PSE commander the opportunity to refute any staff comments if he deems necessary.

---

1. **SITUATION.** This appendix outlines the approval process within XXX HQ for the staffing and approval of PSYOP activities and products.

2. **MISSION.** See Annex.

3. **EXECUTION.** See Annex.

   A. Concept of the Operation.

     (1) General. In order to make PSYOP a timely and responsive player in XXX operations, the staffing and approval process must be as responsive and expedited as possible. COMXXX, or his designated approval authority, is the sole decision maker on the approval or disapproval of PSYOP activities and products.

     (2) Staffing/Approval Process.

      a. Staffing. The POTF/PSE commander is responsible for the packaging, staffing, and final disposition of all staffed PSYOP activities and products. POTF/PSE commander will conduct staffing per SOP. All product/activity approval requests are typically staffed, simultaneously, with Chief IO, POLAD, and SJA. These staffing agencies will not have approval/disapproval authority over any PSYOP products or activities. For planned operations, the POTF/PSE commander will submit PSYOP product/activity staffing requests at 0800 hrs each day. IF NO RESPONSE IS RECEIVED BY CLOSE OF BUSINESS (COB) ON THE DAY OF SUBMISSION, CONCURRENCE IS ASSUMED AND THE PRODUCT/ACTIVITY APPROVAL REQUEST WILL ENTER THE APPROVAL CHAIN. After completion of the staffing process, the POTF/PSE commander will consolidate comments and prepare the request for entry into the approval chain. Staffing sections will make comments on the form provided or attach a point paper with their comments about the product. PRODUCT/ACTIVITY STAFFING REQUESTS WILL NOT RETURN TO THE PDD FOR CHANGES AT ANY POINT IN THIS PROCESS UNTIL FINAL APPROVAL/DISAPPROVAL.

      b. Approval. After all staffing actions are complete, PSYOP products/activity approval requests will be submitted to the G-3 for review and comment. Normally, the G-3 is given approval authority by the commander unless in the case of an Army corps or division, the G-7 is given approval authority. All staffing sections' comments will be available for review with explanations/comments from the POTF/PSE commander. The G-3 or G-7 will recommend approval or disapproval and forward the request through the COS to the COM, or his designated approval authority for final approval.

      c. Postapproval/disapproval actions. Following COMXXX's final decision, the POTF/PSE commander will incorporate any changes directed by the approval chain and prepare the product or activity for execution. If the product or activity is disapproved, the POTF/PSE commander will file the request and determine if an alternate means to achieve the same desired effect can be developed. All staffing and approval sheets will be maintained on file with the POTF/PSE commander for the duration of the operation.

4. **SERVICE SUPPORT.** See Annex.

5. **COMMAND AND SIGNAL.** See Annex.

Figure 6-11. Example of Approval Process Explanation

PHASE VI: PRODUCTION, DISTRIBUTION, AND DISSEMINATION

6-69. This phase of the PSYOP development process is discussed in Chapters 9 and 10. Once product prototypes are designed, translated, and approved, they move into production. The coordination and management of this phase of PSYOP development is normally conducted by the G-3 or S-3. Distribution is the process of moving PSYOP products from the point of production to the place where the disseminator is located. Dissemination is the delivery of a PSYOP product to its intended TA. Once a product has been delivered to a TA, the postdissemination phase of evaluation takes place.

PHASE VII: EVALUATION

6-70. This process is discussed in Chapter 7 and considers both pretesting and posttesting. Evaluation is crucial to the effectiveness of the PSYOP effort. Evaluation will let the POTF or PSE commander know what impact he is having and what changes or modifications are needed. The evaluation process is ongoing throughout the PSYOP effort and its conclusions will be incorporated as soon as possible. There are many sections involved in the evaluation process. The TED has primary responsibility but outside agencies and the POTF or PSE G-2 or S-2, as well as supported unit G-2, are all involved in trying to assess impact indicators.

COUNTERPROPAGANDA

6-71. Counterpropaganda is not considered its own phase in the PSYOP development process because it is incorporated into all phases. During the planning phase, the propaganda capabilities and possible plan of the opponent is considered during the PSYOP estimate. The possible avenues that the opponent may use are considered and incorporated into the initial PSYOP plan. This plan would include any proactive programs that are deemed necessary as a preemptive strike. Once opponent propaganda is obtained by friendly forces, it is analyzed and used to confirm, deny, or modify the initial opponent propaganda plan. As each individual piece of propaganda is analyzed using the SCAME process, the opponent propaganda plan is extrapolated and the information is filtered back into the PSYOP development process. For example, if the source of the propaganda is identified, they become a TA and enter the TAAP. Chapter 11 discusses counterpropaganda in detail.

SUMMARY

6-72. The PSYOP development process is complex and encompasses all aspects of executing a successful PSYOP effort. The process in this chapter has been broken into phases rather than steps because there is a large amount of overlap and congruent activity. Figure 6-12, page 6-30, is a graphic depiction of the PSYOP phases and the path that a specific series would take. Different series can be in different phases at the same time and must be managed and tracked by the POTF or PSE.

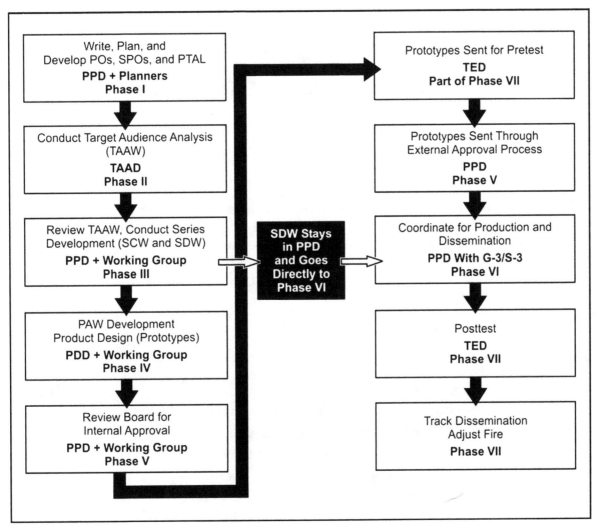

Figure 6-12. The PSYOP Process

Chapter 7

Evaluation of Product Effectiveness

The necessity of procuring good intelligence is apparent and need not be further urged.

General George Washington
26 July 1776

PSYOP personnel use intelligence from various sources in the evaluation process to determine the effectiveness of the PSYOP effort. Ideally, products and symbols are tested on a limited audience prior to full-scale production. Before full-state dissemination and use, the results of testing are analyzed to determine whether to modify the product or symbol, or if necessary, eliminate it completely.

PRODUCT PRETESTING

7-1. Following the development and design of a potential symbol or PSYOP series, PSYOP personnel conduct pretesting. Pretesting allows PSYOP personnel to answer important questions about PSYOP materials, such as—

- Should this line of persuasion be used?
- Are the symbols meaningful to the TA?
- Are the colors used offensive in any way?
- Is the material addressing the correct TA?
- Is the medium used the most effective way to present the material (leaflet, TV, radio)?
- Does each product in the series complement the others?

7-2. PSYOP personnel use pretesting to assess the potential effectiveness of a series of PSYOP products on the TA. The information derived from testing is also used to refine and improve PSYOP products. This section describes the methods PSYOP personnel use to test product effectiveness on the TA.

7-3. Both versions, the English and the translated, should go to the product approval authority. Waiting to translate a product after final approval precludes pretesting and thus prevents one from telling the approval authority how the product was tested or how the TA reacted to it. Again, the product must be translated as accurately as possible before pretesting and approval of the product. The product must also receive a quality control check for printing and translation errors after final product approval and before dissemination. The challenge in PSYOP development is to predict or estimate the product's effect on the TA. There are, in general, several ways to evaluate the potential impact of PSYOP on a selected TA, including surveys and focus groups. Each of these methods has its strengths and weaknesses.

SURVEY SAMPLE

7-4. Survey sampling is the preferred method of evaluating the effectiveness of PSYOP products. With this method, the TA is sampled directly through questionnaires and personal interviews. When the responses are obtained, the PSYOP specialist analyzes the resulting data to develop generalizations. Survey sampling requires personnel trained to collect and interpret data. Access to the TA is required.

7-5. Most personal interviews follow a prescribed formal pattern with the wording and order of questions determined in advance. An informal interview can be based on a detailed list, which indicates the subject matter to be covered. An informal interview permits the interviewer to vary the wording and order of the subject matter to obtain the maximum amount of information. The survey sample is the preferred method of evaluating PSYOP products because it is the method that addresses the TA directly. These surveys help PSYOP personnel determine the potential effects of a PSYOP product on a TA. PSYOP personnel are also able, through pretesting, to determine the effects of products that create a hostile reaction within the TA. By conducting surveys, PSYOP personnel acquire demographic data on the TA.

7-6. PSYOP units use the survey sample to collect responses from a set of respondents about their opinions, attitudes, or behavior toward developed PSYOP products (pretesting) and disseminated PSYOP products (posttesting). The unit uses the survey to make predictions and generalizations about the TA.

7-7. Choosing the sample is the first step in conducting a survey. The larger the sample, the greater the validity of the survey results. The sample should also be random. To obtain a representative sample, the unit conducting the survey randomly selects a sample large enough to represent the entire population adequately. Two types of samples conducted by PSYOP personnel are probability samples and nonprobability samples.

Probability Samples

7-8. Probability samples include simple random samples, stratified random samples, and cluster samples. These categories are explained below.

7-9. **Simple Random Sample.** In the simple random sample, each person in the TA has an equal chance of being included in the sample. To conduct this sample, the sampler needs an alphabetical list of the TA's members. The sample works as follows:

- The sampler starts with an alphabetical listing of 1,000 villagers. He wants to draw a sample of 100.
- The sampler then places pieces of paper numbered from one to ten in a container.
- He draws one slip of paper out to determine the starting point. The starting point would be any of the first ten names on the list. For example, if the selected number was five, the sample begins with the fifth name on the list.

- After selecting the starting point, every tenth name on the list is selected for the sample. The sampler goes through his entire list, selecting 100 names for the sample.

7-10. **Stratified Random Sample.** In the stratified random sample, members of the TA have an unequal chance of being included in the sample. Using two or more characteristics of the TA as a basis, the sampler divides the TA into layers or strata. The sampler then draws a simple random sample from each stratum. The combinations of these subsamples form the total sample group. To conduct this sample, the sampler needs an alphabetical list of the members of the TA and a list of the characteristics that form the layer.

7-11. The sampler wants to find the relationship between wealth and certain attitudes. The sampler knows the total population is 1,000. He also knows the population of the TA consists of 200 wealthy, 600 average, and 200 poor people. If the sampler just draws a simple random sample, the wealthy or poor may be represented unequally in the sample. The sampler, therefore, divides the TA into three groups based on wealth: upper class, middle class, and lower class. Using the alphabetical list for each group, the sampler draws a simple random sample from each group. Each sample includes the same number of people. If the sampler wants a sample of 150, he selects 50 names from each group. By combining the samples from each group, the sampler forms the total sample group with equal representation for each group. The sampler uses the stratified random sample when he knows in advance that a segment of the TA lacks sufficient numbers to be included in a simple random sample. For example, one class greatly outnumbers another.

7-12. **Cluster Sample.** In the cluster sample, the sampler divides the TA into large geographical areas. Next, he performs the same sampling process as when sampling individuals, but the sample begins with a large region. After sampling the region, the sampler then draws samples from the next smaller division. The sample works as described below. Using the procedures for random sampling, the sampler draws a sample from a large region or country. The sample might include the provinces or states within that region or country; for example, the sampler knows he wants to draw a sample from the Commonwealth of Independent States. The sample he draws comes from the Baltic States. The sampler now draws a sample using the next smaller administrative division—the Republic of Estonia. The sampler follows this pattern with the samples becoming smaller until they become individuals within the cities. After sampling the region, the sampler continues with a sample from the countries within the region followed by the districts within the country. He continues this pattern until he draws a sample of individuals within the cities.

Nonprobability Samples

7-13. These samples include accidental samples and quota samples. Examples include man-on-the-street interviews and product surveys of customers in stores. In the accidental sample, the sampler interviews people at a specific location. This sample is the easiest to select; however, it does not accurately represent the TA. For example, the sampler chooses a street corner in a city or village. He then interviews the people who walk by. This sample is inaccurate because it only represents the part of the TA that happened to walk by the street corner when the sample took place. The street corner chosen for the sample may only attract a certain type of person; therefore, it would not truly represent the whole TA. A street corner near a factory would attract different people than a street corner near an exclusive department store. In the quota sample, the sampler interviews a specific type and number of people from the TA. This sample is more desirable than the accidental sample because it designates the type and number of people to be interviewed.

7-14.   One drawback to this method is that the sampler interviews the people who are most available or willing to be interviewed. An individual within a specific category may also represent a special segment of that category. Once the sampler fills his quota from one group, he moves to another category. The sample works as described below.

7-15.   The sampler is tasked to interview the different groups within the TA; for example, farmers, students, laborers, and merchants. The sampler must interview 50 people from each category. The sampler begins the survey with the farmers. Once the sampler interviews 50 farmers, he moves to the students. The sampler continues this process until he interviews the remaining groups.

Preparing the Questionnaire

7-16.   Preparing the questionnaire is the second step in conducting a survey. A questionnaire is a list of objective questions carefully designed to obtain information about the attitudes, opinions, behavior, and demographic characteristics of the TA. Each questionnaire developed by PSYOP or interrogator personnel must have a definite purpose that is linked to obtaining information that will contribute to the success of the PSYOP plan.

7-17.   **Questionnaire Format.** The format of a questionnaire generally includes three basic sections: the administrative section, the identification section, and the problem section.

7-18.   The administrative section is always the first part of the questionnaire. The purpose of the administrative section is twofold—to explain the purpose of the questionnaire and to establish rapport with the individuals being questioned.

7-19.   The identification section gathers information that will help identify subgroups within the TA. Subgroup identification is necessary for the development of lines of persuasion. Because not all groups have the same attitudes and opinions, a PSYOP unit develops different lines of persuasion to suit each distinct subgroup. Some of the questions asked in this section will pertain to the respondent's sex, age, birthplace, family size, occupation, education, and ethnic group. The identification section may follow the administrative section, or it may appear at the end of the questionnaire. The problem section obtains objective information about the behavior, attitudes, and opinions of the TA. Objective information of interest in this section includes such information as—

- Familiarity with mass media.

- Knowledge of previous PSYOP products or actions.

- Behavior relevant to an estimate of the psychological situation.
- Knowledge of events.
- Economic conditions.
- Perceptions, aspirations, and preferences of the TA.

7-20. **Question Guidelines.** PSYOP personnel should ask all members identical questions. They should state questions clearly and simply in a vocabulary suitable for all respondents. A person who does not understand a question may give a response that does not represent his real opinion. Sequencing of the questions is also important. PSYOP personnel should consider the following guidelines when developing questionnaires:

- Begin the questionnaire with warm-up questions. (These questions help maintain the rapport established in the administrative section. Warm-up questions should be easy to answer, they should be factual, and they should arouse the respondent's interest in filling out the questionnaire. Warm-up questions should set the respondent at ease and make him feel comfortable answering. They should not ask intensely personal questions. They should not make the respondent feel threatened.)

- Place sensitive questions between neutral ones (because PSYOP attitude surveys frequently deal with key issues, ones that arouse the TA emotionally). PSYOP personnel must often ask questions sensitive to the TA. In many cases, the respondent may not answer such questions. He may not respond honestly and directly because he feels violated. Placing sensitive questions between neutral ones, however, normally reduces the emotional impact of the sensitive questions upon the respondent. It also promotes his receptivity and objectivity to the questions.

- Avoid leading questions—ones that lead the respondent to a particular choice (stating half the questions in a positive way and the others in the negative helps to avoid leading the respondent). Avoid phrasing questions in a way that causes the respondent to think he should answer in a certain manner; for example, "Your country's leader should resign, shouldn't he?"

7-21. **Types of Questions.** There are three basic types of questions used in a questionnaire. They include open-ended questions, closed-ended questions, and scaled-response questions, as discussed in the following paragraphs.

7-22. Open-ended questions require the respondent to put his answers in his own words. They also allow the respondent to include more information about complex issues. Measuring and analyzing the responses to open-ended questions prove difficult because the answers are so individualistic. Additionally, open-ended questions require more time and effort to analyze than closed-ended questions. This drawback makes open-ended questions difficult in many situations. Examples of open-ended questions are—

- How did you come in contact with the safe conduct pass?
- When did you find the safe conduct pass?

- Were other people with you who picked up safe conduct passes?
- What made you pick up the safe conduct pass?

7-23. Closed-ended questions let the respondent choose between given answers: true or false, yes or no, or multiple-choice items. PSYOP personnel can quickly and easily evaluate closed-ended questions because respondents must use the choices contained in the questionnaire. Closed-ended questionnaires are often relied on because of time and resource limitations. Examples of closed-ended questions are—

- Have you ever seen the safe conduct pass?
  - Yes.
  - No. (If no, do not continue.)
- Did you find the safe conduct pass?
  - Yes.
  - No.
- If no, where did you get the safe conduct pass?
  - A friend.
  - A stranger.
  - Other.
- Were there other safe conduct passes available?
  - Yes.
  - No.
- Did other people want a safe conduct pass?
  - Yes.
  - No.

7-24. When more time is available, PSYOP personnel can prepare elaborate open-ended questionnaires and conduct surveys that may take several weeks. Closed-ended questions are ideal for tactical and operational situations.

7-25. Scaled-response questions are actually statements, rather than questions. Scaled-response questions require the respondent to indicate the intensity of his feelings regarding a particular item. He records his answers on a scale ranging from positive to negative or from strongly agree to strongly disagree. The scaled-response question weighs the choices on a numerical scale ranging from the lowest limit of intensity to the highest. In a series of scaled-response questions, PSYOP personnel alternate the limits of the scale by presenting the lowest limit first part of the time and the highest limit first the rest of the time. This procedure will help prevent the respondent from simply checking choices at one end of the scale rather than carefully thinking through each selection. Questionnaires containing scaled-response questions should provide clear instructions explaining how the scale works and how the respondent is to mark his selection. Figure 7-1, page 7-7, provides an example of a scaled-response question.

7-26. Because no standard formats exist for PSYOP pretest questionnaires, PSYOP personnel must prepare each questionnaire to fit the situation and the echelon level of the unit. Personnel designing the questionnaire get the basic information for developing the questionnaire from the PAWs. After designing the questionnaire, they should test it for clarity. Once PSYOP personnel have completed testing the questionnaire, they can use it to conduct the interview.

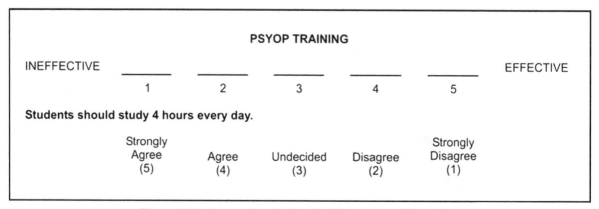

Figure 7-1. Example of a Scaled-Response Question

Individual Interviews

7-27. Individual interviews allow an individual respondent to carefully observe and study a PSYOP product. An interviewer then questions him on important facets of the proposed PSYOP message. When indigenous personnel and EPWs are employed for pretesting, the PSYOP specialist must brief them on the importance of responding as they personally feel about the subject matter. Their responses would not be valid if they gave answers they believe were expected of them.

7-28. Conducting the personal interview is the third step in conducting a survey. The interview is a series of questions devised to get information about the TA. It may be structured or informal. PSYOP personnel conduct structured interviews by reading questions from a printed questionnaire. The interviewer then records the respondent's answers on the questionnaire. PSYOP personnel base informal interviews on a detailed list of subjects to be covered. This method allows the interviewer to vary the wording and order of the questions to get the most information. In either type of interview, PSYOP personnel must not only pay attention to what is being said, but also to how it is being said.

7-29. Before conducting an interview, particularly an interview with someone from a different cultural background, PSYOP personnel should consider the motivation of the respondent. The interviewer must remember that the person he will interview will have his own motivation for whatever he says and does. The respondent's age, cultural background, experience, and training may influence his motivation. These same factors influence the interviewer, so the interviewer should try to understand how his prejudices and experiences color his responses to what the subject of the interview is saying. During an interview, the interviewer must interpret communication on two levels: verbal and nonverbal.

7-30. **Verbal Communication.** This communication includes words and the way they are spoken. The interviewer must remember that every word has a denotation (its literal, dictionary meaning) and a connotation (its suggested meaning). The way in people say a word has influence on its meaning. The interviewer needs to look for vocal cues. These cues include emphasis, volume, tempo, pitch, enunciation, and breaks in speech.

7-31. **Nonverbal Communication.** This communication, or body language, is the second part of communication. The interviewer must properly interpret the body language—facial expressions, territory, body position, gestures, visual behavior, and appearance of the person he is interviewing—to understand fully what is being said. During an interview, the interviewer should look for body language that indicates negative emotions. Examples include—

- Facial expressions, which include lowered brows, narrowed eyes, and a tightened mouth or frown.
- Territory, which involves violating space relationships by standing too close.
- Body position, which includes "closing-up" positions, such as clenched fists, tightly crossed arms or legs, or shifting of body weight from one foot to the other.
- Gestures, which include shaking the head, covering the mouth with the hand, or rubbing the ear.
- Visual behavior, which includes staring or not maintaining eye contact.
- Appearance, which includes dress and behavior inappropriate for the situation.

7-32. **Interpreting Emotions.** Adding both verbal and nonverbal communication, the interviewer should follow these general guidelines when interpreting emotions during an interview:

- Look for cooperation, respect, and courtesy. This behavior may indicate trust.
- Look for embarrassment, crying, or a withdrawn attitude. This behavior may indicate hurt.
- Look for aggression; hostile, sarcastic, loud, or abusive language; lack of cooperation; or a stiff, strong face. This behavior may indicate anger.
- Look for sweating, sickness, running away, freezing in place, nervousness, physical or mental inability to cooperate, excessive cooperation, or submission. This behavior may indicate fear.
- Look for the offering of aid and comfort through word or deed, by listening, or by nodding agreement. This behavior may indicate concern.

7-33. **Listening Habits.** To interpret human behavior accurately, the interviewer must pay close attention to the subject's expressions and movements and develop the following good listening habits:

- Concentrate on the message content (the interviewer should ignore emotion-laden words or phrases that may upset and disrupt the train of thought; he should not become upset over something said and miss the rest of the message).

- Listen first, then evaluate (the interviewer should not decide in advance that a subject is uninteresting).

- Listen for concepts and main ideas, not just for facts (a good listener is an idea listener).

- Adapt note taking to the particular interview (the interviewer should not write notes during the interview if it makes the person nervous; he should write notes immediately after the interview if he cannot take them while the subject is talking).

- Pay attention (the interviewer should indicate that the information he receives is important and significant).

- Tune out distractions and interruptions (the interviewer should move the interview site to a quieter place, if necessary).

- Use thought rate to the fullest advantage (most people speak at a rate of 100 words per minute, while they listen at 400 words per minute; the interviewer should use the timing difference to absorb the ideas being presented and to form questions).

Controlling the Interview

7-34.   The interviewer should control the interview at all times. If the subject of the interview is hostile or disruptive, the interviewer should maintain his composure. Often, an angry person simply needs to vent his strong feelings. The interviewer should develop and maintain courtesy, empathy, respect, and a concerned but calm attitude during an interview by—

- Explaining the reasons for the interview.

- Putting the respondent at ease.

- Informing the respondent that his identity will remain anonymous if he so desires.

- Convincing the respondent to answer according to his convictions. The interviewer should explain that the pretest interview will be used to identify weak and strong points in the PSYOP material.

- Allowing the subject to vent his feelings. Doing so may uncover a psychological vulnerability to exploit.

- Letting the subject know the interviewer recognizes and accepts his feelings.

- Responding to concern with appreciation and calm.

- Responding to fear with concern and assurance. The interviewer must use interpersonal communication skills to keep fear from turning into defiance.

- Responding to trust with courtesy and respect.

- Responding to hurt with empathy and concern.

7-35. Conducting an interview is an important part of taking a survey. When conducting an interview, the interviewer should observe the following guidelines:

- Assemble material.
- Research background information.
- Direct flow of interview.
- Review questionnaire for essential information.
- Transcribe notes.

7-36. An interview is the best method for gauging what the TA is thinking. Surveys, however, take time and access to the TA—luxuries the typical PSYOP unit seldom has.

7-37. Respondents may develop their responses based on their own opinions, values, attitudes, or desires. Well-constructed questionnaires and the development of key attitude indicators can provide insight into the effectiveness of the PSYOP product. PSYOP personnel can gather observer commentaries from uninvolved, but often interested, foreign individuals who live in or near the target area. The accuracy of these reports depends on the expertise of the observer and the type of evidence gathered, such as letters, diaries, and official documents. PSYOP personnel must cautiously evaluate reports from these sources to eliminate bias. If a source's biases are known, they can be taken into account, and the reports can be evaluated with a reasonable assurance of accuracy.

FOCUS GROUPS

7-38. Focus groups are useful as they have the ability to provide in-depth discussion of PSYOP products. Focus groups include the following: a panel of representatives, group consultations, and a panel of experts, which are discussed in the following paragraphs.

Panel of Representatives

7-39. This panel consists of actual TA members or may include EPWs/CIs/DCs, defectors, and others who were formerly part of the TA and now approximate the TA as closely as possible. The evaluator must realize that the conditions that affect a former TA member will not be exactly the same as an actual TA member. Pretests conducted with such groups can indicate what appeals are likely to be effective, what should be emphasized, and what should be avoided. The composition and structure of such a panel can vary from as few as five representatives to as many as a hundred. Two guidelines must be considered when the number of representatives for a panel is being determined: the number must be sufficient to provide for an adequate cross-section of the intended target, and adequate sampling must be obtained for reliability. This form of pretesting can by done by interviewing the group as a whole or by interviewing members of the group individually. By using individual interviews, any inaccuracies or bias due to group dynamics can be overcome.

Group Consultations

7-40. Group consultations call for representatives (5 to 15) to observe, study, and exchange views concerning PSYOP material. The procedure requires the pretester to direct the discussion along prearranged lines and exclude irrelevant comments. The respondents can exchange ideas and feel comfortable since they are among peers, allowing the pretester to obtain diverse opinions of the representatives in a relatively short time. The respondents, however, may tend to agree with the majority to avoid peer group criticism, and controlled discussions may become long and extraneous.

Panel of Experts

7-41. This panel is a group of individuals who have studied the TA and are thoroughly acquainted with its culture. This is the simplest and most frequently used method. The panelists should have lived in the target country recently. The purpose of the panel is to read or listen to the PSYOP material developed for the potential TA and to predict its effect. The panel may answer the following questions about the PSYOP material:

- Will it attract attention?

- Will it be understood?

- What reaction will it produce?

- Will it be accepted and believed?

- Will it change any attitudes or lead anyone to take the action desired?

- How can it be made more effective?

7-42. Criticism and predictions of the panel of experts can be used either to revise the PSYOP material or to decide when and where to disseminate it. The report of the panel of experts will be valid only to the extent that the panel can identify with the TA and anticipate the process by which the audience will respond to the PSYOP material.

FINAL PRETEST DATA

7-43. After completing the pretest of a prototype product, PSYOP personnel make required changes to the product. The unit then produces a limited quantity of the prototype product, usually no more than three to five copies. The unit forwards one copy of the prototype PSYOP product along with the PAWs to higher HQ for approval. It does not produce or disseminate additional copies of the prototype PSYOP product until it receives final program approval from higher HQ.

IMPACT ASSESSMENT AND POSTTESTING

7-44. One means of determining PSYOP effectiveness is to evaluate intelligence and other sources for indicators of behavior or attitudes relative to POs. Another means is to give a posttest of the products, using such methods as the survey sample or focus groups.

FACTORS IN PRODUCT EFFECTIVENESS

7-45. Many factors influence the effect a PSYOP product has on the TA. These factors include the following:

- Type and location of the TA.
- Number and variety of communication channels open to the TA.
- Degree of program saturation.
- Degree to which the PSYOP product conforms to group standards.

COLLECTION TECHNIQUES

7-46. The data collection techniques for pretesting are also useful in determining whether or not the product stimulated behavior and caused the restructuring of attitudes. Indicators of effectiveness may be direct or indirect. Impact assessment allows units to determine the effectiveness of a PSYOP program by studying these indicators. They may be any behavior, action, event, medium, or feedback that displays the behavior desired by the PSYOP objective.

POSTTESTING

7-47. Posttesting is a process that evaluates products after the products have been disseminated. PSYOP personnel use the same posttesting methods as in pretesting. These methods include the survey sample and focus groups.

IMPACT INDICATORS

7-48. Impact indicators are those events that aid in determining the success of the PSYOP effort. All impact indicators are either positive or negative and contain a direct or indirect orientation. They are used to determine the degree to which the TA has been influenced by the PSYOP effort or if the TA received the message.

Positive Impact Indicator

7-49. Positive impact indicators are actions, events, or behaviors that are favorable in orientation to the desired PSYOP objective. For example, if a PSYOP program is attempting to convince opponent forces to surrender, an increase in the number of opponent soldiers giving themselves up would be a positive indicator (also a direct indicator). However, PSYOP personnel should be aware that the defectors might be surrendering because of factors other than the PSYOP program.

Negative Impact Indicator

7-50. A negative impact indicator is an event or a change opposite that desired by the PSYOP unit. One example might be fewer defectors despite a massive program to convince them of the benefits and advantages of defecting (may also be a direct indicator). PSYOP personnel should examine this case to determine why the program is having the opposite effect or if PSYOP had anything to do with it.

Direct Impact Indicator

7-51. Direct impact indicators are changes or events that show the TA's actual behavior in relation to the PSYOP effort. For example, if the SPO was "TA votes" and this election had an increase of 20 percent in voter participation, this would be a direct impact indicator (also positive). The increase in participation was the actual behavioral response being sought by the PSYOP program.

Indirect Impact Indicator

7-52. Indirect impact indicators are changes or events that show the TA's possible behavior in relation to the PSYOP effort. For example, if the SPO was "TA votes" and there was a 5 percent decrease in voter registration, this would be an indirect impact indicator (also negative). Voter registration is not the actual behavior being sought after by the PSYOP effort; however, it does give an indication that the PSYOP program may not be working.

7-53. To determine behavioral change, a baseline or starting point must be established. For attitudinal changes, surveys or studies must exist before or as near to the beginning of the PSYOP effort as possible. Once a baseline is established, then the effectiveness of the PSYOP effort can be assessed. An example would be if the SPO is "TA votes" in upcoming election and last year they had 55 percent voter turnout, this would be the baseline. In this year's election, there was 70 percent turnout. A positive impact indicator would be that the TA voter turnout increased by 15 percent. Whether an indicator is positive or negative is normally easy to determine, but for PSYOP it is usually more important to determine if an indicator has a direct or indirect orientation. A further discussion of direct and indirect is therefore necessary.

7-54. Direct indicators are the desired results themselves. They are the most reliable determinants for assessing effectiveness. Here, the TA displays the behavior desired by the PSYOP objective. The first direct indicator is responsive action. For example, if a specific action, such as writing letters, refusing to obey orders, defecting, or voting is called for and actually takes place, then the PSYOP product was probably the direct cause of the action. However, PSYOP personnel must be able to demonstrate that the action was motivated by PSYOP products and not by some other factor. Often, the product serves as a catalyst for action, particularly when surrender appeals and safe conduct passes are disseminated in conjunction with military actions. PSYOP personnel may also determine effectiveness through participant reports collected from survey sampling.

7-55. Indirect indicators involve the assessment of events in the target area that appear to be the result of PSYOP activities but cannot be conclusively tied to any series of products. Any independent external factors that may have influenced events in the target area must be identified and evaluated before any firm conclusions can be drawn. Indirect indicators may be developed from the following types of evidence:

- Physical actions barring reception of the PSYOP product by the TA.
- Psychological conditioning of the TA.

- Events occurring in the target area that are apparently related to the issues covered in the PSYOP products.

7-56. Once dissemination has begun, the opponent force may try to prevent PSYOP material from reaching the TA. Some typical techniques used to stop reception include barring entry of printed material, organizing takeovers or attacks on television and radio stations, forbidding newspapers to be printed, banning social gatherings, and jamming radio broadcasts.

7-57. A hostile government or other power group can initiate nonphysical actions that cause the TA to avoid PSYOP products. These actions are carried out after the initial messages are transmitted. They include attempts to convince the TA that the source of the material cannot be believed or that the message is untrue. The hostile government may penalize TA personnel who possess PSYOP materials, listen to PSYOP radio transmissions, or watch PSYOP television broadcasts. These related events occur when the TA takes an action not specifically called for in the appeals. These events are usually beneficial to the PSYOP program and national objectives. Sources of indirect indicators include radio communications, newspapers, and other publications. They also include captured documents, opponent propaganda, in-depth interviews, and other intelligence reports.

SUMMARY

7-58. Pretests using samples can determine the effects of products or symbols on a TA, and demographic data on foreign TAs can be acquired. Pretests conducted with EPWs, refugees, defectors, or civilian detainees indicate what lines of persuasion will be effective, what to emphasize, and what to avoid. After pretesting, PSYOP personnel make the required changes to the product and forward a copy of the prototype PSYOP product along with the PAWs, to higher HQ for approval.

7-59. Impact assessment and posttesting allow PSYOP units to determine the effectiveness of products and actions by using a deliberate and systematic evaluation process. Posttesting may uncover why the TA responded in a certain way. For this reason, PSYOP units should posttest all PSYOP products after the products have been disseminated. The data collection techniques used for pretesting also apply to posttesting.

Chapter 8

Tactical PSYOP Functions and Organization

To capture the enemy's entire army is better than to destroy it...
for to win one hundred victories in one hundred battles is not the
supreme of excellence. To subdue the enemy without fighting is the
supreme excellence.

Sun Tzu
The Art of War, 510 B.C.

Tactical PSYOP units organize, plan, and execute operations in support of SOF and conventional forces. They convey selected information and actions in the AO to influence the TA's behavior in favor of the tactical commander's objectives.

TACTICAL PSYOP BATTALION

8-1. The TPB conducts operational- and tactical-level PSYOP at corps level and below, and can support an Army-level or equivalent Marine forces HQ. The TPB staff and elements of the companies conduct planning and operations at the operational and tactical levels for the Army, corps, or division. Rarely does an entire tactical battalion deploy and, in most cases, its component parts are attached to other army units. The tactical PSYOP company will, therefore, be the focus of this chapter.

8-2. Before discussing the details of the TPC, the importance of staff integration to supporting maneuver commanders must be stressed. Due to the varying nature of missions that the TPC supports, there is a tremendous amount of importance on the initial meeting between the PSYOP leader and supported unit. This meeting includes the TPC commander at the division level all the way down to the staff sergeant at the battalion level. This initial meeting will set the tone of the entire relationship and therefore must be polished, professional, and cover several critical areas. These areas include, but are not limited to, capabilities (not only the element the PSYOP leader is representing, but also PSYOP in general), support required from the supported unit, and current status of the supporting unit. A positive initial meeting will lead to successful integration and make mission accomplishment that much easier. When possible, the supporting PSYOP element should work with and integrate themselves with the supported unit for training prior to deployment. This chapter will discuss the various elements of the TPC and focus on the role that each plays when employed in an operational status.

TACTICAL PSYOP COMPANY

8-3. The TPC is the centerpiece of PSYOP support to maneuver commanders. The TPC provides the maneuver commander with the ability to influence, either directly or indirectly, the behavioral responses among neutral, friendly, and enemy TAs. It can develop, produce, and disseminate tactical-level products within the guidance assigned by the approval authority.

8-4. The TPC typically supports component commanders at the division level and falls under the operational control of the G-3; however, during some SOF missions a TPC can support a brigade-sized element, such as a Special Forces group. The TPC consists of a company HQ section, a TPDD, and three TPDs.

8-5. The TPC HQ section usually works as a support element at the division level, along with the TPDD. The TPD works as a support element at the brigade level, while TPTs can be attached to battalions to provide direct support or be retained at the brigade level to provide general support.

COMPANY HEADQUARTERS

8-6. The company HQ section is comprised of the commander; first sergeant; supply sergeant; nuclear, biological, and chemical (NBC) specialist; and commander's driver and clerk. The company HQ plays a limited role operationally with the exception of the commander who ensures execution of the commander's intent and advises the supported commander. The HQ section is responsible for accomplishing several critical functions. They provide all logistic and administrative functions for the company; common Army items are provided by the supported unit. The HQ section facilitates the distribution of products to the TPD and exercises battle tracking of PSYOP personnel. The commander is responsible for submitting a SITREP that combines the information from each detachment, while the first sergeant ensures the health and welfare of all company Soldiers.

TACTICAL PSYOP DEVELOPMENT DETACHMENT

8-7. The TPDD is a 13-Soldier detachment (DET), which provides PSYOP staff planning, TAA, product development, and limited production to division-sized units. The TPDD consists of three teams—the PPT, the TAAT, and the PDT (Figure 8-1, page 8-3).

Plans and Programs Team

8-8. The PPT is the center for action in the TPDD. The PPT consists of two officers, an operations NCO, team leader, and assistant team leader. The PPT conducts mission analysis, PSYOP assessments, and MDMP to provide PSYOP input to COA development. The members facilitate product approval, track and supervise all product development, and maintain contact with the POTF or PSE. PPT members provide guidance to the TPDD sections concerning product development. The PPT also advises the commander and supported G-3 regarding product dissemination. Personnel and primary duties of the PPT are discussed in the following paragraphs.

8-9. **Officer in Charge.** The OIC is responsible for ensuring that PSYOP is fully integrated into all aspects of the supported unit's mission. He analyzes the supported unit's mission and provides input into how PSYOP can support the unit's COA. The OIC participates in the supported unit's targeting meetings and identifies PSYOP priorities. He identifies POs, as well as themes and symbols to be stressed or avoided (only done if the supported unit is the highest element in the mission; otherwise, these will be received from higher HQ). The OIC assists the J-3 or S-3 in preparation of the PSYOP estimate, annex, or plan to the OPORD, as needed.

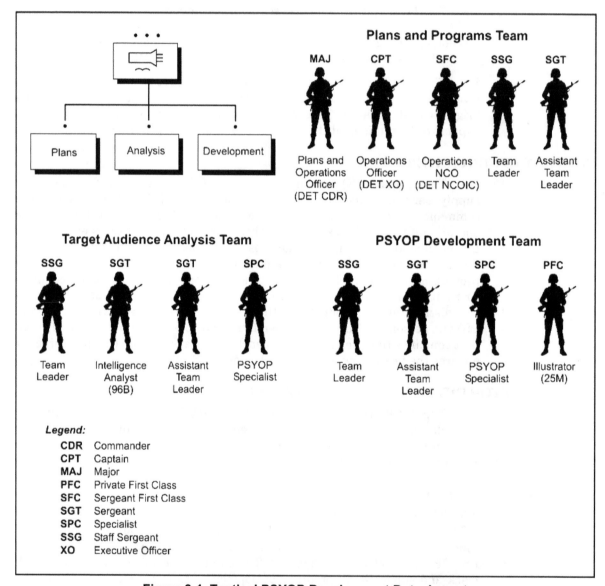

Figure 8-1. Tactical PSYOP Development Detachment

8-10. Operations Officer. The operations officer oversees and manages all operations within the TPDD. Additionally, the TPDD operations officer integrates with the S-2 analysis and control element to monitor all PSYOP IRs and PIR, and is responsible for the archiving of all information related to the TA. The TPDD operations officer serves as the primary link with other PSYOP elements. He also reviews the TAA of the TAAD. The operations officer assists the OIC and executes the duties as the PDD OIC in his absence.

8-11. **Noncommissioned Officer in Charge.** The NCOIC assists the OIC with analyzing the supported unit mission and PSYOP planning. The NCOIC monitors and coordinates with subordinate elements to determine product development priorities and oversees the product development process and assigns each product a tracking number. The NCOIC develops and supervises the TPDD training program. He also conducts liaison with higher-level PSYOP elements, ensuring mutually supportive PSYOP activities.

8-12. **Team Leader.** The PPT team leader assists the NCOIC with the monitoring of subordinate units. The team leader develops the SPOs and identifies potential TAs and available forms of media. The team leader coordinates air operations for movement, leaflet drops, aerial loudspeaker operations, and product support to the TPDs.

8-13. **Assistant Team Leader.** The PSYOP sergeant assists the PPT chief with his responsibilities and is responsible for the battle tracking of all friendly and enemy PSYOP-relevant information in the supported unit's area of influence. The PSYOP sergeant determines the viability of leaflet missions by calculating and mapping leaflet drop patterns. He is also responsible for the setup of the PPT and establishment of communications to all PSYOP elements.

Target Audience Analysis Team

8-14. The TAAT reviews and finalizes the PTAL received from the PPT. The TAAT then analyzes each TA for its conditions, attitudes, beliefs, vulnerabilities, and susceptibilities. TAAT members combine efforts with the TAAD of the PDC to complete a detailed TAA. The members also maintain TA files while monitoring intelligence reports to detect any shifts in attitudes, behavior trends, or conditions of the TA. The TAAT will look for any vulnerability that could be exploited by a series of PSYOP products or actions. The TAAT also analyzes opponent propaganda and conducts a more comprehensive analysis of SCAME reports initially conducted by TPT members. The TAAT must also look for propaganda, such as TV, Internet, radio, or regional news agencies. The TAAT, in concert with PDC assets, then assesses each individual SCAME to determine the opponent propaganda plan (discussed in detail in Chapter 11). The TAAT also determines suitable themes and symbols for each TA and the possible credibility of each media type. The TAAT, in TPDDs, must also fill the role of the TED. Therefore, they must write surveys and conduct pretesting. They will also conduct posttesting and track MOEs (discussed in Chapters 4 and 7). These testing responsibilities should be completed with coordination and assistance of the TED whenever possible. The TAAT is usually the section responsible for conducting aerial loudspeaker missions. Personnel and primary duties of the TAAT are discussed in the following paragraphs.

8-15. **Leader.** The TAAT leader works closely with the TPDD operations officer. He also assists the TPDD NCOIC with the TPDD training program. The TAAT leader supervises the conduct of aerial loudspeaker operations and advises the TPDD OIC on TA information needed for PSYOP planning. The TAAT leader supervises the development of pretests, posttests, and surveys. The TAAT leader also reviews TPD SITREPs to ensure that the TPDD incorporates their requests and observations into all TPDD activities.

8-16. **Intelligence Analyst.** The intelligence analyst reviews intelligence reports prepared by outside agencies for PSYOP-relevant information. He compiles all PIR and IRs from the detachment and submits them to the TPDD operations officer for review. The intelligence analyst is responsible for compiling the various conditions that affect each TA.

8-17. **Assistant Leader.** The assistant leader assists the TAAT leader with his responsibilities, assists in the refining of TAs, supervises the TAA process, and coordinates for aerial loudspeaker operations. The TAAT assistant leader also develops pretests and posttests to ensure PSYOP products, themes, and symbols will have or are having their intended effect. He is also responsible for tracking MOEs.

8-18. **PSYOP Specialist.** The PSYOP specialist conducts TAA (discussed in Chapter 5) and may help conduct aerial loudspeaker operations. The PSYOP specialist assists the intelligence sergeant with collecting information on TAs.

PSYOP Development Team

8-19. The PDT develops and produces products to support achievement of the division commander's mission objectives. The PDT has the TPDD's only illustration and graphics capability with the PDW. The PDW enables the PDT to produce text and graphic visual products to support the commander's maneuver plan. The PDT also has limited audio and audiovisual production capabilities. The PDT develops products based on guidance from the PPT and input from the TAAT. The PDT prepares and executes the production of products or coordinates their production through external assets (POTF or indigenous resources). They also manage picture archives and product archives, maintain product books, and manage TPDD translators and all product translations. Production assets and personnel are often attached to the PDT. Personnel and primary duties of the PDT are discussed in the following paragraphs.

8-20. **Leader.** The PDT leader supervises the PDT during product development and production while assisting the PDD NCOIC with the training programs. The leader monitors the maintenance of all equipment and coordinates for any 20 level maintenance that is necessary. The leader is responsible for coordinating translator support and ensuring the appropriate product is translated at the appropriate time into the correct language. The PDT leader is also responsible for quality control of all products produced by the TPDD.

8-21. **PDT Assistant Leader.** The PDT assistant leader assists the PDT leader with his duties and supervises the product development and production process. He is responsible for maintaining the product archive and product books.

8-22. **PSYOP Specialist.** The PSYOP specialist is responsible for the development and organic production of products. He is also responsible for weekly system maintenance on computers and production equipment.

8-23. **Illustrator.** The illustrator provides assistance to the PSYOP development process by providing graphics and illustrations for products. The illustrator assists during the development process on product layouts and product production with organic assets. He is also responsible for maintaining the picture archive.

8-24. The TPDD operates in a similar fashion to a PDC on a smaller scale. Many of the duties mentioned in this section are discussed in greater detail in previous chapters. The support that the TPDD gives a division is crucial for supporting maneuver commanders; however, many products do not reach the TA without the TPD.

TACTICAL PSYOP DETACHMENT

8-25. The TPD is a 13-Soldier detachment commanded by a captain with a staff sergeant (sergeant first class in reserve units and in future active units) as the NCOIC. The TPD provides tactical PSYOP support to brigade-sized units or battalions when in support of Special Forces groups. The TPD is composed of a four-man HQ section and three TPTs (Figure 8-2) consisting of three Soldiers each. The HQ section conducts staff integration at the brigade level where they assist in mission analysis and COA development. The TPD determines dissemination priorities and is responsible for tracking the dissemination of products. They maintain communications and conduct C4I of all their TPTs. The TPD maintains constant communications with the TPDD and POTF or PSE, forwarding information that the TPTs obtain during operations. The TPD has no product development capability and therefore receives their products from higher HQ. The HQ section of the TPD compiles all TPT SITREPs and sends a detachment SITREP to the PSYOP company HQ.

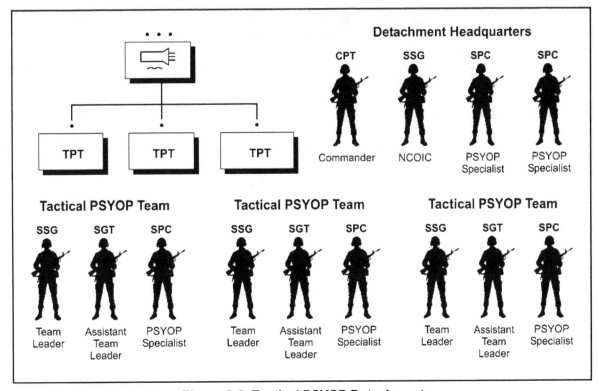

Figure 8-2. Tactical PSYOP Detachment

Tactical PSYOP Team

8-26.   The TPT is a three-man team commanded by a staff sergeant. The TPT provides tactical PSYOP planning and dissemination support to battalion-sized units. The TPT's primary purpose is to integrate and execute tactical PSYOP into the supported battalion commander's maneuver plan. The TPT must also advise the battalion commander and staff on the psychological effects of their operations on the TA in their AO and answer all PSYOP-related questions. The TPT can conduct loudspeaker operations, face-to-face communication, dissemination of approved audio, audiovisual, and printed materials. They are instrumental in the gathering of PSYOP-relevant information, conducting town or area assessments, observing impact indicators, and gathering pretesting and posttesting data. TPTs also conduct interviews with the TA. They take pictures and document cultural behavior for later use in products. TPTs often play a role in establishing rapport with foreign audiences and identifying key communicators that can be used to achieve U.S. national objectives.

8-27.   The TPT is in many ways the most crucial link to the entire PSYOP process. They are typically in continuous contact with the TA and thus have the ability to assess their impact immediately. The feedback they give to the TPD and maneuver commander will often determine the overall success of PSYOP in any given AOR. This is especially true in stability operations where PSYOP, as discussed later in this chapter, have a major role. Several functions of a TPT that are critical to ensuring tactical PSYOP mission accomplishment are discussed in the following paragraphs.

8-28.   **Capabilities Brief.** The capabilities brief is often the first time that a supported brigade, battalion, or company commander is exposed to PSYOP. The essential element of TPD or TPT integration is the capabilities brief. When done effectively, it will quickly gain the supported unit commander's attention and his willingness to have PSYOP support in his AOR. A well-thought-out, tailored, and timely capabilities brief should be directed to the supported unit commander, his S-3, and his XO as soon as possible on arrival to the supported unit. The TPD or TPT leader should, however, be prepared to deliver his brief to any member of the staff. The TPD or TPT leader should always have a briefing prepared to suit the type of unit, mission, and AOR he will support. Prior to deploying to the AOR, there may be time to give a detailed capabilities brief; however, more often than not, there is insufficient time for an in-depth briefing. Often, the TPD or TPT leader will link up with a supported unit that is already in the AOR conducting missions. The supported unit commander and his staff will be consumed with current operations and may have limited time to integrate PSYOP into his staff. The TPD or TPT leader should therefore shorten his brief without compromising effectiveness. The TPD or TPT leader must ensure that the supported commander receives the information he needs to understand and utilize tactical PSYOP effectively. An example that has proven to be effective with maneuver commanders stresses the following three points:

- Tactical PSYOP can increase the supported unit commander's ability to maneuver on the battlefield by reducing or minimizing civilian interference.

- Tactical PSYOP can potentially reduce the number of casualties suffered by the supported unit by reducing the number of enemy forces he must face through surrender appeals and cease resistance messages.

- Tactical PSYOP can assist the supported unit commander in gaining the tactical advantage on the battlefield through the use of deception measures, allowing the commander to have the element of surprise.

8-29. **Occupation of a Broadcast Position (Mounted/Dismounted).** There are several considerations a TPT must be aware of to successfully occupy a broadcast position. The team leader (TL) should begin by obtaining a map of the potential broadcast area (1:50,000 scale) and the location of the TA to be affected. The TL selects the potential broadcast position based on terrain, distance to target, and environmental conditions. He also selects a location in which to conduct a temporary halt prior to the broadcast position. The TL must also assess potential security threats based on a map reconnaissance and intelligence updates. Once the broadcast position is selected, the TL coordinates with the supported unit for security. TPTs should always go out on combat operations with a security element provided by the supported unit when possible. A TPT has only a limited amount of organic weapons systems to defend itself against a hostile force. The team should then determine the best route to the broadcast area and check the engineer map and mine overlay of known routes in the AO. The TL will inform the unit commander of the broadcast position and selected route to prevent fratricide. Once permission to initiate movement has been granted by the supported unit, the TPT begins movement to the broadcast position.

8-30. A temporary halt is conducted prior to reaching the broadcast position. The TPT establishes security and the TL then gets out of the vehicle (if mounted) while the assistant team leader (ATL) mans the M249. The driver (if mounted, or PSYOP specialist if dismounted) observes terrain and maintains security always considering the best evacuation route if the team is engaged. The TL then reconfirms the planned broadcast position's suitability and calls in new coordinates if he changes location from the original determination (the TL asks himself if it is better to broadcast from a remote position). Once the position is confirmed, the TL gives the order to prepare for broadcast.

8-31. The next step is for the ATL to power up the system and notify the TL that he is ready to broadcast. The TPT then moves forward and occupies its broadcast position using the route that gives the most cover and concealment possible. The driver (PSYOP specialist when dismounted) scans the sector maintaining situational awareness at all times. Once the TPT occupies the broadcast position, the TL reports to higher HQ. The TL must verify target area, assess wind and other environmental factors, and then direct the ATL to sight the loudspeaker cones in the proper direction for the target area to receive the message. Once the ATL sights the cones, the TL reports to higher HQ that they are in position and requests permission to broadcast. The TPT maintains 360-degree security throughout the entire process. During and after the broadcast, the TPT should monitor for impact indicators. The team should also maintain communications with higher HQ throughout the entire broadcast.

8-32. **Face-to-Face Communication.** Prior to conducting a face-to-face mission, the TL must confirm the local threat and impact of prior operations or dissemination by coordinating with the battalion S-2 or company commander of the supported unit. The TL should know the name of the village or town leader, if possible. The TL and the security element should do a face to face with the leader as a means to ease dissemination within the area. The TL also coordinates with any friendly or adjacent units within the AO to ensure that ongoing operations will not adversely affect the mission. The TL determines the disseminator (usually himself), security (usually the ATL), recorder (usually the PSYOP specialist), and translator (usually a native speaker) for the mission. The TPT determines security posture, informs supported unit of operating location, and performs communications checks prior to the mission to minimize any possibility of fratricide. The disseminator and translator should discuss potential topics, articulate clear meaning of certain key words or phrases, and establish certain parameters prior to the mission.

8-33. Once all premission planning and coordination has occurred, the disseminator and linguist will conduct dissemination in a nonthreatening manner. Regardless of the uniform required by the supported unit, a smile and approachable attitude are disarming techniques. The individual pulling security constantly monitors the surrounding environment analyzing the threat to the disseminator and general perceptions and attitudes. The TL must continually assess the security posture throughout the engagement. The individual who records, documents, takes photos, or videos for future products must also maintain situational awareness and security responsibilities. In the event propaganda is encountered, the PSYOP specialist prepares an initial SCAME, as outlined in Chapter 11, and forwards it to the TPD as soon as possible.

8-34. **Reaction to Civil Disturbance Using the Graduated Response Method.** If the TPT finds itself surrounded, the TL attempts to first discuss the situation or grievance with the key communicator or agitator. Effective use of the interpreter is essential during this attempt at diffusing the situation. If unsuccessful, the TL attempts to reason with known sympathetic individuals. If the TA poses a threat to personnel or USG property, the TL implements the graduated response techniques IAW the ROE. The TPT maintains security and communication throughout the entire process. Upon mission completion, the TL forwards a SITREP that summarizes his discussion and notes any impact indicators.

8-35. If the face-to-face communication is not well received by the TA, the TL determines whether to continue and if any additional security measures need to be taken. If the TA grows hostile and no local maneuver elements are present, then the TPT should attempt to leave the area.

8-36. If mounted, the TL ensures all doors and hatches on the vehicle are secured. A security person should remain with the vehicle at all times in the objective area. If an interpreter is present, the TL should use him to issue commands to the TA. Noninterference messages should be used. The TPT should attempt to maneuver out of the area by way of the quickest route available. The family of loudspeakers (FOL) (vehicle-mounted loudspeaker system) may be used to facilitate retrograde movement. The siren, trill, or other loud, irritating noises may be used to assist in clearing a path in a nonlethal manner. The supported unit and higher HQ must be notified of the situation and the route being utilized.

8-37. If dismounted, the TPT must retrograde out of the area as quickly as possible. The supported unit and higher HQ must be contacted immediately so that assistance can be provided. Security is paramount and must be maintained at all times. The supported unit and higher HQ must be kept informed of the route being utilized.

8-38. When being deployed to a situation that is deteriorating into a disturbance, the TL should quickly reiterate the ROE to his team and conduct linkup with the supported commander, as necessary. He should then receive an update on the current situation from the supported unit and establish liaison with other quick-reaction force (QRF) or graduated response measure (GRM) components, as required. The team should assess the situation on the ground, maintain communications with higher HQ, and submit SITREPs, as required. The TPT should maintain security at all times, regardless of whether or not another element is present. During the initial stages of the disturbance, the team monitors and attempts to identify facts and assumptions about the TA (crowd). The TPT uses the following questions as a guide to get as complete a picture as possible of the disturbance:

- Identify the key communicator or lead agitator. What is his message?
- What is the general attitude or behavior of the group?
- How many people are present in the group?
- What are the demographics (age and gender)?
- What is the cultural composition of the group?
- What language are they speaking?
- How are they moving (mounted or dismounted)?
- Are signs or banners present and, if so, what is the message?
- Is there any media on site? If so, identify whom they represent.
- Are there any weapons present among the demonstrators?
- Who else is present at the location (police, elected public officials, NGOs, CA, other forces)?
- Is the group from that location or have they come from another location? If from another location, where and why?
- How did the people know or hear about the gathering, rally, or demonstration?
- What are their underlying grievances or stated objectives for the event?

Once these questions are answered, the team will have a fairly well-documented picture of the situation.

8-39. The team should then consult the specified and implied tasks of the supported unit (commander's intent, scheme of maneuver, and coordinating instructions) to see how this disturbance fits into the command guidance. The TPT must know the preapproved lines of persuasion and objectives, resources available to address the needs and grievances of the crowd, and the ROE. The

TL should consider conducting face-to-face communication with the key communicator in an isolated area as this, many times, is the most successful approach to diffusing a crowd situation. The TPT should be prepared to create a message for broadcast, if needed.

8-40. When the commander directs the TPT to broadcast in this environment, the team should adhere to the following guidelines:

- Give simple directions that are clear and concise.
- Always maintain composure.
- When constructing messages, avoid using the word "please" so the team does not display a passive appearance.
- Do not issue ultimatums that are not approved by the commander.
- If the commander does approve an ultimatum, ensure that the crowd has time to conform to its conditions.
- Ensure that the supported commander is prepared to act upon his ultimatum should the crowd fail to respond favorably.
- Use approved lines of persuasion when possible, and conduct impromptu broadcasting only as a last resort.
- Always conduct rehearsals with the translator prior to going "live" unless the situation makes this absolutely impossible.
- Ensure the gender and other social aspects of the translator are credible in the eyes of the TA.
- Always attempt to pick a broadcast position that communicates with the crowd effectively and does not compromise the security of the team.
- Direct the broadcast toward the primary agitators.
- Limit the volume of the broadcast so as not to be overbearing, and do not harass the crowd as this will only exacerbate the situation.

8-41. The team must maintain communication with the supported commander or his representative on the ground throughout the situation. The TL also ensures that PSYOP-relevant information, HUMINT, and PIR are forwarded through appropriate channels.

8-42. **Interview.** TPTs conduct interviews to obtain PSYOP-relevant information or as part of compiling pretest and posttest data. There are a number of things to consider when conducting an interview. The TPT begins by selecting a suitable location that is conducive for an interview and isolated from other TA members. The TL must conduct the interview IAW FM 27-10, *The Law of Land Warfare*, and often must employ the use of a translator. The TL normally is the interviewer, the ATL is the recorder, and the PSYOP specialist serves as an observer. The interviewer needs to practice the questions with the translator prior to the actual interview. The TL must always ensure that the person being interviewed knows which individual is conducting the interview and to whom his responses should be directed. All TPT members should adhere to local customs to facilitate a comfortable environment for the interviewee. The interviewer needs to maintain eye-to-eye contact with the individual being interviewed throughout the entire process. Gaining answers to the following points are not inclusive; however, those that are applicable will elicit a large amount of information:

- Name.
- Age.
- Group with which the interviewee identifies.
- Branch of service.
- Birthplace.
- Years in military.
- Education level.
- How captured or detained (motivation to cooperate or cease resistance).
- Relative status (power, wealth, rank) in group (may be ascertained by clothes or possessions).

After establishing the above-stated basic demographic information, the interviewer then attempts to obtain PSYOP-specific information by asking the following questions:

- How was the information received (radio, TV, newspaper, word of mouth)?
- Have you seen, read, or heard PSYOP information (name particular products in question)?
- How was the particular product perceived (solicit TA's individual perception and their believed perception of how others accepted the message and presentation)?
- Did the product motivate your actions?
- Was the language and dialect understandable?
- Were the messages effective or believable?
- Are the messages believed or thought of as propaganda?

8-43. During this process, the interviewer needs to adjust his personality or behavior as appropriate (compassionate or stern, as required). Prior to finishing the interview, the TL must verify that the information collected and recorded are the interviewee's answers and not the recorder's opinion. The TL then ensures that the information is forwarded to intelligence (S-2), TAAD, or other necessary agencies.

8-44. Using these techniques will allow a TPT to safely conduct some of their critical tasks. A TPT that is able to disseminate products, establish rapport, acquire testing data, diffuse potential disturbances, and interact with the TA will be an asset to any maneuver commander. To ensure that a TPT is ready to conduct their critical tasks, the following checklists are provided that TLs may find helpful.

8-45. As with all military operations, precombat inspections (PCIs) are instrumental to mission success. The following (Figure 8-3, pages 8-13 and 8-14) is a guide to areas that should be addressed. This guide is not inclusive and may be tailored to each TPT and mission needs.

1. **Individual Preparation for a Mission.**

   a. Seasonal uniform worn according to climate and mission along with load-bearing equipment (LBE) properly assembled and serviceable.

   b. Briefed on current mission or situation.

   c. Briefed on prevention of hot and cold weather injuries. Previous hot or cold weather injuries identified and properly marked.

   d. Supported unit SOP and packing list.

2. **Vehicles.**

   a. Current, valid preventive maintenance checks and services (PMCS) and properly dispatched.

   b. Operator's manual for PMCS on hand.

   c. Pioneer tools complete, stored properly, clean and serviceable.

   d. Tools and tool bag complete.

   e. Loaded according to loading plan.

   f. TA-50 loaded per loading plan.

   g. Fuel tanks no less than 3/4 full.

   h. Fuel cans full (2).

   i. Water cans full (2).

   j. Fire extinguishers mounted, sealed, tagged, updated and serviceable.

   k. MRE rations.

   l. First aid kits complete.

   m. Combat lifesaver (CLS) bag complete.

   n. M249 squad automatic weapon (SAW) properly mounted and with ammunition, if applicable.

   o. Advanced System Improvement Program (ASIP) radios (2) with current fill, operational and properly mounted.

   p. Global positioning system (GPS) mounted and functional to the AO.

   q. Additional (2) hand microphones.

   r. Additional batteries for dismounted operations.

3. **PSYOP-Specific Equipment.**

   a. Mounted operations (see technical manual [TM] for further details).

      (1) FOL complete and operational:
      - Low-frequency (LF) speaker cover.
      - Low-frequency module (LFM).
      - High-frequency (HF) speaker cover.
      - HF speaker array.
      - HF array support tray.
      - Control module assembly.
      - Recorder/reproducer.
      - Amplifier array assembly.
      - Speaker stand assembly.
      - HF speaker cables (15 foot [ft] and 50 ft).

Figure 8-3. General Mission Inspection Checklist

- LF speaker cables (15 ft and 50 ft).
- Control cables (6 ft and 25 ft).
- Single-channel ground and airborne radio system (SINCGARS) adapter cable (6 ft).
- System power cable, vehicle.
- Amplifier mounting base.
- Guard assembly, amplifier.
- Loudspeaker, interface, vehicle.

   (2) Additional batteries for mini-disk player and tape player.

   (3) Additional mini-disks and cassette tapes.

   (4) PSYOP products (sounds, leaflets, posters, and so on) present.

   (5) M256A1 kit complete.

   (6) M274 marking kit complete.

   (7) M9 tape (1 roll).

   (8) MP3 player.

b. Dismounted operations (see TM for further detail).

   (1) Tactical loudspeaker manpack (40C) complete and operational:
- Speaker array assembly.
- Amplifier/battery box.
- Control module assembly.
- Recorder/reproducer.
- Speaker cable (3 ft).
- SINCGARS radio adapter cable (6 ft).
- Control cable (6 ft).
- System interconnect cable (25 ft).
- Remote control cable (25 ft).
- Speaker extension cable (50 ft).
- Field pack.
- BA 5590 batteries (3).

   (2) ASIP radios operational with current fill.

   (3) Long and short whip antennas.

   (4) Additional (2) hand microphones.

   (5) Additional AA batteries for mini-disk player and tape player.

   (6) Additional mini-disks and cassette tapes.

   (7) Additional BA 5590 batteries.

   (8) PSYOP products (sounds, leaflets, posters, and so on) present.

   (9) CLS bag complete.

   (10) M256A1 kit complete.

   (11) M274 marking kit complete.

   (12) M9 tape (1 roll).

c. Mounted tactical radio operations.

Figure 8-3. General Mission Inspection Checklist (Continued)

8-46. Once all equipment is inventoried, there are several steps required to ensure equipment is mission-capable. The following (Figure 8-4) are steps to mount and test the vehicle FOL system. The steps to connect, test, and transport the manpack loudspeaker system (MPLS) are shown in Figure 8-5, pages 8-16 and 8-17.

---

1. Mount LFM to vehicle wing (gunner's turret) ensuring all screws are firmly secure. (**NOTE:** This procedure is a two-man lift.)

2. Detach shock plate from the high-frequency module (HFM). Make sure shock plate is stored securely (vehicle, cages, container express [CONEX]).

3. Attach the HFM to the LFM ensuring that all screws are firmly secure.

4. Mount vehicle amp into vehicle making sure that it is seated properly and all the screws are firmly secured. (**NOTE:** This procedure is a two-man lift.)

5. Connect LFM cable to the LFM amp slot (5-prong female end and 6-prong male end on amp).

6. Connect the HFM cable to the amp. Cable is identified as Amp 1, Amp 2, and Amp 3.

7. Connect the power from the direct current (DC) input to the North Atlantic Treaty Organization (NATO) adapter located under the track commander (TC) seat. Ensure that the power switch is selected to the off position.

8. Connect the control module to the control located on the amp.

9. Test the system. The operator—
   - Turns power switch to on. The operator will note that the lights flash on the control box.
   - Making sure that the volume is at the lowest level, initiates the wail function on the control module. The operator presses and holds the low button on the control module until the volume reads no volume.
   - Presses the high button until the (1) volume bar is showing.
   - Presses the function button and holds; the operator presses select button once then lets go of function. This process will enable the wail system.
   - Warns anyone in front of the speakers that they are about to broadcast.
   - Presses the speaker on/off button once on the control module.
   - Ensures that all speakers work. The speaker system is now operational and ready for PSYOP operations.

10. Turn the speaker off by pressing the on/off button once on the control module.

11. Power down the amp.

12. Place the inclement weather cover on the speaker array. This step is done at all times to protect the speakers and the LFM.

NOTE: Drivers need to be aware that the vehicle is now top heavy. They have an additional five (5) feet on top of the vehicle, therefore caution must be taken when driving in heavily vegetated areas or making quick turns.

Figure 8-4. FOL System Checklist

1. Inventory loudspeaker system and conduct system checks.

    a. Insert 3 x BA5590 batteries into the battery box being careful not to damage socket pins.

    b. Ensure spare batteries are serviceable.

    c. Connect all cables tightly at the appropriate connection.

    d. Energize the system (turn toggle switch to "on").

    e. Face speaker away from microphone and away from operator.

    f. Adjust control module assembly:

        (1) Microphone:

- Review script.
- Turn speakers on.
- Adjust volume.
- Talk into the microphone and read message.
- Turn speakers off.

        (2) Digital voice recorder (DVR):

- Record multiple messages.
- Listen to messages (on headset).
- Turn speakers on.
- Adjust volume.
- Play each message (not necessarily in order).
- Put one message on loop.
- Turn speakers off.

        (3) Wail:

- Turn speakers on.
- Turn on wail.
- Adjust volume.
- Turn speakers off.

        (4) Recorder (cassette, mini-disk, CD):

- Cue cassette, mini-disk, or CD.
- Turn speakers on.
- Adjust volume.
- Play message.
- Turn speakers off.

    g. Utilize wireless remote. Test from at least 50 meters away.

    h. Connect (daisy chain) two or more speakers together.

    i. Play message from SINCGARS radio (at least 100 meters away).

2. Pack MPLS in field pack.

    a. The MPLS must be padded sufficiently to avoid damage during normal operations. Specifically, pad and protect the following areas:

- Amp/battery box. Critical parts are the switches and knobs.

Figure 8-5. MPLS Checklist

- Speakers.
- Cable connections.
- Control module assembly.
- Mini-disk/cassette recorders.

b. Padding must be enhanced for airborne and/or fast-rope operations.

c. The on/off switch must be accessible.

d. The control module assembly must be accessible.

e. The speakers must be packed so that they can still broadcast (the bottom of the field pack unzipped [speakers exposed], secured with straps).

NOTE: It is critical to turn down the volume before turning the speakers on and off for both the MPLS and FOL. Failure to do so will cause a "pop" sound, violating noise discipline. Also, if volume is high when power is applied, the speaker may become permanently damaged.

Figure 8-5. MPLS Checklist (Continued)

8-47. Once Soldiers are ready and equipment has been tested, there are a couple of considerations that must be made prior to conducting a mission. The chances that a mission will require a native-speaking translator or include an encounter with the media are extremely high and therefore must always be considered.

8-48. **Native-Speaking Translators.** A detailed discussion about translators is provided in Appendix H; however, a TPT must make these considerations at the very minimum:

- Integrate the translators into the detachment or team prior to using them on a mission; make them feel welcome and comfortable, and always do several rehearsals with them.
- Know their strengths and weaknesses. For example—
  - Are they good at simultaneous translation?
  - Are they stronger conversationally or with written texts?
  - How is their grammar?
  - Can they translate under pressure or stress?
  - Do they understand complex English or must the Soldier speak very simply?
- Know their background and education level. Will talking about politics, religion, or economics confuse them?
- Be aware of any ties they may have, to include political, military, clan, and so on.
- Be aware of their dialect and if it will have a positive or negative impact on the mission to be conducted.
- Ensure translator knows what noise and light disciplines are so they do not compromise the mission.

8-49. **Guidelines on Speaking With the Media.** Speaking with the media in a forward-deployed area can be stressful; however, TPTs should follow these general guidelines set forth by the United States Army Special

Operations Command (USASOC) PAO when articulating what PSYOP is to the media:

- PSYOP is a commander's way of communicating with different groups of people in an attempt to change behaviors that support his objectives in a military theater of operations.
- There are various means that PSYOP Soldiers use to communicate a supported commander's message. Among these are leaflets, radio and loudspeaker broadcasts, face-to-face communication, and video products.
- Truth is always the most powerful tool when using PSYOP in military operations.

Figure 8-6 provides examples of PAO guidance cards.

Points to Remember When Doing Media Interviews:	What to Do When the Media Visits Your Area of Operations:
• Be relaxed, confident, and professional. • Be concise; think about what you will say before you speak. • Avoid using colorful or profane language. • Stay in your lane. Confine your discussions to areas in which you have firsthand knowledge or where you have personal experience. • Deal in facts—avoid speculation and hypothetical questions. • Label your opinions as opinions. Don't get into political discussions. • Stay on the record. If you say it, they'll print it. • You don't have to answer a question, but don't say "no comment." • Don't argue with the reporter. Be firm, be polite, but don't get emotional. • Protect the record. Correct the "facts" if they are wrong. • Speak plainly. Don't use military slang or jargon. • Don't discuss classified information.	• Do not threaten the media representative. • Politely move the media to an area out of harm's way where they do not interfere with the performance of the mission. • Notify the senior person present so he can determine what the media wants. • Cooperate with the reporter within the limits of OPSEC and safety. • If there are OPSEC or safety concerns that make the interview or filming impossible at this time, let the reporter know up front. • At no time should a media representative's equipment be confiscated. If you feel a security violation has occurred, notify your change of command. • If you have problems with the media, report the incident through the chain of command to the area public affairs officer.

Figure 8-6. Examples of PAO Guidance Cards

8-50. PSYOP Soldiers should always consult the PAO guidance for the specific operation they are currently involved in, as well as these general guidelines.

8-51. **PSYOP-Relevant Information.** Perhaps the most important mission for TPT members is gathering PSYOP-relevant information. Tactical PSYOP Soldiers are often in direct contact with the TA, giving the Soldiers the opportunity to obtain specific and accurate information. This contact is a critical link to the PSYOP development process, and when done correctly will help to ensure the success of programs. Tactical PSYOP elements continuously assess the PSYOP situation in the AO to determine effects of the programs on friendly, enemy, and neutral TAs. Gathering PSYOP-relevant information includes, but is not limited to—

- Conducting pretesting and posttesting of PSYOP products, themes, and symbols (Chapter 7).
- Conducting PSYOP area assessments.
- Casual contact and conversation with local populations.
- Observations of living and work conditions and attitude of local populations.
- Examining information from local television, newspapers, radio, and other media.
- Identifying and communicating with key communicators whether they are teachers, principals, religious figures, town elders, or prominent businessmen.
- Conducting interviews with EPWs/CIs/DCs. There is one PSYOP battalion structured specifically for this purpose; however, all PSYOP Soldiers have the ability to assist in this process.

8-52. PSYOP Soldiers must always be aware of the CCIR and PSYOP PIR so they can pass this information on when observed. PSYOP-relevant information must be passed from TPTs to higher echelons as quickly as possible for adjustments to be made to the appropriate program. Attitudes and conditions affecting a TA can change, which makes PSYOP-relevant information highly time sensitive. One means TPTs use to gather and organize PSYOP-relevant information is the area assessment.

8-53. **PSYOP Area Assessment.** This assessment provides detailed information that is useful for the TPT once they arrive in an area and is critical to the TPDD, especially the TAAT. All of this information will not always be applicable; however, as much detail as possible will be extremely valuable for developing effective programs and is critical in the TAA process (Figure 8-7, pages 8-19 through 8-24).

AREA ASSESSMENT FORMAT   DTG_____

1. PURPOSE AND LIMITING FACTORS.

    a. Purpose. Delineate the area being studied.

    b. Mission. State the mission the area study supports.

    c. Limiting Factors. Identify factors that limit the completeness or accuracy of the area study.

2. GEOGRAPHY, HYDROGRAPHY, AND CLIMATE. Divide the operational area into its various definable subdivisions and analyze each subdivision using the subdivisions shown below.

    a. Areas and Dimensions.

Figure 8-7. Example of Area Assessment Format

b. Strategic Locations.

    (1) Neighboring countries and boundaries.

    (2) Natural defenses including frontiers.

    (3) Points of entry and strategic routes.

c. Climate. Note variations from the norm and the months in which they occur. Note any extremes in climate that would affect operations.

    (1) Temperature.

    (2) Rainfall and snow.

    (3) Wind and visibility.

    (4) Light data. Include beginning morning nautical twilight (BMNT), ending evening nautical twilight (EENT), sunrise, sunset, moonrise, and moonset.

    (5) Seasonal effect of the weather on terrain and visibility.

d. Relief.

    (1) General direction of mountain ranges or ridgelines and whether hills and ridges are dissected.

    (2) General degree of slope.

    (3) Characteristics of valleys and plains.

    (4) Natural routes for, and natural obstacles to, cross-country movement.

    (5) Location of area suitable for guerrilla bases, units, and other installations.

    (6) Potential landing zones (LZs) and drop zones (DZs) and other reception sites.

e. Land Use. Note any peculiarities especially in the following:

    (1) Former heavily forested areas subjected to widespread cutting or disconnected bypaths and roads. Also note the reverse, pastureland or wasteland that has been reforested.

    (2) Former wasteland or pastureland that has been resettled and cultivated and is now being farmed. Also note the reverse, former rural countryside that has been depopulated and allowed to return to wasteland.

    (3) Former swampland or marshland that has been drained; former desert or wasteland now irrigated and cultivated; and lakes created by dams.

f. Drainage (General Pattern).

    (1) Main rivers, direction of flow.

    (2) Characteristics of rivers and streams. Include widths, currents, banks, depths, kinds of bottoms, and obstacles.

    (3) Seasonal variations. Note dry beds, flash floods.

    (4) Large lakes or areas with many ponds or swamps. Include potential LZs for amphibious aircraft.

g. Coast. Examine primarily for infiltration, exfiltration, and resupply points.

    (1) Tides and waves. Include winds and currents.

    (2) Beach footing and covered exit routes.

    (3) Quiet coves and shallow inlets or estuaries.

h. Geological Basics. Identify types of soil and rock formations. Include areas for potential LZs for light aircraft.

i. Forests and Other Vegetation.

    (1) Natural or cultivated.

    (2) Types, characteristics, and significant variations from the norm at different elevations.

    (3) Cover and concealment. Include density and seasonal variations.

Figure 8-7. Example of Area Assessment Format (Continued)

j. Water. Note ground, surface, seasonal, and potability.

k. Subsistence.

    (1) Seasonal or year round.

    (2) Cultivated. Include vegetables, grains, fruits, and nuts.

    (3) Natural. Include berries, fruits, nuts, and herbs.

    (4) Wildlife. Include animals, fish, and fowl.

3. POLITICAL CHARACTERISTICS. Identify friendly and hostile political powers and analyze their capabilities, intentions, and activities that influence mission execution.

a. Hostile Power.

    (1) Number and status of nonnational personnel.

    (2) Influence organization and mechanisms of control.

b. National Government (indigenous).

    (1) Government, international political education, and degree of popular support.

    (2) Identifiable segments of the population with varying attitudes and probable behavior toward the United States, its allies, and the hostile power.

    (3) National historical background.

    (4) Foreign dependence or alliances.

    (5) National capital and significant political, military, and economic concentrations.

c. Political Parties.

    (1) Leadership and organizational structure.

    (2) Nationalistic origin and foreign ties (if a single dominant party exists).

    (3) Major legal parties with their policies and goals.

    (4) Illegal or underground parties and their policies and goals.

    (5) Violent opposition factions within major political organizations.

d. Control and Restrictions.

    (1) Documentation.

    (2) Rationing.

    (3) Travel and movement restrictions.

    (4) Blackouts and curfews.

    (5) Political restrictions.

    (6) Religious restrictions.

4. ECONOMIC CHARACTERISTICS. Identify those economic factors that influence mission execution.

a. Technological Standards.

b. Natural Resources and Degree of Self-Sufficiency.

c. Financial Structure and Dependence on Foreign Aid.

d. Monetary System.

    (1) Value of money, rate of inflation.

    (2) Wage scales.

    (3) Currency controls.

e. Black Market Activities. Note the extent and effect of those activities.

f. Agriculture and Domestic Food Supply.

Figure 8-7. Example of Area Assessment Format (Continued)

g. Industry and Level of Production.

h. Unemployment Rate.

i. Manufacture of and Demand for Consumer Goods.

j. Foreign and Domestic Trade and Facilities.

k. Fuels and Power.

l. Telecommunications and Radio Systems.

m. Transportation Adequacy by U.S. Standards.

    (1) Railroads.

    (2) Highways.

    (3) Waterways.

    (4) Commercial air installations.

n. Industry, Utilities, Agriculture, and Transportation. Note the control and operation of each.

o. International and Nongovernmental Organizations in the Area.

5. CIVIL POPULACE. Pay particular attention to those inhabitants in the AO who have peculiarities (including importance or ability to influence others) and who vary considerably from the normal national way of life.

a. Total and Density to Include Age and Gender Breakdowns.

b. Basic Racial Stock and Physical Characteristics. Take pictures or document in some way.

    (1) Types, features, dress, and habits.

    (2) Significant variations from the norm.

c. Ethnic and/or Religious Groups. Analyze these groups to determine if they are of sufficient size, cohesion, and power to constitute a dissident minority of some consequence.

    (1) Location or concentration.

    (2) Basis for disconnect and motivation for change.

    (3) Opposition to the majority or the political regime.

    (4) Any external or foreign ties of significance.

d. Attitudes. Determine the attitudes of the populace toward the existing regime or hostile power, the resistance movement, and the United States and its allies.

e. Division Between Urban, Rural, or Nomadic Groups.

    (1) Large cities and population centers.

    (2) Rural settlement patterns.

    (3) Areas and movement patterns of nomads.

f. Standard of Living and Cultural (Educational) Levels.

    (1) Extremes away from the national average.

    (2) Schools, student attendance, and specifics of teachers and principals.

    (3) Class structure. Identify degree of established social stratification and percentage of populace in each class.

g. Health and Medical Standards.

    (1) General health and well-being.

    (2) Common diseases.

    (3) Standard of public health.

Figure 8-7. Example of Area Assessment Format (Continued)

   (4) Medical facilities and personnel.

   (5) Potable water supply.

   (6) Sufficiency of medical supplies and equipment.

  h. Tradition and Customs (Particularly Taboos). Note wherever traditions and customs are so strong and established that they may influence an individual's actions or attitude even during a war situation.

6. MILITARY AND PARAMILITARY FORCES. Identify friendly and hostile conventional military forces (Army, Navy, Air Force) and internal security forces (including border guards, local police, international police) that can influence mission execution. Analyze nonnational or hostile forces, as well as national (indigenous) forces, using the subdivisions shown below.

  a. Morale, Discipline, and Political Reliability.

  b. Personnel Strength.

  c. Organization and Basic Deployment.

  d. Uniforms and Unit Designations.

  e. Ordinary and Special Insignia.

  f. Overall Control Mechanism.

  g. Chain of Command and Communication.

  h. Leadership. Note officer and NCO corps.

  i. Nonnational Surveillance and Control Over Indigenous Security Forces.

  j. Training and Doctrine.

  k. Tactics. Note seasonal and terrain variations.

  l. Equipment, Transportation, and Degree of Mobility.

  m. Logistics.

  n. Effectiveness. Note any unusual capabilities or weaknesses.

  o. Vulnerabilities in the Internal Security System.

  p. Past and Current Reprisal Actions.

  q. Use and Effectiveness of Informers.

  r. Influence on and Relations With the Local Populace.

  s. Psychological Vulnerabilities.

  t. Recent and Current Unit Activities.

  u. Counterinsurgency Activities and Capabilities. Pay particular attention to reconnaissance units, special troops (airborne, mountain, ranger), rotary-wing or vertical-lift aviation units, counterintelligence units, and units having a mass NBC delivery capability.

  v. Guard Posts and Wartime Security Coverage. Note the location of all known guard posts or expected wartime security coverage for all types of installations. Pay particular attention to security coverage along the main LOC (railroads, highways, and telecommunications lines) and along electrical power and petroleum, oils, and lubricants (POL) lines.

  w. Forced Labor and/or Detention Camps. Note exact location and description of the physical arrangement (particularly the security arrangements).

  x. Populace and Resources Control Measures. Note locations, types, and effectiveness of internal security controls. Include checkpoints, identification cards, passports, and travel permits.

7. RESISTANCE ORGANIZATION. Identify the organizational elements and key personalities of the resistance organization. Note each group's attitude toward the United States, the hostile power, various

Figure 8-7. Example of Area Assessment Format (Continued)

elements of the civilian populace, and friendly political groups. This information is more relevant when supporting SF groups.

a. Guerrillas.

(1) Disposition, strength, and composition.

(2) Organization, armament, and equipment.

(3) Status of training, morale, and combat effectiveness.

(4) Operations to date.

(5) Cooperation and coordination between various existing groups.

(6) Motivation of the various groups and their receptivity.

(7) Quality of senior and subordinate leadership.

(8) General health.

b. Auxiliaries and the Underground.

(1) Disposition, strength, and degree of organization.

(2) General effectiveness and type of support.

8. MEDIA. Identify all the media outlets in the area, as well as any indigenous locations that may be able to produce PSYOP products. Note their location and capabilities.

a. Television.

(1) Identification of each station that is received and its approximate listener.

(2) Programming (independent or state run).

(3) Location, height of antenna, and power of transmitter.

(4) Broadcasting days and times.

(5) Name and background information of any station owner, manager, or journalist.

b. Radio.

(1) Identification of each station that can be received and the primary type of programming.

(2) Programming (independent or state run).

(3) Location, height of antenna, and power of transmitter.

(4) Broadcasting days, times, and frequencies.

(5) Name and background information of any station owner, manager, or journalist.

c. Newspapers.

(1) Name.

(2) Circulation.

(3) Political affiliation.

d. Facilities That Can Produce Any Media.

(1) Location.

(2) Capabilities.

(3) Name and background information of owner, manager, or journalist.

Figure 8-7. Example of Area Assessment Format (Continued)

8-54. TPTs must ensure these area assessments are as complete as possible and forward them up the chain of command so they can be incorporated into higher planning and shared with intelligence sections benefiting all levels of command.

8-55. There is a media guide in Chapter 3 that gives guidance about assessing any media agency; however, TPTs assess radio stations on almost every mission and therefore this shorter guide has been included (Figure 8-8, pages 8-25 and 8-26). This guide is a list of information required to support the TPTs' interaction with HN radio stations. This list of questions is not all-inclusive; additional questions may be necessary in some situations. Some of these questions may not be relevant to all radio stations, especially those pertaining to personal information about the radio station manager. These questions may be too sensitive to inquire about directly, especially on a first visit to the station.

---

1. What is the location of the radio station? (Town name, street name, neighborhood, universal transverse mercator (UTM) coordinates, geo coordinates, proximity to landmarks.)

2. Who is the manager, owner, or POC? (Name, professional background, languages spoken, ethnic group, tribal affiliations, family background, religion, political agenda.)

3. How can we reconnect the station manager or POC? (Telephone number, E-mail, residence.)

4. Who else can act as a facilitator in doing business with this radio station? (Village headman, political party official, and so on.)

5. What other media facilities are collocated with this radio station? (For example, a television station or audio recording studio may be in the same or adjacent buildings.)

6. What are the program times and formats? (For example, music, 0600–1000; news, 1000–1200; music, 1200–1600; talk radio, 1600–2200.)

7. What are the radio station's sources of music broadcast material? (Napster downloads, commercially purchased CDs, black market CDs, tape recordings of local artists, live performers, gifts from NGOs, and so on.)

8. What are the radio station's sources of news broadcast material? (Commercial news services, local newspapers, reporters, Internet, local journalists.)

9. What advertisers are currently doing business with the radio station? (Political parties, local businesses, NGOs, and so on.)

10. How does the radio station charge advertisers? (Barter for free airtime? Price per minute? What national currencies does the radio station accept? What form of payments does the station accept—credit cards, local checks, or cash only?)

11. What broadcast equipment does the radio station use? (CD, cassette, MP3 [manufacturer and model number]. Recommend taking a digital photograph of the radio station's broadcast equipment. We want to provide compatible media for broadcast and maybe replacement parts or upgrades; a photograph will facilitate this.)

12. What electrical power source does the radio station use? (Commercial power or generator. What type of electrical outlets is used in the radio station—American or European, 110V or 220V?)

13. What are the parameters of the radio station's electrical power supply? (Voltage, hertz [Hz], and so on.)

14. What is the reliability of the radio station's electrical power supply? (How often do blackouts and brownouts occur? Surges?)

15. Where is the radio station's antenna located? (Is the antenna collocated with the broadcast studio or is it in a remote location? [UTM, geo coordinates.])

Figure 8-8. Radio Station Assessment Guide

16. What type of antenna does the radio station use? (Dipole or single pole?)

17. What type of soil is prevalent at the antenna site? (Sand, loam, clay, gravel.)

18. What is the radio station's broadcast output? (In watts.)

19. What is the radio station manager's estimate of the broadcast footprint?

20. What nearby terrain features affect the radio station's broadcast footprint? (Mountains, steep valleys, large buildings.)

Figure 8-8. Radio Station Assessment Guide (Continued)

8-56. Reviewing specific techniques for employment of a TPT, consulting premission checklists, testing equipment, and considering translator support and media encounters will prepare a TPT for a successful mission. TPTs must remember the importance of gathering PSYOP-relevant information, and using these assessment formats as guides will allow TPTs to fulfill their critical role in all PSYOP missions regardless of the operation or supported unit. To accomplish some of the aforementioned tasks, the TPT must be able to conduct mounted operations in a variety of operational environments. There are several considerations to keep in mind when conducting mounted operations, as discussed in the following paragraphs.

Mounted Operations

8-57. TPTs often conduct mounted operations and must know the fundamentals of mounted movement using the M1114 (Armored) high mobility multipurpose wheeled vehicle (HMMWV). PSYOP teams, depending on the mission, will either be integrated with another element or will possibly be moving alone. When traveling as part of another element, the TL must be familiar with that unit's SOP. This section will identify some of the considerations a team must make prior to any mounted mission.

8-58. **Duty Descriptions.** The primary driver does the PMCS with assistance from the rest of the team. The driver—

- Assumes most of the vehicle operating duties.
- Ensures that the vehicle is topped off with fuel at the end of each movement and that the vehicle is prepared for the next movement.
- Monitors the fuel, water, and rations level for the vehicle.
- Advises the navigator of the situation before the next movement.
- Conducts the PMCS of the vehicle's communications system.

8-59. The weapons system operator is responsible for the onboard weapons system of the vehicle. Standard armament for a TPT is an M249. The weapons system operator—

- Observes for enemy activity and keeps situational awareness at all times. From his position outside and on top of the vehicle, he has the greatest field of view, and his vision is unrestricted by windows and doors.
- Communicates with the navigator and the driver to alert them to any hazards or obstacles in the path of the vehicle or enemy activity.

- Is accountable for the internal load of the vehicle.

- Ensures after each movement that the internal configuration of the vehicle is squared away, that everything is secured to the vehicle, and that essential equipment is accessible.

- Advises the vehicle commander daily on the vehicle's weapons and ammunition status.

- Ensures spare batteries are accessible in case of battery failure during movement.

- Accounts for all additional equipment that is stored in the vehicle storage bins.

8-60. The navigator/team leader must be able to determine the team's position at any time within 100 meters with a GPS or within one-quarter mile without. The navigator/team leader—

- Conducts the route planning, to include preparing the route-planning log.

- Always makes sure that the correct frequencies and crypto keys are loaded.

- Maintains communications with the supported unit and/or the higher HQ.

- Maintains the GPS and vehicle's compass.

- Monitors progress while en route; calls in all checkpoints, phase lines, and so on.

8-61. **Fundamentals of Movement.** When planning and conducting movement, the TPT must consider the below-listed fundamentals of movement to reduce chances of enemy observation and contact:

- *Cover and concealment*: Use terrain features and vegetation that offer protection from enemy observation. When using cover and concealment to its full advantage, personnel will usually need to compromise between security and speed of movement.

- *Sky lining*: Avoid sky lining. Select routes that avoid high ground that may silhouette the vehicle.

- *Choke points*: Avoid choke points. Choke points or areas where the terrain naturally channels routes are often sites for ambushes or areas that the enemy may have under observation. If a choke point proves impossible to avoid, then reconnoiter it thoroughly before moving through it.

- *Movement discipline*: Practice movement discipline. Movement discipline means adhering to your light, noise, litter, and interval rules. It also means keeping the vehicle speed slow enough so that a large dust signature is not left behind (usually 10 to 12 miles per hour on most surfaces at night, slower during the day).

- *Checkpoints*: Checkpoints are used to track rate and accuracy of movement, and as a means of informing higher HQ to the exact location of the element during movement.

- *Security*: Maintain 360-degree security at all times to avoid being taken by surprise. Unit SOP usually assigns sectors of fire to ensure 360-degree security.
- *Routes and contingencies*: Make sure all team members know the route and contingency plans.

8-62. **Methods of Travel.** There are two methods of travel in the AO. They are on existing tracks, trails, or roads, or traveling cross-country. There are advantages and disadvantages to both methods. For tracks, trails, or roads, advantages include—

- Speed of movement.
- Hard-packed trails that do not easily yield readable prints and signs of passage.
- Quietness of movement.
- Less stress on vehicles and tires.
- Easier navigation (sometimes).

Disadvantages include—

- Greater chance of being seen or compromised.
- Natural lanes of observation and fire for the enemy.
- More probable mechanical and/or manual ambushes.

The U.S. HMMWV leaves a distinctive tire trail unlike any other truck. The TPT must consider this fact during planning.

8-63. For cross-country movement, advantages include—

- Less chance of enemy observation or contact.
- More cover and concealment (usually).
- Less chance of ambush.

Disadvantages include—

- Slower rates of movement.
- More noticeable vehicle tracks and signs of passage.
- Greater tire failure and vehicle stress.
- Navigation that is more difficult. Some desert terrain is so rough that even the HMMWV has trouble traversing it faster than a man can walk.

The team must rehearse cross-country movement in terrain as close as possible to that of the target area before deployment.

8-64. **Navigational Techniques.** Navigation in desert regions is more similar to navigation at sea than in other land environments. Some of the problems associated with vehicular navigation are lack of identifiable terrain features to use as reference points, outdated maps, and difficulty in keeping a vehicle on any set bearing. To minimize these problems, the mounted team must be thoroughly versed in the four levels of mounted navigation, each level supplementing the other. These four levels of navigation are—

- Terrain association.
- Dead reckoning (DR).

- Stabilized turret alignment.
- A combination of the above.

FM 3-25.26, *Map Reading and Land Navigation*, Chapter 12, provides more information.

8-65. **Navigation Duties.** The mounted team's primary navigator/team leader is usually the most experienced at mounted operations and is also the route planner. His primary duty is to ensure that the team arrives at the appropriate destination at the right time. He accomplishes this task by—

- Detailed route planning.
- Keeping a log in which he records planned and actual time, distance, and direction. He can plot or chart this data at convenient intervals to ensure correct course and to estimate times and duration for future movements.
- Estimating, on short notice, the team's position within a reasonable degree of accuracy (400 meters using DR, 200 meters when using terrain association, or 100 meters when using satellite position fixes).
- Making frequent checks on his estimated position using satellites or bearing fixes.
- Finding the objective by methodical search if it is not located when reaching the estimated position of the objective.

8-66. The primary tools the navigator uses, other than maps, are the vehicle compass, odometer, and GPS. The navigator must be proficient with all of these devices. He cannot depend on one device alone; the tool he is counting on the most may be the one to break when it is most needed.

8-67. For a determination of distance traveled, many of the methods used for mounted operations are similar to those used for dismounted operations. To determine distance during mounted operations, the navigator must—

- Ensure that large changes in elevation along a particular route are considered during planning, as it can add several miles to the total distance as seen on a map.
- Consider "wheel slip" and the fact it must be compensated for.

8-68. The speed and time method is the least desirable method for measuring distance because of the need to keep very accurate records of vehicle speed. The navigator computes distance traveled by multiplying the constant vehicle speed by the hours and tenths of hours spent traveling to get total distance traveled.

Example:

	5 miles per hour (constant vehicle speed).
Multiply	5.5 hours (hours/tenths of hours traveled).
Equals	27.5 (total miles traveled).

8-69. The odometer count is the preferred method for measuring distance. Before the team can rely on the odometer, it must be tested at a known distance of at least two miles. Accuracy should be exact on hard-surface roads. Soft sand or loose rocks will cause what is called "wheel slip." Wheel slip occurs when the vehicle's wheels turn overproportionately, causing the odometer to read a greater distance traveled than the actual distance traveled. Wheel slip factor comes with experience, but a general rule is that moderately soft sand will cause the wheel to slip up to 10 percent. Upon determining the wheel slip factor, the navigator multiplies it by the distance to be traveled. The result obtained gives him the odometer reading when the team arrives at their destination.

Example:

	30 miles (distance to be traveled).
Plus	3 (wheel slip factor [10 percent] multiplied by distance).
Equals	33 (odometer reading when destination is reached).

8-70. If the navigator can determine distance traveled, he then needs a method for keeping the vehicle on a bearing (azimuth). The navigator has three primary tools at his disposal to maintain azimuth:

- The liquid-filled, vehicle-mounted compass (adjusted to account for the vehicle's electrical field while engine is running).

- The satellite positioning device.

- The individual Soldier's lensatic compass. (This compass can be used inside the vehicle if the user accounts for the amount of deviation caused by the vehicle, and the compass is used in the same position on the vehicle every time. The electrical field in a running vehicle can throw off a compass 25 to 30 degrees and it is different in every part of the vehicle).

8-71. After determining the correct azimuth, the navigator orients the driver to the direction of travel. The navigator does this by picking a point in the distance and identifying it to the driver. This point can be a terrain feature, a man-made object, or a celestial object.

8-72. Using these methods will allow for a TPT to conduct mounted operations successfully. The following formulas and statistics (Figures 8-9 through 8-11, page 8-31) will help TPT leaders in the planning and execution of mounted operations. During mission preparation and planning, team leaders can use the following formula (Figure 8-9) to estimate fuel requirements.

8-73. During mission preparation and planning, team leaders can use the following formula (Figure 8-10) to estimate water requirements. Figure 8-11 outlines the statistics of the M1114 (Armored) HMMWV.

8-74. Using these formulas and statistics will ensure that TPTs successfully plan and conduct mounted operations regardless of their specific type of mission, which can be many and varied.

Fuel Estimation Formula

	_____ Total miles of mission (mission distance)
divide by	_____ vehicle miles per gallon (mpg) average

light load highway = 12 mpg
heavy load highway = 10 mpg
light load cross-country = 10 mpg
heavy load cross-country = 7 mpg
fully loaded trailer = subtract 5 mpg

equals	_____ gallons necessary per vehicle
plus	_____ % of gallons necessary

1:250,000 = 15%
added for map error 1:100,000 = 10%
1:50,000 = 5%

equals	_____ adjusted gallons necessary per vehicle
multiply by	_____ number of vehicles on mission
equals	_____ gallons necessary for detachment
plus	_____ 15% safety factor
equals	_____ total detachment fuel requirements
minus	_____ gallons carried in vehicle fuel tanks (25 gallons per vehicle tank)
equals	_____ gallons of fuel to be carried in 5-gallon fuel cans
divide by	_____ gallons per can (U.S. fuel can = 5 gallons)
equals	_____ 5-gallon cans necessary for remaining fuel requirements

Figure 8-9. Fuel Estimation Formula Work Sheet

Water Estimation Formula

	_____ number of personnel
multiply by	_____ number of quarts per day (minimum 4–6 quarts)
multiply by	_____ number of days of mission duration
equals	_____ mission water requirements
plus	_____ 15% safety factor
equals	_____ total water requirement
divide by	_____ gallons per can (U.S. water can = 5 gallons)

Figure 8-10. Water Estimation Formula Work Sheet

Curb Weight:	9,800 pounds
Payload:	2,300 pounds
Gross Weight:	12,100 pounds
Engine (Diesel):	6.5 liters
Horsepower:	190
Acceleration 0–30 mph:	8.2 seconds
Acceleration 0–50 mph:	25.1 seconds
Maximum Towed Load:	4,200 pounds
Cruising Range:	273 miles

Figure 8-11. Statistics of M1114 (Armored) HMMWV

OPERATIONS SUPPORTED BY TACTICAL PSYOP

8-75. PSYOP units have the ability to conduct missions across the operational spectrum. FM 3-0, paragraph 1-49, states the following:

When conducting full-spectrum operations, commanders combine and sequence offensive, defensive, stability, and support operations to accomplish the mission. The JFC and the Army component commander for a particular mission determine the emphasis Army forces place on each type of operation. Throughout the campaign, offensive, defensive, stability, and support operations occur simultaneously. As missions change from promoting peace to deterring war and from resolving conflict to war itself, the combinations of and transitions between these operations require skillful assessment, planning, preparation, and execution.

FM 3-0, *Operations*
14 June 2001

8-76. A full-spectrum mission, such as force protection, is conducted throughout offensive, defensive, stability, and support operations. Examples of PSYOP support to force protection could include threat reduction (weapons amnesty [stability operations]), noninterference with military operations (offensive and defensive operations), base defense (informing locals to report suspicious activity or using loudspeakers in a camp scenario [support operations]).

OFFENSIVE OPERATIONS

8-77. Offensive operations seek to seize, retain, and exploit the initiative to defeat the enemy decisively. Army forces attack simultaneously throughout the AO to throw enemies off balance, overwhelm their capabilities, disrupt their defenses, and ensure their defeat or destruction. Attacks, raids, counter-attacks, feints, and demonstrations are examples of offensive operations. PSYOP often support these missions with surrender appeals, noninterference messages, and masking the size or movement of friendly forces by using loudspeakers or leaflets.

8-78. Tactical-level PSYOP support battles and engagements by bringing psychological pressure on hostile forces and by persuading civilians to assist the tactical supported commander in achieving the commander's objectives. Tactical PSYOP are used to achieve rapid results with local and narrowly defined TA.

8-79. During war, PSYOP focus on supporting offensive and defensive operations. PSYOP support to stability and support operations continues but it is usually a lower priority. In times of war, PSYOP strive to undermine the enemy's will to fight. This is, in fact, the chief mission of PSYOP during hostilities. PSYOP personnel will use various media, such as loudspeakers, radio broadcasts, and leaflets, to instill fear of death, mutilation, or defeat in the enemy and undermine the enemy's confidence in their leadership, decreasing the enemy's morale and combat efficiency, and encouraging surrender, defection, or desertion.

8-80. The other primary focus of PSYOP in warfare is to reduce interference with military operations. The modern battlefield is populated not only by enemy soldiers but also civilians. PSYOP personnel assist the commander by encouraging civilians to avoid military operations, installations, and convoys.

DEFENSIVE OPERATIONS

8-81. The purpose of defensive operations is to defeat enemy attacks. Defending forces await the attacker's blow and defeat the attack by successfully deflecting it. Waiting for the attack is not a passive activity. Army commanders seek out enemy forces to strike and weaken them before close combat begins. PSYOP units often support mobile defense by helping to orient attacking forces into a position that exposes them to counterattack.

8-82. An example of PSYOP being used in defensive operations is when loudspeakers and TPT vehicles are used to deceive the enemy as to the supported unit's location, troop position, movements, or strength. Loudspeakers can also broadcast harassment noises that can make enemy reconnaissance of friendly locations more difficult and confuse the enemy during an attack.

8-83. Countering hostile propaganda is an important function of PSYOP. In the information era, battles can be won or lost due to perceptions and attitudes toward the United States and its military forces. The United States' adversaries will attempt to sway those perceptions and attitudes through the use of propaganda. It is PSYOP personnel's role to analyze that propaganda and determine what response is necessary. While counterpropaganda is an ongoing mission in any environment, its importance increases dramatically during times of war.

8-84. Supporting deception is often a consideration for tactical PSYOP. While the planning and execution of deception is a responsibility of the supported unit, PSYOP can provide support in the form of sonic deception. Special care must be taken to ensure that PSYOP personnel's contribution to these operations are coordinated and synchronized thoroughly with the supported unit's deception plan.

STABILITY OPERATIONS

8-85. Stability operations promote and protect U.S. national interests by influencing the threat, political, and information dimensions of the operational environment. They include developmental, cooperative activities during peacetime and coercive actions in response to crisis. Army forces accomplish stability goals through engagement and response. The military activities that support stability operations are diverse, continuous, and often long-term. Their purpose is to promote and sustain regional and global stability. Examples of PSYOP missions during stability operations include humanitarian assistance (HA), CD, antiterrorism, peace (peacekeeping, peace enforcement), NEOs or other flexible deterrent options as directed, demining, FID, and support to insurgencies. Appendix I discusses PSYOP in support of stability operations.

8-86. Tactical PSYOP elements have the capability to perform many different functions across the spectrum of stability operations. TPTs can disseminate products designed and produced by the TPDD, conduct face-to-face communication, gather PSYOP-relevant information, teach tactical PSYOP operations to foreign militaries, assess impact indicators, and conduct pretesting and posttesting. The TPDD, during stability operations, can produce handbills, pamphlets, newspapers, magazines, posters, loudspeaker messages, radio broadcasts, and novelty items.

8-87. Peace includes peacekeeping and peace enforcement. During peace missions, PSYOP's main objectives are gaining acceptance of U.S. or allied forces in the AO, reducing civilian interference with military operations, gaining support and compliance with U.S. and allied policies and directives, and increasing support for HN governments or military and police forces and their policies and directives.

8-88. During CD missions, PSYOP units focus on reducing the flow of illicit drugs into the United States. PSYOP units do this by striving to achieve the following objectives:

- Decreasing the cultivation of illegal narcotic crops.
- Decreasing production and trafficking of drugs by convincing those involved in the drug trade that penalties outweigh profits.
- Persuading people to provide information about illegal drug activities.

PSYOP units also seek to reduce popular support for the drug trade by educating the TA about the negative consequences of drug trafficking.

8-89. NEOs are conducted to remove USG personnel, U.S. citizens, and approved third-country nationals from areas of danger. PSYOP units support these operations by reducing interference from friendly, neutral, and hostile TAs and by providing information to evacuees.

8-90. HA operations are conducted to provide relief to victims of natural and man-made disasters. PSYOP units support these operations by providing information on benefits of programs, shelter locations, food and water points, and medical care locations. PSYOP units also publicize HA operations to build support for the U.S. and HN governments.

8-91. Demining operations are supported by tactical PSYOP through educating the TA on the dangers of mines, how to recognize mines, and what to do when a mine is encountered, leading to a decrease in mine-related injuries. PSYOP units also support demining by encouraging the TA to report locations of mines and UXO; PSYOP personnel can train the HN military on PSYOP techniques, who in turn can educate the TA.

SUPPORT OPERATIONS

8-92. Support operations use Army forces to assist civil authorities, foreign or domestic, as they prepare for or respond to crises and relieve suffering. In support operations, Army forces provide essential support, services, assets, or specialized resources to help civil authorities deal with situations beyond their capabilities. The purpose of support operations is to meet the immediate needs of designated groups for a limited time, until civil authorities can do so without Army assistance. An example of a PSYOP mission in this category is disaster relief. Loudspeakers can be used to provide disaster relief information to victims or make announcements in a camp scenario.

PSYOP SUPPORT TO ARMY SPECIAL OPERATIONS FORCES CORE TASKS

8-93. Army special operations forces (ARSOF) core tasks are conducted by Ranger, Special Forces, Civil Affairs, and PSYOP units. These core tasks are conducted across the spectrum of conflict at all levels of war. ARSOF core tasks include UW, FID, Civil Affairs operations (CAO), IO, direct action (DA), special reconnaissance (SR), counterterrorism (CT), and counterproliferation (CP). PSYOP support these core tasks as discussed in the following paragraphs.

8-94. UW is the support of an insurgency against the current government. The U.S. military provides technical and tactical training to the insurgents and can also assist in planning and conducting operations. PSYOP units support UW by increasing support for the insurgents, primarily by legitimizing their cause and by decreasing support for the current government (Appendix J).

8-95. FID covers a broad range of activities. Its primary intent is to help the legitimate host government address internal threats and their underlying causes. FID is not restricted to times of conflict. It can also take place in the form of training exercises and other activities to show U.S. resolve to and for the region. During FID, PSYOP personnel's main objectives are to build and maintain support for the host government while decreasing support for insurgents.

8-96. Normally limited in scope and duration, DA operations usually incorporate an immediate withdrawal from the planned objective area. These operations can provide specific, well-defined, and often time-sensitive results of strategic and operational critical significance. PSYOP unit's primary objectives in support of DA are to control noncombatants and minimize interference by hostile forces allowing DA elements to successfully accomplish their mission. After the conclusion of operations, PSYOP units may be called upon to explain and legitimize the purpose for DA operations.

8-97. SR complements national and theater intelligence collection assets and systems by obtaining specific well-defined and time-sensitive information of strategic or operational significance. PSYOP units support SR by providing cultural assessments, better preparing SR team members in the event they are compromised. PSYOP personnel will also analyze the psychological impact on the various TAs in the area in the event they compromise the team. If necessary, PSYOP will minimize the effects of compromise. PSYOP can also support deception operations conducted in conjunction with SR missions.

8-98. CT actions are either defensive (antiterrorism) or offensive (counterterrorism). PSYOP units support CT by decreasing popular support for terrorists, terrorist activities, and terrorist causes. PSYOP units also attempt to convince the terrorists that they cannot achieve their goals through terrorist acts. Throughout CT, PSYOP units continually seek to improve support for U.S. and HN goals and governments.

8-99. CP is those activities taken to control the production, trade, and use of weapons of mass destruction (WMD). PSYOP units will attempt to discredit the users of WMD during CP operations and legitimize CP activities.

8-100. CAO conducted during conflict or peace seek to build a rapport with civil governments and populations to facilitate the conduct of military operations. Military commanders must consider not only military forces but also the environment in which they operate. This environment includes a civil populace that may be supportive, neutral, or antagonistic to the presence of military forces, both friendly and opposing. A supportive populace can provide material resources that facilitate friendly operations, as well as a positive moral climate that confers advantages on the military and diplomatic activities the nation pursues to achieve foreign policy objectives. A hostile populace threatens the immediate operations of deployed friendly forces and can often undermine public support at home for the nation's policy objectives.

8-101. Since CAO are designed to "win the hearts and minds" of foreign populations, it is imperative that PSYOP be integrated into all activities. The first objective that PSYOP personnel must achieve is to explain and promote the purpose of CAO activities. Failure to achieve this objective could result in the populace, or opponents, creating their own explanation for the presence of U.S. forces (for example, combat operations, nuclear waste dumps, or so on). PSYOP personnel must then publicize the results of CAO to those portions of the populace that do not have firsthand knowledge of these activities, which will greatly increase the effect of each individual event.

8-102. IO are coordinating activities between several fields dealing with or affecting the information environment. IO are designed to coordinate and deconflict these various fields. It is imperative that PSYOP units provide liaisons to the IO cell.

SUMMARY

8-103. Tactical PSYOP forces are responsive to the ground commander's needs. Their ability to develop, produce, and disseminate products provide a means to rapidly and effectively address changing and unusual tactical situations. Tactical PSYOP forces also provide the commander the ability to communicate both directly and indirectly with combatants and hostile or potentially hostile noncombatants, ensuring they take actions that support the maneuver commander's intent.

Chapter 9

PSYOP Media Production

In the sphere of leaflet propaganda, the enemy has defeated us...The enemy has defeated us, not as man against man in the field of battle, bayonet against bayonet; no, bad contents poorly printed on poor paper have paralyzed our strength.

German Army Report
World War I

This chapter describes techniques used to produce PSYOP products. This chapter also discusses internal and external means and methods to perform these functions. To maximize effectiveness, PSYOP personnel need to use all appropriate media when producing products.

PRODUCTION PROCESS

9-1. The production process ranges from simple to complex. For example, a deployed loudspeaker team prepares a voice message for a target of opportunity. Preparing a field video production to support a PSYOP program, however, requires significant coordination between the requesting PSYOP unit and the production facility. PSYOP personnel need formal training and experience before they can produce video products with quality. This section presents production considerations and methods associated with face-to-face communication, loudspeakers, videotapes, novelties and gifts, printed material, and radio programming, as well as guidelines for briefing those agents that carry out PSYACTs.

9-2. Language in printed, audio, and audiovisual media is the primary form of communication. Messages written or presented by those lacking native language skills may have an adverse effect on the ability of the TA to understand or treat the message as credible. Those with native language proficiency of the TA are critical, not only to media production, but also for proper pretesting and posttesting. Printed media have the advantage of combining both printed instructions and pictures depicting the actions to be taken. If only using printed language, the PSYOP planner must have a clear understanding of the literacy rate and reading level of the TA. The better understanding the PSYOP personnel have of the product and about the product, the more successful they will become in producing a quality product.

ORGANIC PRINT ASSETS

9-3. PSYOP have organic assets—deployable and nondeployable—necessary for limited print capabilities needed for various campaigns within the theater of operation. PSYOP print personnel have experience in product layout and press repair, and are capable of producing multicolor products ranging in size from calling cards, leaflets, posters, handbills, books, and magazines, to tabloid newspapers, which are a major means of conveying propaganda. Various organic PSYOP print capabilities include the following:

- Heavy Print Facility (HPF).
- Modular Printing System (MPS).
- Risograph.
- Deployable Print Production Center (DPPC).
- PDW-Heavy.
- PDW-Light.

USAJFKSWCS Pub 525-5-16 provides detailed information on this equipment.

NONORGANIC PRINT ASSETS

9-4. Due to limited lift assets, PSYOP forces must make use of HN print assets and facilities. Contracting with a local company during the initial stages of military operations is cost-effective and allows for timely and responsive production of PSYOP products. This coordination will be made through the PSYOP contracting officer. The HN interpreters will normally know the names of local printing companies or they can assist in the search for local companies that may still be available. An advantage to using HN assets is that they may have faster turnaround times for the finished product, which will free up personnel to work on new prototypes for approval while approved products are being produced. However, when contracting with an outside company, PSYOP forces must be aware of the control of a new product. PSYOP forces must ensure that sensitive products are produced internally before being disseminated. Products that are steady state (products that are continuing on a certain theme) can be produced through an outside vendor. HN print companies may not have the experience, knowledge, or resources to repair their own broken equipment. Print specialists (MOS/additional skill identifier [ASI] J6) may assist in training the local personnel on the proper ways to fix and service their machines and equipment. This assistance may help establish rapport with the local company, thereby facilitating the printing of products.

VISUAL PRODUCT PRODUCTION

9-5. With the use of PSYOP organic or nonorganic print assets, visual products can convey messages to a TA that otherwise may not be readily accessible. A visual product is a written or pictorial message on a variety of media. Visual media are the most diverse types of PSYOP products. Visual products can be posters, handbills, or leaflets. PSYOP personnel can produce newspapers, pamphlets, and even magazines. In addition, PSYOP personnel have used a myriad of nonstandard visual devices to transmit PSYOP messages. From key chains and tee shirts distributed in the Philippines to comic books distributed in Bosnia to soccer balls given out in Latin America, many visual products have redefined exactly what can be used to distribute a PSYOP message. Although simplistic, if a printed PSYOP message or a PSYOP-relevant symbol or picture can be placed on a product, and the TA will access it, then the product is a visual PSYOP product.

9-6. PSYOP messages are being delivered by new and different means. Emerging technologies have created new opportunities to get the printed PSYOP message out to a wider audience and a narrower audience. E-mail PSYOP messages can target individuals within the governmental and military hierarchies of foreign governments, while Internet web sites can blanket mass audiences with a PSYOP message.

9-7. The more traditional visual products all have the same basic advantages, disadvantages, and production considerations. Nonstandard products have many of the same considerations, as well as some special considerations. For instance, an enemy may use the white space on a soccer ball or Frisbee in just the same manner as on a leaflet or poster. Special considerations arise with products such as novelties. These considerations are often logistical in nature. Special visual products, such as soccer balls or key chains, usually have higher costs associated with them. Production times on such items are often far longer than on a more conventional product, such as a poster. When developing a series concept, the PSYOP planner should balance such concerns against the probable payoff.

NEWSPAPER AND MAGAZINE PRODUCTION

9-8. Newspapers and magazines are extremely powerful means of transmitting a PSYOP message. They have some unique production considerations. Both media can be prohibitively costly. Furthermore, both media may be a waste of effort and resources if used in the wrong phase of operations or with the wrong TA.

9-9. Newspapers are often very effective with a TA in countries or regions that lack news and particularly newspapers. TAs often consider newspapers authoritative and credible. However, if TAA indicates that the TA considers newspapers suspect due to censorship or government control, it is unlikely that PSYOP can create credibility. Newspapers are best used in news- and information-denied areas. They will often be ineffective if the TA continues to receive news by means such as international radio or television news organizations. Newspapers will also often be ineffective if in-country papers are in print.

9-10. Newspapers produced by PSYOP should provide timely, truthful news and entertainment in a format familiar to the TA. Stories should not be exclusively supporting whatever POs and SPOs are contained in the PSYOP plan. These stories, such as the building of a new hospital by coalition forces, should be balanced with pure human interest and some entertainment features. Overt PSYOP messages should be just that. They should be clear PSYOP messages set off in much the same way as advertising with the source clearly visible. News stories must be as unbiased as possible. Credibility is critical. Carrying a story that may initially be damaging to the image of U.S. or HN forces (for example, the truthful covering of an accidental mistargeting of munitions) may pay off in both credibility and positive public opinion further down the road.

9-11. Newspapers should be produced on good quality newsprint with good inks. If some color can be incorporated, it should be considered, although this will raise production costs. A newspaper should not be done if it cannot be sufficient in size and content to be attractive to the TA. The PSYOP-produced newspapers generated in the past have been distributed freely but often sold by members of the TA. Very little can be done about this other than to clearly display that the paper is free on the front page. The practice of the TA selling the PSYOP-produced paper is an impact indicator of its acceptability. The PSYOP newspaper should provide public service space to local charities or legitimate HN government agencies if possible, but no advertising should be done on a commercial basis.

9-12. Newspapers may be printed on a contract basis with HN assets, but the most effective period for a PSYOP-produced newspaper may be when HN assets are incapable of putting out papers of their own. When HN papers begin to publish again, the PSYOP newspaper can cease production or it can transition to production of a magazine on a less frequent production schedule. *The Herald of Peace* magazine in Bosnia is a prime example of such a transition. As Bosnian newspapers began printing again, *The Herald of Peace* became the monthly magazine, *The Herald of Progress*. The magazine was able to retain and build on the credibility and resonance built up by the PSYOP-produced newspaper.

9-13. Production concerns and considerations for magazines are similar to newspapers. A magazine done well on glossy paper with quality color illustrations is expensive. However, a magazine of less-than-high quality is usually a waste of resources and talent. Magazines allow for longer, more scholarly articles supporting PSYOP arguments. However, a magazine also is produced to be desirable to the TA. A magazine should have interesting and entertaining articles and features as well. A magazine may have broad appeal to multiple TAs, but it is impossible for one magazine to be all things to all TAs.

ELEMENTS AND PRINCIPLES OF LAYOUT

9-14. There are several elements common to all visual products, which are called the elements of layout. Although they apply in every case to paper media, the same basic principles apply to novelties, durable goods, and complex visual products (a magazine). The elements of layout should not be ignored, even in areas where at first glance PSYOP personnel may think the elements do not apply, such as graffiti, E-mail PSYOP messages, and cell phone text messaging. The following items are the common elements of layout of visual products:

- *Format.* It is the presentation of visual products in a manner to which the audience is accustomed. Unfamiliar formats may detract from credibility, as well as be incomprehensible to a TA.

- *Display lines.* These include the headline, subheadline, and caption. They should attract attention and enhance the message.

- *Headline.* It must gain the reader's attention. It must also be easily read, quickly understood, and provocative. It is in large type at the top of the article and contains a quick message.

- *Subheadline.* It bridges the gap between the headline and the copy text. It is smaller type than the headline, but larger than the body of text.

- *Captions.* These explain illustrations.

- *Illustrations.* They aid the nonreader. They enable the reader and nonreader to visualize the message without reading the text. Illustrations should contrast with the background so that they are recognizable at distances and tied to the text.

- *Copy text.* This expresses the printed material's line of persuasion. It is a discussion or justification of the appeal, and it is written at the level of the TA. It is critical that this text be correctly translated.

- *White space.* As the name implies, this is the area not used by other format items. PSYOP personnel must keep white space to a minimum. The opponent of any PSYOP message can use white space to negate or reverse the intended message.

9-15. In addition to the elements of layout, there are two overriding principles of layout—balance and eye direction. These, too, apply to all PSYOP products.

9-16. Balance is expressed in four ways: formal balance, informal balance, informal diagonal balance, and grouping. Balance refers to the distribution of the weight (volume) of text and illustration on either side of the optical center. The optical center of a printed product is one-third of the distance from the top edge of a sheet of paper. The optical center of nonstandard visual products can differ or may need to be created by highlighting or mechanical eye direction. Balance includes the following:

- *Formal balance:* The weight is equally distributed on either side of the optical center. It is good for dignity, conservatism, and stability but lacks visual appeal.

- *Informal balance:* Text and graphics are casually spread across a page. It is more dynamic and provocative.

- *Informal diagonal balance:* The weight is distributed diagonally across the optical center. An example would be to place the illustrations and text opposite each other on either side of the optical center.

- *Grouping:* The use of two or more forms of balance in a single presentation.

9-17. The other principle of layout is eye direction. This refers to the ability of the visual material to lead the reader through the presentation from the optical center through the layout to the main message. There are three categories of eye direction:

- *Suggestive eye direction:* Uses tones, shadings, and postures of figures to direct the eye. It is the most effective technique because, when properly executed, the reader is not aware that his attention is being manipulated. It is the subtlest form of eye direction.

- *Sequential eye direction:* Capitalizes on the eye's ability to follow an established logical sequence of shapes, colors, and numbers or letters. The image of a clock face that directs the eye in a clockwise direction is an appropriate example.

- *Mechanical eye direction:* The most obvious of eye directions since it uses guiding lines and arrows to direct the reader's eye to significant points. This is the most obvious method; however, the reader may realize it and resent being manipulated.

9-18.   In addition to the elements and principles of layout, there are physical characteristics, such as permanency, color, and shape that must be considered. Permanency is the durability of the product. Permanency is not necessarily synonymous with indefinite shelf life. A laminated poster that will last for several months has permanency. However, an unlaminated poster that will only last a month does not have permanency.

9-19.   Colors have significance in many cultures. For example, red to an American may signify danger; whereas, in communist countries red may signify loyalty and patriotism. Shapes may convey a message in themselves. Leaflets printed in the shape of a maple leaf or star are examples. Also, geometric shapes often have religious meanings.

9-20.   If possible, a judicious use of color is important in the appearance of a visual product. The type of printing equipment available will limit the number of colors available. When two or more colors can be used, the following factors should be considered:

- To attract attention, color in a leaflet should usually contrast sharply with the predominant color of the terrain over which the leaflet is to be disseminated. On occasions, however, color in a leaflet may be planned to blend with the terrain in areas where punitive or other sanctions have been imposed to limit the reading (and therefore the impact) of enemy leaflets.

- Blended colors give an individual greater opportunity to pick up, handle, or retain a leaflet. Multicolor or near-photo-quality color generally present a more attractive and professional look with leaflets, handbills, posters, and other print media. Cost concerns may prohibit the free use of color in products such as newspapers or magazines.

- Favorite colors of the TA may be used frequently. For example, canary yellow is favored in China, and green in Ireland. Colors included in the national flags of countries are usually "safe" colors to use.

- Colors must be appropriate to the culture of the audience in order to convey an idea and elicit a behavior.

- Colors may be used to harmonize with the moods of the illustrations or message within the frame of reference of the TA. In some countries, red may be used to suggest violence, blue or green for peaceful scenes, and black or white for death.

- Colors can have religious connotations. Green is universally "the color of the faithful" in the Moslem world. In the west, it is often associated with health and nature and generally has no religious significance.

9-21.   Production of printed products on paper follows several general production guidelines. Posters, handbills, and leaflets may have a message printed on one or both sides of the sheet of paper. It is not recommended that any product be printed on only one side. In addition to the obvious chance for an enemy to deface or otherwise negatively alter a product by printing on the blank side, an enemy may welcome the supply of paper to simply print his own message.

9-22. Posters, handbills, and leaflets have no standard size, shape, or format. In selecting the size, shape, and weight of the paper, the primary consideration is that the paper accommodates the message and is easy to distribute. For leaflets, the recommended size, provided the message can be accommodated, is 15.25 centimeters by 7.72 centimeters (6 inches by 3 inches) on 7.25- or 9.06-kilogram paper (16 or 20 pound). Leaflets of this size and weight have very favorable aerial dissemination characteristics. (Appendix K discusses leaflet operations in detail.) Posters generally will not be printed smaller than 11 (27.94 centimeters) by 17 (43.18 centimeters) inches. Handbills are commonly either 5.5 by 8.5 inches or 8.5 by 11 inches.

NOTE: Appendix L consists of conversion tables that may be used to convert measurements from U.S. standard terms to metric when mission requirements or environments change.

9-23. Printed product production is affected by the physical characteristics of paper, such as shape, texture, quality, size, and weight. Paper quality and texture noticeably affect legibility and color reproduction. A high grade of paper is needed for correct color reproduction. Quality also affects durability. The major factors involved in selection of paper weights and product sizes are—

- Message length.
- Artwork required.
- Dissemination means.
- Press capabilities.
- Material available.

9-24. Leaflets require the planner to consider special factors in production. Paper size and weight effect whether or not a leaflet autorotates. This may affect the choice of delivery system. The planner must consider the purpose of the leaflet. For example, safe conduct passes should always be printed on durable, high-quality paper, but special situation leaflets do not require such durability.

9-25. When producing novelties or consumer goods, the quality of materials must be considered on a case-by-case basis. The PSYOP planner must balance good quality with production cost. The general rule with products in this arena is that the product should never be produced with less-than-high-quality materials that have durability. If cost is prohibitive, the PSYOP planner should always err on the side of not producing a product that will not perform its intended role for as long or longer than a similar consumer good available for purchase by the TA. For instance, putting a PSYOP message on a basketball with a poor-quality valve will damage the credibility of the PSYOP element as much or more than an offensive leaflet or radio message. Production of shoddy goods transmits the message that the PSYOP element does not care about the TA.

9-26. There are many advantages of using visual products. Some advantages are as follows:

- Printed word has a high degree of credibility, acceptance, and prestige.
- Printed matter is unique and can be passed from person to person without distortion.
- Illiterates can understand photographs and graphic illustrations.
- Permanent message cannot be changed unless physically altered.
- Dissemination is to, and is read by, a larger, widespread TA.
- TA can reread for reinforcement.
- Complex and lengthy material can be explained in detail.
- Messages can be hidden and read in private.
- Messages can be printed on almost any surface, including useful novelty items.
- Printed material can gain prestige by acknowledging authoritative and expert authors.

9-27. There are also disadvantages of using visual products. Some disadvantages are as follows:

- High illiteracy rate requires the developer to limit the use of text in the printed product.
- Printing operations require extensive logistical support.
- Production, distribution, and dissemination of bulk or nonstandard products can be costly and time-consuming, requiring the use of special facilities and conveyances.
- TA can prevent or interfere with the dissemination.
- Products can be less timely than other means of communication.
- TA can collect and destroy the product.
- TA can alter the message.

9-28. Print products may be categorized as persuasive, informative, and directive. The persuasive product attains its objective through use of reason. Facts are presented so that the audience is convinced that the conclusions reached by the author are valid. The informative product is factual. In presenting facts previously unknown to the audience, this approach attracts a reading public by satisfying curiosity. Directive print material directs action when intelligence indicates the target is receptive. The directive approach is used to direct and control activities of underground forces. This type of product may be used to disrupt enemy production by giving advance warning of bombing attacks and suggesting that workers in enemy production facilities protect themselves by staying away from work. During consolidation and FID operations, directive products assist in maintaining law and order and in publicizing government programs.

9-29. Leaflets are developed for specific uses, such as prepackaged, special situation, safe conduct, and news. Special-situation leaflets are requested when the prepackaged leaflet message is inadequate to exploit a particular opportunity, situation, or objective. These leaflets are developed when intelligence indicates the existence of a specifically exploitable, but transient and presumably nonrecurring, psychological opportunity. Special-situation leaflets are intended for use only once because the circumstances that govern their preparation are seldom duplicated. These leaflets are used in tactical operations. Tactical PSYOP achieve maximum results when leaflets have specific relevance at the moment of receipt, when psychological pressures are greatest, and when a reasonable COA is presented. For example, surrender becomes a reasonable COA only when under current conditions no other alternative action seems plausible.

9-30. Other than surrender appeals, which generally are not as exploitable with posters or handbills (with the exception of long-term FID or UW operations), other printed media can be prepackaged, special situation, safe conduct, or news. Posters and handbills can be the best way to respond to special situations. For instance, a TPT can respond to a specific short-term need by distributing handbills quickly modified from a prepackaged product and printed by their TPDD on a Risograph. Lack of aircraft, timeliness, length of message, or the desirability of the face-to-face distribution of handbills may necessitate such a COA.

9-31. Prepackaged visual products contain general messages intended for repeated use in all types of PSYOP. They are particularly valuable in fast-moving tactical situations when PSYOP units are unable to prepare products to fit rapidly changing situations. The content of prepackaged products used in support of FID, UW, and consolidation operations varies widely. The advantages of prepackaged leaflets apply to other visual products and are as follows:

- Permits rapid dissemination of a variety of propaganda messages.

- Is prepared in advance, stockpiled in bulk, or loaded in disseminating devices for storage or immediate delivery, which provides flexibility for the use of PSYOP at all levels of command.

- Permits standardization of selected themes or messages, ensuring consistency of content.

- Allows cataloging. Prepackaged products are easily cataloged. The availability of catalogs of standard leaflets simplifies the task of integrating selected leaflets into tactical operations.

- Permits the most efficient use of large, high-speed presses at theater-Army level and maximum use of commercial facilities.

- Permits a joint production agency to better control printed materials and allows pretesting well in advance of dissemination.

- Ensures continuation of the PSYOP effort even though reproduction equipment may be destroyed or temporarily disabled.

Disadvantages of prepackaged visual products are as follows:

- Prepackaged products are usually less effective than products tailored for a specific action or situation.

- They are subject to deterioration.

- Circumstances and conditions make them obsolete.
- Stockpiles of products become a logistical burden.

Since space and other considerations limit the text of a PSYOP message, the writer must persuade the intended TA succinctly and economically.

9-32. Objectivity is the keynote of effective, copy text writing. Although difficult to do, the efficient PSYOP writer puts aside all personal prejudices and biases when writing for enemy consumption. The writer depends upon intelligence agencies and TAA for information upon which to base his appeals. This information must not be adapted to fit the writer's own personal views. Rather, the information must fit the emotional state and thought process of the audience and be pertinent to the primary interests of its members.

9-33. Assertion, not negotiation, is the stock in trade of the PSYOP writer. The PSYOP writer has, without doubt, the toughest selling job in the world. Every facility at the disposal of the enemy, from domestic propaganda to military strength, is aimed at discrediting or refuting the writer's statements. A negative attitude, therefore, is interpreted by the enemy as a sign of weakness. Only positive appeals can wear down the psychological barrier the enemy has erected against the PSYOP writer. Furthermore, enemy propaganda may be designed to influence the opponent to deny something, and if the PSYOP writer retaliates by categorically denying enemy accusations, he may be supplying data for which the enemy has been probing.

9-34. The composition of copy text is very important in the development of the message. Although leaflets are generally small, they should contain comparatively large print, particularly when directed toward the enemy. However, a small leaflet with large print makes it necessary to use a text that is brief, to the point, and immediately attractive. Since enemy personnel and civilians in areas under enemy control are prohibited from picking up or reading leaflets from external sources, the large print enables them to read the message without touching the leaflet. In case the reader wishes to hide the leaflet and read it surreptitiously, a small leaflet is more easily concealed.

9-35. Type must be large enough to be perfectly legible and familiar to the audience. Although the heading and subheading may vary in size, body type should be eight points or larger. If the Roman alphabet is not used in the target area, provision must be made to obtain the proper type of reproduction capability. Factors contributing to effective message writing include the following:

- A good, practical knowledge of the TA language, including current idioms and slang, to enable the writer to effectively translate the ideas to be incorporated into the product.
- Recent residence in the target location and familiarity with current happenings in that area. (Politics, cultural patterns, and even language vernacular often change rapidly, and the skillful writer must be abreast of all these changes.)
- Familiarity with the organization of the TA's leadership, equipment, and arms should enable the writer to know the average TA member's

emotional and sociological background, including his ambitions, prejudices, likes, and dislikes.

- Familiarity with the civilian population and the political, sociological, economic, and psychological environment within which the writer functions.

  - Access to personnel with experience in one or more of the following fields:

    - Advertising.

    - Journalism.

    - Public relations.

    - Marketing.

9-36. The PSYOP planner needs to consider all of the principles of writing copy text with the production of novelties and consumer goods. Many times the product itself will mandate very short, concise messages. With things like school supplies or sports equipment, a single visually appealing, but linguistically simple, message is often the best approach. Text messaging cannot be verbose. The effective text message will make its point in a single short phrase or sentence. E-mail messages targeting individuals can be more detailed. The PSYOP planner should avoid writing overly lengthy messages. A key leader or official who might not click on the delete icon, but actually read a concise paragraph or two, may very well decide to delete if the message is too long.

9-37. In many cases with consumer goods, the "less is more" approach may be superior. Often, the food package with "Gift of the United States" printed on it is the PSYOP message. There can be great PSYACT value with simply distributing goods either unilaterally or with coalition partners. Any further PSYOP message may be resented at the time. A further message may be interpreted as "strings." The TA may feel the PSYOP planner is attempting to buy compliance. What is more, in some cultures giving gifts with any condition attached is unacceptable. In all cases, the PSYOP planner must balance any written message against the PSYACT value of distributing useful or essential goods with implicit rather than explicit messages.

AUDIO AND AUDIOVISUAL ASSETS

9-38. The PSYOP production broadcast detachments provide complete audio and audiovisual production and broadcast transmission support and are responsible for the setup and operation of organic radio and TV transmitters. A secondary mission is to repair, interface with, and operate HN or foreign TV production and broadcast facilities. TPTs use loudspeakers to broadcast messages that adhere to many of the same production guidelines and parameters as radio. (Chapter 10 includes a detailed discussion of loudspeaker operations.) In addition, TPTs conduct face-to-face communications, which are one of the most powerful means of audiovisual communications.

AUDIO MEDIA

9-39. PSYOP personnel produce audio, radio, loudspeaker, and telephonic messages at the PDC or TPDD. Radio and telephonic messaging are addressed in the following paragraphs.

9-40. Radio provides entertainment, news, and instructions along with the desired PSYOP message. As with all other media, selecting to use the radio will depend greatly on the availability of and access to radios by the TA and the ability of the signal to reach the target. Truthful, credible, and accurate news reporting is the best way to gain and hold attention. Radio broadcasts can be transmitted to local audiences, across national boundaries, and behind enemy lines. Political boundaries or tactical situations may hinder radio broadcasts, but they are not complete barriers. Since radio can reach mass TAs quickly, radio is useful for all types of PSYOP. Where radio stations are not common and receivers are rare or nonexistent, receivers may be airdropped or otherwise distributed to key communicators, public installations, and selected individuals. Public listener systems may also be set up.

9-41. PSYOP personnel can contact local radio stations to have a live on-air show that broadcasts weekly to speak with the local populace, as a means to disseminate PSYOP messages and command information. In addition, they can contact and coordinate with the area commanders and key communicators for interviews on local radio stations. This contact provides direct interaction with, and access to, the local populace and helps reinforce the objectives of the area commander while adding credibility to the message. Advantages of radio include—

- *Speed*. Radio programs can be quickly prepared for broadcast. Speed is important when attempting to capitalize on targets of opportunity.

- *Wide coverage*. Radio programs can reach members of large and varied audiences simultaneously.

- *Ease of perception*. Radio requires little or no effort to visualize the radio message. Illiteracy does not prevent the listener from forming his individual image as he listens.

- *Versatility*. Radio is easily adaptable to drama, music, news, and other types of programs.

- *Emotional power*. A skilled radio announcer can exert tremendous influence on the listener simply with pitch, resonance, inflection, or timing.

- *Availability of receivers*. Where availability or ownership of receivers is common, listening to radio is a habit. Ownership of receivers has increased greatly with the invention of transistors.

Disadvantages of radio include—

- *Enemy restrictions*. The target group may be subjected to severe censorship, thereby reducing the effectiveness of radio broadcasts. Some countries have only single-channel radios with the frequency set to the government-owned station. In some areas, central receivers are connected to household receivers to control listening.

- *Jamming possibilities*. Jamming may prevent the target group from receiving radio broadcasts.

- *Technical problems*. The signal may be made inaudible or distorted by fading or static due to unfavorable atmospheric conditions.

- *Lack of receivers*. In certain areas, so few receivers are available that radio may not be an effective medium.

- *Fleeting impressions*. Oral media do not have the permanency of written media. Messages may be quickly forgotten or distorted.

9-42. Radio programming consists of planning the schedule, content, and production of programs during a stated period. Words, music, and sound effects are put together in various ways to produce the different kinds of programs. Some of the major types of radio programs are—

- Straight news reports (without commentary).

- Musical (whatever genre is popular with the TA).

- Drama. Although this genre has virtually disappeared from American radio programming, many foreign countries still produce popular radio dramas that range from soap operas to radio theater.

- Speeches, talks, discussions, or interviews. So-called "talk radio" is increasingly a worldwide phenomenon. With the proliferation of cell phones and increase in landlines in third- and fourth-world countries, remote locations on the globe have radio call-in shows.

- Sports.

- Special events, such as on-the-spot coverage of an election or the arrival of an important visitor.

- Religious.

- Variety—a combination including music, skits, or comedy.

- Announcements.

Radio principles include the following factors:

- Regularity is an essential element of programming. The radio programmer must create habitual program patterns to build a regular audience. Content, style, and format should follow an established pattern.

- Radio programming builds listenership by following a set time schedule. Listeners must know when they can tune in for the programming they want to hear. This allows the TA to form a regular habit of listening to the PSYOP program. If the time schedule varies on a daily basis, listeners will become frustrated and turn to another station.

- Repetition is necessary for oral learning; therefore, key themes, phrases, or slogans should be repeated to ensure the TA gets the desired message. If a certain message is only aired once or is only aired at one time every day, the listener has a good chance of missing the information.

- The radio program must suit the taste and needs of the audience. Program style and format should follow the patterns to which the audience is accustomed.

- Discussion or presentation of banned books, plays, music, and political topics is readily received by the audience. The same is true for news withheld by censors. In breaking censorship, the psychological operator must be certain that the reason for censoring the items was political and not moral.

- Announcers with attractive voice features are essential to successful radio operations. Some factors to consider include—

  - The emotional tone conveyed by the voice may influence the listener more than the logic of arguments.

  - Announcers whose accents are similar to those of unpopular groups should not be used.

  - Female voices are used to exploit nostalgia, sexual frustration, or to attract female audiences. However, in some parts of the world, due to the status of women, female voices are resented.

Radio programs are classified according to—

- *Content.* The most common and useful radio program classification is by content. News reporting, commentaries, announcements, educational or informative documentaries, music, interviews, discussions, religious programs, drama, and women's programs are the most common examples.

- *Intent.* Classification by "intent" is useful in planning to obtain a desired response with a particular broadcast. Programs are produced to induce such emotional reactions as confidence, hope, fear, nostalgia, or frustration.

- *Origin.* Classification by "origin" pertains to the source of the message; for example, official, unofficial, authoritative, high military command, or political party.

9-43. Planning effective loudspeaker messages requires the availability of current and appropriate PSYOP intelligence and PSYOP-relevant information. The loudspeaker scriptwriter, as part of a TPDD or PDC, should follow all normal product development procedures when preparing a loudspeaker script as part of a program. The TPT leader should also know the TA and be prepared to conduct an abbreviated TAA when preparing a short-notice loudspeaker script in support of exploitation situations. The TPT leader should be aware of approved themes and symbols, and can obtain additional information through the TPD and the S-2 to help evaluate the TA's current situation. Information on the TA's order of battle, morale, and matters that are currently troubling or worrying the TA is of great value to the scriptwriter in the formulation of the loudspeaker message. Other requirements that are basic to planning effective loudspeaker messages include the following:

- The prior establishment and the continuous maintenance of credibility.

- An experienced scriptwriter who understands the mission at hand.

- Consistency in the content of loudspeaker messages, tempered with adaptability to frequently changing TA situations.
- Coordination with friendly forces concerned with the loudspeaker mission.
- Linguistic capabilities of the operator.

9-44. Ideally, the text of each loudspeaker message should be specifically tailored for a given situation. However, peacetime contingency requirements often demand that PSYOP messages be prepared in advance as part of a specific OPLAN. Nevertheless, experience has established the principles of script preparation for all loudspeaker messages. The following paragraphs discuss these principles.

Openings That Gain Attention

9-45. In any type of loudspeaker message, the writer should use an opening that will immediately attract the attention of the TA. The TA may not hear or understand the first sentence of a broadcast because he is not expecting the broadcast and has not set his mind to listen. For this reason, there must be some opening expression or phrase to alert the listener and to draw his attention to what is to follow, such as "attention, attention." The opening can contain the formal designation or the nickname of the unit addressed, or the opening can identify where the troops are located. Again, the opening phrase might announce the source of, or authority for, the broadcast such as, "This is a message from the United Nations Command!" If a cooperative EPW delivers the message, he may identify himself by name or he may use the names of former comrades in addressing his unit. This personalization is likely to gain the interest and attention of the TA.

Brevity

9-46. In exploitation or similar fast-moving situations, each individual broadcast should be kept as short as possible—90 seconds at the most. This limit does not apply to static, retrograde, or consolidation situations in which messages of somewhat greater lengths may be used, but loudspeaker teams must always take care to keep the broadcast short enough so the audience does not lose interest.

Applicability

9-47. The message must apply directly to the listener's situation. The message must be in the form of a clear and concise statement of the military situation or of other circumstances surrounding, or difficulties confronting, the TA.

Bottom Line

9-48. Loudspeaker messages should make their principal point or argument early in the text. Because of the potential for a hostile reaction by the TA or time limits, important points should be stated quickly and explained later.

Simplicity

9-49. The message should be phrased in simple, easily understood terms and be tailored to the TA. There may be only one opportunity to deliver the broadcast, so it must be kept simple enough to be understood without repetition. The writer should refrain from involved or argumentative messages. These messages have little power to convince the opponent and, if not heard in their entirety, lose effectiveness.

Repetition

9-50. The loudspeaker team should repeat important phrases in its message to ensure that the TA understands them and to increase the emphasis and force of the message. Repetition also minimizes interruptions in the broadcast's intelligibility caused by battle noises or other sounds. Not only may individual phrases or sentences within the text be repeated, but the entire message should also be rebroadcast if the situation permits.

Authoritativeness

9-51. Every loudspeaker message should have an authoritative tone. If the message is demanding positive action on the part of its audience, then PSYOP personnel should deliver the message in an authoritative voice. Statements such as, "I am speaking for the American armored force commander," or "General Jones sends you this message," will impress the TA with their power and authority. Such expressions are particularly effective in surrender appeals.

Instructiveness

9-52. Loudspeaker messages that ask the audience to perform, or refrain from performing, some specific action must include precise instructions as to how individuals or groups are expected to act. For example, detailed assurances and instructions must be included in the surrender message when the opponent soldier is asked to leave the relative security of his fighting position and possibly expose himself to fire from U.S. troops and, in some cases, his own troops. He should have valid promises that he will not be fired upon by U.S. forces and be given a workable plan for escaping from his own lines. Failure of a surrender attempt by a man who follows instructions can lead to loss of credibility.

Personalization

9-53. The capability of the loudspeaker to pinpoint its target enables PSYOP personnel to personalize the message and increase its psychological impact. The scriptwriter may personalize the message with order of battle intelligence from the supported S-2. The message may include the designations and locations of units and the names of unit leaders or other personnel. Indexes of unit morale are invaluable in preparing a personalized message for a particular unit, and to a lesser extent, civilian line crossers provide additional sources of information. The height of personalization occurs when a captured opponent soldier broadcasts to his former comrades in arms. In his message, he identifies some by name, describes his good treatment and his ease of escape through the lines, and finally advises them to follow his example.

Avoidance of Scripts That Antagonize

9-54. The writer of the loudspeaker script or message is ostensibly the friend of his listeners, seeking to benefit them by sound advice. A message that angers the opponent is worse than useless, since this type of message will induce him to fight harder and delay surrender.

Credibility

9-55. Credibility is faith on the part of the TA in the reliability of the loudspeaker message. Credibility must be established and carefully guarded, for once an opponent loses belief in a message, all other broadcasts become suspect. For example, a surrender appeal in the Korean conflict stated that prisoners already in I/R camps received eggs and white bread for breakfast. Although this fact was true, subsequent intelligence revealed that opponent soldiers could not believe that the UN forces had enough eggs or, if they had, would waste them on prisoners. As a result, credibility for the entire appeal was lost.

9-56. Telephonic messaging is an extension of face-to-face communication in some aspects. It is, however, more limited than conventional face-to-face communication in that the sender cannot always judge the feedback of the receiver and cannot communicate with him nonverbally. In telephonic messaging, the TA is very narrowly defined. Telephonic messaging will target individuals who have the ability to effect radical change. Telephonic messaging targets ruling elites. Although a general script should be followed, like face-to-face communications, telephonic messaging must adapt to the feedback received during the conversation. The sender must avoid entering into a "negotiation." This medium, like any other PSYOP medium, is for the transmittal of a clear PSYOP message with the presentation of the specific behavior desired of the individual.

AUDIOVISUAL MEDIA

9-57. Audiovisual media combine the impact of sight and sound. They are the most powerful communications system in history. TV, movies, and now video transmitted over the Internet have the power to invoke deep emotional responses. The proliferation of TVs, videocassette recorders (VCRs), and video compact disc (VCD) and DVD players has brought electronic audiovisual products into remote locations. Satellite technology has brought real-time news to the poorest of countries. Areas lacking any other viable infrastructure may have Cable News Network (CNN) playing on a battery-operated television. Video production technology is available in a majority of countries and the development of the portable videotape camera has made the expensive and time-consuming process of making films easy in PSYOP. Although the mechanics of producing a video are important, PSYOP personnel should not forget the psychology of the message. Without ideas, creativity, and the ability to apply them, the machines are nothing but plastic, metal, and glass.

FACE-TO-FACE COMMUNICATIONS

9-58. Perhaps the most powerful form of audiovisual communication, face-to-face, remains a bedrock of PSYOP. When a PSYOP Soldier may have no other means to get his message out, interpersonal, face-to-face communication remains an option. Face-to-face communication provides feedback to the sender instantly. The PSYOP Soldier can determine what effect his message is having and can "adjust fire" on the spot. When combined with the dissemination of handbills, the distribution of HA, a medical civic action program (MEDCAP), or even a social event, face-to-face communications can not only get the PSYOP message out, it can build rapport. When face-to-face communication is combined with something like HA, it becomes a PSYACT as much as a psychological operation. In short, nothing is more powerful than the human contact of face-to-face communication when it is done well.

9-59. Face-to-face communication is an art rather than a science. When conducting face-to-face communication, the PSYOP Soldier should have prewritten guidelines but not a script. Scripted face-to-face communication will sound insincere. It will be rigid and unresponsive to the reaction of the TA. A PSYOP Soldier must know the borders of his message. The PSYOP Soldier must never make promises that he cannot keep or promises that are outside of the PSYOP arena.

9-60. An important aspect of face-to-face communication is the collection of impact indicators on the spot. The PSYOP Soldier may be able to see the results of the PSYOP message instantly. However, the behavior displayed at the time may be contrived. The TA may just wish to please the individual doing the face-to-face communication because of a positive relationship. Production of face-to-face products should incorporate a general plan to collect feedback in a codified form. Face-to-face communication presents another unique production consideration. Face-to-face communication provides a chance to do TAA, as well as deliver the PSYOP message. Production of a face-to-face plan should include specific TAA questions to be answered by passive observation or questions that do not detract from the message being presented. When considering what to ask, the PSYOP Soldier must balance the TAA value of information obtained against detracting from the message. The message must come first over any collection.

VIDEO MEDIA

9-61. Over the past decade, the development and advancement of new technology has greatly increased the needs and capabilities for audiovisual means of dissemination. As PSYOP forces have expanded their scope for production, distribution, and dissemination, they have increased the value of audiovisual assets. New advancements in technology have led to the use of digital cameras and the Internet. PSYOP personnel have the ability to access the Internet, as well as the ability to employ the use of the digital camera for the production of new, more efficient, and advanced products. These items are crucial in the development of new products for the PDC.

9-62. POTF elements, PSEs, and TPTs can take the digital cameras into the AO and gather pictures of the local countryside and the local populace carrying out their everyday activities. POTFs, TPTs, and PSEs use organic electronic news gathering (ENG) kits to gather audiovisual products. The audiovisual PSYOP personnel can also go along with the TPTs and use this opportunity to film the local populace with their audiovisual cameras. This filming opportunity gives PSYOP personnel and the PDC valuable new raw footage and photos for producing new products that relate better to the TA. The PDC then downloads the digital pictures of the raw footage and compiles all the data. When collecting raw material footage for new products, PSYOP personnel ensure that they film this footage on digital videotape of the highest possible clarity. Digital video better preserves the footage during postproduction or format conversion.

9-63. The optimum way for PSYOP personnel to analyze the captured footage is through the input of interpreters. Interpreters will be able to determine the best footage to use, what pictures may be meaningful to the local populace, and why. Ensuring that interpreters are involved in the decision-making process of a new product may provide valuable insights into why a certain product or decision will be successful or not. Interpreters will also be able to offer reasons for other prime locations to gather footage that may have a positive or negative effect on a final product. This information will give PSYOP personnel a clearer understanding about attitudes and opinions, which may expand on the feelings of the local populace in reference to a particular program that is being developed. When PSYOP personnel use new advancements in technology in addition to the interpreter's opinions, PSYOP effectiveness is optimized within the AO and a greater quality of products is generated. Appendix H provides information for the proper use and supervision of interpreters.

9-64. The PDC receives guidance from the POTF commander or the operations officer in reference to what products are being developed and the most efficient means of dissemination. Audiovisual production is a major undertaking and will entail the input from the 37Fs, 25Vs, interpreters, and other personnel in the PSYOP organization at the product review board (PRB). PSYOP personnel work off the PAW for guidance. PSYOP personnel review initial drafts internally before creating the final drafts of a new product. Once a finalized draft is produced, the product will have to be seen at the PRB for the PSYOP commander's approval. If this process is done correctly and efficiently, no more than 2 weeks should be needed for final approval of the product. The PDC officer will maintain contact with the approval authority and will be notified of the approval process and determination of the new product. Once the product is approved, copies of the product can be made to disseminate at either the POTF or the PDC at the detachment level.

9-65. There are various organic PSYOP audio and audiovisual capabilities. The MOC located at Fort Bragg, North Carolina, has the capacity to produce commercial-quality graphic, photographic, audio, and audiovisual products. USAJFKSWCS Pub 525-5-16 provides detailed information on the MOC. The inventory of audio and audiovisual production equipment includes several deployable systems. In addition, ever-growing reachback capability through satellite systems sending broadcast and data streams over broadband assists production downrange.

CONTRACTED PRODUCTION ASSETS

9-66. This process will take place externally of the PSYOP production, which may allow PSYOP personnel to produce greater quality products by more efficient means. For the use of audiovisual products, the POTF contracting officer may be able to establish contracts with one of the local TV stations to help produce, edit, and make copies of approved products in correct formats for distribution and dissemination. Local TV stations normally are more than cooperative and can assist PSYOP personnel, if needed, on newer or more advanced audiovisual equipment. PSYOP forces may also use outside contractors who can assist with proper maintenance of audiovisual equipment. The PSYOP OIC can contact the POTF and coordinate cross training with TV personnel who operate TV production equipment at the POTF. Normally, these personnel are from other countries with years of knowledge and experience in television production. They can help cross train the audiovisual personnel if needed, or the PSYOP personnel may be able to train with the Soldiers on similar equipment. Another asset to consider for audiovisual production is contracting with local companies like the Theater Actors Guild or a modeling agency for personnel to narrate and become a spokesperson or newscaster for PSYOP audiovisual products. This type of asset will catch the attention of the TA and may add credibility to the PSYOP message or story being aired.

9-67. PSYOP personnel may be able to use other assets within the AO; for example, the PAO has audiovisual production and editing capabilities within a section known as the mobile public affairs detachment (MPAD). The MPAD equipment is only available in NTSC video standard, but their public affairs personnel have knowledge of the digital nonlinear editing systems (which is organic to PSYOP broadcast assets) and may be able to assist PSYOP personnel in editing and production. The JCCC coordinates inputs from the individual Services' combat camera units. Combat camera units can be a valuable source of visual and audiovisual products. Another option that may be researched is the Coalition Press Information Center (CPIC). They may have audiovisual capabilities in-theater that may be useful in making copies of approved products. The PSYOP LNO will have contacts to all the key personnel for these capabilities. PSYOP personnel may also have the POTF produce the audio and audiovisual copies needed to disseminate throughout the AO.

OTHER PRODUCTION ASSETS

9-68. PSYOP forces conduct operations directed by the President and SecDef in close cooperation with or under the supervision of other agencies, the UN, and NGOs. Often due to limited assets, PSYOP forces must make use of the production assets and facilities of the HN. PSYOP forces may use some of the HN fixed facilities or contract out with local companies for various media production assets. PSYOP forces can also use the experience and expertise of other Services within the U.S. military. The Navy has the capability to produce audiovisual products from the Fleet Audio-Visual Command, Pacific; Fleet Imagery Command, Atlantic; fleet combat camera groups; various film libraries; and Naval Imaging Command. Naval assets have the capability to broadcast AM/FM radio and produce documents, posters, articles, and other materials for PSYOP. Administrative capabilities ashore and afloat exist to produce various quantities of printed materials. Language capabilities exist in naval intelligence and among naval personnel for most Asian and European languages. The USAF has a variety of aircraft with a vast range of capabilities that lend themselves to PSYOP across the range of military operations. Several types of military aircraft are specially modified for the PSYOP role. AFSOC is equipped with a number of aircraft capable of accomplishing broadcast and leaflet operations. Six EC-130 (COMMANDO SOLO) aircraft, assigned to the Pennsylvania Air National Guard, broadcast PSYOP as their primary mission. These aircraft are equipped for airborne broadcasting of radio and television signals. The Marine Corps have units similar to CA units where some of their marines are PSYOP-qualified and may be working within the same AO as PSYOP personnel. These units may have some important information that they can share to assist PSYOP in the production or dissemination of materials and products. The PSYOP S-3 will assist in the coordination with these various Services and the HN.

9-69. New equipment programs are being developed to enhance the capabilities of the PSYOP community. USAJFKSWCS Pub 525-5-16 provides more information on these programs.

SUMMARY

9-70. This chapter discussed the different organic and nonorganic production techniques and processes available to PSYOP. Also discussed were print, audio, and audiovisual techniques along with advantages and disadvantages of each. Using these techniques and the resources available, PSYOP forces will maintain the ability to produce effective quality products.

Chapter 10

Distribution and Dissemination of PSYOP Products

Public sentiment is everything. With public sentiment nothing can fail. Without it nothing can succeed. He who molds opinion is greater than he who enacts law.

President Abraham Lincoln
Debate With Stephen Douglas, 21 August 1858

In today's Information Age, there is an increasing reliance on sophisticated, near-real-time media dissemination. Information, and its denial, is power. The state or entity most able to effectively control or manage information, especially managing the perceptions of particular TAs, will be the most influential. Once PSYOP programs and messages have been chosen, the PSYOP commander must decide the most effective way to convey them to the TA. This chapter discusses the distribution and dissemination methods and factors. Though each process is unique, they are interrelated.

DISTRIBUTION METHODS

10-1. Distribution is the movement of products, either physically or electronically, from the production location to the disseminators. Products may be employed through various media—visual (newspaper, pamphlets, handbills), audio (radio, loudspeakers), and audiovisual (TV). Maneuver commanders can request products in support of operations. Product distribution within the theater often consists of using ground or air couriers to physically deliver products to PSYOP units for dissemination. PSYOP dissemination involves transmitting products directly to the TA via desired media. There are several methods for the distribution and retrieval of products currently available. The following paragraphs describe several of these methods and their characteristics.

PRODUCT DISTRIBUTION FACILITY

10-2. This facility houses product distribution hardware that enables PSYOP units to distribute products throughout the world via SIPRNET and into Europe via the Bosnia command and control augmentation (BC2A) system—the satellite communications system used throughout Europe, including Bosnia. USAJFKSWCS Pub 525-5-16 provides more information on this facility.

4TH POG(A) SECURE WEB PAGES

10-3. The 4th POG(A) maintains secure web pages on the POAS secure servers located at Fort Bragg. These pages can be accessed through the

SIPRNET or a dedicated secure connection into the POAS system. The S-6, 4th POG(A), maintains a hierarchy of web pages under the 4th POG(A) web site for each PSYOP battalion. Products can be developed and forwarded to the S-6 for inclusion on the web pages. These web pages can be accessed using a secure computer with a web browser (such as Internet Explorer, Mosaic, or Netscape) and a connection to the SIPRNET or the POAS router. These web pages provide a logical, hierarchical way to organize and store PSYOP information and products for subsequent retrieval by deployed PSYOP units. Length of retrieval time is dependent upon several factors, such as size of the file and available bandwidth. This system is ideal for storing products for retrieval by deployed units. However, drawbacks include the inability to "push" products to the user and use of additional bandwidth overhead to navigate to the appropriate subpage and download nonessential web page information, such as embedded graphics and text prior to retrieving the desired product. Therefore, it is critical that web pages that deployed units will access contain no unnecessary graphics that require additional bandwidth.

FILE TRANSFER PROTOCOL

10-4. FTP is a service much like a web server, but is text-based and is designed exclusively for transferring files over a transmission control protocol/Internet protocol (TCP/IP) network, such as SIPRNET or NIPRNET. Although not as intuitive as using a web browser, FTP is very useful for a trained user and avoids many of the overhead problems associated with using web pages. The user must know the exact location and file name of the file desired. The user logs into the FTP server site, uses disk operating system (DOS)-like commands to navigate to the appropriate directory where the desired file is stored, and then issues a command to get the file (transfer the file to his computer across the network). An advantage of FTP over web pages is that FTP can be both a "pull" and a "push" system—users can both send and retrieve files to and from the FTP server. Like a web page, a "virtual" point-to-point connection is established, and the file is transferred immediately without any intermediate "store-and-forward" sites in between. If the appropriate software is used, the deployed user can establish an FTP server site, and products can be pushed to the deployed site without intervention on the receiving end. Additionally, "FTP outbox" software is available which allows a user to send a file to an outbox from which the system will send the files in order without constant supervision by the sender. This type of software is particularly useful when connected to a busy network where frequent timeouts occur and files must be resent.

SIPRNET/NIPRNET

10-5. The SIPRNET/NIPRNET is a commercial off-the-shelf International Business Machines (IBM)-compatible computer system with network adapter. This computer system is used for secure and nonsecure product research and distribution.

REACHBACK

10-6. To make the best use of all available technologies and resources, PSYOP elements use reachback capabilities. The main capabilities required by the deployed PSYOP element to implement reachback are access to POAS, access to the 4th POG(A) web servers, point-to-point file transfer, access to SIPRNET and NIPRNET for file transfer and E-mail, and intertheater distribution of PSYOP products. This concept allows a portion of PSYOP forces that support forward-deployed elements to transfer products and ideas instantaneously. Current and emerging technologies (both military and commercial) will support the reachback concept by providing secure, digital communications paths for transferring PSYOP products between Fort Bragg and deployed PSYOP units. They use secure communication links including, but not limited to, the SIPRNET, the POAS, and the PSYOP Special Operations Media System-B (SOMS-B).

10-7. Under reachback, a portion of the PDCs of the regional PSYOP battalions remains with the POTF (Rear) and the MOC, depending on mission requirements. These personnel work on long-range planning, develop products based on mission requirements, and then provide them to the POTF (Forward). Deployed forces will develop, produce, and disseminate products at the tactical and operational levels using internal assets or other military or civilian assets in the AOR. The POTF (Rear), however, may move forward as the situation dictates.

ELECTRONIC MAIL

10-8. Secure and nonsecure E-mail is available through the SIPRNET and NIPRNET, respectively, providing the capability to send both C2 as well as PSYOP products over a network. E-mail can be sent to one or many recipients, and is primarily a "push" system. An advantage of the system is that files can be sent directly from a user workstation without having to post to an FTP or web site. A disadvantage is that E-mail is a store-and-forward system. The sent message can be delayed by each E-mail host along the way before it is forwarded onto the next, resulting in what could be very significant delays. E-mail host administrators concerned about disk space can set arbitrary limits on maximum message size and can block messages over a certain size (often 1 to 2 megabytes [MB]). E-mail also poses a significant challenge in distribution of the right product at the right time to the right place. Users can send E-mail to the wrong place, consume massive bandwidth by sending it to multiple users, or lose track of the original file or the correct version after sending it.

POINT-TO-POINT FILE TRANSFER

10-9. Two computers can transfer files directly between them without using a TCP/IP network by using PROCOMM or similar software and a communications channel. This process is similar to FTP using a dedicated communications channel rather than a network. This file transfer can be done over commercial or military telephone lines or a point-to-point communications data link, such as single channel tactical satellite (TACSAT) or international maritime satellite (INMARSAT). The major limitation of this capability is that it is strictly point-to-point. Data destined for other locations must be either transferred to a system with one of the above capabilities or via another point-to-point connection.

PSYCHOLOGICAL OPERATIONS AUTOMATED SYSTEM

10-10. POAS is an automated database containing intelligence reports and country information prepared by analysts within the 4th POG(A). POAS has a superior search capability that enables users to retrieve detailed information based on specified search criteria. POAS can be accessed through several means—dedicated POAS terminals connected to the POAS secure network, dial-up telephone connections using STU-III data modems, or through the SIPRNET. A future enhancement for POAS will include a CA database containing information for CA units.

CONTRACTED DISTRIBUTION

10-11. PSYOP personnel may use local delivery companies to deliver products to various parts of an AO. Large quantities of magazines or posters can be delivered to different areas within the country. PSYOP personnel may contract out with a local company for delivery on a weekly, biweekly, or monthly basis. This agreement will ensure the delivery of the products and will not tie up military transportation assets. The PSYOP contracting officer coordinates these actions and outside contracts. The contracting officer works out all the legal issues with payment, insurance, and delivery companies.

HOST NATION ASSETS

10-12. PSYOP personnel must employ the HN's assets that may become available. Existing facilities will have the power and range required to reach an existing TA with radio or TV. Programming can be introduced onto the airways immediately, without having to wait for the installation of transportable systems. PSYOP personnel should strive to build bonds with the HN by working together with their military, OGAs, or the NGOs. By working with the local military (if feasible) or NGOs, PSYOP forces will be able to coordinate combined distribution efforts to many of the areas that need to be reached. This coordination helps in establishing a greater working relationship between PSYOP forces and the HN, and places PSYOP in a positive light with parts of the local populace that see these coordinated efforts as favorable.

10-13. The PSYOP operations officer should be able to help coordinate these programs or joint ventures. Some of the organizations that may be of service are the—

- United Nations High Commissioner for Refugees (UNHCR).
- International Police Task Force (IPTF).

10-14. The list of NGOs in any given area may be quite extensive. The United States Agency for International Development (USAID) publishes a yearly report entitled Voluntary Foreign Aid Programs. The PSYOP commander should be able to obtain this report from the combatant commander's library.

OTHER DISTRIBUTION ASSETS

10-15. New equipment programs are being developed to enhance the capabilities of the PSYOP community. The following equipment is in various stages of development, procurement, and fielding:

- Psychological Operations Distribution System (PDS).
- Theater Media Production Center (TMPC).

USAJFKSWCS Pub 525-5-16 provides more information on this equipment.

DISSEMINATION FACTORS

10-16. Dissemination is the actual delivery of the PSYOP message to the TA. Having multiple means of dissemination is most preferred. For example, the Gulf War brought a whole new meaning to the use of multimedia in PSYOP. Radio and TV broadcasts, leaflets, and loudspeakers used the themes of Arab brotherhood, allied and air power, and Iraqi isolation to induce large numbers of enemy soldiers to desert. Selecting dissemination techniques is influenced by a combination of several factors, including political, military, and geographic considerations; countermeasures; weather; and availability of dissemination devices. By carefully considering the political effects of these factors and using the unique delivery techniques of each medium to their full extent, PSYOP units can successfully disseminate PSYOP products to the TA. Audiences vary greatly in their ability to understand the message because of language, cultural, or other barriers, whether that medium is radio, TV, or print. As soon as possible in the PSYOP planning process, PSYOP personnel should decide on the best means of dissemination. To determine the most effective methods of dissemination, PSYOP personnel must assess the following dissemination and communication factors:

- Existing communication structure.
- Media availability and credibility.
- Language (to include dialects, slang usage).
- Musical likes and dislikes.
- Social taboos.
- Control of the media.
- Capability of the media; for example, power of TV transmitters.
- Physical conditions (geography and climatology).
- Graffiti.
- Opponent's means to disrupt.

PRODUCT DISSEMINATION SYSTEMS AND METHODS

10-17. PSYOP has numerous dissemination platforms used to disseminate finished, approved PSYOP visual, audio, and audiovisual products to designated TAs within an AOR or JOA. These dissemination systems include the following:

- Mobile Audiovisual System (MAVS).
- Loudspeaker systems (FOL manpack, LSS-40C/MPLS, FOL airborne loudspeaker system [ALS]).

- M129E1, M129E2, and PDU5/B leaflet bombs.
- Portable AM transmitter - 400 watt (PAMT-400).
- Transportable AM transmitter - 10 kilowatt (TAMT-10).
- Transportable AM transmitter - 50 kilowatt (AN/TRQ-44).
- Portable FM transmitter - 1000 watt (PFMT-1000).
- Portable FM transmitter - 2000 watt (PFMT-2000).
- Flyaway Broadcast System (FABS) stand-alone AM, FM, shortwave (SW), and TV transmitters.
- SOMS-B.

PRINT DISSEMINATION SYSTEMS AND METHODS

10-18. To best use the dissemination techniques for printed products, PSYOP forces need to consider the availability of assets at their disposal and the most efficient and effective way to get the product to the TA. Obviously, printed products directed at an illiterate target or written in the wrong language have little effect on the target. Also, using a symbol with an indistinct meaning to an illiterate target or written in the wrong language has little effect on the target. However, using a symbol with a distinct meaning to an illiterate target may have a significant effect. The following paragraphs discuss specific dissemination systems and methods available to PSYOP forces.

Face-to-Face Dissemination

10-19. Of the many dissemination techniques available, PSYOP forces may choose to use handbills, leaflets, posters, or novelty items for face-to-face communication and dissemination. Face-to-face communication is the conveyance of a message by the sender in the sight or presence of the receiver. This communication may be by one individual to another or one speaker addressing a large group. These individuals are known as agents of action. Face-to-face communication ranges from two or more individuals in informal conversation to planned persuasion among groups. The credibility of the PSYOP messages delivered by face-to-face communication is increased when the communicator is known and respected. By disseminating through face-to-face communication, PSYOP forces have the opportunity to interact with the local populace and get direct and immediate feedback and reactions from the TA that would normally not be available as quickly.

10-20. PSYOP personnel may place posters up within their specific AO using tape, staples, or poster paste. Poster paste is the preferred method as paste makes tearing the product down more difficult. PSYOP personnel should consult with local leaders prior to disseminating posters. These leaders can provide PSYOP personnel information as to the best locations to put up posters to gain maximum visibility. Care should also be taken when placing posters at sensitive locations, such as religious facilities. PSYOP personnel should check with the facility manager; there may be specific guidelines for where, how, and when a poster is put up due to fears of retribution or other perceived threats. Printing novelty items with the PSYOP message is an extremely effective means to reach more people, especially children. PSYOP personnel use novelty items, such as notebooks, soccer balls, pens and pencils, and T-shirts, all with the PSYOP message printed on them. An effective dissemination technique is to hand out products at the same time and place on a regular schedule. When PSYOP personnel distribute these products, they inform the local populace that they will be back on a certain date and time. This practice sets up a specific dissemination location where the TA knows they will receive new products and information on a regular basis. (PSYOP personnel employ this practice only in a mature theater and not in a hostile environment.) In time, messages will reach the parents by reading what their children bring home, and, after some time, the children may start to ask their parents questions about the message and persuade their parents to think differently. PSYOP personnel should target the youth, as their opinions are not as ingrained. When passing out handbills and novelty items, PSYOP personnel should take care to adhere to cultural nuisances. For instance, some cultures frown on adults other than parents having direct contact with or talking to children. Cultural awareness is key to gaining the trust and respect of the TA.

10-21. PSYOP forces should maintain a close working relationship with CA personnel within the AO. Many common areas are covered between the two organizations whereby PSYOP and CA, by sharing information, can provide mutually beneficial information to be exploited more advantageously by each organization. Through working with the CA units, PSYOP forces can also coordinate the mutual dissemination of products.

10-22. There are many advantages of face-to-face communication. Some examples include the following:

- *Relationship.* Face-to-face communication employs an interpersonal relationship.

- *Audience selection.* The audience can be deliberately selected and the appeal directed and tailored for the audience.

- *Assessment of impact.* Feedback is immediate. The communicator can immediately assess the impact of his message and adjust his approach to obtain the desired response.

- *Requirement for limited support.* Limited technical and logistical support is required.

- *Credibility.* Face-to-face communication can be more credible than other methods because the TA can evaluate the source.

- *Presentation.* Complex material can be presented in detail. Frequent repetition and slight variations can be readily used to influence the audience.

- *Expeditiousness.* In some instances, particularly in primitive areas, face-to-face communication may be the most expeditious method of disseminating propaganda.

10-23. There are also disadvantages of face-to-face communication. Some examples include the following:

- *Limited use in tactical situations.* Use is limited in war due to the inaccessibility of the target individual or group. Use is limited in combat since the psychological Soldier has little face-to-face communication with the adversary until they are captured or they defect.

- *Close control necessary.* Face-to-face dissemination must be controlled, especially at the lowest levels where each communicator has the responsibility to interpret policy and objectives. The control factor is best illustrated by trying to pass an oral message, one person at a time, throughout a group. By the time the message reaches the end of the group, it does not resemble the original message. Reinforcement by other media is necessary to eliminate this problem.

- *Limited use in secure areas.* Security considerations limit the conduct of face-to-face communications. As the security situation improves and more areas are secure, area coverage can be extended.

- *Able communicators required.* Effective communication requires knowledgeable, orally persuasive individuals who can convince the TA that the program and policies are irresistible and inevitable.

- *Indigenous personnel required.* For effective communications, indigenous personnel are normally required.

- *Limited range of voice.* The range of the human voice and the need for visual contact limit this method to relatively small audiences.

10-24. A keen awareness of the TA's culture coupled with skillful face-to-face communication can lead to successful PSYOP. PSYOP personnel can use face-to-face communication to present persuasive appeals and complex material in detail. They can repeat portions of the communication as required and use slight variations to influence a specific TA. The importance of appropriate gestures and physical posture in the communication process must not be overlooked. What may be an appropriate gesture in one culture may be viewed quite differently in another. The most important part of face-to-face communication is the immediate feedback that can be obtained from the TA. PSYOP personnel can obtain valuable information from this feedback and may realize the true meaning of the message that PSYOP personnel may have overlooked due to a lack of the political or cultural differences. This information may change the message intent or the message itself. PSYOP personnel should take every opportunity to hone and enhance their ability to conduct effective face-to-face communication. PSYOP personnel need to rehearse face-to-face communication to practice favorable body language while eliminating unfavorable gestures and posture. Body language is as important as the verbal message and should appear natural, not labored or uncomfortable.

10-25. To learn more about gestures, posture, and other mannerisms used when communicating face-to-face, PSYOP personnel should consult individuals who have lived in the HN and are aware of these customs. A good source of this information is to talk with and ask questions of the interpreters that are assigned in the AO. Another excellent source of additional information is the Culturgram series published by Brigham Young University. Each Culturgram lists the latest information about greetings, eating, gestures, and travel under the "Customs and Courtesies" heading and also includes the headings "The People," "Lifestyle," "The Nation," and "Health." The *Do's and Taboos Around the World* book contains chapters on hand gestures and body language, giving and receiving gifts, a quick guide to the ways of the world, and information about the importance of colors, jargon, slang, and humor. The ethnic composition of a working PSYOP team should be as diverse as possible. This practice will prevent hostile propaganda about the use of a specific ethnic group to achieve certain goals. A diverse ethnic composition within the TPT demonstrates a willingness to work with all races.

Leaflet Dissemination

10-26. Another means available for mass dispersal of a product to areas that are difficult to reach is the leaflet. If leaflet dissemination is the primary means to be used, PSYOP personnel must determine which methods will be used—surface delivery or air-to-ground delivery. Coordination must be made with the G-3 Air for scheduling the proper aircraft, depending on which method of dissemination is used. The POTF G-3 will handle this coordination. When preparing for leaflet dissemination, the method of delivery depends on a variety of factors. PSYOP personnel should examine the following items for their effect on the mission:

- Political or military denial to the TA.
- Opponent countermeasure capabilities.
- Seriousness of punishment inflicted upon TA members caught in possession of the product.
- TA population density.
- Geographical denial.
- Number and size of printed material.
- Availability of delivery devices.
- Availability of air sorties.
- Weather.
- Multiple leaflet dissemination.
- Production time.
- Mixed media requirements.
- Product priority.
- Enemy countermeasures.

10-27. Paper quality affects the drift of airdropped leaflets. If a leaflet, which offers little or no wind resistance, is dropped from a flying aircraft, the leaflet will be blown at about the same speed and direction as the wind. If there are updrafts or downdrafts, the leaflet will still follow the general direction of the wind. In areas of no turbulence, the constant pull of gravity acting upon the leaflet will cause it to fall at a fairly constant rate. The basic objective of leaflet drops is to place sufficient leaflets on the ground to ensure that every member of the TA will see (not necessarily possess) a leaflet. PSYOP personnel use several air-to-ground delivery methods:

- *Aerial distribution.* Leaflets printed or distributed in areas of high humidity tend to stick together. Ruffling one or both ends of the leaflet stack ensures complete dispersion.

- *Airdrop by hand (low altitude).* Leaflets are dropped by hand through aircraft doors, ports, or specially fabricated chutes in areas where low-level delivery is feasible. Leaflets should be dropped in small quantities at very close intervals. This method results in an almost continuous release of leaflets evenly distributed downwind and parallel to the flight of the aircraft. Two men can dispense thousands of leaflets per minute using this efficient, inexpensive technique.

- *High-altitude free fall.* Leaflets are dispensed from aircraft flying at altitudes up to 15,000 meters (50,000 feet). This technique is well suited for leaflet drops directed at large general target areas. This technique requires long-range planning and preparation to ensure prompt reaction to favorable wind conditions. PSYOP personnel must know the characteristics of different-sized leaflets to ensure that the proper "mix" of leaflets is used to obtain dissemination throughout the target area.

- *Static-line technique.* At high altitudes, the use of leaflet bundles or boxes opened by static line has proven effective. Through use of rollers on the deck of the aircraft, boxes weighing up to 50 kilograms (110 pounds) can be ejected with minimum exertion. The box is rolled out of the aircraft, and as the container comes to the end of the static line, the sides of the box split. In effect, the box is turned inside out and the leaflets fall away followed by the empty box.

- *Balloon operations.* These operations are useful for penetrating denied areas and can be conducted up to a range of 2,400 kilometers (1,500 miles). Balloons are made of paper, rubber, or polyethylene. The weather, wind, air currents, and gas pressure determine flight patterns. Although the maximum payload is 9 kilograms (about 20 pounds), balloons are an inexpensive means of disseminating leaflets.

- *Remotely piloted vehicles (RPVs).* RPVs are capable of conducting a variety of combat missions, including leaflet delivery, surveillance, reconnaissance, electronic warfare, and strike. The remote pilot is able to detect and identify targets, change the course of the RPV, and make decisions to initiate and terminate operations in the target area. Pinpoint accuracy is possible. RPVs can be flown into enemy territories where the gun and missile antiaircraft defenses are very intense and the losses of manned aircraft might be unacceptable. RPVs can be fitted with modified wing pods, providing a large leaflet capacity per mission.

- *Leaflet bomb.* The M129E1 and M129E2 leaflet bombs are Air Force items, obtained through Air Force ordnance channels. Each leaflet bomb weighs about 52 kilograms (115 pounds) empty and about 100 kilograms (225 pounds) when loaded. The leaflet bomb can carry approximately 30,000 16-pound machine-rolled leaflets (13 x 20 centimeters [5 1/4 x 8 inches]). Before the leaflets are placed in the bomb, the detonating cord is placed in the seam between the two halves. When the bomb is released, the fuse functions at a predetermined time, detonating the primer cord separating the two body sections, detaching the fins, and releasing the leaflets.

10-28. The PDU-5/B leaflet bomb (SUU-76C/B without leaflet payload) is an Air Force item, obtained through Air Force ordnance channels. It weighs about 140 pounds empty and has a maximum carrying capacity of 152 pounds. The PDU-5/B can be loaded with 20 rolls of 3- x 6-inch leaflets. Each leaflet roll will measure 11 inches in diameter, and total fiber tube weight (with leaflet rolls) must be between 148 and 152 pounds. Other leaflet sizes include—

- 3- x 4-inches, 20 rolls, weighing 7.5 pounds per roll.
- 4- x 4-inches, 15 rolls, weighing 10 pounds per roll.
- 6- x 6-inches, 10 rolls, weighing 15 pounds per roll.

Appendix L consists of conversion tables that may be used to convert measurements from U.S. standard terms to metric when mission requirements or environments change.

AUDIO AND AUDIOVISUAL DISSEMINATION SYSTEMS AND METHODS

10-29. The audiovisual media used to disseminate PSYOP products fall into three categories: face-to-face communication, TV broadcasting, and movies. Audiovisual media have a great appeal as they add motion to the perceptions of sight and sound and have become one of the most effective means over the past decade for PSYOP to disseminate products. When selecting a form of audiovisual media, the PSYOP planner must weigh all factors before making a media decision. In some cases, more than one type of medium may be desired to ensure full dissemination of the message. Product dissemination not only depends on the types of media selected, but also on the media availability to provide coverage and accessibility to the TA.

Audio Methods

10-30. The audio media used to disseminate PSYOP products fall into two categories: radio broadcasting and loudspeaker operations. Radio broadcasts reach local and worldwide TAs quickly and simultaneously by providing broad coverage and the speed to capitalize on opportunities. Radio reaches beyond borders and into denied areas to help shape the attitudes, opinions, beliefs, and behavior of the TA. Whenever possible, PSYOP personnel should broadcast on HN radio equipment. In hostile situations, PSYOP personnel should use captured radio facilities, when available. The PSYOP staff officer assigned to the supported unit must ensure maneuver commanders are informed about the need to limit or prevent damage to radio facilities in the AO. This information is communicated to the JTCB to be placed on the restricted fires list.

10-31. **Radio Broadcasting.** PSYOP forces have numerous dissemination platforms used to disseminate finished, approved PSYOP audio products to designated TAs within an AOR or JOA. The radio broadcasting equipment includes the following:

- PAMT-400.
- TAMT-10.

- AN/TRQ-44.
- PFMT-1000.
- PFMT-2000.
- SOMS-B (AM/FM/SW).

USAJFKSWCS Pub 525-5-16 provides details on these systems.

10-32. **Loudspeaker Operations.** Of the many media employed to communicate PSYOP messages to TAs during combat operations, only the loudspeaker affords immediate and direct contact. The loudspeaker can move rapidly to wherever an exploitable PSYOP opportunity is found and can follow the TA when the TA moves. The loudspeaker achieves, in effect, face-to-face communication with the adversary. Loudspeakers can convey speeches, music, and sound effects to the audience. Tapes and CDs can be used to augment or replace live performers. Messages can be rehearsed and prerecorded. Loudspeakers are commonly mounted on a tactical wheeled vehicle (HMMWV), or mounted in a rucksack; however they can also be carried on a larger truck, tank, boat, or an aircraft. The loudspeaker can be directed to be broadcast at opponent forces that have been cut off, urging them to surrender or cease resistance. Loudspeakers can also be used to issue instructions to persons in fortified positions and locations, and used for deception operations by broadcasting sounds of vehicles or other equipment. Loudspeakers can also be employed to control the flow of refugees and DCs, and to issue instructions to reduce interference by civilians on the battlefield. During loudspeaker broadcasts, the TA becomes a captive audience who cannot escape the messages being delivered. In addition, if the message is properly tailored and has been well conceived, the TA will not be able to escape the psychological impact of the message. Loudspeakers can be used to exploit any opportunity that suddenly arises, and can reach the target faster than other media do.

10-33. One of the best examples of the successful use of loudspeakers occurred during the Gulf War. The allied coalition effectively isolated a large element of the Iraqi forces on Faylaka Island. Rather than attack the island with a direct assault, a TPT from the 9th Battalion aboard a UH-1N helicopter flew aerial loudspeaker missions around the island with Cobra gunships providing escort. The message told the adversary below to surrender the next day in formation at the radio tower. The next day, 1,405 Iraqi soldiers, including a general officer, waited in formation at the radio tower to surrender to the Marine forces without a single shot being fired.

10-34. PSYOP personnel must consider several factors when planning the use of loudspeakers in support of tactical operations. These factors include the following:

- *Weather.* Weather conditions have a considerable effect on how the loudspeaker sounds to the TA. Since dry air carries sound better than humid air, and cold air better than warm air, cold and dry weather creates the greatest audibility range. The exception to this rule occurs when snow is on the ground because snow absorbs and muffles sound. Wind is another important factor. When the wind is blowing from behind the broadcast site and toward the target, audibility ranges increase several hundred meters. Broadcasting into the wind reduces the range. When coming from the side, wind deflects the sound in the same manner as wind deflects a rifle bullet; therefore, the loudspeaker cones must be aimed to the right or left of the target, just as windage is considered on a rifle sight. Winds with velocities exceeding 15 knots make all except very short-range broadcasts impractical. Likewise, a heavy rain or thunderstorm destroys audibility at normal ranges.

- *Terrain.* Terrain also has important effects on loudspeaker broadcasts. In hilly or mountainous country, PSYOP personnel emplace the loudspeaker on the forward slope facing the opponent. In built-up areas, the loudspeakers are positioned so structures do not come between them and the target. Trees and brush—like snow—absorb and muffle sound. Echoes reduce or destroy the intelligibility of the message, but the sound of the broadcast remains audible to the opponent. Using loudspeakers near water or flat land maximizes audibility.

- *Equipment limitations.* Current loudspeaker sets are a compromise between power output, transportability, and ruggedness. A more powerful set would require the sacrifice of one or both of the other qualities. Although it is possible under ideal conditions to achieve a range of 3,200 meters (10,500 feet), a single set under average battle conditions cannot be expected to be effective beyond 1,400 meters (4,600 feet). Loudspeaker teams prefer to operate at a range under 1,000 meters (3,300 feet) whenever possible.

- *Opponent counteraction.* Opponent commanders often try to prevent their troops from listening to loudspeaker broadcasts. They sometimes open fire to destroy or drown out the loudspeaker.

- *Personnel.* The human factor in loudspeaker operations is extremely important. In addition to personnel with highly developed and widely varied skills needed for loudspeaker operations, the team also needs Soldiers who are effective with weapons and trained in tactical movements.

- *Support operations.* The key to a successful loudspeaker operation lies in correct employment of PSYOP messages in a given situation. A cardinal rule in all tactical loudspeaker operations is that any loudspeaker broadcast, to be effective, must be carefully tailored to fit the situation. Loudspeakers are particularly useful in tactical support of exploitation, retrograde movement, and static situations, as well as in support of consolidation and counterinsurgency operations.

- *Exploitation.* When friendly forces are exploiting the breakthrough of opponent lines, the loudspeaker can achieve its most spectacular results. Opponent units that are surrounded, isolated, or bypassed become ideal targets for surrender or cease resistance broadcasts. Roadblocks, towns containing opponent troops, and other points of opponent resistance also provide excellent targets. The primary mission of the loudspeaker in exploitation is to persuade the opponent to surrender or cease resistance. The loudspeaker may also be used to deliver ultimatums or to bring about "white flag" missions in which the opponent commander or his representative is requested to discuss capitulation. Successful loudspeaker missions speed the advance of friendly forces and reduce casualties.

- *Retrograde movement.* During a withdrawal, the loudspeaker supports military operations by assisting in clearing roads for military traffic, controlling refugee movements, and warning the civilian populace against acts of sabotage.

- *Static situations.* When lines are stabilized or when a truce situation exists (such as during the Korean conflict when peace negotiations were in progress), loudspeakers are used for the long-range mission. The objective is to undermine the opponent's morale and reduce combat efficiency by exploiting his weaknesses—tactical, economic, psychological, and other. Loudspeaker messages play on tensions known to exist among opponent troops and exploit nostalgic themes with music and female voices to make the opponent soldier discontented and worried about affairs at home. News is broadcast regularly, particularly items opponent leaders are likely to withhold from their troops and items the TA can verify. These broadcasts build credibility for the entire PSYOP effort and, in particular, build audience acceptance of loudspeaker broadcasts. Such broadcasts may be the only source of news for the opponent frontline soldier. In this situation, primary objectives are not to obtain surrenders but to lower the opponent's morale and, consequently, reduce his fighting effectiveness by encouraging dissatisfaction, malingering, and individual desertions. Loudspeakers may also be used in a static situation to support counterguerrilla operations.

- *Consolidation operations.* In newly occupied or liberated territory, PSYOP personnel can effectively use the loudspeaker to broadcast instructions and proclamations to civilians and to help CA personnel control the population. Loudspeakers are also used for traffic control, particularly to prevent refugees from clogging roads and hindering military movement, and in crowd control.

- *Counterinsurgency operations.* PSYOP personnel can support tactical operations using loudspeakers to broadcast a wide variety of PSYOP messages to the civilian population or the insurgents. PSYOP personnel can extend the range greatly by mounting the cones on aircraft and broadcasting over areas believed to contain guerrillas or their supporters.

10-35. There are many advantages of using loudspeakers. Some examples include the following:

- Targets of opportunity can be exploited.
- Persuasive messages can be transmitted to the target as the situation changes.
- Loudspeakers can be an extension of face-to-face communication.
- The operator can pinpoint his target.
- The TA can be illiterate.
- The loudspeaker can be used to undermine enemy morale.

- Operators can be easily and readily trained.
- PSYOP personnel can move to and operate anywhere a potential TA is located.
- Large, powerful, fixed loudspeakers can broadcast messages considerable distances into enemy territory.
- Loudspeakers can be mounted on either wheeled or tracked vehicles.
- Small portable loudspeaker systems can be backpacked by dismounted troops.
- Loudspeaker systems can be mounted in rotary-wing aircraft. Use of aircraft broadens the areas accessible for loudspeaker operations. Since aircraft must operate at low altitudes for the message to be understood on the ground, the sophistication and intensity of the enemy air defenses are prime considerations.
- Loudspeaker missions, based on the mission type, can provide immediate feedback and impact indicators.

10-36. There are also disadvantages to using loudspeakers. Some examples include—

- Range is limited by environmental conditions.
- The enemy can readily take countermeasures, such as concentrating artillery or other weapons on loudspeaker personnel and equipment.
- Messages may be forgotten and distorted with the passage of time.

10-37. In an urban setting, loudspeakers are used to communicate with assembled groups and in localized street broadcasting. Loudspeakers effectively extend the range of face-to-face communications and are the most responsive medium that can be used to support tactical operations. Unsophisticated loudspeaker messages can be developed on the spot and delivered live in fast-moving situations. Loudspeaker broadcasts are usually prerecorded to ensure accuracy. Occasionally, standard tapes are developed, mass produced, and distributed from the theater or national level.

10-38. Close coordination by the loudspeaker team with personnel of the supported unit and with other supporting elements is essential. Commanders within audible range of the broadcasts must be informed about support for loudspeaker operations. Commanders must ensure that troops are briefed on the opponent's possible reaction to the broadcast. Examples include enemy soldiers attempting to surrender or enemy fire directed at the loudspeakers. Troops must also be briefed on what procedures to follow in the event of these reactions. If the loudspeaker message is an ultimatum—threatening artillery fire or air attacks—arrangements must be made so one or the other will take place as announced. Lack of follow-through contributes to decreased credibility.

10-39. Without thorough and continuing coordination of activity, the most carefully made plans for PSYOP support cannot achieve maximum effectiveness. Coordination is required in several directions. Command and staffs at higher, lower, and adjacent echelons must know about the PSYOP program and its results. If artillery and air support are required for loudspeaker operations, the PSYOP planner must make precise and detailed coordination with the supported unit's operations staff. Coordination may involve the FSCOORD, theater airlift liaison officer (TALO), tactical air control party (TACP), and the maneuver element commander. PSYOP personnel must ensure that requirements are clearly spelled out in the unit's concept of the operation and execution portion of the OPORD so that all involved understand what is to happen. Without coordination, the many hours of planning and preparation that precede a loudspeaker mission are wasted or counterproductive.

10-40. As organized military PSYOP developed in World War II, the Korean conflict, Vietnam, Grenada, Panama, and Operation DESERT STORM, the loudspeaker has accounted for an ever-increasing percentage of output for combat PSYOP. Since this trend is likely to continue in future conflicts, loudspeaker messages must be based on sound PSYOP principles. Similar to the leaflet developer and radio scriptwriter, PSYOP loudspeaker scriptwriters must follow established doctrine, use relevant themes, make effective use of PSYOP intelligence, and deliver the message in understandable, persuasive language. In fluid situations, plans must be flexible to meet changing conditions.

10-41. To achieve maximum effect in the loudspeaker broadcast, certain rules governing speech delivery must be observed. PSYOP personnel—

- Speak loudly, but do not shout.
- Speak deliberately and take time for message delivery.
- Maintain a constant voice volume with an even rate of delivery.
- Never slur over or drop words.
- Avoid a singsong delivery.
- Sound each syllable of each word.
- Sound the final consonant of each word.
- Think of each word as it is spoken.
- Speak into the microphone.

Audiovisual Methods

10-42. Television is a proven means of persuasion worldwide and, therefore, a vital asset in PSYOP dissemination. TV appeals to a number of senses, making it the closest medium to face-to-face communication. TV has been responsible for swaying the opinion of entire nations. A thoroughly prepared PSYOP TV product can be extremely effective if PSYOP planners fully understand the unique properties of TV and do not limit their imagination in its use. TV, including videotape recording (VTR), is one of the most effective mediums for persuasion. TV offers many advantages for propaganda operations, and its wide application in other fields contributes to its acceptance and use. TV is appropriate for use across the full spectrum of operations and is particularly effective in FID and consolidation operations. In places where TV is not a common communication medium, receivers may be distributed to public facilities and selected individuals. A possible limitation in enemy countries, however, is that TV receivers may be set to allow reception on only one or two channels under government control. TV is an all-encompassing mass communication medium. Like radio, TV makes use of the sense of hearing to convey an idea. Like printed material, TV makes use of the sense of sight, adding the element of motion. Moreover, like the motion picture, TV combines sight, sound, and motion. TV is immediate; in effect, it places the viewer in two locations simultaneously, creating the illusion of participating in a distant event.

10-43. PSYOP has numerous dissemination platforms used to disseminate finished, approved PSYOP audiovisual products to designated TAs within an AOR or JOA. These dissemination systems include the following:

- SOMS-B.
- FABS TV transmitter.

USAJFKSWCS Pub 525-5-16 provides details on this equipment.

10-44. There are many advantages of TV. Some examples include—

- *Speed.* TV programs can reach large segments of the TA rapidly. The transmission of events can be instantaneous.

- *Audience illiteracy.* Illiteracy is not a barrier; an audience need not be able to read.

- *Unification.* TV brings people in widely separate locations closer together by exposing them visually to the same ideas and concepts.

- *Aural-visual effect.* TV appeals to two senses, each reinforcing the other, and gives the viewer a sense of involvement.

10-45. There are also disadvantages of TV. Some examples include—

- *Range.* Geography and atmospheric conditions affect the strength and range of the signal. The signal may, however, be boosted with relay stations, airborne transmitters, or satellite relay to increase the transmission range. Airborne antenna relay domes extend the range of a central transmitter but at great expense.

- *Reception.* TV sets are unevenly distributed throughout the world. Messages disseminated by TV will normally be received only by those within an above-average income range and economic class in many areas of the world, particularly in developing nations. In some developing nations, however, group listening and viewing centers may be available, negating the link between income and access to television. The association should be carefully determined for each target country.

- *Equipment incompatibility.* Receivers in the target area may not be compatible with the transmission equipment.

- *Power.* Most TV receivers require an outside source of electric power. Many areas of the world lack this power. The introduction of self-contained power packs partially eliminates this problem. If broadcasts are to be made from areas lacking power facilities, special generators and a fuel supply may be needed.

- *Vulnerability.* Equipment and parts are fragile and extremely vulnerable to damage. Stations are easily identified and make excellent targets. Receivers are difficult to hide.

- *Program requirements.* A substantial production staff and supporting equipment are required to produce daily programs. Each day's operation requires a large amount of film, videotape, and live programming to sustain a program schedule.
- *Maintenance.* Maintenance is highly technical, requiring trained and skilled technicians and engineers; such people are difficult to find.
- *Personnel.* Television is a complicated communication medium, demanding specialized personnel with a wide range of scarce skills.
- *Audience accessibility.* Difficulty in reaching audiences in hostile areas due to incompatibility of receivers, extreme distortions caused by multiple transmitters on the same wavelength, jamming, and censorship limit the use of TV broadcasts to hostile areas.

10-46. To take full advantage of TV as a medium, PSYOP personnel must realize that TV has always been primarily a means of entertainment. However, the vast majority of viewers accept events seen on the TV screen as fact. The implied actions of the characters we see on the TV screen manipulate our understanding of what we see. This impact is what sets TV apart from all other media. Before selecting TV as a PSYOP medium, PSYOP personnel must determine the degree of credibility TV holds for the TA and its degree of access. The TA's accessibility to TV may be limited. In remote areas, videotape may be the proper alternative to TV. Advantages of videotape include the following:

- The results of the "take" can be seen immediately; if editing is necessary prior to release to the audience, the editing can be done electronically as the material is being produced. There is no time lag as with film, which requires chemical processing.
- Videotape can be reused a number of times, erasing itself as it is run through the recorder, or it can quickly be erased on equipment made for that purpose, and then reused.
- Videotape is virtually indestructible and can be used in almost any environment in which humans live.
- Videotape can be placed on readily available videocassette players that feed directly into commercial TV receivers. With special equipment, videotaped scenes can be projected onto large motion picture viewing screens. The requirement for special projection equipment is not unique, as special equipment is also required to project filmed scenes on television screens.
- Videotape can instantaneously project scenes in black and white or color, with natural or dubbed sound, on open (public) or closed (limited audience) circuits.
- Scenes may be recorded for a permanent record or for future use.

Disadvantages of videotape are the same as those inherent in the television medium.

10-47. An analysis of TV in the area of intended PSYOP provides valuable information about its specific regional characteristics. Popular programs provide models for PSYOP TV products and help keep the message subtle.

Before developing or producing a new product, PSYOP personnel should ensure that they research the information about a nation's popular TV programs and shows. This research may provide answers and insight into what is credible within that AO. PSYOP personnel should also seek the opinions of interpreters, as they may be able to give thorough insight into the views of the TA (Appendix H). PSYOP personnel may research information in the libraries and universities, as well as the local marketing companies that do market research in the AO. Area studies produced by universities are valuable, along with information from religious organizations with missionaries in the host or target nation. PSYOP personnel can also determine a great deal of information through research about literacy rate, viewing habits, opinions, distribution of TV sets, and political views. The local marketing companies can be extremely useful as well by gathering survey information and categorizing by demographics, age, location, most frequently viewed program, best times to air, and so on. U.S. agencies, such as the Voice of America and the United States Information Service (USIS), conduct audience research and are a great source of information. The POTF G-3 will be responsible for coordinating the dissemination of the videos to their respective areas and TV stations. TV has been responsible for swaying the opinions of entire nations. Using the information that is available through research and investigation, PSYOP elements are capable of producing superior products. A thoroughly prepared PSYOP TV product can be extremely effective if PSYOP planners fully understand the unique properties of TV and do not limit their imagination in its use.

OTHER DISSEMINATION ASSETS

10-48. PSYOP forces have other dissemination assets they may choose to employ. The following paragraphs discuss these assets in detail.

Internet

10-49. The Internet has become an integral part of U.S. and other societies, and has become an incredible source of information. Establishing a web site for the purpose of using the Internet for PSYOP dissemination must be authorized through the chain of command in-theater and then up through DOD. The PSYOP commander, operations officer, or LNO must go through division level to establish a web site. The PSYOP officer may also coordinate with the IO section, which may have greater resources available to assist PSYOP personnel with a web site. IO may also have a web site already established that PSYOP personnel may use. The PAO usually has links and sites already established, and PSYOP may be able to piggyback on the site with a few articles.

10-50. PSYOP personnel must ensure that they check web sites that are sending antipropaganda over the Internet to give PSYOP personnel a better understanding of others' capabilities. PSYOP personnel cannot underestimate opposition capabilities. Viewing Internet propaganda will assist PSYOP personnel in developing quality products. The PSYOP operations officer can obtain web sites by contacting either the G-2 section or the IO section, and should be able to assist in the search for such web sites. PSYOP personnel should search the web for downloads of pictures, themes, and quotes that may be used for products. PSYOP forces must use the Internet as a dissemination tool for messages and as a distribution tool to link developers, producers, and disseminators of information.

Contracted Dissemination

10-51. The PSYOP contracting officer will help establish external means of dissemination within the AO to maximize the effectiveness of the PSYOP message to the TA. Using all necessary means of external media available, PSYOP personnel can ensure the dissemination of products reaches the widest range of the TA. The contracting officer will establish contracts with local newspapers, radio stations, television stations, and billboard companies. The contracting officer will work out the legal issues with payment, insurance, and establishment of purchasing time and space with each of the media assets. Through maximizing all media assets within the AO and contracting with local companies, PSYOP personnel will expand their range of dissemination to reach the TA and influence attitudes and behavior.

New Equipment Programs

10-52. New equipment programs are being developed to enhance the capabilities of the PSYOP community. The following equipment is in various stages of development, procurement, and fielding:

- Leaflet Delivery System (LDS).
- Unmanned Aerial Vehicle-Payloads (UAV-P).

USAJFKSWCS Pub 525-5-16 provides details on this equipment.

SUMMARY

10-53. This chapter covered the various internal and external means of distribution and dissemination of PSYOP products. Through studying and understanding the advantages and disadvantages of each means of the various delivery systems, PSYOP forces will be able to maximize their effectiveness and exposure of their products to the chosen TAs. By using the various internal and external capabilities and resources that are available, PSYOP forces will maintain their ability to influence the conditions and attitudes of their chosen TA and prove that they are an effective force multiplier.

Chapter 11

Propaganda Analysis and Counterpropaganda

*Propaganda more than ever is an instrument of aggression, a new means
for rendering a country defenseless in the face of an invading army.*

Alfred McLung Lee and Elizabeth Bryant Lee
The Fine Art of Propaganda, 1939

Historically, opponents have always used information in support of their
objectives and operations. In the current Information Age, the use of
information as a weapon has reached unprecedented levels. The former
Soviet Union and the United States waged an ongoing propaganda war
throughout the 1970s and 1980s. The breakup of Yugoslavia
demonstrated again the power of information or, more correctly,
propaganda—a lesson learned earlier in Europe during the Nazi regime.

Future adversaries will be more likely to attempt to rely upon their
ability to subvert U.S. foreign policy goals through the use of
sophisticated propaganda on their own populace, as well as on
international audiences, rather than confront the United States through
traditional military means. This chapter discusses the five major tasks
associated with propaganda analysis and counterpropaganda. Once
propaganda analysis is completed and counterpropaganda has been
considered, the PSYOP unit can advise the supported commander of the
available options to prevent adversary propaganda success or to counter
the propaganda.

TERMINOLOGY

11-1.   Propaganda has traditionally been considered in the context of armed
conflicts. Nevertheless, disinformation, misinformation, propaganda, and
opposing information are all being used by adversaries around the world.
PSYOP personnel analyze propaganda for the purpose of determining
suitable techniques for potentially countering it.

11-2.   Propaganda can be classified as White, Gray, or Black. White
propaganda is propaganda disseminated and acknowledged by the sponsor or
by an accredited agency thereof. The information is accurate and attempts to
build credibility. With Gray propaganda, the source may or may not be
correctly identified and the accuracy of the information is uncertain. Black
propaganda is credited to a false source and spreads lies, fabrications, and
deceptions. The following paragraphs describe the different types of
propaganda operations.

DISINFORMATION

11-3. Disinformation is information disseminated primarily by intelligence organizations or other covert agencies designed to distort information and deceive or influence U.S. decision makers, U.S. forces, coalition allies, and key actors or individuals via indirect or unconventional means. Disinformation includes covert propaganda operations, contaminating or altering friendly internal and external databases, creating illegitimate political groups and empowering them to act via demonstrations and rumor programs, distorted intelligence reports, and other means. Deception planners, computer network defense (CND) units, communicators, the intelligence community, counterintelligence organizations, the public affairs community, and OGAs are normally tasked to counter disinformation. Disinformation is often extremely sensitive and usually designed against decision makers, databases, key leaders and staff, or other target groups. Disinformation is the most difficult counter information to detect and often requires comprehensive actions and measures to counter.

11-4. An example of disinformation is the former Soviet Union's effort to blame the creation of Acquired Immune Deficiency Syndrome (AIDS) on the United States. This program was designed to discredit the United States and disrupt the movement of U.S. forces, especially naval personnel, from using critical port facilities in and around the world. In 1985, the Soviets began a concerted program claiming that a U.S. laboratory at Fort Detrick, Maryland created the AIDS virus. The Soviets used their own media and other unwitting media around the world to accomplish this disinformation program. Articles in Soviet and international newspapers amplified their story of the development of AIDS. Eventually, the stories were reinforced by an article in the *London Sunday Express*, a conservative publication. With the Express publication, the story took hold, having the effect the Soviets sought. Once the story was published in the Express, other respected newspapers throughout the world picked up the story and reprinted it in various versions. Quick reaction and rebuttals from the USIA and the State Department helped to reverse acceptance of the original Soviet story by the international media. However, the Soviets were successful in this disinformation effort. Today, in many parts of the world, U.S. forces are not welcome for port calls because local governments believe they could spread the AIDS virus. To counter the disinformation, U.S. authorities eventually reverted to extensive AIDS testing of all U.S. military personnel before deployments and sending the results of these tests to HNs. The costs and man-hours lost for AIDS testing is still being calculated.

MISINFORMATION

11-5. Misinformation is unintentionally incorrect information emanating from virtually anyone for reasons unknown, or to solicit a response or interest that is not political or military in origin. The recipient of this information could be anyone. CNN publicized a story regarding the use of chemical weapons by U.S. Special Forces Soldiers during Operation TAILWIND in Laos during the Vietnam War. The facts were not verified and later proved inaccurate or completely false. CNN unwittingly assisted in spreading misinformation, prompting a government investigation that lasted for months, costing countless man-hours and dollars.

11-6. Misinformation is often best countered by either ignoring the information altogether or providing the truth. However, it is important to note that even providing the facts can be a time-consuming affair that may not be worth the effort. The credibility of the military is often pitted against a credible news agency and there may be no clear winner. Therefore, it is often the best policy to be open and objective when faced with the possibility of misinformation. This COA may mean establishing a more cooperative relationship with the media and using the military public affairs staff as a conduit.

PROPAGANDA

11-7. Propaganda is intentionally incorrect or misleading information directed against an adversary or potential adversary to disrupt or influence any sphere of national power—informational, political, military, or economic. This information is normally directed at the United States, U.S. allies, and key audiences in the JOA or AOR. The broadcasts of Lord Haw Haw (William Joyce) to the British Isles during the Battle of Britain, and Tokyo Rose in the Pacific theater during World War II are excellent examples of this type of skewed information. These programs are deliberately designed to attack the will of nations to resist and the will of Soldiers to fight. These propagandists attempt to mix truth and lies in a way that is imperceptible to the listener. Countering propaganda is usually the responsibility of PSYOP units within an AOR and JOA. OGAs will counter propaganda on an international scale and within the United States. Often, PSYOP forces must depend upon the information networks of U.S. allies to counter propaganda within their own borders. However, PSYOP forces may provide assistance when requested. The ideal counterpropaganda plan incorporates a loose network of organizations with common themes and objectives. All elements of IO can and will support the counterpropaganda plan, but the focal point for such operations should remain with the PSYOP forces.

11-8. The Internet has presented PSYOP units with a new medium for exploitation by both friendly and opposing forces. Figure 11-1 shows an example of electronic media propaganda.

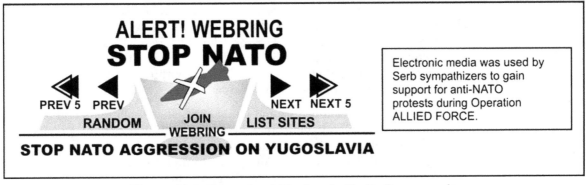

Figure 11-1. Example of Electronic Media Propaganda

OPPOSING INFORMATION

11-9. Opposing information is intentional or unintentional truth based on information coming from anyone that represents an opposing view based upon factual evidence. This counter information would also be directed against the U.S. military, U.S. allies, key audiences within the JOA or AOR, or even U.S. adversaries and potential adversaries or nonaligned parties. Key U.S. decision makers must understand the impact U.S. forces are having in a JOA or AOR, and react in such a way as to minimize negative images and amplify positive images of U.S. policy and operations. All good policies and actions taken by a military, the government, and coalitions will have equal and opposite adverse impacts and reactions within a JOA or AOR. When American troops are deployed outside the continental United States (OCONUS), they can create problems by their presence. For example, during humanitarian operations to build schools and hospitals in Central America, indigenous Indian populations demonstrated against the U.S. forces because the construction did not facilitate their needs. Local populations complained that the Americans bought all the construction materials in the area and escalated prices. Local businessmen complained that Americans were signing contracts and working with minority and small businesses while not attempting to work with them, although they offered lower prices in many instances. These opposing attitudes and beliefs, if not monitored and addressed quickly, can create an image of the force that will nullify the success of an operation. Normally, the PSYOP unit crafts the image of the force in a JOA or AOR with support from the assigned public affairs and CA staff.

COUNTERPROPAGANDA PROCESS

11-10. The process by which U.S. military personnel determine when, if, and how to counter opponent propaganda can be subdivided into two basic tasks with subordinate tasks. Propaganda analysis encompasses collecting, processing, and analyzing, while counterpropaganda encompasses advising and executing.

PLANNING

11-11. Counterpropaganda planning is not a separate step, but is embedded throughout the PSYOP planning and development processes. In the initial PSYOP tab or annex, planners and analysts begin to identify potential objectives, themes, and the TA that an opponent may use to implement a propaganda campaign against U.S. or friendly forces. This initial planning may involve a separate appendix or annex to the PSYOP tab or annex and may even require a dedicated organization within the POTF or PSE to analyze and counter opponent propaganda.

11-12. As the operation begins and plans are realized, planners and analysts attempt to identify any indicators of any potential opponent propaganda campaign developing. As indicators arrive, they are integrated into the intelligence and TAA process. Analysts attempt to confirm or deny their initial anticipated opponent plan and fill in any holes.

11-13. As PSYOP products and activities are developed and planned, planners, analysts, and product developers begin to embed potential counterpropaganda themes into TAAWs, and ultimately into products and actions. This proactive measure will assist in setting the stage for any later counterpropaganda operations.

11-14. While counterpropaganda planning continues throughout the operation, there are certain events or activities that PSYOP planners can anticipate will generate significant amounts of opponent propaganda. During Operation IRAQI FREEDOM, Saddam Hussein's government attempted to capitalize on some of these events with mixed results. Some examples of these events and activities that could trigger opponent propaganda include—

- Initial force entry.
- Air strikes and bombings.
- Civilian casualties, including children.
- Collateral damage.
- Friendly force mishaps.
- Friendly force prisoners of war (PWs) and MIA.
- Friendly force KIA.
- Detainment of public figures.
- War criminal activities.
- Civil disorder.
- Raids and seizures.

11-15. PSYOP planners can war-game the possibility of these events, anticipate the opponent's reactions, and attempt to mitigate those reactions early. Doing so reduces the amount of time required to develop counterpropaganda products, but requires that PSYOP planners be included in all the supported unit planning for such operations. PSYOP planners can and should offer different options for executing operations to assist in any anticipated counterpropaganda plan later. Again, such planning greatly increases the likelihood of a successful counterpropaganda execution.

COLLECTING

11-16. PSYOP personnel must use all available assets to collect the wide variety of information and propaganda existing in an area. Due to the sheer volume of information and potential sources, PSYOP forces do not have the organic ability to collect all available information. In addition, PSYOP personnel may be lured by the obvious propaganda appearing in the AO and miss collecting the more subtle and potentially effective propaganda being disseminated through the local media. Adversaries aware of PSYOP capabilities in the supported force may deliberately disseminate obvious propaganda to draw PSYOP personnel away from other events or information. For example, an adversary may display a particularly graphic poster in several towns in the AO, while subtler and potentially more damaging editorials appear in the local newspapers. The requirement for native speakers fluent in the local dialect exacerbates this problem. A proven method of collecting information is media analysis.

11-17. Media analysis is the structured, deliberate tracking and analysis of opponent and neutral media (TV, radio, Internet, and print). Properly performed media analysis, although time-consuming and linguist-intensive, can identify trends and become predictive when the supported force considers a potentially unpopular activity. To be truly effective, media analysis must be conducted on a daily basis. PSYOP units usually do not have the organic personnel sufficient to accomplish this task. The TAAD of the PDC is best suited for conducting media analysis. Attached translators and linguists can also be given the role of monitoring local media and providing input to the TAAD. The use of attached linguists is best used as an early warning device to identify hostile reports in the local media, as the linguists frequently have other duties to perform in the PSYOP organization. Some organizations capable of conducting media analysis or sources are—

- *Intelligence organizations.* The J-2 or G-2 sections have access to hostile media reporting and can assist in the analysis. For example, the Task Force Eagle G-2 section in Bosnia produced a daily report of media analysis in the task force's AO. PSYOP personnel should explain clearly to the intelligence sections exactly what they are looking for to maximize the use of these assets.

- *Public affairs.* Public affairs personnel and units frequently review and analyze media reports at the international and local levels. These analyses are often produced for the supported commander on a regular basis. In larger operations, allied and coalition PAOs operate specific media analysis cells. PSYOP personnel often work with public affairs personnel in identifying media outlets in the AO and, sometimes, on the specific analyses.

- *Department of State.* Most U.S. Embassies have information officers (formerly known as USIS personnel) who collect and analyze international and local media reports. With their long-established knowledge and experience in the AO, these personnel present excellent sources for PSYOP personnel to use in the collection of propaganda and media reports.

- *Foreign Broadcast Information Service.* FBIS reports are detailed and methodical in their analysis; however, there is usually a 24-hour delay in the receipt of the detailed reports. FBIS is an excellent resource, but may not cover all media in the AO; often they will report only on the larger media outlets. PSYOP forces can establish accounts with FBIS or obtain the reports through intelligence channels.

- *International organizations and NGOs.* Many of these organizations conduct media-monitoring activities. In certain peacekeeping missions, some of these organizations are chartered with the task of media moni-toring. Frequently, these organizations have significant expertise in the area and can provide valuable information and analysis. PSYOP personnel must exercise caution in using information from these organizations as they may be biased in their views of the situation in the AO.

- *Local media.* PSYOP personnel often work with the local media on a regular basis. In the course of routine business, PSYOP personnel can acquire valuable information concerning media reporting in the AO. After friendly working relationships are established, this information may be easier to obtain and be more accurate.

- *The Internet.* Many media outlets maintain web sites on the Internet. These sites frequently have the most recent editions of their reports posted in both the local language and in other languages. Many governments also maintain official web sites on which they post news releases (with their own slant) and other forms of information. Some of these government-sponsored sites are actually sources of propaganda that should be closely monitored.

During Operation ALLIED FORCE, PSYOP soldiers in the TAAD of 6th PSYOP Battalion regularly monitored and analyzed a variety of Serb web sites, notably the Serbian Ministry of Information web site. The TAAD then produced a daily propaganda analysis report for use by the JPOTF in Germany. Over time, the TAAD was able to reverse engineer the Serb propaganda plan and become predictive in its analyses. The quality of these daily reports was such that they became one of the most requested and most-often-forwarded E-mail attachments during the operation. The Defense Intelligence Agency, among others, requested inclusion on the distribution list.

11-18. The collection task presents several significant challenges—time, personnel, and integration. Time is a challenge because the analysis of propaganda and information often requires translation and careful studying. The use of outside sources can assist in overcoming this challenge. Personnel shortages and multiple requirements within the PSYOP forces present challenges for leaders in terms of prioritization of tasks. Again, the effective use of outside personnel and organizations will assist PSYOP forces in overcoming the shortage of personnel. PSYOP personnel must identify and coordinate with all available collection assets and integrate their capabilities.

PROCESSING

11-19. Processing opponent information and propaganda refers to the movement of the information through non-PSYOP and PSYOP channels. PSYOP personnel must ensure that their supported unit HQ and all of its subordinate units understand where suspected opponent propaganda and information is sent. All collection agencies must know that PSYOP units have the mission of analyzing opponent propaganda and information. Once in the PSYOP force, the G-2 or intelligence representative logs the item and keeps a copy, if necessary. The propaganda or information should pass to the PDC in the POTF or the TPDD in a TPC. Although the plans and programs section or detachment initially receives the suspected propaganda, ultimately the TAAD or section receives the product and begins the detailed analysis of it. During the processing of suspected propaganda and information, PSYOP personnel should, if possible—

- Establish a log of the items as they arrive. Critical information to be acquired is the location of the item (if news, then the medium found in, date, page number, author, channel, time of day broadcast, radio station heard on, and so on), unit or persons collecting the information, geographic location (if applicable), and reactions of others.

- Visually display the items. This display allows for comparison with PSYOP products and serves as a motivator for PSYOP personnel.
- Maintain electronic and hard copies of the item for archive purposes.
- Categorize the information by date or topic, as the situation dictates.
- Incorporate the item into command briefings.
- Compare and contrast the item with other similar items of propaganda and information.

ANALYZING

11-20. When analyzing an adversary's propaganda, PSYOP personnel work with two levels of analysis: the analysis of individual items of propaganda and propaganda program analysis.

Individual Item Analysis

11-21. This analysis includes several methods available to analyze specific propaganda products. PSYOP personnel analyze opponent propaganda by attempting to identify the—

- Overall objective of the product (PO).
- Behavior expected of the intended TA (SPO).
- Ultimate TA.
- Themes and symbols used.
- Frequency of use.
- Description of product.

Propaganda Program Analysis

11-22. This analysis includes several methods available to analyze the specific propaganda programs. PSYOP personnel analyze opponent propaganda programs by attempting to identify the—

- Propaganda program's organization and structure.
- Purpose of the program.
- Context in which the program occurs.
- Media used for the program.
- TAs and their susceptibility to the program.
- Ultimate target or object of the program.
- Effectiveness of the program.

11-23. There are two major methods of analysis: objective and subjective. Each technique has advantages and disadvantages. PSYOP personnel should use both techniques in analyzing opponent propaganda.

Objective Analysis

11-24. This method of propaganda content analysis requires the establishment and continuous update of databases. PSYOP personnel categorize opponent propaganda in a database, allowing for rapid analysis. This technique works best when used in tracking media-based propaganda, and allows PSYOP personnel to anticipate responses as events occur. Over time, each media outlet will develop a pattern of reporting that PSYOP personnel can use in developing counterpropaganda messages in anticipation of hostile media reports. This technique is time-consuming and requires depth in translators. PSYOP personnel may often need to seek assistance in the collection and translation tasks. If established correctly, this technique allows for accurate and timely trend analysis and prediction. Categories for use are—

- Media source (names of newspapers, radio stations, and so on).
- Themes used.
- Intended objectives of the propaganda.
- TAs.
- Media techniques used (TV, radio, and magazines).

11-25. Categories are chronological and are timed against supported unit actions. Objective analysis requires considerable time and effort, but enables PSYOP units to more effectively predict and counter opponent propaganda. Figure 11-2 is an example of objective propaganda analysis.

Figure 11-2. Example of Objective Propaganda Analysis

Subjective Analysis

11-26. In this method, PSYOP personnel rely on their judgment, experience, background, and knowledge of the local area to evaluate opponent propaganda. This technique allows for analyst bias, and information can be lost if that particular analyst departs the organization. The subjective technique is more often used in analyzing propaganda items other than those that appear in the media, such as posters or handbills. There are numerous techniques in conducting propaganda analysis; the SCAME technique described below is just one of several. An alternate technique is the process of reverse engineering the propaganda using PSYOP doctrinal terms. In this method, the analyst attempts to determine the PAW for the propaganda, which then allows greater insight into the overall plan of the opponent.

SCAME Technique of Analysis

11-27. PSYOP personnel often use the SCAME technique of analyzing opponent propaganda. PSYOP personnel should avoid "forcing" information into this format if they do not know the actual information. Often, the true information will appear after the propaganda has been analyzed or after other forms of intelligence data have been revealed.

11-28. **Source.** A source is the individual, organization, or government that sponsors and disseminates the propaganda. Source analysis should consider all of the various players involved in the design, development, and dissemination of the propaganda or information. Correct identification of the various sources behind a particular item of propaganda can assist in providing a clearer picture of the opponent's capabilities and intent. The source may also be classified as White, Gray, or Black, if known. The following are types of sources:

- *Actor*. An actor can be a true "actor" in the film or stage sense, or an actor can be the individual, animal, or representative that the opponent has selected to use to convey the message of the propaganda.

- *Author*. The author is the individual who created or wrote the message or propaganda. The author is readily identifiable in many media forums. In addition to the individual authors, PSYOP personnel should attempt to identify the production location where the propaganda was created or developed; for example, a TV studio or print plant.

- *Authority*. Authority is the propaganda source's means to establish credibility in the eyes of the intended TA. Authority can be manifested by means of individuals, symbols, slogans, or representations of items that resonate with the TA. An example is the use of the presidential seal on written documents produced in the USG. Another example is the Iraqi Minister of Information during Operation IRAQI FREEDOM. While the Iraqi Minister of Information's inaccurate statements minimized impact on any Western audiences, his position as a member of the government did establish his authority to the Iraqi people initially. As it became obvious that Iraq was losing the conflict, his stubborn defiance (and continued misrepresentation of the situation) became a source of pride to some in the Arab world.

I can say, and I am responsible for what I am saying, that they have started to commit suicide under the walls of Baghdad. We will encourage them to commit more suicides quickly.

Mohammed Saeed al-Sahaf
Iraqi Minister of Information

- *Disseminator.* PSYOP personnel should attempt to identify who disseminated the propaganda. Sometimes, the dissemination means is obvious, as in the retransmission of a TV product via terrestrial retransmission sites. In many cases, PSYOP personnel can identify the dissemination source by applying other known facts about events in the AO to the situation. Potential dissemination sources are—

  - Government agencies.
  - Police.
  - Political parties.
  - Mass media.
  - Military organizations.
  - Hired personnel.
  - Volunteers.
  - International media.
  - Underground networks.

11-29. **Content.** Content analysis reveals what the propaganda message says and what is trying to be achieved regarding the TA. This analysis can also reveal the source's intent, motives, and goals. Content analysis reveals the meaning of the message, the reason the message was disseminated, the intended purpose or objective, and the manner in which the message was presented to the TA. PSYOP personnel analyze the content of propaganda by evaluating—

- Objectives.
- Lines of persuasion used.
- Morale.
- Involuntary information.
- Biographic information.
- Economic data.
- Propaganda inconsistencies (Figure 11-3, page 11-12).
- Geographic information.
- Intentions.

11-30. **Audience.** In this aspect of propaganda analysis, PSYOP personnel attempt to determine which TAs are being reached by the propaganda and which TAs were specifically selected by the opponent. By viewing the TA via opponent propaganda, PSYOP personnel may become more aware of themes and symbols that are more effective; these themes and symbols can later be used in the development of PSYOP products. This aspect of propaganda is critical as it will, to a large part, determine which TA PSYOP forces will target in their counterpropaganda campaign. Audience analysis must be conducted in concert with content analysis, as content analysis will discover what behavior or attitude the opponent seeks in the TA.

This anti-NATO propaganda contains inconsistencies. If the intended target audience is Americans, then the message of global domination by the United States via NATO does not resonate. If the target audience is other than Americans, the symbol of the pyramid and eye from a U.S. one dollar bill is unknown to most non-Americans and means nothing. Although the product is graphically of high quality, the execution is flawed. Proper planning by PSYOP personnel prevents obvious errors of this sort.

Figure 11-3. Example of Propaganda Inconsistencies

11-31. The establishment of a Taliban web site in English represents a viable attempt to harness a worldwide dissemination tool. Further examination of the web site reveals themes targeting the Muslim community as the ultimate TA. The use of English as a language could be an attempt to use a common, worldwide language to reach Muslims around the world, who may not speak Afghan or Arabic. Western (sympathetic) Muslims are an additional potential TA. Another TA may be the English-speaking Afghan Diaspora, though such a small TA seems hardly worth the effort. Propaganda analysis involves the exploration of all possible TAs targeted by the opponent. Audience analysis identifies four major classifications of TAs:

- *Apparent:* Upon first observation, the propaganda appears to be intended for this TA. The audience may or may not be the real intended or final targets of the propaganda. The opponent may have selected this TA deliberately or may be trying to deceive PSYOP forces. Closer examination and analysis may reveal a true TA beneath that which is obvious (Figure 11-4, page 11-13).

- *Intermediate:* The opponent uses this TA to assist in getting the message across to the ultimate TA. This audience may or may not be part of the ultimate TA.

- *Unintended:* These TAs are those for whom the propaganda was not intended, but nonetheless received it.

- *Ultimate:* These TAs are those for whom the opponent intended the message to get to, or those targets in which the opponent desires a change of behavior or attitude.

| IMAGINEZ UN INSTANT | Upon initial observation, the apparent target audience of this propaganda is the French population; however, after some initial analysis, the impact of a famous monument in flames in the heart of a major European capital possibly strikes a chord in the minds of all Europeans. Europeans well remember the bombings of capital cities during WW II; this appears to be the theme sought by the creators of this product. The ultimate target audience may potentially then be the European population. This product was also used as a backdrop behind a location from which international reporters were forced to report. |

Figure 11-4. Example of Questionable Propaganda Audience

11-32. **Media.** This aspect of propaganda analysis determines why a particular medium was selected, what media capabilities the opponent has, and how consistent the message was across a variety of media. Propaganda can be disseminated via visual, audio, and audiovisual means. Propaganda transmission modes may also be overt or covert.

11-33. Disseminated propaganda can show opponent weaknesses. Propaganda printed on inferior grades of paper may indicate supply shortages. Weak broadcast signals, interrupted programs, poor production techniques, and a shortage of broadcast platforms may also indicate a lack of support, both logistically and from the opponent's HQ. PSYOP personnel should not evaluate the effectiveness of opponent propaganda based only on production quality. The opponent may have deliberately lowered the quality of the propaganda to make it more acceptable to the TA. The following common terminology is used when analyzing media selection:

- *Frequency* refers to how often a medium is disseminated. Newspapers or magazines may be daily, weekly, or monthly. Radio and TV may be daily, hourly, or weekly broadcasts. Propaganda may appear multiple times across different mediums.

- *Placement* is the physical location of opponent propaganda in a medium. In printed media, propaganda may be located in various parts of the paper. In audio and audiovisual mediums, propaganda can be located in a wide variety of places. PSYOP personnel are able to evaluate the legitimacy of the propaganda by its placement in media.

- *Place of origin* is the production source of the propaganda. Examples are print plants, TV production studios and broadcast stations, radio production studios and broadcast stations, advertising agencies, marketing firms, and print media firms.

- *Technical characteristics* include such information as frequency, channel, modulation, signal strength, bandwidth, and other electronic signature means. TV propaganda characteristics include picture quality, sound quality, and color (Figure 11-5). Printed media may be classified by size and quality of paper, print colors, and print quality.

- *Method of dissemination* is similar to dissemination source, as stated earlier in the source analysis.

Belgrade television developed several television spots like this one in English and broadcast them on their TV stations daily. International media, such as CNN and British Broadcasting Corporation (BBC), then rebroadcast the spots onto Western stations, assisting the Serbs in disseminating their messages. The spots were of very high quality and were produced by a Serbian marketing firm in Belgrade using state-of-the-art digital technology.

Figure 11-5. Example of Television Propaganda

11-34. **Effects.** The most important, and often the most difficult, aspect of propaganda analysis to determine is its effectiveness on the ultimate TA. The ultimate measure of opponent propaganda effectiveness is the changes in behavior or attitude of the TAs involved. Effects analysis is similar to determining the impact of friendly PSYOP on its intended TAs; direct and indirect impact indicators are significant indicators of effectiveness. Direct and indirect impact indicators are discussed at length in Chapter 7.

11-35. PSYOP planners may not always be able to gather actual impact indicators to evaluate the effects of an opponent's propaganda, and may have to analytically evaluate its impact. Below is a portion of an analysis of Osama bin Laden's recruitment video by Richard Williams Bulliet of Columbia University. The evaluation goes beyond effects, but evaluates many other aspects of the video. Such input can be very helpful to PSYOP personnel in propaganda analysis.

There is no way to calculate the effectiveness of this videotape. Some young Arab men who watch it find it gripping; some feel it contains nothing new. Effective propaganda often contains nothing new, however. It works by triggering latent feelings, by manipulating familiar words and images. Looked at strictly from a structural standpoint, the bin Laden videotape shows a highly professional mind at work. The psychological understanding of how propaganda can move people to action is of a very high order, as are the technical skills deployed in the video and sound editing. Though some propagandists for the American side in the current conflict portray Osama bin Laden as the enemy of America's modern technological civilization, this tape proves that he is capable of using both the techniques and the professional production skills of the modern television industry to convey his message. Though never named in the tape or accorded a rank or title confirming his implicit leadership, Osama bin Laden's face, voice, and thinking dominate it throughout. Whoever the actual producer, the animating intelligence is that of bin Laden, a man who shows himself here as a master of propaganda and an intelligent, ruthless, and, yes, modern adversary.

Richard Williams Bulliet
Columbia University

11-36. If necessary, PSYOP units may decide to test the opponent propaganda on the TAs by survey sampling, focus groups, or any of the other means of product pretesting and posttesting. A drawback of this action is that PSYOP personnel actually are further disseminating the propaganda. Another means of determining the effect of opponent propaganda is to execute surveys of the TAs involved.

11-37. PSYOP personnel may often find that the behavior or attitudes of the TAs are impacted by a variety of sources, one of which is opponent propaganda. PSYOP personnel should evaluate the impact of opponent propaganda on all applicable TAs—apparent, unintended, intermediate, and ultimate. This analysis may reveal errors or vulnerabilities for future exploitation.

11-38. While conducting effects analysis, PSYOP personnel also identify any linkages between the propaganda being analyzed and other known items of similar design. This step marks the beginning of a transition from individual propaganda analysis to analysis of a potential propaganda program. Figure 11-6, pages 11-15 and 11-16, provides an example of the SCAME format.

Source Analysis: What is the real source?   **DTG:** When last updated?

1. Elements of the source:
   a. Actor:
   b. Authority:
   c. Author:
2. Type: White _____ Gray _____ Black _____
3. Credibility of each source element:
   a. Actor:
   b. Authority:
   c. Author:

Content Analysis: What does the propaganda say? What is it trying to get the TA to do?

1. Objective of the message:
2. Line of persuasion used:
3. Morale of the source:
4. Involuntary information in the message (news, opinions, and entertainment):
5. Biographical information (new leader, and so on):
6. Economic information:
7. Propaganda inconsistencies:
8. Intentions/agenda of the source:
9. Geographic information:

Figure 11-6. Example of SCAME Format

Audience Analysis: Who are the audiences?

1. Apparent audience:
    a. Perception of the message:
    b. Reason selected:
2. Ultimate audience:
    a. Perception of the message:
    b. Reason selected:
3. Intermediate audience:
    a. Perception of the message:
    b. Reason selected:
4. Unintended audience:
    a. Perception of the message:
    b. Reason selected:

Media Analysis: What media are used and why?

1. Type: Radio _____ Television _____ Print (specific type) _____

    Newspaper/Magazine _____ Internet _____ Other _____

2. Frequency:
3. Placement:
4. Place of origin:
5. Technical characteristics:
6. Method of dissemination:
7. Transmission mode:

Effects Analysis: What impact is this propaganda having?

1. Methods used in analysis:
2. Impact indicators (direct and indirect):
3. Conclusions:

Figure 11-6. Example of SCAME Format (Continued)

Program Analysis

11-39. Analysis of an opponent's propaganda program begins with what the PSYOP unit anticipates will happen. The collection of information confirms or denies the presence of such a program and enables the PSYOP analyst to "flesh out" the opponent's plan. This analysis involves searches in the international media and local media, detailed propaganda analysis as items arrive, and population and TA actions and reactions. The themes, TA, and objectives all build to complete a "picture" for the PSYOP analyst.

11-40. Once PSYOP personnel suspect that an opponent propaganda program is present in the AO, they must begin to analyze and anticipate the program. Individual product analysis feeds the program analysis and can clarify missing information. Program analysis is critical to the PSYOP unit because this analysis will serve as the basis for deciding when, if, and how to execute counterpropaganda operations. In conducting opponent program analysis, PSYOP personnel focus on the—

- Overall objectives of the opponent (for example, to justify an invasion by the opponent).
- Intermediate objectives of the program (for example, reduce the TA's faith in the JTF's ability to protect them).
- Potential TAs of the program.
- Potential means (media) by which the program will be executed.
- Possible themes used by the opponent, to include future themes as the situation develops.
- Timing of the campaign.
- Potential key communicators or intermediate TAs.
- Opponent's reaction to supported force operations.
- Potential effectiveness of the program.
- Common themes across different TAs and mediums.
- Identification of repeated attempts to target a specific TA.
- Use of similar symbols in different media.
- Use of similar content or verbiage across different media.
- Repeated attempts to reach TAs.
- Past propaganda efforts (many themes will remain the same).
- Changes in TA behavior toward friendly forces.

11-41. PSYOP analysts then try to fit these pieces together to form a picture of the opponent's plan. Once the opponent's plan is verified, PSYOP personnel can begin to counter it by anticipating actions and reactions and disseminating products and conducting activities in advance of expected opponent propaganda. One portion of a possible campaign analysis of the Iraqi propaganda campaign during Operation IRAQI FREEDOM is discussed in the following paragraph.

11-42. While the obvious overall objective was to stop the operation, Saddam Hussein's government appeared to seek the following supporting objectives (not inclusive) in its propaganda campaign prior to and during Operation IRAQI FREEDOM:

- Bolster the Iraqi population against a prospective allied invasion.
- Try to divide Arab allies from the United States.
- Try to divide Europeans and others apart from the United States.
- Reduce international support for the operation (increase condemnation).
- Increase Muslim countries' opposition to the operation.

Some techniques and methods the Iraqi regime used in their campaign were—

- Crafting tragedy.
- Exploiting suffering.
- Exploiting Islam.
- Corrupting the public record.
- Staged suffering and grief.

- Collocation of military assets and civilians.
- Restricting journalists' movements.
- False claims or disclosures.
- False man-in-the-street interviews.
- Self-inflicted damage.
- On-the-record lies.
- Covert dissemination of false stories.
- Censorship.
- Bogus, edited, or old footage and images.
- Fabricated documents.

ADVISING

11-43. PSYOP personnel advise the supported commander and coordinating staff of the current situation regarding the use or anticipated use of adversary propaganda in the AO. PSYOP personnel advise commanders on the recommended defense against adversary propaganda and recommend the appropriate material to be included in command information programs. This task also includes advice on available options for use of counterpropaganda based on—

- Propaganda analysis.
- Current intelligence.
- Planning considerations (discussed in the following section on counterpropaganda).
- Impact of adversary propaganda.

EXECUTING

11-44. Part of the challenge of counterpropaganda is deciding whether or not to execute a counterpropaganda program. In an active sense (due to constraints, silence may be an option), it may be far more damaging to initiate a weak counterpropaganda plan and have it fail than to employ the silent option. PSYOP personnel may employ some preventative measures before the appearance of opponent propaganda. These techniques can be used in conjunction with PAO actions in the AO.

Preventative Action

11-45. Preventative actions take the form of propaganda awareness programs that inform and expose military (U.S. and allied) forces and civilian populations to the nature of opponent propaganda. The objective of most preventative measures is to reduce a potential TA's vulnerability to opponent propaganda. PSYOP personnel generally develop exposure programs for military forces and information-based programs for civilian populations. The following paragraphs discuss the components of preventative action.

11-46. **Command Information.** This information is normally disseminated through a unit chain of command concerning facts about an ongoing or upcoming operation. Command information seeks to keep Soldiers as informed as possible about their missions, roles, and expected end state.

Although the unit chain of command is the primary source of this information, PSYOP personnel advise unit commanders about potentially exploitable vulnerabilities and how to address them. PSYOP personnel do not perform the actual informing of the Soldiers, but monitor their status and advise the chain of command. Extended duration operations also see the use of different media dedicated to command information. Examples include the *Talon* magazine used in Multinational Division North (MND-N) in Bosnia and the Armed Forces Network (AFN) radio and TV stations in use around the world. PAO personnel normally operate these stations without PSYOP involvement.

11-47. **Information Articles.** PSYOP personnel can publish articles in professional military magazines highlighting the nature and types of hostile propaganda that have been observed or that may be used. These articles serve as an exposure to potential propaganda and assist unit commanders in reducing Soldiers' vulnerabilities. Because U.S. Soldiers have not been susceptible to opponent propaganda in past conflicts, PSYOP personnel have not performed this preventative action often.

11-48. **Institutional Training.** If required, PSYOP personnel could provide propaganda exposure training in various military training institutions. This component would also serve to expose military personnel to potential propaganda and therefore reduce their potential susceptibility.

11-49. **Exposure.** In this component, PSYOP personnel develop and disseminate propaganda during command post exercises (CPXs) and field training exercises (FTXs) to reduce Soldiers' susceptibility to potential opponent propaganda. PSYOP personnel actually operate dissemination equipment, such as loudspeakers, to demonstrate the impact of opponent propaganda to units as they prepare for an operation. PSYOP personnel create the propaganda using potential themes resulting from their analysis of the opponent's capabilities and advise the unit commander on the best way to deal with the opponent propaganda.

11-50. **Civilian Information.** This component of preventative action is critical to eliminating potential vulnerabilities of foreign TAs. In concert with public affairs units, PSYOP personnel analyze the potential responses to friendly force operations and attempt to eliminate any fear and speculation among the local populace. This action is especially critical before a major deployment to set conditions favorable for the introduction of forces. This action differs from the counterpropaganda conditioning technique in that PSYOP personnel address potential vulnerabilities of the TAs instead of addressing specific themes.

Opponent Propaganda Techniques

11-51. Opponents may use a wide array of propaganda techniques against friendly forces. Historically, these techniques have been limited to combat situations; however, PSYOP forces have encountered more direct propaganda in peacekeeping and other noncombat operations. PSYOP forces have observed the following opponent propaganda techniques:

- Direct propaganda against the population back home (PSYOP units do not counter this propaganda).

- Seek to divide the force along national lines (for example, Bosnian Serbs sought to separate the French forces in the Stabilization Force [SFOR] from the remainder of the organization to weaken the force as a whole).

- Pose questions to Soldiers regarding the overall mission that they are supporting from a humanitarian or legal point (for example, Why are you here? Are you carrying out the work of political masters?).

- Use a theme establishing a monolithic threat (for example, the rumors concerning the UN seeking world domination).

- Limit the force's effectiveness by increasing the force protection threat via propaganda and selected violence.

- Target the local populace to deter any cooperation with the friendly force.

- Use lies, misinformation, and disinformation to keep the supported force away from important issues.

11-52. Opponent propaganda personnel use a wide variety of themes against friendly forces. These themes may include—

- Officer and enlisted differences.

- Fear of death and mutilation.

- Family-at-home themes.

- Racial differences.

- Moral or religious superiority.

- Emotional appeals to undermine friendly resolve (Figure 11-7).

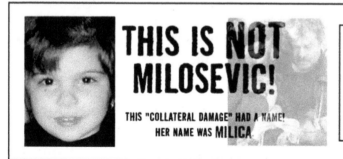

Emotional appeals are often difficult to counter with objective information as the emotional approach strikes the "gut" and the heart, as opposed to the mind. This product was aimed at Western populations, particularly Americans at home.

Figure 11-7. Example of Emotional Appeal

11-53. Based upon the advice of PSYOP personnel, supported unit commanders will decide whether to initiate a deliberate counterpropaganda program. PSYOP personnel must exercise caution against haphazardly advising supported unit commanders without a complete evaluation of the situation. Some planning considerations are—

- *Propaganda analysis (program and individual item).* What are the results of all individual and program analyses? Is the opponent's program having an effect? Can the program potentially have an effect in the future if left unchecked? PSYOP personnel must fully evaluate all aspects of the opponent's propaganda program, understand its strengths and weaknesses, and be prepared to exploit those weaknesses.

- *TA analysis.* PSYOP personnel must continue the TAA and evaluate the TA's response to opponent propaganda. PSYOP personnel must also ensure that they have sufficient information regarding the targets of opponent propaganda before initiating a counterpropaganda program.

- *Timeliness.* PSYOP personnel must evaluate the amount of time required for them to counter opponent propaganda. If they are unable to effectively counter the propaganda in a reasonable amount of time, the supported unit may suffer more damage to its credibility through a late counterpropaganda program, as opposed to not countering the propaganda at all. PSYOP planners should include development, production, and dissemination times in the overall time assessment and must evaluate the entire timeline from decision to execute to the arrival of counterpropaganda products among the TAs.

- *Resources.* Counterpropaganda programs can consume many, if not all, of the PSYOP force's available resources. If sufficient resources do not exist, planners should not hesitate to request assistance immediately from the supported unit. PSYOP planners must consider the availability of the following resources:

  - Time.

  - Analyst support.

  - Funds.

  - Electronic media (TV, radio, Internet).

  - Dissemination personnel and units.

  - Printed materials (paper, ink).

  - Contracted media support.

- *Impact on ongoing PSYOP programs.* PSYOP planners must consider the impact of executing a counterpropaganda program on the overall PSYOP plan. Opponents may try, especially if the PSYOP plan is having an impact, to deliberately draw the supported force into a counterpropaganda program to reduce the effectiveness of the PSYOP plan. Counterpropaganda programs also draw resources away from the overall PSYOP plan, thus limiting its effectiveness.

- *Technique selection.* Specific counterpropaganda techniques are covered in detail later, but PSYOP personnel must apply the correct techniques based upon their evaluation of the situation at hand. Some techniques require more time and resources to execute than others.

- *Impact of additional publicity.* Some counterpropaganda techniques draw more external publicity than others. PSYOP personnel should advise the supported unit of this impact when recommending if and how to counter opponent propaganda. Credibility of the supported unit is paramount. Once the planners advise the supported units to counter opponent propaganda, they should also war-game all potential responses, to include the response and attention of the international media.

- *Counterpropaganda potential for success.* The single most important consideration for PSYOP planners is the potential for them to be successful in their counterpropaganda program. Planners must be forthright in advising the supported unit of their ability to successfully counter opponent propaganda. A detailed evaluation of all planning considerations should be used in advising the supported unit. PSYOP personnel should also advise the supported unit of all possible ramifications should their counterpropaganda program fail.

Counterpropaganda Techniques

11-54. A wide variety of techniques exist for countering propaganda. There is no "correct" or "best" technique; the techniques must be based upon the situation at hand. More than one technique may be used in concert with another in a single PSYOP product or action. The following are some of the more recognized techniques used:

- *Direct refutation.* This technique is a point-for-point rebuttal of opponent propaganda allegations or themes. This technique is best used in a very timely manner when PSYOP personnel have complete access to factual information regarding the allegation. Personnel use this technique when they are confident that they can refute the propaganda with complete accuracy. Often, PSYOP personnel can request that the PAO assist in using this technique at press conferences or in press releases. A disadvantage of using this technique is that direct refutation may draw added publicity, strength, and credibility to the opponent's allegations. Additionally, this technique may draw additional publicity to the opponent's propaganda by repeating and then refuting the information. PSYOP personnel should avoid becoming involved in a "mudslinging" contest when using this technique, so that damage to the supported force's credibility, in addition to the credibility of the PSYOP force, is not done.

In 1994, the USIA submitted a report to the UN entitled, "The Child Organ Trafficking Rumor: A Modern Urban Legend." This report sought to counter rumors that had been circulating worldwide since 1987 that children were being kidnapped so that they could be used as unwilling donors in organ transplants. Although the report was over forty pages in length and was not published for several years after the rumor first appeared, the report serves as an example of detailed direct refutation. Each version of the rumor is laboriously examined and refuted through the use of factual information. In its concluding paragraph, the report stated that "this myth derives its credibility from the fact that it speaks to widespread, largely unconscious anxieties about mutilation and death that have been stimulated by the dramatic advances made in the field of organ transplantation in recent years."

- *Indirect refutation.* This technique seeks to question the validity of some aspect of the opponent's allegations or the source of the propaganda, thus challenging its credibility. This technique is often seen in courtroom trials where one side seeks to lower the credibility of "expert" witnesses. An advantage of using this technique is that indirect refutation does not bring added publicity or credibility to the propaganda by repeating certain aspects. PSYOP personnel should ensure that the facts used to damage the credibility of the propaganda are accurate and have some importance in the minds of the TA. When seeking to lower the credibility of the source of the propaganda, personnel should avoid "name calling," as this may potentially damage the credibility of the supported force.

Recently, the chairman of Microsoft, Bill Gates, used this technique in a subtle fashion by appearing in a series of television commercials following the negative outcome of the antitrust trial against his company. He appeared in a relaxed setting, seated in an armchair, and spoke of the positive impact that Microsoft had on the lives of most Americans. He spoke at length of the commitment of Microsoft to the youth of America and to American families in general. At no time did he speak of the trial itself or the court's final ruling. He did, however, attempt to damage the credibility of the ruling by highlighting the positive impact of Microsoft on Americans, and insinuating the question, "How could a company which is so dedicated to Americans be treated so badly by the courts?" While not overtly stated, this notion appeared to be the desired reaction of his indirect refutation.

- *Diversion.* This technique involves the presentation of more important or relevant themes (in the eyes of the intended TA) to draw attention away from the opponent propaganda. A critical factor in succeeding with this technique is to select an important topic to use as the diversion. The attempted diversion must be well planned and subtly executed. If the diversion is obvious to the TA, then the attempt will appear clumsy and consequently damage the credibility of the supported force. Media selection is critical in using this technique, as the media used must be able to reach large numbers of the TA and divert their attention.

Slobodan Milosevic used a diversionary technique during Operation ALLIED FORCE as he drew the world media focus away from his forces' actions in Kosovo to the damage wrought by NATO bombings in Belgrade. Milosevic's forces continued, and even intensified, their efforts in Kosovo while the international media, under his manipulation, focused on NATO miscues during the bombing effort. His use of this technique was successful in part due to his control of what the international media was allowed to see and report upon within the Former Republic of Yugoslavia.

- *Silence.* This technique does not respond to the opponent propaganda in any way. One exception to this technique is the use of remarks alluding to the opponent's propaganda as being "unworthy of comment." An advantage of this technique is that silence does not publicize the propaganda further or provide the opponent with potential feedback. This technique is used when the use of another technique may prove dangerous or when the situation and TA response is uncertain. One drawback of this technique is that the TA may question the absence of a response from the supported force.

- *Restrictive measures.* This technique denies the intended TA access to the propaganda. Jamming, physical destruction, and occupation of media outlets are some examples of this technique. Restrictive measures must be evaluated for their potential negative feedback potential before being implemented. This technique may also bring additional attention to the propaganda and encourage the TA to seek out the propaganda via covert means. When used in peacekeeping operations by U.S. forces, restrictive measures (such as shutting down radio stations) invite hostile propaganda against the supported unit concerning freedom of the media and freedom of speech. In addition, these measures are often used by repressive regimes, inviting the inevitable comparison.

- *Imitative deception.* When using this technique, PSYOP personnel alter opponent propaganda to decrease or nullify its impact. The propaganda is subtly altered so that the information appears to be unchanged; the true message, however, has been physically changed by the PSYOP personnel. The item is then reintroduced to the TA so that the information appears to be from the true source. This technique is considered black PSYOP and is dangerous to the supported force's credibility if found out. For this reason, this technique is not often used. PSYOP personnel must exercise considerable restraint in advising this technique to a supported force.

During World War II, the German Army began dropping the Skorpion morale leaflet on their troops in November 1944. The leaflets attempted to hold out the hopes of new super weapons, new sources of manpower, and the hope of German victory. Allied psychological warfare personnel obtained copies of the Skorpion and soon made subtle changes and prepared pseudo Skorpion leaflets—exact copies with an allied slant to the information. The allies then airdropped millions of these pseudo Skorpion leaflets on German troops in the field. One pseudo Skorpion authorized German Soldiers to shoot their officers if they did not display sufficient "National Socialist zeal." German Field Marshal Walter Model, who first believed the pseudo Skorpion leaflets were the real thing, commented that if his people could be made fools of so easily, they had better get out of the business. The true Skorpion was soon discontinued.

- *Conditioning.* Conditioning is a nonspecific means of eliminating potential vulnerabilities in the TA before they can be exploited. This technique is preemptive in nature. Conditioning is very similar to a preventative action measure. PSYOP personnel educate and inform a wide range of TAs concerning the supported force's mission, intent, and operations. This technique does not specifically address potential themes that the opponent may use in a propaganda program against the force, but seeks to remove or reduce potential vulnerabilities before they can be exploited. A common PSYOP role using this technique is force entry to an area; PSYOP personnel explain the force's reason for being there, legal justification for being there (UN resolution, and so on), and departure criteria. When using this technique, PSYOP personnel must avoid the use of specific end dates for operations, as political forces may change those dates. For example, while the President of the United States declared in 1995 that U.S. forces would be in Bosnia for only one year, PSYOP personnel did not use this artificial date with the TAs. Instead, PSYOP personnel and the Implementation Force (IFOR) stated the conditions that must exist in Bosnia for IFOR to depart. Public affairs units assist greatly in using this technique.

- *Forestalling.* This preemptive technique anticipates the specific themes the opponent may use in their propaganda and counters them before they reach the TA. PSYOP personnel must know the opponent and be able to anticipate their reactions to an event or operation. This technique uses war gaming in analyzing the different possible outcomes from a planned event, from best-case scenario to worst-case. PSYOP personnel then use counterpropaganda themes to bring the potential themes or issues to the TA before the opponent does. PSYOP personnel must have timely and accurate information concerning the planned event and its impact as it occurs to effectively counter hostile propaganda. A detailed knowledge of opponent propaganda techniques and themes assists greatly when using this technique. This technique differs from conditioning in that PSYOP personnel preemptively address specific themes that the opponent may use.

In 1997, SFOR attempted to detain two Bosnian-Serb indicted war criminals near the town of Prijedor, Bosnia. One individual was killed in the operation and the other was peaceably detained. Bosnian-Serb propaganda against SFOR was immediate and intense. PSYOP personnel, however, were unaware of the operation and were, for the most part, unable to effectively counter the hostile propaganda. Later that year, PSYOP personnel were brought in to assist in planning a similar operation to detain several Bosnian-Croat indicted war criminals. The PSYOP personnel war-gamed the Bosnian-Croat response, and developed, pre-positioned, and disseminated large numbers of counterpropaganda products as the operation unfolded. Opponent propaganda and hostile reaction was minimal; PSYOP personnel ceased this preemptive counterpropaganda campaign 10 days after it started due to lack of response.

- *Minimization.* When using this technique, PSYOP personnel acknowledge selected elements of the opponent's propaganda, but minimize the importance of the information to the TA. PSYOP personnel can use this technique as a "set" for a follow-on technique. A disadvantage of this technique is that opponent propaganda gains some credibility if PSYOP personnel do not fully minimize its importance in the eyes of the TA. Personnel may elect to use minimization if the supported unit feels that it cannot remain silent on an issue. This technique may also build some level of increased credibility in the eyes of the TA, as PSYOP personnel appear to be acknowledging some truthful aspects and not just refuting them.

Following the SFOR detainment of two Bosnian-Serb indicted war criminals, Bosnian-Serb propaganda claimed that there was a "secret list," built by Bosnian Muslims, consisting solely of Bosnian-Serb individuals. SFOR acknowledged that the names were on "sealed indictments," as opposed to a "secret list." After acknowledging this aspect of the hostile propaganda, PSYOP personnel then attempted to alleviate Bosnian-Serb fears by explaining how and why the sealed indictments were used and why average Bosnian Serbs had nothing to fear if they had not participated in war crimes. In one counterpropaganda product, PSYOP personnel initially used this technique and then used other techniques following it. The attempt was to regain some element of trust among Bosnian Serbs and add credibility to the product as a whole.

11-55. PSYOP personnel often disregard counterpropaganda as there is not always an obvious threat or the task appears to be too difficult. In some cases, other organizations and agencies will fill the void in the absence of a concerted PSYOP effort. This tendency diminishes the value of PSYOP in the eyes of the supported commander and makes involvement in the supported force's plan more difficult for PSYOP personnel. Opponent propaganda may appear with little or no warning, and when the propaganda does appear, the supported force will want analysis, decisions, and actions rapidly. At this point, it is too late to conduct a methodical analysis and planning effort. PSYOP personnel must be prepared for the event of opponent propaganda and have contingency plans, products, and actions in place (approved and translated) to respond.

SUMMARY

11-56. Propaganda analysis involves collecting, processing, and analyzing. Counterpropaganda involves advising the supported force and then executing the counterpropaganda plan. To be effective at these tasks, PSYOP forces must have an in-depth knowledge of the AO and its inhabitants. Cultural expertise and an understanding of the political, social, and religious impacts of friendly force actions are absolutely essential.

11-57. Propaganda analysis and counterpropaganda are critical tasks for all PSYOP forces. Counterpropaganda, in particular, is a task that carries long-range impact for the supported force's credibility. PSYOP personnel must plan for these tasks, anticipate the opponent's response, and strive to maintain the initiative.

Chapter 12

PSYOP Support to Internment/Resettlement

In soliciting and taking in enemy soldiers: if they come in good faith there is great security, because deserters harm the enemy more than casualties.

Flavius Vegetius Renatus
General Rules of War (Epitoma Rei Militaris), c. 378

Unlike EPW/CI operations in the past, I/R operations include additional detained persons. I/R operations include handling, protecting, and accounting for the following classifications of detained persons: EPWs, CIs, retained persons (RPs), other detainees (ODs), DCs, and U.S. military prisoners. I/R PSYOP forces are trained and equipped to support all I/R operations except the handling of U.S. military prisoners. I/R PSYOP forces may be employed across the spectrum of conflict, from major theater war to small-scale contingency operations. I/R PSYOP forces can also be employed during peacetime HA operations. This chapter provides techniques, procedures, and considerations for employment of I/R PSYOP forces and other PSYOP units task-organized to support I/R operations.

MISSION

12-1. The I/R PSYOP unit (or other PSYOP unit assigned the mission) plans and conducts PSYOP in support of theater, JTF, or corps-level I/R operations in any mission environment. The purpose of the mission is to assist military police (MP) or other units assigned an I/R mission to maintain order and to provide the POTF with information relevant to the ongoing PSYOP programs. PSYOP units supporting I/R operations will be prepared to support other PSYOP missions and units as directed by the POTF.

MISSION-ESSENTIAL TASKS

12-2. I/R PSYOP units provide the POTF with a unique and useful capability by collecting timely PSYOP-relevant intelligence and other important information from representatives of actual TAs. In addition, I/R PSYOP units provide the geographic combatant commander or JTF commander with a valuable asset by executing PSYOP programs that pacify I/R camp populations. These programs reduce MP guard requirements, freeing scarce MP resources to conduct other missions. To support effectively, I/R PSYOP units must perform the following essential tasks:

- Pretest and posttest PSYOP products as directed by the POTF.
- Assist I/R holding facility guard force in controlling the facility population during emergencies.

- Collect, analyze, and report PSYOP-relevant intelligence.
- Determine effectiveness of current and previous PSYOP campaigns.
- Develop and provide PSYOP products in support of POTF operations, such as EPW-recorded surrender appeals.
- Collect and verify demographic information about TAs.
- Determine the effectiveness of opponent's internal propaganda, such as propaganda directed by the opponent at his own forces.
- Ascertain targets and objectives of hostile PSYOP.
- Conduct PSYOP to pacify, obtain cooperation of, and condition I/R holding facility population to accept U.S. authority.
- When directed, conduct PSYOP to achieve other POTF objectives, such as reorientation or reeducation of the I/R holding facility population.
- Assist in improving relations with the local populace to minimize interference with camp operations.
- Conduct tactical PSYOP on order.

OPERATIONAL CONCEPTS AND PROCEDURES

12-3. Since I/R operations can vary greatly in many aspects, to include PSYOP support requirements, each mission must be planned and tailored to meet unique mission requirements. One I/R detachment of ten personnel is capable of supporting an I/R facility operated by a battalion with a maximum capacity of 8,000 detainees. If more than one detachment is required, then an element from the I/R company HQ will be required, with a mix of personnel and skills based on specific mission requirements. Ideally, the span of control for the I/R company should not exceed five detachments. Also, one audiovisual (AV) team should be assigned per two I/R detachments. AV teams can be attached to I/R detachments, retained under company control, or organized into a detachment to support specialized dissemination, print, and limited product development requirements.

12-4. If mission requirements exceed the ability of the company HQ to provide C2 and administrative support, an element from the I/R battalion HQ can be organized with the minimum necessary personnel to meet mission needs (Figure 12-1, page 12-3). Any additional support teams required for the mission (print teams, for example) will be attached directly to the company or battalion HQ.

INTERNMENT/RESETTLEMENT DETACHMENT

12-5. I/R detachments (Figure 12-2, page 12-3) deploy to I/R facilities during the construction phase. Figure 12-3, page 12-4, and FM 3-19.40, *Military Police Internment/Resettlement Operations*, include examples of typical I/R facility layouts. The detachment is attached to the I/R MP battalion (or other unit) responsible for the camp, while remaining OPCON to the detachment's parent organization (or the POTF). Arrival at the camp during the construction phase ensures adequate time for the detachment to coordinate operating procedures, communications, and logistical support with the supported battalion. Early arrival also allows time to develop and produce the products necessary when the detainees arrive, such as printed and recorded camp rules in the language of the facility population.

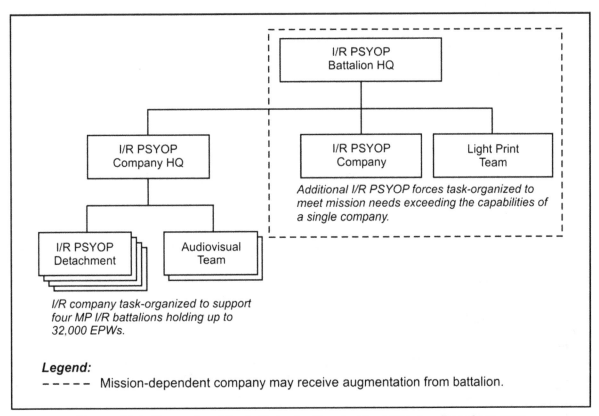

Figure 12-1. Example of Task Organization to Meet Mission Requirements

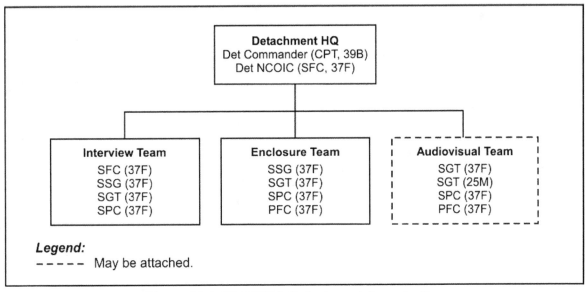

Figure 12-2. I/R PSYOP Detachment Organization

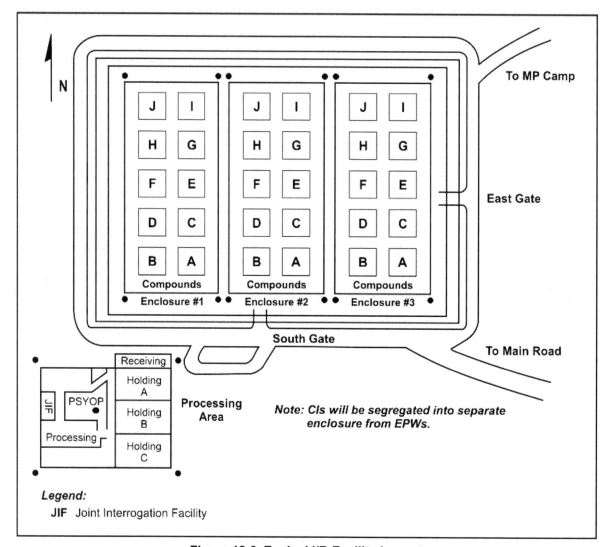

Figure 12-3. Typical I/R Facility Layout

12-6. The I/R PSYOP detachment commander functions as the PSYOP staff officer for the camp commander. The detachment commander is responsible for advising the camp commander on the psychological impact of all actions within the camp, and all actions external to the camp that affect the camp population. This support is critical to prevent misunderstandings that may lead to subsequent disturbances by the facility population. Differences in culture, custom, language, religious practices, and dietary habits can be of such magnitude that misunderstandings are not always completely avoidable. However, investigation, information briefings, and proper handling can minimize misunderstandings.

12-7. Upon arrival at the camp, the I/R PSYOP detachment commander briefs the camp commander and subordinate enclosure commanders on the detachment's mission and capabilities. He, or his designated representative, attends all camp command and staff meetings. These meetings provide the most effective means to communicate on a daily basis with the various facility commanders, their staffs, and other supporting units. Before the arrival of detainees at the camp, the detachment commander and enclosure team NCOIC brief the MP guards who will work directly with the facility population.

12-8. All I/R PSYOP personnel must be thoroughly familiar with the laws, regulations, and current policies governing the treatment of detainees. Chief among these are the Geneva Convention of 12 August 1949, paragraph 1, Article 3: The Hague Conventions; Army Regulation (AR) 190-8, *Enemy Prisoners of War, Retained Personnel, Civilian Internees, and other Detainees*; FM 3-19.40; and FM 27-10. Ensuring all facility personnel observe these rules validates the team's credibility with the facility population, as well as with facility guards. In addition, following these rules prevents embarrassing incidents that can be exploited by hostile actors or bring discredit on the United States. These rules apply even when hostilities are not declared.

12-9. During stability operations and support operations, such as HA or peace support operations, special rules for handling civilians apply. Procedures for treatment of CIs and DCs should be coordinated with the camp commander and the Judge Advocate General or competent legal authority.

12-10. The I/R PSYOP detachment executes command information and pacification programs using a variety of media. Music and news (from approved sources), camp rules, and in-processing instructions are broadcast using semipermanent camp loudspeaker systems. Supporting AV teams produce and disseminate audio, video, and audiovisual products, as well as limited numbers of signs, posters, information sheets, camp newspapers, and other printed products. Additional and large-quantity print products will be produced by supporting light print teams or through reachback capability. All products not directly related to camp command information are subject to the POTF-established approval process.

12-11. By international convention and Army regulation, all information presented to the facility population must be in their language. Translators and interpreters must be fully integrated into I/R PSYOP detachment operations. These personnel provide the team with the capability to address the facility population in their native language and to screen products for language accuracy and content. U.S. or allied military personnel, contracted civilians, or cooperative Detainees may provide translator and interpreter support. Team members must exercise caution to safeguard classified material and sensitive POTF operations.

12-12. Limitations on resources available for camp construction, combined with large surges of detainees arriving at the camp, may result in temporary overcrowding. Potential for disturbances increases dramatically when I/R facilities experience overcrowded conditions. The PSYOP detachment commander should ensure that enclosure commanders include PSYOP loudspeaker support in all activities involving mass transfers between compounds; for example, health and welfare inspections. I/R PSYOP personnel provide an MP force multiplier in these situations.

INTERVIEW TEAM

12-13. The interview team is comprised of experienced PSYOP personnel trained to conduct interviews. If available, the team should be augmented with qualified 97E interrogators to increase team effectiveness. The interview team normally operates in the facility processing area screening all, or a representative sample, of the incoming detainees. Although military intelligence (MI) units will likely be present in the facility, it is important for the interview team to maintain a separate operation. Nevertheless, the team must coordinate closely with MI and other assets to obtain any PSYOP-relevant information those assets may gather.

12-14. The team uses interview notes and database software tailored to the purpose to collect information about each detainee and provides the data to the company HQ. The company compiles this data and forwards it to the battalion or directly to the POTF for TAA. Information collected includes—

- Race or ethnicity.
- Sex.
- Age.
- Political affiliation.
- Religious affiliation.
- Geographic origin.
- Education levels.
- Length, depth, and type of involvement.
- Previous or current occupation.
- Standard of living and personal finances.
- Previous military training.
- Political and military indoctrination.
- PSYOP vulnerabilities and susceptibilities.

12-15. Detainees who are cooperative, or who possess information, skills, or characteristics of interest to the PSYOP team are interviewed in depth as time permits. Interview team personnel look specifically for the following:

- Malcontents, rabble-rousers, trained agitators, and political officers who may attempt to organize resistance or create disturbances within the camp. Once these individuals are identified, the guards will normally confine them in isolated enclosures to deny them access to the general population.
- Detainees willing to cooperate with setting up informant networks. These detainees should be referred to counterintelligence personnel, as it is their responsibility to run informant networks within the facility.
- Detainees with special skills who can assist with camp operations. Such skills include language, construction, engineering, medical, education, entertainment, and so on.
- Detainees willing to assist with product development, such as taping audio surrender appeals.
- Detainees willing to participate in pretesting or posttesting.

12-16. Ready access to members and former members of the TA allows the interview team to conduct pretesting and posttesting that provides accurate, meaningful feedback to the POTF. Data collected during these surveys is passed to the POTF through the I/R PSYOP company and battalion. The interview team must maintain secure, reliable communications with higher HQ, and ensure the timely, secure transport of the product prototype and testing results.

12-17. The interview team, along with other camp personnel, must take precautions to safeguard the identities of cooperative detainees to protect them from reprisal. PSYOP personnel must always exercise discretion when dealing with cooperative detainees. Guards must be thoroughly briefed on proper handling procedures.

12-18. Discovering detainees with false identities is an important security measure that can reduce potential problems and ensure smooth camp operations. Interview team personnel can discover false identities during initial processing or subsequent interviews. They look for—

- Documents that do not match or agree.
- An interview response that does not match the response given during earlier interview.
- Identification that does not agree with another document or information from another source, such as the International Committee of the Red Cross (ICRC).
- Slow verbal response to simple questions such as date of birth. The detainee may be making up responses or trying to remember false information.
- A detainee without documentation. This situation requires careful investigation. Did detainee throw away ID?
- A detainee who suddenly refuses to cooperate at any point during processing.
- Detainee names that appear in the "black book," or on list of sought-after persons.

ENCLOSURE TEAM

12-19. The enclosure team conducts face-to-face PSYOP and collects vital information within the facility. To perform their mission, enclosure team personnel must have unrestricted access to the camp population. Close coordination with MP guards is necessary to ensure the safety of PSYOP personnel when operating inside the camp. Enclosure team personnel and MP guards develop a system of signals before conducting operations.

12-20. Enclosure team personnel build rapport with detainees by distributing recreational equipment, conducting morale support activities, and performing other actions designed to gain the trust of detainees. Although it is important for the enclosure team to maintain close communication with other PSYOP team elements, such communication should be discreet and conducted away from the view of the camp population. If they are not identified with the authoritarian elements of camp administration, enclosure team personnel will usually enjoy greater rapport with the camp population.

12-21. Information is critical to the effective management of an I/R PSYOP program. Enclosure team personnel capitalize on their access to the camp population to collect information about the population and to watch for any potential problems. Enclosure team personnel look for—

- Leaders. Leaders are not necessarily those wearing higher rank. Enclosure team personnel should look for respect being paid to a private. He may be a high-ranking person hiding his identity.
- A detainee who is the center of attention in a group.
- Loners. Detainees who shun others may be mentally ill or may be hiding their true identity. They may be intelligence operatives or members of a special operations unit.
- Unusual groups. Their presence may indicate someone is organizing.
- Items passed from one person to another.
- New soil in the compound. Someone may be tunneling.
- Lookouts. Does this person warn others? Does a group scatter at the approach of a guard?
- Signals and codes. Are detainees tapping out messages, waving rags, or using hand signals? The use of codes is common in I/R facilities and usually indicates something is going on that requires secrecy.
- Individuals who move from one group to another and whose presence forces the topic of conversation to change. They may be political officers or intelligence officers.
- Individuals who speak for a group but maintain eye contact with another person in that group. The speaker may be a front man for the real leader.
- Individuals who immediately make friends with MP guards and are readily accepted back into the camp population. They may be key communicators.
- Detainees who express interest in camp construction or materials and equipment used in camp construction. These detainees could be planning escape or weapons manufacture.

12-22. Enclosure team personnel must be alert for detainees who attempt to contact them discreetly. Contact attempts may be manifested in the following manner:

- Detainee hails the guard asking for asylum.
- Detainee is unusually friendly or cooperative.
- Detainee feigns illness.

12-23. Guard and PSYOP enclosure team personnel must watch for missing items. Dining facility items, such as knives, forks, spoons, and most other common kitchen items, can be used as weapons or digging tools. I/R facilities usually have construction of some sort underway. All construction materials and tools must be accounted for daily. Any other items that detainees can use for escape, such as ropes, ladders, uniform items, documents, and cameras, must also be accounted for daily.

AUDIOVISUAL TEAM

12-24. The AV team normally supports one or two I/R detachments. The AV team utilizes the MSQ-85B mobile audiovisual system and Product Development Workstation–Light (PDW-L) to produce and disseminate products to the facility population. The team supports the facility PSYOP program by disseminating entertainment products, such as videos and music. This asset gives the I/R detachment the ability to influence detainee behavior by providing or withholding something of value to the facility population. When directed, the AV team disseminates products that support other POTF programs, such as reeducation, reorientation, or posthostility themes.

12-25. The MSQ-85B audiovisual system is capable of producing audiovideo presentations, photographic slides, and loudspeaker broadcasts, as well as a limited quantity of print material. Housed in an S-250 shelter, the system is mounted on an M1037 shelter carrier. A ten-kilowatt generator towed by an additional vehicle provides primary power. The system is transportable by a single C-130 sortie.

12-26. At a minimum, the AV team should have the capability to edit audio in digital formats, provide recorded audio products in mini-disk and CD formats, edit and disseminate video products in VHS or DVD formats, record and edit digital still photographs, and print limited numbers of color products in various sizes and paper thickness.

QUICK-REACTION FORCE

12-27. The I/R PSYOP detachment commander coordinates with enclosure commanders to include PSYOP loudspeaker support as part of the facility's QRF. The QRF is a predesignated element that serves as an emergency tactical response force for the compounds or other locations determined by higher command. This force is ready 24 hours a day, every day.

12-28. The I/R PSYOP detachment commander maintains contact with the QRF element through the supported unit's radio net or by other means. Soldiers designated to support the QRF must be prepared to rapidly execute the QRF mission. The I/R PSYOP detachment commander or his designated representative must accomplish these premission tasks:

- Brief the QRF leader on PSYOP capabilities and employment.
- Coordinate linkup plan with the QRF.
- Rehearse linkup procedures with each new QRF element.
- Rehearse likely emergency scenarios and perform reconnaissance of the sites.
- Prepare audio products and scripts for likely scenarios.
- Ensure interpreters are briefed and available.

SUMMARY

12-29. I/R PSYOP forces not only provide a force multiplier to the forces tasked to support I/R missions, but also are critical in collecting PSYOP-related intelligence and assisting the product development process through pretesting and posttesting. Careful adherence to all provisions of the Geneva Conventions and relevant laws and regulations must be maintained. Legal consultation may prevent incidents that could be used against the United States in opponent propaganda. In addition, the attitudes and opinions of former detainees toward the United States can have a long-term impact on relations with their nation in the future. A positive attitude may lessen the chance of future armed conflict.

PSYOP and the Targeting Process

This appendix discusses the targeting process. To be effective, PSYOP planners must understand the targeting and coordination process. They should also have an effective means of expressing their ideas so that non-PSYOP personnel can understand and apply them to their own planning processes. Targeting is the process of selecting targets and determining the appropriate response to them, taking into account operational requirements and force capabilities. Targeting and joint fires are intended to delay, disrupt, divert, or destroy the enemy's military potential throughout the depth of the AO.

OVERVIEW

A-1. At the JTF level, targeting and joint fire support are derived from the guidance of the JFC and from the concept for the campaign or operation. To effectively employ all joint forces against an adversary, the CJTF must prioritize, deconflict, and synchronize all actions of the joint forces. Through the J-3, the CJTF provides targeting guidance and priorities, apportions and allocates resources, establishes the timing and specific effects required on each target, and tasks components to strike targets or to support those strikes. Apportionment is the determination and assignment of the total expected air effort by percentage or by priority that should be devoted to the various air operations for a given period of time. Allocation is the translation of the air apportionment decision into total numbers of sorties by aircraft type available for each operation or task.

A-2. In general, the JFC relies on his JTCB to implement his guidance. The JTCB must ensure unity of effort across the JTF's spectrum of fire. This is no easy task, given the frequently overlapping and sometimes competing interests among the various components of the JTF.

PSYOP TARGETING

A-3. The JPOTF J-3 primarily uses the PSYOP targeting matrix as a tool for war-gaming possible effects of PSYOP, PSYACTs, or other activities in relation to each other; for sequencing of PSYACTs; for ensuring unity of effort; and for prioritizing PSYOP fires. The matrix offers a format that is recognizable to conventional force planners from all Services, and it provides a smooth process of integrating PSYOP nonlethal fires into a standard targeting and fire support architecture.

A-4. PSYOP targeting is perhaps the single most important element of PSYOP planning. Its role is especially critical in making the PSYOP plan relevant to the other elements of the JTF. PSYOP targeting synchronizes the

PSYOP plan with the overall OPLAN of the supported commander and, if properly formatted, gives the other planners something concrete on which to link.

A-5. To maintain a common frame of reference, PSYOP planners must use the same terminology used by the other planners with whom they work. The target categories are—

- *Links:* Connections, human or mechanical/electronic, between nodes.
- *Nodes:* Key centers of power and influence, human or mechanical/ electronic.
- *Human factors:* Intelligence, attitudes, emotions, beliefs, values, morality, personality, and so on.
- *Weapon systems:* Primarily mechanical systems; however, a weapon system could be human (for example, a suicide bomber).
- *Databases:* Computer data, software and hardware, and electronic media.

A-6. A critical node is an element, position, or communications entity whose disruption or destruction would immediately degrade an adversary's abilities. A vulnerable node is one that is susceptible to PSYOP attack, is a realistic target, and is accessible by means at the JTF's disposal or means available to others that the JTF understands and can access. (A PSYOP target will most likely need to be a demonstrably critical node to warrant the apportionment of a JTF commander's assets to attack it.)

A-7. Targets are further characterized as HVTs and HPTs. An HVT is critical to the success of the enemy's mission. An HPT is critical to the success of the friendly unit's mission. Figure A-1 is an example of a PSYOP targeting matrix.

Target #	Priority	HVT/ HPT	Type Target	PSYOP PIR	Trigger	PSYACT	Attack Guidance	Feedback	Planned Effect
1									
2									
3									
4									
5									
6									
7									
8									

Figure A-1. PSYOP Targeting Matrix

A-8. The first block of the targeting matrix assigns a number to the target. Any number of PSYACTs can be executed against the same target. The second block assigns a priority to the target, based upon the supported commander's guidance and an analysis of the TA. The J-3 and the chief of the PDC assign priority. The third block is simply a yes-or-no answer for HVT or HPT criteria.

A-9. The fourth block identifies the type of target to be attacked: link, node, human factor, weapon system, or database. The fifth block expresses briefly the priority intelligence needed to determine the attack guidance. For example, "Will interceptor pilots fly in response to cross-border air operations?" In this case, the target would be the interceptor pilots. The sixth block is the trigger or the event that would cause the JPOTF to execute PSYOP fires against the target. In this example, the trigger could be the increased activity of the ground-support personnel at the interceptor air base.

A-10. The seventh block describes the PSYACT itself, such as a leaflet drop to a denied area. The eighth block shows the attack guidance derived from a TAA and a mission analysis. In the example of the air base, for instance, analysis of the TA might show that leaflets would be the proper medium for communicating the desired message. A mission analysis might indicate that because of the air defense threat, only fast-moving aircraft would be capable of reaching the target, so the attack guidance would be PDU-5/B leaflet bombs.

A-11. The ninth block is the source of feedback once the PSYACT has been executed. In the example of the air base, a good source of feedback would be reconnaissance photos of the airfield during the days following the leaflet drop. The tenth block describes the desired effect of the PSYACT, such as reduced activity of ground-support personnel at the airfield and a decreased likelihood of sorties in the near term.

A-12. To guarantee the synchronization of lethal and nonlethal fires, the PSYOP targeting process must be coordinated with the JTF's targeting process. The JPOTF J-3 is the focal point for planning and integrating the PSYOP plan with the JTF plan or theater campaign plan. To be of value to the JTF, the JPOTF must provide its targeting input in a timely manner. Figure A-2, page A-4, graphically represents the ATO cycle and Figure A-3, page A-5, provides general planning guidance for integrating PSYOP targets into the JIPTL.

A-13. The ATO is a continuous planning evolution that operates on a 72-hour cycle. The end product for each planning cycle is an ATO. The ATO is usually identified by a letter (for example, ATO A) that promulgates the guidance, coordination, and mission orders for one day of JFACC-controlled air assets to support the JFC plan for the military operation. On every day, there are five ATOs in the various stages of being developed, executed, or evaluated.

A-14. The cycle starts with the coordination between the JFC and all component commanders for the requirements for air power support to the JFC intent and scheme of maneuver. The result of this coordination is a JFACC recommendation for the apportionment of air power. Apportionment is the assignment of the total expected air effort by priority that should be devoted to each of the sixteen air power mission areas; for example, counter air, strategic attack, close air support, and counter-information. The apportionment recommendation and decision is expressed in terms of a percentage of air effort; for example, 30 percent of assets dedicated to counter air, 20 percent dedicated to strategic attack, and so on, which will add up to 100 percent of the available air effort. A JFC apportionment decision that reflects a percentage of air assets dedicated to PSYOP dissemination is crucial to the JPOTF's ability to use fixed-wing assets to disseminate leaflet or broadcast missions. In the ATO process, the JFACC makes the apportionment recommendation and the JFC makes the decision.

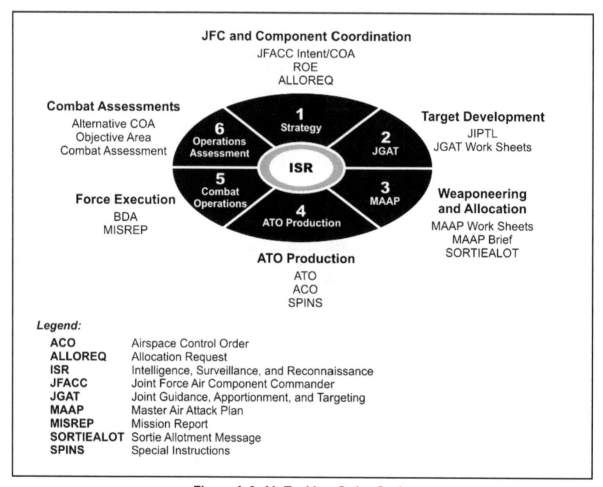

JFC and Component Coordination
JFACC Intent/COA
ROE
ALLOREQ

Combat Assessments
Alternative COA
Objective Area
Combat Assessment

Target Development
JIPTL
JGAT Work Sheets

Force Execution
BDA
MISREP

Weaponeering and Allocation
MAAP Work Sheets
MAAP Brief
SORTIEALOT

6 Operations Assessment
1 Strategy
2 JGAT
ISR
5 Combat Operations
3 MAAP
4 ATO Production

ATO Production
ATO
ACO
SPINS

Legend:

ACO	Airspace Control Order
ALLOREQ	Allocation Request
ISR	Intelligence, Surveillance, and Reconnaissance
JFACC	Joint Force Air Component Commander
JGAT	Joint Guidance, Apportionment, and Targeting
MAAP	Master Air Attack Plan
MISREP	Mission Report
SORTIEALOT	Sortie Allotment Message
SPINS	Special Instructions

Figure A-2. Air Tasking Order Cycle

A-15. Once the apportionment decision is made—before desired mission execution—the JPOTF must provide target nominations for targets to be serviced with PSYOP to the JTF joint fires element (JFE) and J-2 targets section. The JPOTF must ensure that its desired target nominations are input into the appropriate JTF and JFACC staff sections IAW the JTF battle rhythm to be integrated into the JTF-approved JIPTL. All targets must be on an approved JIPTL before they can be serviced with lethal or nonlethal fires. Concurrently with the target nomination, the JPOTF must work with the JFACC planners in the weaponeering allocation—determination of number of aircraft, and leaflets and canisters required to service the targets.

A-16. The result of this process is the allocation decision, which translates the JFC's apportionment decision into total numbers of sorties by aircraft type available for each operations or task, to include PSYOP dissemination. JFACC makes this decision and publishes it 72 hours before desired mission execution. The allocation decision is promulgated in the form of the MAAP, which provides the guidance for the JFACC staff planners in the JGAT section to develop the ATO to support the JTF commander's intent. The result of the JGAT planning effort is the actual ATO and associated SPINS, which delineate mission orders to the various flight squadrons to conduct their individual mission planning. The ATO and SPINS are published 24 hours before the desired mission execution to allow squadron and pilot commanders to conduct detailed mission execution planning. The targets are then serviced during the force execution phase when that ATO is flown. Results are assessed during the combat assessment, which provides recommended input to the JFC and component coordination for the next evolution of the ATO planning cycle.

	Operations Process Activity	Targeting Process Activity	Targeting Task
Assessment	Planning	Decide	**Mission Analysis** • Perform target value analysis to develop HVTs. • Develop targeting guidance and targeting objectives. **COA Development** • Designate potential HPTs. • Designate and coordinate potential HPTs. • Deconflict and coordinate potential HPTs. **COA Analysis** • Develop HPT list. • Establish target selection standards (TSS). • Develop attack guidance matrix (AGM). • Determine criteria of success for BDA requirements. **Orders Production** • Finalize HPT list. • Finalize TSS. • Finalize AGM. • Submit IRs/RFIs to G-2.
	Preparation Execution	Detect	• Execute collection plan. • Update PIR/IRs as they are answered. • Update HPT list and AGM.
		Deliver	• Execute attacks IAW the AGM.
		Assess	• Evaluate effects of attacks. • Monitor targets attacked with nonlethal means.

Figure A-3. Four-Phase Land and Maritime Targeting Process

A-17. The targeting cycle is an integrated intelligence and operations continuous planning evolution that operates concurrently within the ATO production cycle. In many respects, the targeting cycle mirrors and operates within the timelines, constraints, parameters, and guidelines of the ATO cycle. One of the key outputs of the targeting cycle is the JIPTL. To service targets by JTF lethal and nonlethal fires, nominated targets must be on the JFC-approved JIPTL. This process ensures that targets are prioritized, vetted, and approved IAW the JFC priorities and legal, political, and operational constraints imposed by law of armed conflict, ROE, collateral damage restrictions, political considerations, and operational requirements to minimize potential for fratricide.

A-18. Commander's guidance and objectives provide mission guidance for target selection, priorities, and weight of effort to meet the JFC intent and objectives. JTF staff elements and components then provide target nominations concurrently to the JTF JFE in the J-3 and J-2 Targets (J2T) section to be serviced IAW this guidance. In the target development phase (conducted primarily by intelligence staff), target folders for each target are developed with required information (grid coordinates, radar, or graphic imagery) to ensure clear identification of the target and constraints imposed for engagement.

A-19. Targets are identified in two basic categories—fixed and mobile targets. For fixed targets, which include nonmobile man-made structures and facilities, targets are assigned a basic entry (BE) number (an 8-digit alphanumeric code) unique to each specific target, which is maintained in a database by the Defense Intelligence Agency. For mobile targets, which include movable equipment and military units, JTFs and unified commands establish their internal target folder identification system.

A-20. During the target development process, both categories of targets are then prioritized against commander's guidance and objectives, and vetted against legal, political, and operational constraints (for example, no-fire areas [NFAs], restrictive fire areas [RFAs], and fire support coordination lines [FSCLs]) imposed on or by the JTF. An important consideration for the JPOTF planners is that many of these fire support coordination measures apply only to lethal fires and do not apply to nonlethal fires, such as leaflet dissemination and radio or TV broadcasts. JPOTF planners must work closely with JTF JFE and J2T elements to ensure that PSYOP target nominations within these NFAs, RFAs, and beyond the FSCLs, are on the JIPTL. The output of this process is the JIPTL, which includes targets to be serviced for both lethal and nonlethal fires.

A-21. In the next phase, targets are weaponeered to ensure the appropriate weapon or fire is used to achieve the desired effect. For a PSYOP nonlethal target, this process includes planning for the use of leaflet bombs vice box drop from fixed- or rotary-wing aircraft or engaging with radio broadcasts from EC-130 (COMMANDO SOLO).

A-22. In the force application phase, planning is conducted by Soldiers to ensure that the engagement platform, such as an F-16 loaded with PDU-5/Bs, can reach, engage, and return safely from the target area. This phase would include considerations, such as requirements for defensive counter area, suppression of enemy air defense, electronic warfare, and air-to-air refueling. Force execution involves the physical servicing of the target, while combat assessment evaluates the results achieved by attacking the target.

A-23. The PSYOP targeting board is chaired by the JPOTF J-3 and is attended by the JPOTF J-2 and Air LNO, as well as by representatives from the PDC. The board meets before the daily JTF targeting board so that the JPOTF's targeting board product can be integrated into the JTF targeting board.

A-24. The PSYOP targeting board begins with J-3 giving a quick synopsis of the current friendly and enemy situation. This synopsis includes the number of sorties currently on the ATO and any significant shift in the JTF's targeting priorities or in the upcoming ATO. The JPOTF Air LNO and J-3 Plans and Future Operations then give a rundown of the JTF's enemy templating for the next two ATO cycles. The J-3 follows with a restatement of the JTF commander's intent.

A-25. Next, the PDC chief briefs all ongoing PSYOP and PSYACTs, including any not scheduled in the ATO. The PDC chief presents the evaluation by the PDC and the SSD of the enemy's vulnerable nodes and submits his nominations for PSYACTs in support of current, future, and planned operations. The J-3 validates these PSYACTs and the board members prioritize them. The PSYOP targeting board then submits its final product, the PSYOP targeting matrix, to the JPOTF commander for concurrence and validation. The matrix then serves as the vehicle for the JPOTF to nominate targets at the JTCB. Figure A-4 provides an example of a planning matrix that enables the JPOTF to track selection and development of products and nomination of targets within the time constraints of the ATO.

A-26. The JPOTF Air LNO and future operations planner represent the JPOTF at the JTCB. They nominate targets and request the allocation of resources through the same process that the other components use.

General Planning Guidance							
D-7	D-6	D-5	D-4	D-3	D-2	D-1	D
Product Request	Product Complete	JTF Staffing				Begin Packing PDU-5/Bs	Fuze Munitions
Product Concept	PDC CDR Approval	JPOTF Target Nominations Developed	JTF CDR Approval	Translation Approval			Load Aircraft
	Product Board		JTF Target	Begin Print Production	Complete Print and Cutting	Complete Packing PDU-5/Bs	Time on Target
	POTF CDR Approval		JTCB Apportionment	JFACC ATO Input	Move Products to Departure Airfield	Targeting Data to Air Planners	

Figure A-4. Example of Planning Matrix

Appendix B

Reserve Mobilization

Following the dramatic and well-publicized successes of PSYOP during Operations DESERT STORM, ENDURING FREEDOM, and IRAQI FREEDOM, the demand for PSYOP support to conventional military operations has steadily increased. Ongoing peacetime operations, such as peace support in the Balkans and humanitarian demining, further escalate the demand for PSYOP. With almost 70 percent of total Army PSYOP strength resident in the RC, it is important for PSYOP planners and commanders to know how to access this force. This chapter contains procedures and planning considerations for mobilizing, deploying, redeploying, and demobilizing PSYOP forces.

COMMAND RELATIONSHIPS AND RESPONSIBILITIES

B-1. The following organizations share the responsibilities for directing and executing the mobilization, deployment, redeployment, and demobilization of PSYOP units.

CONGRESS

B-2. The U.S. Congress, exercising its constitutional authority to advise and provide consent to the executive branch, may authorize partial mobilization. Only Congress may authorize full mobilization by declaring war or national emergency. Congress also has the authority to enact legislation to reinstate conscription under the Selective Service Act.

SECRETARY OF DEFENSE

B-3. The SecDef provides leadership for the DOD and is the principal assistant to the President on all matters relating to the maintenance and employment of the Armed Forces. The SecDef directs mobilization and demobilization of RC units and manpower through the military departments. The SecDef oversees the Army in compliance with existing laws, policies, and directives.

JOINT CHIEFS OF STAFF

B-4. The Joint Chiefs of Staff (JCS) serve as the principal military advisors to the President, the SecDef, and the National Security Council (NSC). The CJCS has no executive authority to command combatant forces, but does approve OPLANs and recommends assignment of forces to combatant commands.

COMBATANT COMMANDS

B-5. Combatant commands are those unified and functional commands either planning for, or engaged in, military operations. These include the geographic combatant commanders and the commanders of the United States Transportation Command (USTRANSCOM), USSOCOM, United States Space Command (USSPACECOM), United States Strategic Command (USSTRATCOM), and United States Army Forces Command (FORSCOM). In peacetime, the responsibilities of the commanders include legislation, military department and Service policy, budgetary considerations, and local conditions. During crisis or war, the geographic combatant commander's authority expands to include the use of facilities and supplies of all forces under his command. Commands are designated as supported (normally the geographic combatant commanders with regional responsibility) or supporting (usually those with global responsibilities who provide forces and logistics, but may include other geographic combatant commanders). Supported and supporting commanders provide requirements for PSYOP forces requiring mobilization to USSOCOM and the JCS for validation; approval by the President, SecDef, and/or Congress; and execution by Headquarters, Department of the Army (HQDA), and USASOC.

HEADQUARTERS, DEPARTMENT OF THE ARMY

B-6. HQDA is responsible for the assignment, preparation, and support of land forces necessary for employment across the operational continuum. Specifically, HQDA is responsible for recruiting, training, mobilizing, modernizing, administering, organizing, and demobilizing Army forces; constructing buildings; and repairing equipment. These functions are executed under the supervision of the Secretary of the Army (SECARMY) and the Chief of Staff, United States Army (CSA), and are consistent with the authority granted to the combatant commands over assigned forces.

UNITED STATES TRANSPORTATION COMMAND

B-7. USTRANSCOM is the DOD single manager for transportation. USTRANSCOM provides air, land, and sea transportation to meet national security objectives, including those required to support mobilization, deployment, redeployment, and demobilization.

UNITED STATES SPECIAL OPERATIONS COMMAND

B-8. USSOCOM is a supporting combatant command principally responsible for providing trained and ready SOF to the combatant commanders. USSOCCOM exercises combatant command (COCOM) over CONUS-based Active Army and RC SOF, and coordinates RC mobilization requirements with HQDA and FORSCOM. USSOCOM normally executes its responsibilities regarding mobilization of RC PSYOP forces through USASOC.

OFFICE OF THE CHIEF OF ARMY RESERVE

B-9. The Chief of the Army Reserve (CAR) advises the CSA on all matters pertaining to the development, training, mobilization, readiness, and maintenance of the Army Reserve. The CAR participates with other Army staff agencies to formulate and develop DA policies for the Army

Reserve. The CAR also serves as the Commander, United States Army Reserve Command (USARC), and as the Deputy Commanding General (Reserve Components), FORSCOM.

UNITED STATES ARMY FORCES COMMAND

B-10. FORSCOM is both a specified command and a major command (MACOM). As a MACOM, FORSCOM is the Army CONUS executive agent for mobilization, deployment, redeployment, and demobilization (MDRD). Acting in this capacity, FORSCOM provides guidance and verifies planning, development, training, mobilization, maintenance, and readiness of all Army RC forces. FORSCOM issues directives regarding MDRD to other Army MACOMs, including USASOC. The FORSCOM Mobilization and Deployment Planning System (FORMDEPS) provides detailed guidance to accomplish the MDRD mission.

UNITED STATES ARMY TRAINING AND DOCTRINE COMMAND

B-11. The United States Army Training and Doctrine Command (TRADOC) supports the execution of MDRD by developing doctrine, directing training, and expanding the mobilization training base, as required. TRADOC establishes and operates CONUS replacement centers (CRCs) and CONUS demobilization centers (CDCs) for non-unit (individual) Soldiers.

UNITED STATES ARMY SPECIAL OPERATIONS COMMAND

B-12. USASOC is both a component command of USSOCOM and an Army MACOM. USASOC commands, organizes, trains, equips, and ensures the combat readiness of both Active Army and RC CONUS-based ARSOF, including all PSYOP forces. When directed by USSOCOM, USASOC coordinates with other Army MACOMs to support the mobilization, training, equipping, deployment validation, and subsequent deployment of CONUS-based ARSOF. USASOC mobilizes and attaches RC PSYOP forces to mobilization stations pending OCONUS deployment or reassignment within CONUS on orders published by USASOC. USASOC also coordinates with HQDA and FORSCOM to call up, mobilize, demobilize, and release selected RC personnel and units. USASOC has the following roles and responsibilities:

- *USACAPOC*: Designated as the lead and responsible agency for all matters relating to the mobilization, deployment, redeployment, and demobilization of USAR CA and PSYOP forces.

- *USAJFKSWCS*: Designated as the lead and responsible agency for all matters relating to the institutional training, doctrine, and force development requirements for the mobilization, deployment, redeployment, and demobilization of all RC ARSOF assigned to USASOC.

- *SOSCOM*: Responsible to support as required the mobilization, deployment, redeployment, and demobilization activities of all RC ARSOF assigned to USASOC.

MOBILIZATION

B-13. Mobilization considerations include many factors. Each of these factors is discussed in the following paragraphs.

AUTHORITY

B-14. The authority to order mobilization resides with the President and Congress. The SecDef, with the advice and recommendation of the Service Secretaries and the JCS, recommends to the President and Congress the level of mobilization required to support a given contingency, OPLAN, or national emergency. The SecDef directs mobilization of RC units and manpower through the various military departments.

LEVELS

B-15. Selective mobilization is authorized by Congress or the President, in situations not involving a threat to U.S. national security; for example, domestic emergencies, such as postal strikes, floods, earthquakes, and hurricanes.

B-16. Presidential Reserve Call-Up Authority is used to augment the active force of all Services with up to 200,000 Soldiers of the Selected Reserve serving up to 270 days, in support of an operational requirement. Units and individuals of the Selected Reserve may be involuntarily mobilized under provisions of Title 10, United States Code (USC), Section 12304. The President may also consider the mobilization of volunteers under Title 10, USC, Section 123019(d), or activating military retirees under Title 10, USC, Section 688. Mobilization under PRCA does not require a declaration of national emergency. The President, however, must report to Congress regarding the situation and the anticipated use of the forces within 24 hours of PRCA approval.

B-17. Partial mobilization is approved by the President or Congress and is limited to 1,000,000 ready reservists (units and individual reservists), along with the resources needed for their support, for a period not to exceed 24 months. Partial mobilization is intended to meet the requirements of war or other national emergency involving an external threat to U.S. national security.

B-18. Full mobilization is authorized by the Congress and includes mobilization of all RC units in the existing force structure; all individual, standby, and retired reservists; retired military personnel; and the resources needed for their support for the duration of a declared emergency, plus six months. Full mobilization is also intended to meet the requirements of a war or other national emergency involving an external threat to U.S. national security.

B-19. Total mobilization is the expansion of the Armed Forces by the Congress and the President to organize or generate additional units or personnel beyond the existing force structure, as well as the resources needed for their support. Total mobilization is designed to meet the full requirements of a war or other national emergency involving an external threat to U.S. national security.

PHASES

B-20. Mobilization is conducted in five phases. Each of these phases is discussed in the following paragraphs.

Phase I: Planning

B-21. This phase includes the normal day-to-day efforts of each RC PSYOP unit at its home station (HS). During this phase, RC PSYOP units plan, train, and prepare to accomplish assigned mobilization missions. They prepare mobilization plans and files as directed by FORMDEPS, USSOCOM, USASOC, and USACAPOC. Units also attend mobilization coordination conferences, provide required planning data to mobilization stations (MSs), conduct mobilization training, and develop postmobilization training plans, as required. The overall objective of this phase is for each RC PSYOP unit to complete as many administrative processing actions as possible before being ordered to federal active duty. Plans for movement to the MS must also be completed during this phase. Phase I ends when the RC PSYOP unit receives its official mobilization alert notification.

Phase II: Alert

B-22. This phase includes all those actions taken by RC PSYOP units following official receipt of the alert. RC PSYOP units initiate specific actions to prepare for transition from reserve to active status. Actions such as personnel screening and cross leveling are essential during the alert phase. When time and resources permit, units may conduct an HS annual training (AT) during this phase to complete these actions and conduct additional training. This phase ends on the effective date of unit mobilization at HS.

Phase III: Home Station

B-23. This phase begins on the effective date of unit mobilization. Once mobilized, RC PSYOP units normally have 72 hours to be ready to move to their MS. During this phase, the unit takes action to facilitate its transition to active status. Such actions include inventory and loading of unit property and dispatch of an advance party to the MS. Movement from HS to MS will be by the most expeditious and practical means available. Detailed unit movement planning will be IAW FORSCOM Regulation 55-1, *Unit Movement Planning*. The unit will coordinate directly with the MS before departing HS, and keep USACAPOC informed. Mobilizing PSYOP units will continue to request assistance and support through their peacetime channels until directed otherwise. This phase ends with arrival of the unit at its MS.

Phase IV: Mobilization Station

B-24. This phase begins with arrival of the PSYOP unit at its MS and encompasses all actions necessary to meet required deployment criteria. Actions at the MS include the processing of personnel and equipment and the accessioning of the unit into the active force structure. The goal of the unit during this phase is to attain operational readiness in the shortest possible time, consistent with its planned deployment or operational mission. This phase also includes any necessary individual or collective training, as well as appropriate cross-leveling actions, Soldier Readiness Processing (SRP), POM, and validation for deployment. Phase IV ends with arrival of the unit at the port of embarkation (POE). Phase IV and Phase V may overlap since equipment moving by surface transportation may begin Phase V earlier than deploying personnel.

Phase V: Port of Embarkation

B-25. This phase begins with arrival of the PSYOP unit at the POE. This phase encompasses all activities at the seaport of embarkation (SPOE) or the aerial port of embarkation (APOE). These activities include both manifesting and loading of personnel. This phase ends with departure of PSYOP personnel and equipment from the POE.

LOGISTICAL REQUIREMENTS

B-26. The intent of the SOR process as outlined in FM 100-25, *Doctrine for Army Special Operations Forces*, and Chapter 11, FM 3-05.30, is to identify and validate additional logistical needs early in the planning cycle.

B-27. Each mobilizing PSYOP unit must conduct a comprehensive mission analysis, identify all additional logistical needs, and describe these needs in writing using the SOR format. The unit then forwards this SOR to its higher HQ.

B-28. Receiving organizations will validate the SOR, provide to the initiating unit all items available and on hand at that level, and forward the balance of the SOR to the next-higher HQ.

B-29. This process is repeated at every organizational level until the SOR has been validated by the USASOC Deputy Chief of Staff for Operations and Plans (DCSOPS) and forwarded to the USASOC Deputy Chief of Staff for Logistics (DCSLOG) for fill. Only after every effort has been made to satisfy the SOR within USASOC will the DCSLOG initiate fill actions with non-USASOC units.

B-30. To complete the SOR process, the USASOC DCSLOG will forward unsatisfied support requirements to the theater special operations command (SOC) for validation. Once this validation is completed, the SOC forwards SOF-unique requirements to USSOCOM for fill. Requirements for Army common equipment and remaining supplies and materials are forwarded by the SOC to the theater Army component command (TACC) for fill.

INDIVIDUAL MANPOWER REQUIREMENTS

B-31. Plans for contingencies are continuously updated. Sources of individual manpower support must be continually identified. The following are sources of individual manpower to meet established requirements:

- *Individual mobilization augmentees (IMAs)*. IMAs are members of the Selected Reserve who are preassigned to Active Army positions that must be filled either upon, or shortly after, mobilization. IMAs are available for call-up as part of PRCA or any other level of mobilization. IMAs may volunteer for active duty at any time.

- *Volunteers*. As a rule, RC Soldiers, regardless of affiliation, may volunteer for active duty at any time under Title 10, USC, Section 12301(d). Appropriate commands must approve members of reserve units and IMAs by verifying that loss of the Soldier will not adversely impact upon the unit's capability to perform its mobilization mission. Retirees and Individual Ready Reserve (IRR) members must coordinate with the Commander, United States Army Reserve

Personnel Center (ARPERCEN) to volunteer. End-strength constraints and funding ceilings will restrict the number of volunteers approved in each category.

- *Individual Ready Reserve.* The IRR is composed of trained, non-unit reserve personnel who are liable for involuntary active duty in time of war or national emergency declared by the Congress or by the President. In peacetime, the commander, ARPERCEN commands the IRR.

- *Retired Reserve.* Retired Soldiers who have completed 20 years of active duty are subject to recall to active duty at any time the SECARMY determines a need. These retirees are a valuable source of trained manpower. They are available for most military assignments and deployments, subject to physical or other restrictions dictated by HQDA. Members of the Retired Reserve are also available to replenish critical civilian positions. All other retirees are also available at the discretion of the SecDef, but only after Congress has declared war or a national emergency. Retirees may volunteer for active duty to meet specific operational requirements at any time; however, recall to active duty is subject to approval on a case-by-case basis by the SECARMY.

- *Standby Reserve.* The Standby Reserve consists of officer and enlisted Soldiers with or without remaining military service obligations, but who have no statutory requirements for peacetime training. Members of the Standby Reserve can be involuntarily ordered to active duty only under conditions of full mobilization.

B-32. Information supporting the manpower fill of Active Army and mobilized RC PSYOP units to wartime requirement levels is derived from personnel reports and updates from units at HSs and those located at MSs. USASOC, through USACAPOC, is responsible for determining fill requirements for assigned RC PSYOP units and reporting to HQDA and USSOCOM those shortages that cannot be filled internally.

PERSONNEL AND ADMINISTRATION

B-33. Upon receipt of an alert order, all members assigned to an RC PSYOP unit will be mobilized with that unit unless otherwise directed by regulation, SECARMY guidance, or operational-unique instructions. Standard exceptions are high school students, those Soldiers who have not completed initial entry training, Reserve Officer Training Corps (ROTC) cadets assigned to units under the Simultaneous Membership Program, and Soldiers who have received reassignment or transfer orders. Effective upon the HS mobilization date, all personnel management actions (except for those pertaining to pay and promotions) must comply with Active Army regulations. Commanders at every level must ensure that all assigned Soldiers are fully qualified and prepared for mobilization.

MOBILIZATION STATIONS

B-34. MSs process, accommodate, train, and deploy specified units and equipment; process, validate, and deploy mobilized RC units; and process and move to CRCs those individuals designated as non-unit-related personnel. MSs may perform additional missions, such as—

- Regional marshaling area support for deploying forces.
- POE/port of debarkation (POD) processing support (arrival/departure airfield control group [A/DACG] and port support activity [PSA]), at USTRANSCOM-directed POEs and PODs.

OTHER MOBILIZATION CONSIDERATIONS

B-35. Other considerations during mobilization include, but are not limited to, financial management, contracting, and host-nation support (HNS). The following paragraphs discuss these considerations in detail.

Financial Management

B-36. HQDA issues resource management guidance to MACOM commanders. This guidance defines how USASOC, CONUS power projection platforms, and MSs should capture and cover costs associated with MDRD. Although other financial activities, such as military pay and travel, may receive considerable attention, procurement support is considered the most critical wartime finance mission. This function is divided into two areas: contracting operations and commercial vendor services operations. Both of these functions involve the payment of commercial accounts for goods and services obtained through formal contracting procedures and may include all classes of supply, laundry and bath operations, transportation, real estate, and maintenance. All such requirements are generally the funding responsibility of the theater Army component HQ. Requests for funding of these activities must be closely managed and, if contested or disapproved by theater Army resource managers, will be forwarded to the USASOC resource management and contracting directorates for coordination and action.

Contracting

B-37. Contracting plays a vital role in MDRD. The key to obtaining optimum support from contracting is early and thorough planning. Contracting can bridge the gap at the installation level for increased support during mobilization for the following types of support requirements:

- Billeting.
- Medical supplies.
- Food services.
- Repair parts.
- Transportation.
- Construction.
- Consumable supplies.
- Maintenance.
- Miscellaneous services.

B-38. Additionally, contracting support of these activities may continue during the deployment phase by filling the gap until the logistics civilian augmentation program (LOGCAP) and/or the HNS program become fully operational and integrated into the support plan. During the redeployment phase, contracts for transportation of materiel and maintenance will be used extensively to reconstitute the force. The USASOC contracting directorate provides contracting support for all mobilizing PSYOP units. Mobilization plans should fully integrate contracting support. The USASOC contracting directorate must be contacted early in the planning process and remain involved throughout the life of the contract.

Host-Nation Support

B-39. PSYOP planners should consider HNS capabilities but not depend exclusively upon them. HNS should be closely and extensively coordinated, and routinely exercised during peacetime. Based upon the general state of logistical preparation within the theater, HNS could play a substantial and vital role in providing the procurement needs (supplies and services) of deployed PSYOP units and Soldiers.

DEPLOYMENT

B-40. The ability to project military power is more important now than ever before. PSYOP planners and unit commanders must prepare to deploy forces to any region and ensure that these forces are sustained, even in areas where pre-positioning of equipment will not always be feasible, where adequate bases may not be available, or where poorly developed infrastructure exists. PSYOP mobility strategy demands that personnel and equipment are moved to the scene of a crisis at a pace and in numbers sufficient to achieve quick, decisive success of the mission.

DEPLOYMENT PLANNING CONSIDERATIONS

B-41. The amount of time available for planning is a critical factor in determining the planning procedures to be used. When time is unconstrained, deliberate planning procedures are used. When the time available for planning is short and the near-term result is expected to be an actual deployment or employment of PSYOP forces, crisis-action procedures are used.

MOBILITY OPTIONS

B-42. Mobility options to meet regional requirements are limited only by available military air, sea, and surface lift; requisitioned U.S. commercial ships; the civil reserve air fleet (CRAF); and the widely varying array of allied transport. Options include—

- *Strategic lift.* The ultimate success of force projection and sustainment operations is based upon the adequacy of the strategic mobility triad (airlift, sealift, and pre-positioning) and the proficiency and preparedness of deploying organizations. Deploying PSYOP units can improve the effectiveness and efficiency of airlift and sealift by achieving and maintaining optimum readiness, and by timely planning and preparing of unitized loads of ammunition, supplies, and equipment. The JOPES TPFDD reflects both air and sea movement priorities.

- *Sealift.* The U.S. strategic sealift capability is comprised of a combination of ships from various sources and is managed by the U.S. Navy. Sealift assets currently available to deploy forces include fast sealift ships (FSS), Ready Reserve Force (RRF) ships, and afloat pre-positioning force (APF) ships.

- *Airlift.* The U.S. strategic airlift capability includes organic aircraft primarily in the Air Force's Air Mobility Command (AMC) and selected commercial aircraft containing military-useful compartments. Commercial charter contracts or CRAF aircraft may augment AMC assets. USTRANSCOM administers the CRAF program in coordination with the Department of Transportation. Types and quantities of CRAF aircraft available to support deployments change monthly based upon service, maintenance, and ownership. The use of CRAF aircraft incorporates limiting factors, such as lengthy loading and unloading times and requirements for specialized cargo-handling equipment. Because of these requirements, CRAF cargo assets may reduce organic airlift effectiveness and constrain cargo delivery and off-load. CRAF will normally not be used in lesser regional contingency scenarios.

- *Ground movement.* Rail is the preferred method for moving all tracked vehicles. Rail is also the preferred mode of travel for wheeled vehicles when travel to the POE exceeds one day's driving distance. The commercial railroad industry normally requires up to seven days to position railcars at installations in support of deployments. To overcome this time lag, the commercial railroad industry routinely coordinates with FORSCOM and the Military Traffic Management Command (MTMC) to pre-position military-owned and military-managed strategic port railcars. To support rail movements and staging requirements, installations normally maintain rail tracks, adequate loading ramps, facilities, and staging areas for deployment missions. It is important to note that deploying PSYOP units are responsible for coordinating and procuring blocking, bracing, and tie-down equipment throughout the deployment. Military convoy is the preferred method of moving wheeled vehicles to ports and other facilities that are within one day's driving distance.

- *Unit movement.* PSYOP planning for strategic deployment or unit movement by air or sea is influenced by existing automated unit equipment lists (AUELs), OPORDs, the commander's intent, pre-positioned equipment, available lift, and METT-TC. Units moving in response to an OPORD are programmed for movement via the JOPES, as modified by the supported commander's updated plan of operations. PSYOP units responding to short-notice contingencies without preexisting plans must be prepared to quickly assess unit status and movement requirements. PSYOP units must provide the necessary Status of Resources and Training System (SORTS) transactions (unit status report and mobilization or change report). PSYOP units must use Transportation Coordinator's Automated Command and Control Information System (TC-ACCIS) to update unit movement data. These actions assist USTRANSCOM in computing lift requirements and in determining times of embarkation.

- *Deployment concept.* The ability of USASOC to project PSYOP forces, with adequate support, ensures PSYOP a central role in our nation's land forces with missions ranging from peacetime engagement, to conflict, to war. Depending upon the mission, the size of the required force, and the anticipated duration, RC PSYOP forces may be mobilized to participate. Regardless of the force size or category, PSYOP units must be prepared for rapid task-organizing, echeloning, and tailoring for deployment.

- *Task-organizing process.* For deployment purposes, task-organizing is the process of forming combined arms task forces with limited self-sustaining capabilities for rapid deployment. Task-organizing, centered primarily on maneuver elements, is a predeployment activity.

- *Echeloning.* Echeloning is the process of organizing units for movement. Like task-organizing, echeloning is a predeployment standard operation procedure that establishes a priority for movement within the task force to accommodate available lift. Echelons may be divided, for example, into advance parties, a main body, and a trail force. Within each echelon, there must be appropriate combat, CS, and CSS elements. Planning for each echelon must include numbers of vehicles and personnel, consumable supply requirements, updated unit movement data (UMD), and AUELs.

- *Tailoring.* Tailoring occurs after the initial strategic lift requirements and availability have been identified, pre-positioned assets have been confirmed, and HN or contract services or assets have been determined. Whereas task-organizing and echeloning are preplanned, tailoring is situational-dependent. PSYOP units and UMD may be added to, or subtracted from, a planned task organization, based upon the mission, available lift, pre-positioned assets, or HN or contract services.

TIME-PHASED FORCE AND DEPLOYMENT DATA

B-43. The TPFDD is the supported geographic combatant commander's SORs by unit type, time period, and priority for arrival in the theater. The TPFDD further defines the supported geographic combatant commander's non-unit-related cargo and personnel requirements, to include Army civilians, required to sustain his forces. The TPFDD is a document describing force requirements and transportation movement priority. The ultimate objective of deployment is the arrival of the force at the right place and at the right time. The TPFDD is a dynamic document constantly refined by the supported combatant commander. Some of the factors that may require TPFDD adjustments include—

- Nonvalidated forces or sustainment commodities added to the flow.

- Adjustments to the latest arrival date (LAD) of validated forces.

- UMD adjustments to deployment equipment lists (DELs) necessitating changes in strategic lift type and quantity.

- Available-to-load date (ALD) or ready-to-load date (RLD) adjustments for validated forces.

- Delayed POE/POD arrivals and departures affecting subsequent strategic lift.
- Emergency requirements for additional forces or sustainment.

B-44. The supported commander's required date (CRD) for arrival of forces at their destinations is the ultimate objective for all common-user transportation planning. The supporting combatant commander establishes milestones for loading and transporting units and their accompanying supplies to the POE, embarking them aboard strategic lift, and transiting them to the POD. The supported commander must resolve as early as possible the sequence in which Army units deploy in relation to the movement of forces of the other Services and alliance or coalition forces.

B-45. Efficient and timely use of limited amounts of available strategic lift is the key to successful deployment operations. Early resolution of the sequencing of forces into the theater will solidify the TPFDD, determine the time required to deploy forces, and provide the basis to initiate the theater distribution plan.

B-46. The supported geographic combatant commander performs the ultimate phasing, prioritization, and validation of all requirements. Proper sequencing of PSYOP forces into the AO will allow for rapid buildup of capabilities and permit the supported combatant commander to seize the initiative and conduct successful decisive operations as early as possible. Simultaneous deployment of tactical and operational HQ early in the operation is essential for initiating operations, facilitating future planning, and coordinating with HN or allied forces. Additionally, simultaneous deployment allows for the rapid employment of follow-on reinforcing units.

B-47. Appropriate logistical and administrative support must deploy with the initial force. Throughout the deployment, PSYOP planners must maintain the flexibility to reconfigure units and adjust deployments should the supported commander's needs change while the deployment is in progress.

B-48. The needs of the force commander and the requirement for rapid deployment will initially take priority over maximizing the efficiency of lift. Even if the strategic intent is to attempt to deter an opponent, the operational focus must be on seizing the initiative and creating an offensive capability to fight and win should deterrence fail.

DEPLOYMENT PHASES

B-49. The five deployment phases are discussed in the following paragraphs. Concurrent with, and resulting from, the deployment of forces and logistics, the combatant commander conducts lodgment, stabilization, and restoration of conditions favorable to U.S. interests.

Phase I: Predeployment Activities

B-50. During normal peacetime operations, USASOC, through USACAPOC, prepares its units for crisis-action and force-projection missions. Based on the operational requirements of the supported geographic combatant commander, USASOC organizations are designated, equipped, trained, and led with force projection capabilities in mind. Commanders must adhere to USASOC standards for task-organizing, echeloning, and tailoring units. Units must conduct routine collective deployment training to ensure USASOC deploys the balance of PSYOP forces, individual manpower, and materiel to meet the combatant commander's needs.

Phase II: Movement to the Port of Embarkation

B-51. Based on the mobilization process and Phase I (predeployment activities), units have completed POM and have been validated. Units update AUELs to DELs and submit them to the appropriate authority. Whether deploying for training or in response to a crisis, unit loads are configured for combat contingencies. This configuration provides the capability to redeploy while en route to training or other activities.

B-52. Based on information provided to JOPES regarding the readiness of units and individual manpower for movement, USTRANSCOM provides movement guidance for movement to the POE. This phase concludes with the departure of the strategic lift at the POE, wheels up for aircraft, or passage of the last buoy marking the departure channel for vessels. Unless otherwise specified in the OPORD, command of the departing forces and non-unit-related personnel (NRP) is automatically transferred from the supporting combatant commander to the supported combatant commander at the conclusion of Phase II.

Phase III: Strategic Lift

B-53. This phase begins with departure of the strategic lift from the POE and ends with arrival of forces or cargo in the theater. USTRANSCOM is responsible for in-transit visibility (ITV) of forces and supplies. ITV data, coupled with the actions of unit movement coordinators, can combine to provide force-tracking (FT) information critical to the supported combatant commander.

Phase IV: Theater-Based Reception

B-54. This phase begins with the arrival of PSYOP units and their sustainment materials at the in-theater POD and ends with their departure from the POD. Obtaining necessary port clearances is a theater responsibility.

B-55. The supported combatant commander is responsible for developing the theater reception and onward movement plan for arriving forces and sustainment. Except in instances where the forcible entry of forces is required, CS and CSS forces may either precede or arrive concurrently with the combatant forces to support POD processing and to either begin establishing the theater distribution infrastructure or establish connectivity with the existing infrastructure.

B-56. A/DACG (air) and military or military-contracted port commands (sea), augmented by PSA organizations, must be established to process PSYOP units and sustainment equipment and supplies through the POD. When possible, units should send advance parties to coordinate the orderly processing of deploying forces. Additionally, advance ship manifests are used for POD planning for off-loading and marshaling.

B-57. One of the primary requirements during Phase IV is coordinating the onward movement of deploying forces. This function requires personnel provided by deploying organizations who are knowledgeable regarding the unit, its movement configuration, the nature and extent of pre-positioned war reserve stock (PWRS) received, and the unit's ultimate destination in the theater. These personnel coordinate with the combatant commander's designated representatives for sustainment and movement to develop the requisite planning and documentation necessary to move the units to their theater destination and sustain the forces throughout deployment.

Phase V: Theater Onward Movement

B-58. This phase begins with the linkup of personnel and equipment, continues through the reconfiguration of PSYOP forces, if required, initiation of the sustainment plan, and receipt of PWRS at designated marshaling areas. Phase V concludes with arrival of PSYOP units at the gaining command's staging areas or at basing locations where continued combat preparation occurs. In this phase, ITV and FT are the responsibility of the supported commander.

B-59. The supported combatant commander is responsible for the health, welfare, and support of forces and assisting with their onward movement. In this capacity, the supported combatant commander sustains the NRP forces until they arrive in the theater. Through the theater Army movement control agency (TAMCA), units obtain assistance for intratheater movement. In joint or combined operations, the OPLAN must delineate the reception and onward movement responsibilities of participating organizations.

LOGISTICS REQUIREMENTS

B-60. All sustainment requirements are shipped to theaters based on the priorities of the supported combatant commander. USASOC is responsible for providing units and equipment.

Reception

B-61. In all theaters, initial deploying and reinforcing units must be received and prepared for further deployment and employment. Even forward-presence forces stationed in the theater during peacetime frequently require repositioning before employment. The Air Standardization Coordinating Committee (ASCC) is responsible for receiving, equipping, and assisting deploying units, NRP, and those forward-deployed forces requiring repositioning.

B-62. Normally, PSYOP units deploy the majority of their personnel and equipment by air, with the balance moving by sea. Planners must synchronize these arrivals to accommodate the supported commander's intent. Once unit personnel and equipment arrive, they must be quickly consolidated and prepared for onward movement. Typically, arrival sites are located in the communications zone (COMMZ). The CSS requirements for supporting these operations are normally assigned to the ASCC, which directs the movement of forces and sustainment commodities.

Contracting

B-63. Contracting may be used to support deployment operations by filling the gaps until LOGCAP and HNS become fully integrated into the support plan. The theater Army contracting activity provides contracting support to deployed units.

B-64. Units should plan to satisfy low-dollar-value requirements through the use of ordering officers appointed from within the unit. Selection and training of these ordering officers must be accomplished before deployment. Units should coordinate with supporting installation directorates of contracting to obtain the necessary training and certification.

REDEPLOYMENT

B-65. Redeployment considerations include many factors. Each of these factors is discussed in the following paragraphs.

REDEPLOYMENT PLANNING CONSIDERATIONS

B-66. Redeployment must be planned and executed in a manner that facilitates the immediate use of redeploying forces, equipment, supplies, and sustainment commodities to meet new crises. Redeployment movement is, in most instances, nontactical. Redeployment returns PSYOP forces and individuals through demobilization stations (DMSs) or CDCs to HSs.

B-67. Upon completion of the crisis resolution process, the combatant commander constructs a TPFDD database to be implemented to redeploy forces upon cessation of hostilities. Concurrently, supporting commanders initiate planning to support the combatant commander's redeployment OPLAN.

B-68. In preparation for redeployment, a decision-making process occurs to determine who, what, when, where, and how the operation will proceed. This decision will be influenced by the following factors:

- The JCS residual force mission statement.
- JCS requirements to reconstitute a response capability.
- Other theater needs.
- Occupation, nation assistance, and humanitarian missions.
- Establishment of PWRS in the AO.
- Security of the force.
- Constraints on RC forces and individuals in-theater.
- Alliance or coalition force considerations (when applicable).
- Availability of strategic lift.
- Political considerations.

B-69. Redeployment involves forces (units), manpower (individuals), and materiel (equipment). The supported geographic combatant commander uses the above considerations to develop a redeployment plan, to include the sequencing of movement in coordination with the supporting commanders.

During redeployment, timely and accurate command and public information are critical to the morale of the Soldier and to maintain public support.

B-70. Unit integrity should be maintained to the maximum extent possible. Operational requirements may have necessitated some changes to unit structure during the employment phase. To facilitate demobilization, these units must reconstitute before redeployment.

B-71. Recent operational experiences have featured redeploying units leaving certain residual equipment in the theater. For RC organizations, approval authority for leaving residual equipment in the theater rests at HQDA level.

REDEPLOYMENT PHASES

B-72. Redeployment is conducted in six phases. Each of these phases is discussed in the following paragraphs.

Phase I: Reconstitution for Strategic Movement

B-73. After completion of the operational requirements for which forces were deployed, these forces move back to designated tactical assembly areas. The major focus for units at this point must be regaining unit integrity and establishing accountability for subordinate units, individuals, materiel, supplies, and equipment. Operational requirements may have necessitated changes to unit structure during the employment phase. These units should be reconstituted before redeployment to facilitate accountability and return to peacetime activities. The unit or its parent command is responsible for actions at the tactical assembly area. These include—

- Reconstitution and initial cross leveling.
- Repacking and loading containers under U.S. Customs and U.S. Department of Agriculture supervision. Generally, containerization should be accomplished as far forward as possible depending upon the availability of inspection personnel.
- Reconciling UMD through documentation review, inventory accountability, and coordination of movement instructions with TAMCA representatives.

B-74. Commanders must report excess equipment and materiel to the Materiel Management Center (MMC) for recovery, palletizing, and rewarehousing or redistribution. During this phase, commanders initiate personnel actions, to include the following:

- Processing decorations and awards.
- Processing officer evaluation reports (OERs) and NCOERs.
- Completing personnel records entries and finance action updates.

Phase II: Movement to Redeployment Assembly Areas

B-75. Upon receipt of movement instructions, forces, individuals, and materiel move to redeployment assembly areas (RAAs). At the RAA, the commander conducts activities that he could not accomplish at the tactical assembly area. These activities include—

- Washing and cleaning major items of equipment.
- Affixing required shipment placards and labels.
- Obtaining U.S. Customs and Department of Agriculture inspections on all unit equipment.
- Finalizing unit movement data.

B-76. Based upon the size of the redeploying force and available resources in the theater, intermediate and final staging areas may be used to move units to the POE for out loading. At the final staging area, all remaining strategic-lift preparatory requirements are satisfied. These include—

- Continued supply accountability and maintenance actions.
- Final U.S. Customs and Department of Agriculture inspections for all personnel and equipment.
- Palletization of equipment.
- Completion of labeling.

B-77. The accountable unit officer must ensure the property book and all related documentation, such as the document register, remain with the main body of unit equipment. If equipment is staged for shipment following departure of the main body, the property book and related documents should remain with the rear detachment OIC. It is essential that these documents accompany the majority of unit equipment to support inventory and accountability at all times during redeployment.

B-78. The theater senior logistics commander is responsible for the movement of forces from the tactical assembly area. He is further responsible for actions at, and support of, the RAA. These responsibilities include—

- All actions not completed at the tactical assembly area up to, but not including, those final preredeployment activities conducted at the POE processing center.
- Cleaning and consolidating cargo to U.S. Customs and Department of Agriculture standards.
- Final changes to the AUEL.

B-79. The movement of individuals not redeploying under a TPFDD unit line number (ULN) is coordinated by the unit of assignment through the TAMCA representative and IAW guidance from the supported combatant commander and USTRANSCOM. Personnel redeploying as individuals will remain under the administrative control of their assigned unit or the theater personnel command (PERSCOM) until completion of redeployment POE processing.

B-80. The tactical assembly area and RAA may be combined depending upon the size of the theater and the combatant commander's guidance. The redeployment sequence is based upon theater constraints and guidance provided by the combatant commander.

B-81. In all cases, the TPFDD process is the primary method of redeployment planning and execution. Other methods of redeploying cargo and personnel not scheduled for movement with the main body should be accomplished through established USTRANSCOM procedures, such as requesting additional ULN allocations. Commanders may request ULN allocations through the joint planning and execution community (JPEC) representative functioning as part of the JOPES process. Commanders may also request ULN allocations on an exception basis. With concurrence of the supported geographic combatant commander, commanders may request authorization to transfer accountability of unit cargo to other organizations redeploying to the same locations for later movement with those units.

Phase III: Movement to Port of Embarkation

B-82. Based on instructions provided by the TAMCA, forces, individuals, and materiel are moved to the POE where they are processed for strategic movement.

B-83. At all POE facilities, units must maintain security, supply and maintenance activities, and continued accountability of equipment in preparation for strategic lift. Upon acceptance by the A/DACG at the departure airfield or by the PSA for redeployment by sealift, departing forces, individuals, and materiel are quarantined and loaded aboard strategic lift for movement.

B-84. PSYOP unit movement officers will coordinate with the Theater Army Area Command (TAACOM) for the following actions to be accomplished at the POE processing center:

- Processing baggage and accompanying cargo according to U.S. Customs regulations.
- Configuring cargo and passenger loads according to transportation component command standards.
- Verifying the final manifest and other required documentation.

B-85. The redeployment itinerary is reported through JPEC representatives to USTRANSCOM and the supported commander, who develops and maintains the redeployment TPFDD. USTRANSCOM coordinates both intra-CONUS and intertheater movement.

Phase IV: Strategic Lift

B-86. This phase begins with wheels up for aircraft or passage of the last buoy marking the harbor channel for vessels departing the seaport of debarkation (SPOD). At this point, command of redeploying forces is transferred from the supported geographic combatant commander to the supporting geographic combatant commander, while control is temporarily exercised by USTRANSCOM. Accurate and precise movement schedules and the thorough manifesting of personnel and cargo characterize efficient strategic lift. Phase IV ends with arrival at the POD.

Phase V: Reception at Port of Debarkation

B-87. This phase begins with the arrival of forces, their equipment, and their sustainment supplies at the POD. The phase ends with the departure from the POD after receiving U.S. Customs and Department of Agriculture clearances.

B-88. The commander receiving the forces, equipment, and sustainment supplies develops a reception and onward movement plan for all arriving forces. This plan includes provisions for the necessary port support structure to manage the effort.

B-89. When possible, commanders must provide advance parties to reception facilities to coordinate the orderly reception and processing of redeploying forces. These advance parties will assist in coordinating the onward movement of deploying forces to their follow-on destinations. The advance parties work with MTMC representatives, supporting installation transportation officers (ITOs) or TAMCAs in completing the required documents for moving the forces, equipment, and sustainment to DMSs or CDCs and HSs. The preferred methods for onward movement from the POD mirror those specified for movement from the POE to unit assembly areas or base locations, as prescribed for deployment.

Phase VI: Onward Movement From Port of Debarkation

B-90. This phase begins with the reconfiguration of forces, equipment, and sustainment supplies at a designated marshaling area outside the processing area, and concludes upon arrival at HS or other designated locations. In the marshaling area, unit representatives will conduct a visual inspection of equipment to be moved via convoy or by rail. Equipment requiring further preparation or maintenance prior to movement will be identified and diverted until necessary actions are completed.

B-91. The supporting installation commander is responsible for the health, welfare, and support of arriving forces and for assisting with their onward movement. In this capacity, the supporting installation commander sustains the forces and individuals until they arrive at their prescribed destination, to include assisting them in obtaining intratheater airlift, commercial and military highway, military convoy, rail, or other modes for moving forces and individual manpower to their destinations.

B-92. Follow-on locations for individuals returning separately from units must be clearly designated. These locations may include DMSs, CDCs, follow-on assignment installations, or separation and transition points. Supporting commanders must be prepared to support individual Soldiers carrying sensitive items (weapons, classified material, and so on).

B-93. Follow-on locations for civilians are normally the locations from which deployment originated. These individuals redeploy using the same support structure used by Soldiers redeploying as individuals.

B-94. Follow-on locations for materiel being returned to CONUS or being redistributed elsewhere are determined by the automated redistribution process or through deliberate management decisions. AMC, HQDA (DCSLOG), and Defense Logistics Agency (DLA) render these decisions.

OTHER REDEPLOYMENT CONSIDERATIONS

B-95. The following constitute other areas for consideration during redeployment planning and execution.

Identification of Support Activities

B-96. To conduct effective and efficient redeployment operations, PSYOP planners must identify and allocate specific units, individuals, and equipment and supplies. Early in the process, PSYOP planners must identify a structure to support the redeployment operation. From reception at the arriving port or airfield, to the return to HS or other designated location, medical care, life support, and other services, supplies, and materiel must be provided.

B-97. As units prepare for and execute redeployment, commanders should plan and prepare for reuniting Soldiers with their families and loved ones. This planning should focus on preparing both the Soldiers and their families for the Soldier's reintroduction into the peacetime military environment and into family relationships. Unit chaplains and installation human services agencies may assist in these efforts.

B-98. Units will generally redeploy in increments—advance party, main body, and rear detachment or trail force. The number of increments and the composition of each are determined by the size of the unit, the requirement to support sustainment operations during redeployment, the requirement for equipment movement support activities, and the availability of redeployment transportation assets.

Cargo Accountability and Documentation

B-99. Commanders must ensure that equipment and materiel accountability and documentation accuracy continues throughout redeployment. The rush to return to HS may bring about severe problems without continued command emphasis in these critical areas.

B-100. As noted earlier, maintaining integrity of unit personnel and equipment during redeployment is critical to unit readiness. Every effort should be made to avoid separating personnel and equipment during any phase of redeployment. In those instances where such a separation is necessary, the unit must be reconstituted at the next possible opportunity. Special attention must be directed to cargo (containerized and non-containerized) not redeploying with the unit to ensure that this equipment rejoins the organization as early as is practicable.

Redistribution of Supplies and Materiel

B-101. Redistribution is a key factor in reconstituting supplies and materiel for future operations. Significant national resources are invested in supplies and materiel to support military operations. Therefore, recovery and redistribution of excess materiel are critical efforts.

B-102. Excess nonorganic equipment and supplies are redistributed according to plans developed by HQDA, with input from combatant commanders. Priority of effort is generally to Army forces committed to

JCS-approved OPLANs. Other recipients may include host countries, AMC, DLA, and General Services Administration (GSA) distribution centers.

B-103. Excess equipment may be redistributed in a serviceable or unserviceable condition. In the latter case, the receiving command is normally responsible for returning the equipment to a serviceable condition.

DEMOBILIZATION

B-104. Demobilization considerations include several factors. The following section discusses these factors.

DEMOBILIZATION PHASES

B-105. Demobilization is conducted in five phases. Each of these phases is discussed in the following paragraphs.

Phase I: Demobilization Planning

B-106. Demobilization planning is initiated concurrently with mobilization planning, continues throughout deployment, employment, and redeployment, and ends with the decision to release units and individuals from active duty. Demobilization planning consists of an almost continuous analysis of the workload required to efficiently complete the demobilization process.

B-107. Demobilization planning focuses on precise management of critical resources. These critical resources include medical support, supplies and equipment, maintenance support, transportation support, support personnel, and time. Plans must address comprehensive property accountability measures, equipment maintenance, materiel cross-leveling and requisition, personnel actions, awards, decorations, evaluation report processing, and family support activities.

Phase II: Area of Operations Demobilization Actions

B-108. This phase begins with the initiation of reconstitution actions in the theater of deployment and ends when the units or individual Soldiers report to the POE for onward movement.

B-109. Actions during this phase include initiation of service awards and other decorations, completion of reports, inquiries and investigations assigned by the deployment chain of command, diversion and cancellation of requisitions for items no longer required, and thorough and comprehensive property inventories at all levels of supervision. Reports of survey for equipment considered combat loss or otherwise not accounted for should be initiated during this phase.

B-110. Medical and dental actions required before demobilization should be initiated in the theater of deployment, contingent upon the availability of resources and treatment facilities.

Phase III: Port of Embarkation to Demobilization Station or CONUS Demobilization Center Actions

B-111. This phase overlaps with redeployment phases to move Soldiers to the DMS or CDC. An example of a demobilization process that may occur during this phase is a welcome ceremony for returning Soldiers at the CONUS POD before arrival at the DMS or CDC.

Phase IV: Demobilization Station or CONUS Demobilization Center Actions

B-112. This phase begins with the arrival at the DMS or CDC and ends when the unit or individuals depart for HS or home-of-record. Coordination should be made with the installation for housing, feeding, and transportation for the demobilizing units and individuals.

B-113. Coordination with the supporting installation must be initiated to ensure that all medical and dental actions, finance record entries, legal and entitlements briefings, personnel records updates, and property records are current before units or Soldiers are released from active duty. Required medical examinations, ongoing line-of-duty determinations, and finance actions to compute final pay and entitlements must be completed before issuance of DD Forms 214 and before Soldiers are released from active duty.

B-114. Installations should be prepared for expanded family support requirements and media coverage during this stage. Welcome home ceremonies are vital components of the demobilization process and should be supported to the maximum extent possible. Families of demobilizing Soldiers should be invited to attend and participate where possible. Welcome home ceremonies should be brief but meaningful. Logistics actions to be completed during this phase include—

- Updating prescribed load list (PLL) and authorized stockage list (ASL) accounts.
- Shipping equipment to HSs, equipment concentration sites, and mobilization and training equipment sites.
- Preparing movement orders for unit members to return to HS and for individuals to return to their homes of record.

Phase V: Home Station and Home-of-Record Actions

B-115. This phase begins with departure from the DMS or CDC and ends with release of units at their HSs and individuals at their homes of record.

B-116. Upon demobilization, the unit reverts to RC status based on a date and time determined by the USASOC commander. Unit members are not always released at the same time. Transition leave, medical hold, rear detachment requirements, and stay-behind personnel may require different release dates. The specific release date for unit members will be noted on the orders issued by USASOC HQ.

B-117. During an extended conflict, RC units may lose their pure RC composition through extended cross-attachment, redistribution, and replacement actions. Units mobilized as pure United States Army Reserve (USAR) may contain both USAR and Army National Guard (ARNG), and even regular Army (RA) personnel when demobilized. Equipment on hand at demobilization may not be clearly identifiable as to source component. Planning, preparation, flexibility, patience, and perseverance are required to resolve these issues as they arise.

B-118. Once demobilization is initiated, HQDA identifies the DMS for all units (personnel and equipment). Active duty personnel are reassigned according to the HQDA reconstruction plan. Strategic reconstruction of the total force is initiated at HQDA as part of the demobilization planning process.

DEMOBILIZATION PROCESS

B-119. Demobilization is the process by which units, individuals, and materiel are transferred from active to reserve status. Although the focus is generally on units and individuals, significant resources, such as supplies, materiel, and support activities, are dedicated to the demobilization process.

B-120. Completion of equipment recovery operations and actions to reconstitute units to premobilization levels of readiness require additional resources, to include manpower support, funding, and time. Therefore, the demobilization process does not lend itself to a rigid approach and must be modified based on the situation governing the successful execution of the OPLAN.

B-121. Generally, four options are available for commanders to demobilize units and redeploy their equipment:

- Units and personnel return to their HSs with their equipment via strategic sealift.
- Units and personnel return with their equipment via strategic airlift.
- Units and personnel return by strategic lift and equipment follows at a later date. Unit equipment scheduled to return to CONUS, but which does not accompany personnel, remains in an Active Army equipment status until returned to the unit at its HS.
- Personnel and units return by strategic lift and all or a portion of the unit equipment remains in the AOR for lateral transfer to either the supported commander or the gaining unit.

Demobilization of Units

B-122. As a rule, RC PSYOP units process through the same MS used during mobilization. For deployed units, the supported commander releases the units. Unit personnel redeploy to an aerial port of debarkation (APOD) and are returned to their original MS for demobilization processing. Personnel who were reassigned to serve in other locations are returned to their original units of assignment before demobilization.

B-123. Reassignment of civilians frequently occurs simultaneously with the demobilization of reservists. HQDA issues specific guidance regarding returning civilians to previous duty stations and release of contractor personnel.

B-124. Demobilization logistics applies an almost exclusive focus on restoring equipment, materiel, and supplies to a prescribed level of readiness and placing them at locations that best support future plans or contingencies. Upon completion of demobilization, the desired logistics end state is complete restoration of equipment to support the execution of future operations.

Demobilization Soldier Support

B-125. Personnel actions required to demobilize RC personnel support the transition of the Soldier back to civilian life. The most critical actions center on medical and finance processing and issuance of separation documents (DD Form 214, *Certificate of Release for Discharge From Active Duty*). These actions represent a legal relationship between the Army, the Soldier, and the Soldier's civilian employer and must be completed to the highest standards.

B-126. Other personnel actions (awards submission, OER and NCOER processing, and records update) are completed before demobilization. The DMS must conduct a review of all such actions that may have been completed before arrival at the DMS to ensure that all necessary actions are completed before Soldiers are released from active duty.

B-127. Finance support during demobilization is equal in importance to that rendered during mobilization and ensures a smooth Soldier transition back to RC pay status. Finance personnel out-process demobilizing Soldiers by computing and paying all final entitlements and travel claims. In addition, finance personnel convert Soldiers from Active Army to RC status and separate those individuals reverting back to full-time civilian status using DA Form 3685, *Joint Uniform Military Pay System/Joint Service Software (JUMPS/JSS) Pay Elections*. Demobilizing unit commanders must review any pending pay actions for all assigned Soldiers, ensure that each Soldier is aware of his entitlements, and cause all Class A agents to reconcile and close their accounts.

Appendix C

PSYOP Mapping Symbols

Symbol Title	Description	Symbol
Psychological Operations (PSYOP)	The location of PSYOP.	
PSYOP Written	The location for hand dissemination of PSYOP leaflets, handbills, flyers, and posters.	
PSYOP Leaflets, Helicopter (Rotary-Wing)	The location for the helicopter dissemination center of impact area of PSYOP leaflets.	
PSYOP Leaflets, Aerial (Fixed-Wing)	The area for the airborne dissemination center of impact area of PSYOP leaflets. Military or commercial fixed-wing aircraft may make delivery.	
PSYOP Target Audience Location	The location of a PSYOP target audience.	
PSYOP Loudspeaker Broadcast, Wheeled-Vehicle Mounted	The location of a ground-based mounted PSYOP loudspeaker broadcast event or loudspeaker team.	
PSYOP Loudspeaker Broadcast, Helicopter (Rotary-Wing) Mounted	The location of a helicopter- (rotary-wing) mounted loudspeaker, PSYOP broadcast mission or event, or a helicopter loudspeaker system or unit.	
PSYOP Broadcast, Aerial (Fixed-Wing) Station	The location of an aerial broadcast transmitted over radio or television frequencies, or a location of an aerial broadcast PSYOP system or unit.	
PSYOP Radio Broadcast	The location of a civilian- or military-operated radio broadcast tower or station used to broadcast PSYOP messages.	
PSYOP Television Broadcast	The location of a civilian- or military-operated TV broadcast tower or station used to broadcast PSYOP messages.	

Symbol Title	Description	Symbol
PSYOP Face-to-Face	The location of direct face-to-face of tactical PSYOP, used in establishing legitimacy and credibility of messages with foreign populations.	
PSYOP Printing Service	The location of a civilian- or military-operated print facility used to print PSYOP messages.	
PSYOP Distribution Center	The location of a civilian- or military-operated distribution facility or area used as a holding or distribution point for PSYOP messages.	

Advertising and Social Marketing

This appendix examines the social marketing model of persuasive communication, which is useful for the development of PSYOP products and as an instructional instrument to enhance PSYOP effectiveness. Understanding TAs—to focus on their needs and perceptions while developing appropriate messages—is essential to the success of the social marketing model. Well-designed PSYOP plans using this model, supported by the local population for long sustainment, can have both a significant and an enduring impact on TA behavior. This appendix also emphasizes the importance of synchronizing PSYOP plans with the supported commander's objectives, developing a technique of persuasion that causes a TA to behave in ways that support the commander's objective, and choosing the type of information that is needed to influence a TA's behavior.

INTRODUCTION

D-1. The intent of PSYOP is to influence TA behaviors that support U.S. national policy objectives and the combatant commander's intentions at the strategic, operational, and tactical levels of warfare. Therefore, PSYOP forces must plan, develop, and conduct operations in support of national objectives, combatant commanders, U.S. Country Teams, OGAs, and multinational forces across the range of military operations from peace through conflict to war. PSYOP planning begins with an analysis of the supported unit's missions. From this analysis, the planner derives the PSYOP mission. Once the mission is derived, the PO determines the TAs that can help accomplish the supported mission. The mission objectives will assist in selecting the appropriate audience, and analysis will help to decide how to influence the audience. Strategies developed for well-defined audiences have the greatest chance for success.

D-2. After all specified and implied POs are gleaned from the supported commander's objectives and mission statement, PSYOP planners will examine each objective to ensure TA effectiveness, vulnerability, susceptibility, and accessibility.

D-3. Once the POs and SPOs are determined, it is essential that PSYOP forces identify the PSYACTs and the PSYOP enabling actions and products required for accomplishing the mission. PSYACTs amplify the objectives of the PSYOP force and have immense psychological impact.

FOCUS

D-4. An important first point to understand is the need to focus on the TA rather than to focus on the PSYOP product. Certain advertising methods use a product orientation approach in which the TA is convinced that a product is so wonderful that the TA would desire it. The product, instead of the TA, becomes the focus of attention. Many times emotions or desirable lifestyles are promoted as a feature of the product instead of considering the culture, beliefs, and attitudes of the TA.

D-5. In contrast, social marketing starts with TAs and their needs, wants, and perceptions. This is recognition that influencing behavior change cannot effectively happen by promoting the benefits of some new COAs, but by appealing to the values, attitudes, and beliefs of the TA. Strategy is based on research. Research suggests the best way to reach the audience, what type of message is most effective in changing behavior, and the type of media that is most effective. The behavior to be promoted, the ways in which the message will be delivered, the TA's perception of the message, and the difficulty to change behavior all need close attention.

TARGET AUDIENCE ANALYSIS

D-6. TAA is done to identify the TA to achieve the desired PSYOP objectives and what means must be used to influence them. PSYOP forces depend upon the intelligence network of the supported commander, which includes military and civilian organizations, to collect this intelligence and maintain the necessary databases. PSYOP planners should also start the process to obtain polling data and surveys from government holders and contracted agencies in the area. Additionally, tactical PSYOP units will collect information as they interact with the local community.

D-7. Upon receipt of the mission, the PSYOP planner collects information that may impact the PSYOP mission. PSYOP planners will derive the majority of their analysis by applying the political-military factors. There are fourteen political-military factors that PSYOP planners use to gather information that will ultimately determine the effectiveness, vulnerabilities, susceptibilities, and the accessibility of the TAs. The process will highlight the key communicators that make decisions, the people that may influence the decision makers, and the people that carry out the policies of the leadership. During this process, the planner would also complete an analysis of additional TA activities, such as media analysis data, the telecommunications infrastructure, and an electromagnetic spectrum analysis. Attention also needs to be given to both competitive messages and messages from other agencies that reinforce the chosen themes.

D-8. TAA is a key part of the PSYOP development process, which is part of the IPB. The IPB is the second step of seventeen steps found in the mission analysis phase of the MDMP. The political-military factors are regional perspectives, ideology, natural environment, political system, history, religion, national interests, political economy, role of media, ethnicity, role of the military, foreign influence, leadership, and cultural environment.

D-9. The planner not only researches the existing traits of the TA, but he also examines the trends of the factors, the reasons the TA behaves a certain way, and important influences on their behavior. To produce an effective product, the planner—

- Needs to recognize what the TA values are.

- Ensures that the costs of new behavior are not greater than the old way of acting.

- Ensures the TA understands the value of the new behavior.

- Effectively communicates to the audience the benefits of the new behavior.

- Ensures that the new behavior is possible for the audience at the appropriate time and place.

D-10. Additionally, the planner must engage in designing, pretesting, and evaluating the messages introduced to change behavior. Success will require grouping the audiences for similar characteristics and behavior traits. The planner needs to recognize and adjust products, if necessary, to ensure the new directed behavior is easier, more desirable, and less costly for the audience.

RESEARCH METHODS AND PROCEDURES

D-11. With the focus on the TA, several research methods and procedures may be used to collect pertinent facts and data on the TA. As mentioned earlier, grouping the audience is important since the more specific they are, the greater the potential impact for the product. This information may also prove useful as it helps to develop relevant messages and to identify the media channels most likely to reach audience members. Although groups are the preferred PSYOP TAs, individuals may also be selected for targeting new behavior.

D-12. PSYOP doctrine indicates that TAA is vital to understand what the TA perceives as barriers to change, the role of significant social pressure groups, and the cost to change behavior.

D-13. Culture needs special attention—culture is the set of shared meanings by which people understand their world and make sense of their own behavior and that of others. An important part of developing viable messages is an understanding of the culture of the TA that is being reached. Culture affects how people respond to messages communicated through various channels, such as mass media, community events, and face-to-face encounters. Incorporating cultural sensitivity and effectiveness, and using images, symbols, and language, will create an information flow that is viewed and accepted as part of the culture. The line of persuasion needs to appeal to what is important to the TA and clearly indicate the benefits of the new behavior.

D-14. Culture incorporates the shared values, traditions, norms, customs, arts, history, and institutions of a people. Culture shapes how people see their world and structure their community and family life. Culture also defines what people value and what they determine to be significant in their lives. Examining the TA and its culture present several questions to the PSYOP planner:

- Does the planner have a feel of the message from his point of view that overshadows the audience's perspective?

- Does the planner understand whose wants and needs are being met by the proposed new behavior?

- Does the planner understand the audience's cost to begin the new behavior and what type of media is best suited to reach them?

D-15. A process develops for an effective social marketing strategy. After research is completed to provide insights of the targeted audience, a core marketing strategy is developed based on that analysis, reviewing the goals and objectives. This strategy includes the selection of messages, materials, vulnerabilities, susceptibilities, and accessibility of the TA. Pretesting is done on selected members of the TA and message changes are adjusted as needed. These concepts are incorporated into the PSYOP functions of developing, producing, distributing, and disseminating products, which will establish the marketing structures and systems for an effective program. PSYOP personnel implement the messages, followed by monitoring the impact indicators to determine whether the program is having the intended effects. To improve the credibility of the message, to reinforce the effects of adopting the behavior, and to establish a long-term relationship for success, PSYOP personnel need to implement the plan while working closely with community leaders. PSYOP personnel review and revise the plan as necessary so that an honest, detailed assessment report of behavior intervention and outcome can be completed.

D-16. In review, the social marketing concept is a systematic approach that can be used by many organizations for behavior change, to include PSYOP. This concept can be illustrated by examining how the Office for Substance Abuse Prevention used this process as part of its technical assistance training to agencies working in the alcohol and other drug use prevention field. The substance abuse prevention program places an emphasis on knowing the TA's needs and perceptions, so messages can be targeted specifically to the intended audience for greater impact and success. The program consists of four concepts within a five-stage program, as explained in the following paragraphs.

FOUR CONCEPTS

D-17. The first concept requires making a decision on which behavior is desired for the specified TA, to include an understanding of the TA's attitudes and beliefs. The next concept is understanding what sacrifices the TA has to make to adapt the new behavior. The third concept is determining the themes and symbols for persuading the TA to change the behavior. The last concept is a media analysis to decide how the message should be disseminated.

D-18. The substance abuse prevention program wants teenagers to refuse to drink with peers (first concept). Research, conducted face to face by listening to the people doing the drinking, determined current knowledge and beliefs.

The sacrifice for this action could be the risk of peer rejection (second concept). The theme could stress that not drinking is the smart behavior (third concept). The last concept could be a mass media operation.

FIVE-STAGE PROGRAM

D-19. The first stage of the social marketing process is critical for a successful program. Establishing the objective, selecting the related TA desired behavior, and analyzing research information about the audience are part of this stage. This is also the appropriate time for propaganda analysis. The objectives and the related TA will determine the impact indicators that are chosen to define success. The planner should understand what the TA must give up to receive the benefits of the program. In addition, research should show the means for persuading the TA that the new behavior is worth adapting.

D-20. The more that is known about the TA, the greater is the potential for success. In this example, the agency would review all in-house information and then contact outside sources of information. A description of the problem would reveal current effects on individuals and community; causes and preventive measures; and solutions, treatments, and remedies. TAs are often segmented for similar attitudes and behaviors to aid in the development of messages.

D-21. There are standard sources of information about TAs; however, the issue, the type of TA, the objective, and the local community may vary the other methods of obtaining TA information. Polling companies, which can obtain audience beliefs and attitudes, may be readily available in one area, but special arrangements might be needed to contract their services in other areas. In this example, health organizations, community service agencies, and the library could be data sources. Interviews, in this case, can indicate what drinking means to young people.

D-22. As the initial assessment of the TA is completed, the second stage begins—planning for mission review and objectives, while strategy specifies methods to influence TA behavior. The goals and objectives of the drug use prevention program will indicate the TA. The TA should be vulnerable, susceptible, and accessible for the program to be effective.

D-23. Developing messages and materials comprise the third stage. Deciding on key communicators and the type of media, themes, and symbols is part of this stage. An important point is that the message must not conflict with the information provided by similar sources or with previous messages. One product is often built on the themes and symbols of previous messages. Pretesting to determine audience reaction is a critical part of this stage.

D-24. Implementing the program, the fourth stage, puts the plan into action and begins the process of observing the TA behavior using the predetermined impact indicators as an ongoing process. Media analysis is also completed to learn strengths and weaknesses of methods used. Tracking of the messages and the corresponding media is also a crucial part of determining success.

D-25. Assessing effectiveness and obtaining feedback will be a continuous part of the final stage. The final stage is an examination of behavior, as well as how the program changed beliefs and attitudes. This stage is a continuation of the program evaluation that was decided upon during the first stage. The drug use prevention program would gather information about the TA's awareness of the information, attitude change, and intentions, as well as changes in long-term alcohol consumption. Feedback will determine the accuracy of the TA information that could be used in future programs.

FIVE-STEP CIRCULAR PROCESS

D-26. The social marketing concept can also be portrayed as a five-step circular process in which the last stage of monitoring and evaluating behavior outcomes leads into the first stage of research, analysis, and listening to the TA.

D-27. A key issue in step one is to listen, through research, to the TA's needs, wants, and perceptions. Decisions on planning and strategy (based on mission) result from a consideration of the TA, not on the product or the PSYOP vision. For the most effective message decision and behavior change, the TA is segmented into groups.

D-28. Marketers stress the behavior the audience is to adopt, the audience's perception of what must be given up to benefit, how the message is disseminated, and the theme used to persuade the TA. PSYOP practitioners can clearly benefit from a greater understanding of these concepts. PSYOP doctrine explains the functions of development, production, distribution, and dissemination to indicate task force capabilities. The next step, planning programs, includes a review of goals, themes, and strategies to influence, and variables, such as values, attitudes, and culture. Other considerations are partnerships with key leaders, media choices, and message design. PSYOP planners use the political-military factors when they begin analyzing the vulnerabilities, susceptibilities, and accessibilities of TAs. These factors are part of phase one of the eight-phase MDMP used as a tool that assists the PSYOP commander and staff in developing a plan.

D-29. Examining staff, the organization, systems, and related programs that can deliver effective programs are part of the structuring step. At this stage, establishment of partnerships for reinforcement and maintenance of new behavior has begun. The PDC, which develops programs of products or actions, has several sections that work in a mutually supportive coordination. The PDC normally has personnel from several elements within the PSYOP unit, as well as indigenous personnel, when operating in a foreign environment.

D-30. Pretesting is the next step to gauge potential effectiveness of new messages, emphasizing that the audience is the expert on what works best for them. Pretesting allows the planner to look at the planned operation through the TA's eyes instead of the organization's perception. The message format, as well as the message itself, needs careful examination to choose among alternative executions of various strategy elements and potential problems with chosen executions.

D-31. During the implementation step, the behavior design is carried out. At this time, the TA will move toward the desired behavior in stages, choosing alternatives based on perceived consequences. The planner's challenge is to move the TA to the next stage of the process, as the influences are different in each stage. Careful choice of media, message designs, key communicators, and themes overcome barriers to action, such as lack of exposure or attention. The audience becomes aware of the new behavior as an acceptable part of their culture. They will consider benefits and costs of the proposed behavior, of the peer group pressure, and whether they have the power to make the behavior happen. To sustain the desired behavior, the individuals need to be rewarded for what they have done and resolve any conflicts.

D-32. Monitoring, part of the last step, is a vital part of a behavioral change program management. The TA is again examined for behavior outcomes to evaluate program effectiveness and indications of needed corrections. To remain effective, commanders must adjust PSYOP continually as the battle damage assessment of programs is made. Assessments are done to understand the benefits to a new behavior so a change does not become more costly. Monitoring tells planners what is going right so it can be reinforced, and what is going wrong so changes can be made. PSYOP planners look for competing messages as every attempt to change behavior faces competition. The competition can be other messages or just the desire not to change current behavior. PSYOP planners must consider that the competition is everywhere and never ending. Planners must also understand what is appealing and unappealing about their competitor's proposed alternative behavior. This competitiveness also applies to propaganda analysis and counterpropaganda. Propaganda analysis is an ongoing mission because there will not be an absence of propaganda.

D-33. Social marketing research programs require contact between representatives of the social marketing program and TAs. PSYOP personnel generate tactical intelligence. The HUMINT at this level is intensive because of the interface with the local population. Each of these encounters is an opportunity for a PSYOP Soldier to have an important positive effect on the TA, or he can quickly destroy the program. The easiest way to destroy a marketing program is if the TA believes that the Soldier does not understand the TA's needs and wants. Soldiers' attitudes and behaviors may negatively change the behaviors of the audience they want to assist and influence.

D-34. PSYOP personnel need to be trained to assess TA behavior in relation to the proposed behavior. They need to understand the TA's needs and wants, and understand how to use the information as the basis of a persuasive strategy to move the audience closer to the desired behavior. PSYOP personnel are given the special challenge to have the TA understand that the Soldier has the audience's interest first, while operating in an environment prone to culture clashes. Additionally, PSYOP personnel must give attention to an audience's perceived costs, social influences, and behavioral control. Training Soldiers in the social marketing approach can be a major step in accomplishing this necessary mindset and orientation.

Appendix E

Trip Report Format

Unit Attention Line   Date_____

MEMORANDUM THRU Commander, Product Development Company, XXX Psychological Operations Battalion (Airborne), Fort Bragg, NC 28310 *[if applicable]*

Commander, XXX Psychological Operations Battalion (Airborne),
ATTN: S-3, Fort Bragg, NC 28310

Commander, Xth Psychological Operations Group (Airborne), ATTN: S-3, Fort Bragg, NC 28310

FOR Commander, United States Army Civil Affairs and Psychological Operations Command (Airborne), ATTN: AOCP-OP-SM, Fort Bragg, NC 28310

SUBJECT: Trip Report, _____

1. REFERENCES: *(Examples are JCET joint mission commander's responsibilities, other related message traffic, initiating directives, and so on.)*

2. MISSION: *(PSYOP-specific mission.)*

3. TASK ORGANIZATION: *(Show where/how PSYOP fits into the exercise organization.)*

4. CONCEPT OF OPERATION:
   a. Overview. *(In one paragraph, provide a synopsis of the mission. Synopsis will cover all events from start to finish.)*
   b. Phases. *(Break down exercise into phases specific to PSYOP personnel.)*
   c. PSYOP Training. *(Briefly describe PSYOP-specific training that is planned.)*

5. SUMMARY OF ACTIVITIES:
   a. Conference Itinerary. *(In chronological order, list the major/significant events or activities that occurred during the conference.)*
   b. Highlights of Coordination Activities. *(This area will be specific. Write as if someone else will attend the next conference and participate in the exercise. Write as if you are taking over a new mission in mid-stream and this document is the only continuity/handoff you will receive. Subparagraphs can include, but are not limited to, military interdepartmental purchase request (MIPR)/budget requirements, communications, transportation, memorandums of agreement, programs of instruction [POIs], training locations/facilities, billeting, rations/meals, laundry, medical facilities, or future planning conferences.)*
   c. Points of Contact. *(List POCs with job title, phone, address, and E-mail.)*

6. ISSUES: *(Summary of issues. Be specific.)*
   a. Issue: #1.
      (1) Discussion.
      (2) Recommendation.

b. Issue: #2.

    (1) Discussion.

    (2) Recommendation.

7. EXERCISE MILESTONES: (*In chronological order, list all relevant dates, conferences, suspenses, and so on. Publish subsequent milestones as truth changes.*)

8. POINT OF CONTACT AND PHONE NUMBER:

Signature Block

Encl (*Can include, but is not limited to, memorandums of understanding [MOUs], MIPR requests, operating fund requests, calendars, and so on.*)

After Action Report Format

Unit Attention Line   Date_____

MEMORANDUM THRU Commander, Product Development Company, XXX Psychological Operations Battalion (Airborne), Fort Bragg, NC 28310 *[if applicable]*

Commander, XXX Psychological Operations Battalion (Airborne), ATTN: S-3, Fort Bragg, NC 28310

Commander, Xth Psychological Operations Group (Airborne), ATTN: S-3, Fort Bragg, NC 28310

FOR Commander, United States Army Civil Affairs and Psychological Operations Command (Airborne), ATTN: AOCP-OP-SM, Fort Bragg, NC 28310

SUBJECT: After Action Report, _____

1. SUMMARY: *(In summary form, provide an overview of the element/team participation in the operation/exercise. This paragraph is designed to provide the reader a general overview of the mission which includes Who, What, Where, and Why. Divide into subparagraphs if necessary. The How is contained in paragraph 2.)*

2. BACKGROUND:
   a. General. *(Provide the specific details of how the mission came to the unit.)*
      (1) Mission Tasking (MITASK). *(Submit as enclosure 1, as applicable, the tasking order or any other similar documentation.)*
      (2) Mission Concept (MICON). *(Submit as enclosure 2, as applicable, the MICON or CONOPS.)*
      (3) Mission Support Request (MSR). *(Submit as enclosure 3, as applicable, any support request, such as MIPRs, Class A funds, or taskings required from outside the battalion.)*
      (4) Operations Summary (OPSUM). *(Enclosure 4.)*
      (5) Other details/documents as required. *(Enclosures XX.)*

3. ISSUES/RECOMMENDATIONS: *(In this paragraph, discuss all issues and/or recommendations that will benefit other individuals, elements and/or teams deploying on future similar missions. Be specific. Provide viable recommendations to issues presented.)*
   a. Issue #1:
      (1) Discussion.
      (2) Recommendation.
   b. Issue #2:
      (1) Discussion.
      (2) Recommendation.

4. LESSONS LEARNED: (*Address each of the areas listed below as applicable. Information from this paragraph will be incorporated into the Joint Universal Lessons Learned System [JULLS] and the Army Automated Repository for Special Operations Lessons Learned [ARSOLL].*)

    a. Funding.

        (1) Observation.

        (2) Discussion.

        (3) Lesson Learned.

        (4) Recommended Action.

        (5) Comments.

    b. United States Army Reserve Unique Issues.

        (1) Observation.

        (2) Discussion.

        (3) Lesson Learned.

        (4) Recommended Action.

        (5) Comments.

    c. Doctrine.

        (1) Observation.

        (2) Discussion.

        (3) Lesson Learned.

        (4) Recommended Action.

        (5) Comments.

    d. Organization.

        (1) Observation.

        (2) Discussion.

        (3) Lesson Learned.

        (4) Recommended Action.

        (5) Comments.

    e. Training.

        (1) Observation.

        (2) Discussion.

        (3) Lesson Learned.

        (4) Recommended Action.

        (5) Comments.

    f. Leadership.

        (1) Observation.

        (2) Discussion.

        (3) Lesson Learned.

        (4) Recommended Action.

        (5) Comments.

g. Materiel.

    (1) Observation.

    (2) Discussion.

    (3) Lesson Learned.

    (4) Recommended Action.

    (5) Comments.

h. Soldier Support.

    (1) Observation.

    (2) Discussion.

    (3) Lesson Learned.

    (4) Recommended Action.

    (5) Comments.

5. POINT OF CONTACT AND PHONE NUMBER:

Signature Block

Encl *(As required)*

Appendix G

Product Numbering Country Codes

The DOS recognizes 192 sovereign nation states. In addition, the DOS recognizes several other political entities. These entities range from disputed territories to autonomous regions. Some of the other categories of special administrative areas are territories, special administrative zones, and commonwealths. All DOS-recognized sovereign states and other recognized areas have a two-letter country code. This is the standard that will be used for all PSYOP products in the numbering system. It is the first field in the product number.

DOS does not recognize all disputed territories or special administrative areas with a code. In addition, contingencies may arise that require identification of a smaller political entity than a recognized nation as the target area. If an area is not recognized in the following table (Table G-1, pages G-1 through G-11) and is not the subject of a named operation, the POTF commander in a joint or combined operation will provide guidance for a two-letter code. In a PSYOP support element, the commander will coordinate with the approving authority to establish a two-letter code.

Table G-1. Product Numbering Country Codes

STATE			
Short-Form Name	**Long-Form Name**	**FIPS Code (Note 2)**	**Capital**
* - Diplomatic relations with the United States; + - Member of United Nations.			
Afghanistan *+	Transitional Islamic State of Afghanistan	AF	Kabul
Albania *+	Republic of Albania	AL	Tirana
Algeria *+	People's Democratic Republic of Algeria	AG	Algiers
Andorra *+	Principality of Andorra	AN	Andorra la Vella
Angola *+	Republic of Angola	AO	Luanda
Antigua and Barbuda *+	(no long-form name)	AC	Saint John's
Argentina *+	Argentine Republic	AR	Buenos Aires
Armenia *+	Republic of Armenia	AM	Yerevan
Australia *+	Commonwealth of Australia	AS	Canberra
Austria *+	Republic of Austria	AU	Vienna
Azerbaijan *+	Republic of Azerbaijan	AJ	Baku

Table G-1. Product Numbering Country Codes (Continued)

Short-Form Name	Long-Form Name	FIPS Code (Note 2)	Capital
Bahamas, The *+	Commonwealth of The Bahamas	BF	Nassau
Bahrain *+	Kingdom of Bahrain	BA	Manama
Bangladesh *+	People's Republic of Bangladesh	BG	Dhaka
Barbados *+	(no long-form name)	BB	Bridgetown
Belarus *+	Republic of Belarus	BO	Minsk
Belgium *+	Kingdom of Belgium	BE	Brussels
Belize *+	(no long-form name)	BH	Belmopan
Benin *+	Republic of Benin	BN	Porto-Novo
Bhutan +	Kingdom of Bhutan	BT	Thimphu
Bolivia *+	Republic of Bolivia	BL	La Paz (administrative) Sucre (legislative/judiciary)
Bosnia and Herzegovina *+	(no long-form name)	BK	Sarajevo
Botswana *+	Republic of Botswana	BC	Gaborone
Brazil *+	Federative Republic of Brazil	BR	Brasília
Brunei *+	Negara Brunei Darussalam	BX	Bandar Seri Begawan
Bulgaria *+	Republic of Bulgaria	BU	Sofia
Burkina Faso *+	Burkina Faso	UV	Ouagadougou
Burma *+	Union of Burma	BM	Rangoon
Burundi *+	Republic of Burundi	BY	Bujumbura
Cambodia *+	Kingdom of Cambodia	CB	Phnom Penh
Cameroon *+	Republic of Cameroon	CM	Yaoundé
Canada *+	(no long-form name)	CA	Ottawa
Cape Verde *+	Republic of Cape Verde	CV	Praia
Central African Republic *+	Central African Republic	CT	Bangui
Chad *+	Republic of Chad	CD	N'Djamena
Chile *+	Republic of Chile	CI	Santiago
China *+ (Note 3)	People's Republic of China	CH	Beijing
Colombia *+	Republic of Colombia	CO	Bogotá
Comoros *+	Union of Comoros	CN	Moroni
Congo (Brazzaville) *+ (Note 4)	Republic of the Congo	CF	Brazzaville
Congo (Kinshasa) *+ (Note 4)	Democratic Republic of the Congo	CG	Kinshasa
Costa Rica *+	Republic of Costa Rica	CS	San José
Côte d'Ivoire *+	Republic of Côte d'Ivoire	IV	Yamoussoukro
Croatia *+	Republic of Croatia	HR	Zagreb

Table G-1. Product Numbering Country Codes (Continued)

Short-Form Name	Long-Form Name	FIPS Code (Note 2)	Capital
Cuba +	Republic of Cuba	CU	Havana
Cyprus *+	Republic of Cyprus	CY	Nicosia
Czech Republic *+	Czech Republic	EZ	Prague
Denmark *+	Kingdom of Denmark	DA	Copenhagen
Djibouti *+	Republic of Djibouti	DJ	Djibouti
Dominica *+	Commonwealth of Dominica	DO	Roseau
Dominican Republic *+	Dominican Republic	DR	Santo Domingo
East Timor *+	Democratic Republic of Timor-Leste	TT	Dili
Ecuador *+	Republic of Ecuador	EC	Quito
Egypt *+	Arab Republic of Egypt	EG	Cairo
El Salvador *+	Republic of El Salvador	ES	San Salvador
Equatorial Guinea *+	Republic of Equatorial Guinea	EK	Malabo
Eritrea *+	State of Eritrea	ER	Asmara
Estonia *+	Republic of Estonia	EN	Tallinn
Ethiopia *+	Federal Democratic Republic of Ethiopia	ET	Addis Ababa
Fiji *+	Republic of the Fiji Islands	FJ	Suva
Finland *+	Republic of Finland	FI	Helsinki
France *+	French Republic	FR	Paris
Gabon *+	Gabonese Republic	GB	Libreville
Gambia, The *+	Republic of The Gambia	GA	Banjul
Georgia *+	Republic of Georgia	GG	Tbilisi
Germany *+	Federal Republic of Germany	GM	Berlin
Ghana *+	Republic of Ghana	GH	Accra
Greece *+	Hellenic Republic	GR	Athens
Grenada *+	(no long-form name)	GJ	Saint George's
Guatemala *+	Republic of Guatemala	GT	Guatemala
Guinea *+	Republic of Guinea	GV	Conakry
Guinea-Bissau *+	Republic of Guinea-Bissau	PU	Bissau
Guyana *+	Cooperative Republic of Guyana	GY	Georgetown
Haiti *+	Republic of Haiti	HA	Port-au-Prince
Holy See *	Holy See	VT	Vatican City
Honduras *+	Republic of Honduras	HO	Tegucigalpa
Hungary *+	Republic of Hungary	HU	Budapest
Iceland *+	Republic of Iceland	IC	Reykjavík
India *+	Republic of India	IN	New Delhi
Indonesia *+	Republic of Indonesia	ID	Jakarta

Table G-1. Product Numbering Country Codes (Continued)

Short-Form Name	Long-Form Name	FIPS Code (Note 2)	Capital
Iran +	Islamic Republic of Iran	IR	Tehran
Iraq +	Republic of Iraq	IZ	Baghdad
Ireland *+	(no long-form name)	EI	Dublin
Israel *+	State of Israel	IS	Jerusalem (Note 5)
Italy *+	Italian Republic	IT	Rome
Jamaica *+	(no long-form name)	JM	Kingston
Japan *+	(no long-form name)	JA	Tokyo
Jordan *+	Hashemite Kingdom of Jordan	JO	Amman
Kazakhstan *+	Republic of Kazakhstan	KZ	Astana
Kenya *+	Republic of Kenya	KE	Nairobi
Kiribati *+	Republic of Kiribati	KR	Tarawa
Korea, North +	Democratic People's Republic of Korea	KN	Pyongyang
Korea, South *+	Republic of Korea	KS	Seoul
Kuwait *+	State of Kuwait	KU	Kuwait
Kyrgyzstan *+	Kyrgyz Republic	KG	Bishkek
Laos *+	Lao People's Democratic Republic	LA	Vientiane
Latvia *+	Republic of Latvia	LG	Riga
Lebanon *+	Lebanese Republic	LE	Beirut
Lesotho *+	Kingdom of Lesotho	LT	Maseru
Liberia *+	Republic of Liberia	LI	Monrovia
Libya *+	Great Socialist People's Libyan Arab Jamahiriya	LY	Tripoli
Liechtenstein *+	Principality of Liechtenstein	LS	Vaduz
Lithuania *+	Republic of Lithuania	LH	Vilnius
Luxembourg *+	Grand Duchy of Luxembourg	LU	Luxembourg
Macedonia, The Former Yugoslav Republic of *+	The Former Yugoslav Republic of Macedonia	MK	Skopje
Madagascar *+	Republic of Madagascar	MA	Antananarivo
Malawi *+	Republic of Malawi	MI	Lilongwe
Malaysia *+	(no long-form name)	MY	Kuala Lumpur
Maldives *+	Republic of Maldives	MV	Male
Mali *+	Republic of Mali	ML	Bamako
Malta *+	Republic of Malta	MT	Valletta
Marshall Islands *+	Republic of the Marshall Islands	RM	Majuro
Mauritania *+	Islamic Republic of Mauritania	MR	Nouakchott
Mauritius *+	Republic of Mauritius	MP	Port Louis

Table G-1. Product Numbering Country Codes (Continued)

Short-Form Name	Long-Form Name	FIPS Code (Note 2)	Capital
Mexico *+	United Mexican States	MX	Mexico
Micronesia, Federated States of *+	Federated States of Micronesia	FM	Palikir
Moldova *+	Republic of Moldova	MD	Chisinau
Monaco *+	Principality of Monaco	MN	Monaco
Mongolia *+	(no long-form name)	MG	Ulaanbaatar
Morocco *+	Kingdom of Morocco	MO	Rabat
Mozambique *+	Republic of Mozambique	MZ	Maputo
Namibia *+	Republic of Namibia	WA	Windhoek
Nauru *+	Republic of Nauru	NR	Yaren District (no capital city)
Nepal *+	Kingdom of Nepal	NP	Kathmandu
Netherlands *+	Kingdom of the Netherlands	NL	Amsterdam The Hague (seat of gov't)
New Zealand *+	(no long-form name)	NZ	Wellington
Nicaragua *+	Republic of Nicaragua	NU	Managua
Niger *+	Republic of Niger	NG	Niamey
Nigeria *+	Federal Republic of Nigeria	NI	Abuja
Norway *+	Kingdom of Norway	NO	Oslo
Oman *+	Sultanate of Oman	MU	Muscat
Pakistan *+	Islamic Republic of Pakistan	PK	Islamabad
Palau *+	Republic of Palau	PS	Koror
Panama *+	Republic of Panama	PM	Panama
Papua New Guinea *+	Independent State of Papua New Guinea	PP	Port Moresby
Paraguay *+	Republic of Paraguay	PA	Asunción
Peru *+	Republic of Peru	PE	Lima
Philippines *+	Republic of the Philippines	RP	Manila
Poland *+	Republic of Poland	PL	Warsaw
Portugal *+	Portuguese Republic	PO	Lisbon
Qatar *+	State of Qatar	QA	Doha
Romania *+	(no long-form name)	RO	Bucharest
Russia *+	Russian Federation	RS	Moscow
Rwanda *+	Rwandese Republic	RW	Kigali
Saint Kitts and Nevis *+	Federation of Saint Kitts and Nevis	SC	Basseterre
Saint Lucia *+	(no long-form name)	ST	Castries
Saint Vincent and the Grenadines *+	(no long-form name)	VC	Kingstown

Table G-1. Product Numbering Country Codes (Continued)

Short-Form Name	Long-Form Name	FIPS Code (Note 2)	Capital
Samoa *+	Independent State of Samoa	WS	Apia
San Marino *+	Republic of San Marino	SM	San Marino
Sao Tome and Principe *+	Democratic Republic of Sao Tome and Principe	TP	São Tomé
Saudi Arabia *+	Kingdom of Saudi Arabia	SA	Riyadh
Senegal *+	Republic of Senegal	SG	Dakar
Serbia and Montenegro*+	(no long-form name)	YI	Belgrade
Seychelles *+	Republic of Seychelles	SE	Victoria
Sierra Leone *+	Republic of Sierra Leone	SL	Freetown
Singapore *+	Republic of Singapore	SN	Singapore
Slovakia *+	Slovak Republic	LO	Bratislava
Slovenia *+	Republic of Slovenia	SI	Ljubljana
Solomon Islands *+	(no long-form name)	BP	Honiara
Somalia *+	(no long-form name)	SO	Mogadishu
South Africa *+	Republic of South Africa	SF	Pretoria (administrative) Cape Town (legislative) Bloemfontein (judiciary)
Spain *+	Kingdom of Spain	SP	Madrid
Sri Lanka *+	Democratic Socialist Republic of Sri Lanka	CE	Colombo Sri Jayewardenepura Kotte (legislative)
Sudan *+	Republic of the Sudan	SU	Khartoum
Suriname *+	Republic of Suriname	NS	Paramaribo
Swaziland *+	Kingdom of Swaziland	WZ	Mbabane (administrative) Lobamba (legislative)
Sweden *+	Kingdom of Sweden	SW	Stockholm
Switzerland *+	Swiss Confederation	SZ	Bern
Syria *+	Syrian Arab Republic	SY	Damascus
Tajikistan *+	Republic of Tajikistan	TI	Dushanbe
Tanzania *+	United Republic of Tanzania	TZ	Dar es Salaam Dodoma (legislative)
Thailand *+	Kingdom of Thailand	TH	Bangkok
Togo *+	Togolese Republic	TO	Lomé
Tonga *+	Kingdom of Tonga	TN	Nuku'alofa
Trinidad and Tobago *+	Republic of Trinidad and Tobago	TD	Port-of-Spain
Tunisia *+	Tunisian Republic	TS	Tunis
Turkey *+	Republic of Turkey	TU	Ankara
Turkmenistan *+	(no long-form name)	TX	Ashgabat
Tuvalu *+	(no long-form name)	TV	Funafuti

Table G-1. Product Numbering Country Codes (Continued)

Short-Form Name	Long-Form Name	FIPS Code (Note 2)	Capital
Uganda *+	Republic of Uganda	UG	Kampala
Ukraine *+	(no long-form name)	UP	Kiev
United Arab Emirates *+	United Arab Emirates	AE	Abu Dhabi
United Kingdom *+	United Kingdom of Great Britain and Northern Ireland	UK	London
United States +	United States of America	US	Washington, DC
Uruguay *+	Oriental Republic of Uruguay	UY	Montevideo
Uzbekistan *+	Republic of Uzbekistan	UZ	Tashkent
Vanuatu *+	Republic of Vanuatu	NH	Port-Vila
Venezuela *+	Bolivarian Republic of Venezuela	VE	Caracas
Vietnam *+	Socialist Republic of Vietnam	VM	Hanoi
Yemen *+	Republic of Yemen	YM	Sanaa
Zambia *+	Republic of Zambia	ZA	Lusaka
Zimbabwe *+	Republic of Zimbabwe	ZI	Harare
OTHER			
Taiwan *(Note 6)*	(no long-form name)	TW	T'ai-pei

NOTES

Note 1: In this listing, the term "independent state" refers to a people politically organized into a sovereign state with a definite territory recognized as independent by the United States.

Note 2: Federal Information Processing Standard (FIPS) 10-4 codes.

Note 3: With the establishment of diplomatic relations with China on January 1, 1979, the U.S. Government recognized the People's Republic of China as the sole legal government of China and acknowledged the Chinese position that there is only one China and that Taiwan is part of China.

Note 4: "Congo" is the official short-form name for both the Republic of the Congo and the Democratic Republic of the Congo. To distinguish one from the other, the U.S. DOS adds the capital in parentheses. This practice is unofficial and provisional.

Note 5: Israel proclaimed Jerusalem as its capital in 1950. The United States, like nearly all other countries, maintains its embassy in Tel Aviv.

Note 6: Claimed by both the Government of the People's Republic of China and the authorities on Taiwan. Administered by the authorities on Taiwan *(Note 3)*.

Source: Office of The Geographer and Global Issues, Bureau of Intelligence and Research, U.S. Department of State, Washington, D.C.

DEPENDENCIES AND AREAS OF SPECIAL SOVEREIGNTY

Short-Form Name	Long-Form Name	Sovereignty	FIPS Code (Note 1)	Capital
American Samoa	Territory of American Samoa	United States	AQ	Pago Pago
Anguilla	(no long-form name)	United Kingdom	AV	The Valley

Table G-1. Product Numbering Country Codes (Continued)

Short-Form Name	Long-Form Name	Sovereignty	FIPS Code (Note 1)	Capital
Antarctica	(no long-form name)	None (Note 2)	AY	None
Aruba	(no long-form name)	Netherlands	AA	Oranjestad
Ashmore and Cartier Islands	Territory of Ashmore and Cartier Islands	Australia	AT	Administered from Canberra
Baker Island	(no long-form name)	United States	FQ	Administered from Washington, D.C.
Bermuda	(no long-form name)	United Kingdom	BD	Hamilton
Bouvet Island	(no long-form name)	Norway	BV	Administered from Oslo
British Indian Ocean Territory (Note 3)	British Indian Ocean Territory	United Kingdom	IO	None
Cayman Islands	(no long-form name)	United Kingdom	CJ	George Town
Christmas Island	Territory of Christmas Island	Australia	KT	The Settlement (Flying Fish Cove)
Clipperton Island	(no long-form name)	France	IP	Administered from French Polynesia
Cocos (Keeling) Islands	Territory of Cocos (Keeling) Islands	Australia	CK	West Island
Cook Islands	(no long-form name)	New Zealand	CW	Avarua
Coral Sea Islands	Coral Sea Islands Territory	Australia	CR	Administered from Canberra
Falkland Islands (Islas Malvinas)	Colony of the Falkland Islands	United Kingdom (Note 4)	FK	Stanley
Faroe Islands	(no long-form name)	Denmark	FO	Tórshavn
French Guiana (Note 5)				
French Polynesia	Territory of French Polynesia	France	FP	Papeete
French Southern and Antarctic Lands (Note 6)	Territory of the French Southern and Antarctic Lands	France	FS	Administered from Paris
Gibraltar	(no long-form name)	United Kingdom	GI	Gibraltar
Greenland	(no long-form name)	Denmark	GL	Nuuk (Godthåb)
Guadeloupe (Note 5)				
Guam	Territory of Guam	United States	GQ	Hagatna
Guernsey (Note 7)	Bailiwick of Guernsey	British Crown Dependency	GK	Saint Peter Port
Heard Island and McDonald Islands	Territory of Heard Island and McDonald Islands	Australia	HM	Administered from Canberra
Hong Kong	Hong Kong Special Administrative Region	China (Note 8)	HK	None

Table G-1. Product Numbering Country Codes (Continued)

Short-Form Name	Long-Form Name	Sovereignty	FIPS Code (Note 1)	Capital
Howland Island	(no long-form name)	United States	HQ	Administered from Washington, D.C.
Jan Mayen	(no long-form name)	Norway	JN	Administered from Oslo (Note 9)
Jarvis Island	(no long-form name)	United States	DQ	Administered from Washington, D.C.
Jersey	Bailiwick of Jersey	British Crown Dependency	JE	Saint Helier
Johnston Atoll	(no long-form name)	United States	JQ	Administered from Washington, D.C.
Kingman Reef	(no long-form name)	United States	KQ	Administered from Washington, D.C.
Macau	Macau Special Administrative Region	China (Note 10)	MC	Macau
Man, Isle of	(no long-form name)	British Crown Dependency	IM	Douglas
Martinique (Note 5)				
Mayotte	Territorial Collectivity of Mayotte	France	MF	Mamoudzou
Midway Islands	(no long-form name)	United States	MQ	Administered from Washington, D.C.
Montserrat	(no long-form name)	United Kingdom	MH	Plymouth
Navassa Island	(no long-form name)	United States	BQ	Administered from Washington, D.C.
Netherlands Antilles (Note 11)	(no long-form name)	Netherlands	NT	Willemstad
New Caledonia	Territory of New Caledonia and Dependencies	France	NC	Nouméa
Niue	(no long-form name)	New Zealand	NE	Alofi
Norfolk Island	Territory of Norfolk Island	Australia	NF	Kingston
Northern Mariana Islands	Commonwealth of the Northern Mariana Islands	United States	CQ	Saipan
Palmyra Atoll	(no long-form name)	United States	LQ	Administered from Washington, D.C.
Paracel Islands	(no long-form name)	undetermined (Note 12)	PF	None
Pitcairn Islands	Pitcairn, Henderson, Ducie, and Oeno Islands	United Kingdom	PC	Adamstown
Puerto Rico	Commonwealth of Puerto Rico	United States	RQ	San Juan
Reunion (Note 5)				

Table G-1. Product Numbering Country Codes (Continued)

Short-Form Name	Long-Form Name	Sovereignty	FIPS Code (Note 1)	Capital
Saint Helena (Note 13)	(no long-form name)	United Kingdom	SH	Jamestown
Saint Pierre and Miquelon	Territorial Collectivity of Saint Pierre and Miquelon	France	SB	Saint-Pierre
South Georgia and the South Sandwich Islands	South Georgia and the South Sandwich Islands	United Kingdom (Note 4)	SX	None
Spratly Islands	(no long-form name)	undetermined (Note 14)	PG	None
Svalbard	(no long-form name)	Norway	SV	Longyearbyen
Tokelau	(no long-form name)	New Zealand	TL	None
Turks and Caicos Islands	(no long-form name)	United Kingdom	TK	Grand Turk
Virgin Islands, U.S.	United States Virgin Islands	United States	VQ	Charlotte Amalie
Virgin Islands, British	(no long-form name)	United Kingdom	VI	Road Town
Wake Island	(no long-form name)	United States	WQ	Administered from Washington, D.C.
Wallis and Futuna	Territory of the Wallis and Futuna Islands	France	WF	Matâ'utu
Western Sahara	(no long-form name)	undetermined	WI	None

NOTES

Note 1: Federal Information Processing Standard (FIPS) 10-4 codes.

Note 2: Antarctica consists of the territory south of 60 degrees south latitude. This area includes claims by Argentina, Australia, Chile, France, New Zealand, Norway, and the United Kingdom, the legal status of which remains in suspense under the terms of the Antarctic Treaty of 1959. The United States recognizes no claims to Antarctica.

Note 3: Chagos Archipelago (including Diego Garcia).

Note 4: Dependent territory of the United Kingdom (also claimed by Argentina).

Note 5: French Guiana, Guadeloupe, Martinique, and Reunion are departments (first-order administrative units) of France, and are therefore not dependencies or areas of special sovereignty. They are included in this list only for the convenience of the user. The Department of Guadeloupe includes the nearby islands of Marie-Galante, La Desirade, and Iles des Saintes, as well as Saint Barthelemy and the northern three-fifths of Saint Martin (the rest of which belongs to Netherlands Antilles). The islands of Bassas da India, Europa Island, Glorioso Islands, Juan de Nova Island, and Tromelin Island are administered from Reunion; all these islands are claimed by Madagascar, and Tromelin Island is claimed by Mauritius.

Note 6: "French Southern and Antarctic Lands" includes Île Amsterdam, Île Saint-Paul, Îles Crozet, and Îles Kerguelen in the southern Indian Ocean, along with the French-claimed sector of Antarctica, "Terre Adélie." The United States does not recognize the French claim to "Terre Adélie" (Note 2).

Note 7: The Bailiwick of Guernsey includes the islands of Alderney, Guernsey, Herm, Sark, and nearby smaller islands.

Note 8: Under a Sino-British declaration of September 1984, Hong Kong reverted to Chinese control on July 1, 1997. It is now a semi-autonomous entity that exists pursuant to international agreement and maintains its own government apart from the People's Republic of China.

Table G-1. Product Numbering Country Codes (Continued)

Note 9: Administered from Oslo, Norway, through a governor resident in Longyearbyen, Svalbard.

Note 10: Under the Sino-Portuguese Joint Declaration on the Question of Macau signed in 1987, Macau reverted to Chinese control on December 20, 1999. It is now a semi-autonomous entity that exists pursuant to international agreement and maintains its own government apart from the People's Republic of China.

Note 11: Netherlands Antilles comprises two groupings of islands: Curaçao and Bonaire are located off the coast of Venezuela; Saba, Sint Eustatius, and Sint Maarten (the Dutch two-fifths of the island of Saint Martin) lie 800 km to the north.

Note 12: South China Sea islands occupied by China but claimed by Vietnam.

Note 13: The territory of Saint Helena includes the Island group of Tristan da Cunha; Saint Helena also administers Ascension Island.

Note 14: South China Sea islands claimed in entirety by China and Vietnam and in part by the Philippines and Malaysia; each of these states occupies some part of the islands.

Source: Office of The Geographer and Global Issues, Bureau of Intelligence and Research, U.S. Department of State, Washington, D.C.

Appendix H

Use of Interpreters

During PSYOP, there are occasions when PSYOP Soldiers will lack the linguistic ability to communicate personally and effectively with the local populace in the AO. The use of interpreters is often the best or only option. The proper use and supervision of interpreters can play a decisive role in the mission.

INTERPRETER SELECTION

H-1. Whenever possible, the interpreters used should be U.S. military personnel or at least U.S. citizens. In some operational or training settings abroad, the PSYOP Soldiers will not be faced with the problem of selecting an interpreter—they will simply be assigned one by the chain of command or host government. In other cases, interpreters are chosen from a pool provided by the host government. Finally, in many operational situations, interpreters will be hired from the general HN population. Whatever the case, the following guidelines will be critical to the success of mission accomplishment. The PSYOP Soldier can use this opportunity to truly influence the outcome of the mission. Interpreters should be selected based on the following criteria:

- *Native speaker.* The interpreters should be native speakers of the socially or geographically determined dialect. Their speech, background, and mannerisms should be completely acceptable to the TA so that no attention is given to the way they talk, only to what they say.

- *Social status.* In some situations and cultures, interpreters may be limited in their effectiveness with a TA if their social standing is considerably lower than that of the audience. Examples include significant differences in military rank or membership in an ethnic or religious group. Regardless of the PSYOP Soldier's personal feelings on social status, he should remember the job is to accomplish the mission, not to act as an agent for social reform in a faraway land. The PSYOP Soldier must accept local prejudices as a fact of life.

- *English fluency.* An often-overlooked consideration is how well the interpreter speaks English. As a rule, if the interpreter understands the PSYOP Soldier and the PSYOP Soldier understands the interpreter, then the interpreter's command of English should be satisfactory. The PSYOP Soldier can check that "understanding" by asking the interpreter to paraphrase, in English, something the PSYOP Soldier said; the PSYOP Soldier then restates the interpreter's comments to ensure that both persons are in sync. In addition, interpreting goes both ways. The interpreter must be able to convey the information expressed by the interviewee or TA.

- *Intellectual intelligence.* The interpreter should be quick, alert, and responsive to changing conditions and situations. He must be able to grasp complex concepts and discuss them without confusion in a reasonably logical sequence. Although education does not equate to intelligence, generally speaking, the better educated the interpreter, the better he will perform due to increased exposure to diverse concepts.

- *Technical ability.* In certain situations, the PSYOP Soldier may need an interpreter with technical training or experience in special subject areas. This type of interpreter will be able to translate the "meaning" as well as the "words." For instance, if the subject is very technical or specialized, with terms such as nuclear physics, background knowledge will be useful.

- *Reliability.* The PSYOP Soldier should beware of the potential interpreter who arrives late for the interview. Throughout the world, the concept of time varies widely. In many less-developed countries, time is relatively unimportant. The PSYOP Soldier should make sure that the interpreter understands the military's preoccupation with punctuality.

- *Loyalty.* If the interpreter used is a local national, it is safe to assume that his first loyalty is to the HN or subgroup, not to the U.S. military. The security implications are clear. The PSYOP Soldier must be very cautious in how he explains concepts to give interpreters a greater depth of understanding. Additionally, some interpreters, for political or personal reasons, may have ulterior motives or a hidden agenda when they apply for the interpreting job. If the PSYOP Soldier detects or suspects such motives, he should tell his commander or security manager.

- *Gender, age, and race.* Gender, age, and race have the potential to seriously affect the mission. One example is the status of females in Muslim society. In predominantly Muslim countries, cultural prohibitions may render a female interpreter ineffective in certain circumstances. Another example would be the Balkans where the ethnic divisions may limit the effectiveness of an interpreter from outside the TA's group. Since traditions, values, and biases vary from country to country, it is important to check with the in-country assets or area studies for specific taboos or favorable characteristics.

- *Compatibility.* The PSYOP Soldier and the interpreter will work as a team. For the interpreter to be most effective, he should become a psychic extension of the PSYOP Soldier. The TA will be quick to recognize personality conflicts between the PSYOP Soldier and the interpreter, which can undermine the effectiveness of the communication effort. If possible, when selecting an interpreter, the PSYOP Soldier should look for compatible traits and strive for a harmonious working relationship.

H-2. If several qualified interpreters are available, the PSYOP Soldier should select at least two. This practice is of particular importance if the interpreter will be used during long conferences or courses of instruction. The exhausting nature of these type jobs makes approximately four hours of active interpreting about the maximum for peak efficiency. Whatever the mission, with two or more interpreters, one can provide quality control and assistance to the active interpreter. Additionally, this technique is useful when conducting coordination or negotiation meetings, as one interpreter is used in an active role and the other pays attention to the body language and side conversations of the others present. Many times, the PSYOP Soldier will gain important side information that assists in negotiations from listening to what others are saying amongst themselves outside of the main discussion.

TARGET ANALYSIS

H-3. Implied throughout the preceding points is the need for a careful analysis of the target population. This type of analysis goes beyond the scope of this lesson. Mature judgment, thoughtful consideration of the audience as individual human beings, and a genuine concern for their receiving accurate information will go a long way toward accomplishing the mission. The PSYOP Soldier must remember that the individual from a farm or small village is going to have markedly different expectations than the jet-setting polo player.

EVALUATION CRITERIA

H-4. As mentioned, it is safe to assume that if the interpreter is not U.S. military or at least a U.S. citizen, his first loyalty will be to his country or subgroup and not to the United States.

H-5. The security implications of using local nationals are clear. The PSYOP Soldier must be cautious about what information he gives his interpreter. The PSYOP Soldier must always keep possible security issues in mind.

H-6. Certain tactical situations may require the use of uncleared indigenous personnel as "field expedient" interpreters. Commanders should be aware of the increased security risk involved in using such personnel and carefully weigh the risk versus the potential gain. If uncleared interpreters are used, any sensitive information should be kept to a minimum.

H-7. The interpreters must be honest and free from unfavorable notoriety among the local inhabitants. Their reputation or standing in the community should be such that persons of higher rank and standing will not intimidate them.

RAPPORT ESTABLISHMENT

H-8. The interpreter is a vital link to the TA. Without a cooperative, supportive interpreter, the mission could be in serious jeopardy. Mutual respect and understanding is essential to effective teamwork. The PSYOP Soldier must establish rapport early in the relationship and maintain rapport throughout the joint effort. The difficulty of establishing rapport stems most of the time from the lack of personal contact.

H-9. The PSYOP Soldier begins the process of establishing rapport before he meets the interpreter for the first time. The Soldier should do his homework. Most foreigners are reasonably knowledgeable about the United States. The PSYOP Soldier should obtain some basic facts about the HN. Useful information may include population, geography, ethnic groups, political system, prominent political figures, monetary system, business, agriculture, and exports. A good general outline can be obtained from a recent almanac or encyclopedia. More detailed information is available in the area handbook for the country, and current newspapers and magazines, such as New York Times, Washington Post, Newsweek, and U.S. News and World Report.

H-10. The PSYOP Soldier should find out about the interpreter's background. The Soldier should show a genuine concern for the interpreter's family, aspirations, career, education, and so on. Many cultures place a greater emphasis on family over career than the United States, so the Soldier should start with understanding the interpreter's home life. The PSYOP Soldier should also research cultural traditions to find out more about the interpreter and the nation in which the Soldier will be working. Though the Soldier should gain as much information on culture as possible before entering an HN, his interpreter can be a valuable source to fill gaps. Showing interest is also a good way to build rapport.

H-11. The PSYOP Soldier should gain the interpreter's trust and confidence before embarking on sensitive issues, such as religion, likes, dislikes, and prejudices. The Soldier should approach these areas carefully and tactfully. Although deeply personal beliefs may be very revealing and useful in the professional relationship, the PSYOP Soldier must gently and tactfully draw these out of his interpreter.

ORIENTATION

H-12. Early in the relationship with interpreters, the PSYOP Soldiers should ensure that interpreters are briefed on their duties and responsibilities. The Soldiers should orient the interpreters as to the nature of their duties, standards of conduct expected, techniques of interview to be used, and any other requirements necessary. The orientation may include the following:

- Current tactical situation.
- Background information obtained on the source, interviewee, or TA.
- Specific objectives for the interview, meeting, or interrogation.
- Method of interpretation to be used—simultaneous or alternate:
  - Simultaneous—when the interpreter listens and translates at the same time.
  - Alternate—when the interpreter listens to an entire phrase, sentence, or paragraph, then translates during natural pauses.
- Conduct of the interview, lesson, or interrogation.
- Need for interpreters to avoid injecting their own personality, ideas, or questions into the interview.
- Need for interpreter to inform interviewer (PSYOP Soldier) of inconsistencies in language used by interviewee. An example would be someone who claims to be a college professor, yet speaks like an uneducated person. During interrogations or interviews, this information will be used as part of the assessment of the information obtained from the individual.
- Physical arrangements of site, if applicable.
- Possible need for interpreter to assist in AARs or assessments.

INTERPRETER TRAINING

H-13. As part of the initial training with the interpreter, the PSYOP Soldier should tactfully convey that the instructor, interviewer, or interrogator (PSYOP Soldier) must always direct the interview or lesson. The Soldier should put the interpreter's role in proper perspective and stress the interpreter's importance as a vital communication link between the Soldier and the TA. The PSYOP Soldier should appeal to the interpreter's professional pride by clearly describing how the quality and quantity of the information sent and received is directly dependent upon the interpreter's skills. Also, the PSYOP Soldier should mention how the interpreter functions solely as a conduit between the Soldier and the subject.

H-14. The PSYOP Soldier must be aware that some interpreters, because of cultural differences, may attempt to "save face" by purposely concealing their lack of understanding. They may attempt to translate what they think the PSYOP Soldier said or meant without asking for a clarification or vice versa. Because this situation can result in misinformation and confusion, and impact on credibility, the PSYOP Soldier should let the interpreter know that when in doubt he should always ask for clarification. The Soldier should create a safe environment for this situation as early in the relationship as possible.

H-15. Other points for the PSYOP Soldier to cover while orienting and training the interpreter are—

- Importance of the training, interview, or interrogation.
- Specific objectives of the training, interview, or interrogation, if any.
- Outline of lesson or interview questions, if applicable.
- Background information on the interviewee or TA.
- Briefing, training, or interview schedules. It may take double or triple the amount of time needed when using an interpreter to convey the same information. For that reason, the interpreter may be helpful in scheduling enough time.
- Copy of the briefing, questions, or lesson plan, if applicable. Special attention should be given to develop language proficiency in the technical fields in which the interpreters are expected to be employed. In general, a copy of the material will give the interpreter time to look up unfamiliar words or ask questions to clarify anything confusing.
- Copies of handout material, if applicable.
- General background information on subject.
- Glossary of terms, if applicable.

INTERVIEW PREPARATION

H-16. The PSYOP Soldier selects an appropriate site for the interview. He positions and arranges physical setup of the area. When conducting interviews with very important persons (VIPs) or individuals from different cultures, this arrangement can be significant.

H-17. The PSYOP Soldier instructs the interpreters to mirror the Soldier's tone and personality of speech. The Soldier instructs the interpreters not to interject their own questions or personality. He also instructs the interpreters to inform him if they notice any inconsistencies or peculiarities from sources.

INTERVIEW CONDUCT

H-18. Whether conducting an interview or presenting a lesson, the PSYOP Soldier should avoid simultaneous translations; that is, both the Soldier and the interpreter talking at the same time. The Soldier should speak for a minute or less in a neutral, relaxed manner, directly to the individual or audience. The interpreter should watch the Soldier carefully and, during the translation, mimic the Soldier's body language as well as interpret his verbal meaning. The PSYOP Soldier should observe the interpreter closely to detect any inconsistencies between the interpreter's and PSYOP Soldier's manners. The Soldier must be aware not to force the interpreter into literal translation by being too brief. The Soldier should present one major thought in its entirety and allow the interpreter to reconstruct it in his language and culture.

H-19. Although the interpreter will be doing some editing as a function of the interpreting process, it is imperative that he transmit the exact meaning without additions or deletions. As previously mentioned, the PSYOP Soldier should insist that the interpreter always ask for clarification, prior to interpreting, whenever not absolutely certain of the Soldier's meaning. However, the Soldier should be aware that a good interpreter, especially if he is local, can be invaluable in translating subtleties and hidden meanings.

H-20. During an interview or lesson, if questions are asked, the interpreter should immediately relay them to the PSYOP Soldier for an answer. The interpreter should never attempt to answer a question, even though he may know the correct answer. Additionally, neither the Soldier nor interpreter should correct the other in front of an interviewee or class; all differences should be settled away from the subject or audience.

H-21. Just as establishing rapport with the interpreter is vitally important, establishing rapport with interview subjects or the TA is equally important. The PSYOP Soldier and the interpreter should concentrate on rapport. To establish critical rapport, the subjects or audiences should be treated as mature, important human beings that are capable and worthy.

COMMUNICATION TECHNIQUES

H-22. An important first step for the PSYOP Soldier in communicating in a foreign language is to polish his English language skills. These skills are important even if no attempt is made to learn the indigenous language. The clearer the Soldier speaks in English, including diction, the easier it is for the interpreter to translate. Other factors to consider include use of profanity, slang, and colloquialisms. In many cases, such expressions cannot be translated. Even those that can be translated do not always retain the desired meaning. Military jargon and terms such as "gee whiz" or "golly" are hard to translate. In addition, if a technical term or expression must be used, the PSYOP Soldier must be sure the interpreter conveys the proper meaning in the target language. The Soldier should speak in low context, simple sentences. For instance, he may want to add words usually left off, such as "air" plane, to ensure the meaning will be obvious and he is not talking about the Great Plains or a wood plane.

H-23. When the Soldier is speaking extemporaneously, he must think about what he wants to say. He should break his thoughts down into logical bits, and say them a small piece at a time using short, simple words and sentences and low context, which can be translated quickly and easily. As a rule of thumb, the PSYOP Soldier should never say more in one sentence than he can easily repeat word for word immediately after saying it. Each sentence should contain a complete thought without verbiage.

Transitional Phrases and Qualifiers

H-24. These tend to confuse and waste valuable time. Examples are "for example," "in most cases," "maybe," and "perhaps." The Soldier should be cautious of using American humor. Cultural and language differences can lead to misinterpretations by foreigners. The Soldier should determine early on what the interpreter finds easiest to understand and translate meaningfully. In summary, the PSYOP Soldier should—

- Keep the entire presentation as simple as possible.
- Use short sentences and simple words (low context).
- Avoid idiomatic English.
- Avoid tendency toward flowery language.
- Avoid slang and colloquial expressions.

H-25. Whenever possible, the Soldier should identify any cultural restrictions before interviewing, instructing, or conferring with particular foreign nationals. For instance, when is it proper to stand, sit, or cross one's legs? Gestures, being learned behavior, vary from culture to culture. The interpreter should be able to relate a number of these cultural restrictions, which, whenever possible, should be observed in working with the particular group or individual.

Do's and Don'ts

H-26. The following are some do's and don'ts for the PSYOP Soldier to consider while working with an interpreter. The PSYOP Soldier **should**—

- Position the interpreter by his side (or even a step back). This method will keep the subject or audience from shifting their attention, or fixating on the interpreter and not on the Soldier.
- Always look at and talk directly to the subject or audience. Guard against the tendency to talk to the interpreter.
- Speak slowly and clearly. Repeat as often as necessary.
- Speak to the individual or group as if they understand English. Be enthusiastic and employ the gestures, movements, voice intonations and inflections that would normally be used before an English-speaking group. Considerable nonverbal meaning can be conveyed through voice and body movements. Encourage the interpreter to mimic the same delivery.

- Periodically check the interpreter's accuracy, consistency, and clarity. Have another American, fluent enough in the language, sit in on a lesson or interview to ensure that the translation is not distorted, intentionally or unintentionally. Another way to be sure is to learn the target language so that the interpreter's loyalty and honesty can be personally checked.

- Check with the audience whenever misunderstandings are suspected and clarify immediately. Using the interpreter, ask questions to elicit answers that will tell whether the point is clear. If not clear, rephrase the instruction differently and illustrate the point again. Use repetition and examples whenever necessary to facilitate learning. If the class asks few questions, it may mean the instruction is "over the heads" of the audience, or the message is not clear to the audience.

- Make the interpreter feel like a valuable member of the team. Give the interpreter recognition commensurate with the importance of his contribution.

The PSYOP Soldier **should not**—

- Address the subject or audience in the third person through the interpreter. Avoid saying, "Tell them I'm glad to be their instructor." Instead say, "I'm glad to be your instructor." Address the subject or audience directly.

- Make side comments to the interpreter that are not expected to be translated. This action tends to create the wrong atmosphere for communication.

- Be a distraction while the interpreter is translating and the subject or audience is listening. The Soldier should not pace the floor, write on the blackboard, teeter on the lectern, drink beverages, or carry on any other distracting activity while the interpreter is actually translating.

PSYOP in Support of Stability Operations

Stability operations promote and protect U.S. national interests by influencing the threat, political, and information dimensions of the operational environment through a combination of peacetime developmental, cooperative activities and coercive actions in response to crisis (FM 3-0) (Figure I-1). Army forces accomplish stability goals through engagement and response. The military activities that support stability operations are diverse, continuous, and often long-term. Their purpose is to promote and sustain regional and global stability. This appendix provides guidance for the planning and execution of PSYOP in support of the following four stability operations—NEOs, CD operations, humanitarian mine action (HMA) programs, and peace operations.

Types of Military Operations	Offense	Defense	Stability	Support
Types of Stability Operations and Their Subordinate Forms	**Peace Operations** • Peacekeeping • Peace Enforcement • Operations in Support of Diplomatic Efforts **Foreign Internal Defense** • Indirect Support • Direct Support • Combat Operations **Security Assistance** **Humanitarian and Civic Assistance** **Support to Insurgencies** • Unconventional Warfare • Conventional Combat Actions		**Support to Counterdrug Operations** • Detection and Monitoring • Host-Nation Support • C4 • Intelligence, Planning, CSS, Training, and Manpower Support • Reconnaissance **Combatting Terrorism** • Antiterrorism • Counterterrorism **Noncombatant Evacuation Operations** **Arms Control** • Inspection • Protection • Destruction **Show of Force** • Increased Force Visibility • Exercises and Demonstrations	

Figure I-1. Stability Operations

PSYOP IN SUPPORT OF NONCOMBATANT EVACUATION OPERATIONS

I-1. NEOs are conducted under Executive Order 12656. The Executive Order assigns responsibility for the protection of American citizens abroad and their property to the DOS. NEOs are operations directed by DOS, DOD, or other appropriate authority whereby noncombatants are evacuated from areas of danger overseas to safe havens or to the United States. The Chief of Diplomatic Mission or principal officer of DOS is the head official in the threat area responsible for the evacuation of all U.S. noncombatants. Chiefs of mission will issue the order for the evacuation of civilian noncombatants. DOD is responsible to DOS for advising and assisting in the preparation and implementation of NEO plans. During execution of a NEO plan, DOD operates in support of DOS.

I-2. A NEO may occur in any of the three operational environments: permissive, uncertain, or hostile. In a permissive environment, there is no apparent physical threat to the evacuees. The host government will not oppose their orderly departure or U.S. military assistance. In an uncertain environment, the degree of danger is uncertain. The host government may or may not be in control and cannot ensure the safety of the evacuees. In a hostile environment, the host government or other forces are expected to oppose evacuation and U.S. military assistance.

I-3. PSYOP units support NEOs by assessing the psychological climate in the AO and determining the most effective application of PSYOP to influence the indigenous population. The JTF commander uses PSYOP to project and define his intentions to the HN government, military, and populace. PSYOP forces also disseminate the ROE to the indigenous population. Execution of the PSYOP program may involve radio, loudspeaker, and leaflet operations. Execution of PSYOP during the earliest phases of the NEO will minimize the potential for hostilities. PSYOP forces will also conduct information programs directed at AMCITs and designated foreign nationals (DFNs). These programs provide evacuation instructions and guidance to facilitate evacuation marshalling and processing operations.

I-4. The decision to employ PSYOP by the JTF commander should be coordinated with the ambassador and the embassy staff. The PSYOP officer or NCOIC should provide a capabilities brief and a concept brief to the Ambassador, and at a minimum, to the Defense Attaché Office (DAO). The PSYOP officer obtains the Ambassador's approval for PSYOP products and execution of the PSYOP plan while seeking to have approval delegated to the JTF commander.

I-5. PSYOP activities are designed to discourage interference, persuade TAs to comply with JTF requests and directives, and facilitate the smooth evacuation of AMCITs and DFNs. The following are some examples of PSYOP objectives in support of a NEO:

- Enhance the safety and security of JTF personnel and evacuees.
- Dissuade interference with U.S. operations, minimize casualties, and protect the force.
- Demonstrate the resolve and capabilities of the JTF to protect evacuees and accomplish its mission.
- Gain and maintain active support from neighboring states, regional organizations, and international organizations for JTF efforts.
- Provide evacuation instructions for all evacuees.

Examples of PSYOP themes to stress include—

- JTF personnel are in HN only to withdraw selected noncombatants and will depart upon their successful evacuation.
- JTF personnel will maintain resolve and successfully complete designated operations.
- JTF personnel will defend themselves and others in their custody if threatened.
- JTF personnel are and will operate under the provisions of international law.
- The HN population should continue their lawful activities throughout the NEO.

Examples of PSYOP themes to avoid include—

- Themes that appear to favor one faction over another.
- Themes that imply the JTF is establishing itself as a military government.
- Degradation of local ethnic, cultural, or religious values.
- Any actions by JTF personnel that convey a lack of resolve to complete the evacuation or the intent to use force in self-defense.

I-6. The psychological impact of a NEO is enormous as it demonstrates U.S. resolve to protect its citizens. PSYOP units facilitate the evacuation of noncombatants by keeping potential evacuees informed, and influencing the local populace, HN military, police, and other potential belligerent groups through employment of appropriate media, the appropriate language, and appropriate themes. Judicious use of PSYOP can preclude escalation from a permissive NEO to nonpermissive, and can ensure a safe, orderly, and rapid evacuation, safeguarding U.S. forces while minimizing HN interference and disturbance.

I-7. The following are examples of NEO products (Figures I-2 through I-6, pages I-3 through I-5).

LOUDSPEAKER SCRIPTS

ATTENTION! ATTENTION!
We are moving you onto the helicopter in as timely and safe a manner as possible. Anyone needing special assistance boarding the helicopter, please move to the front of the line. All others please form an orderly line to speed boarding. Thank you for your cooperation.

ATTENTION EVACUEES! ATTENTION EVACUEES!
Please form an orderly line in front of the processing team. Have your bags open and passports ready and give the team your full cooperation. We are searching you to ensure your safety and welfare. Anyone ill or needing special assistance please move to the front of the line. We will process you through as quickly as possible. Thank you for your patience and cooperation.

Figure I-2. Example of NEO Product

Poster to be displayed in the vicinity of NEO AO.

When Reporting to the Evacuation Points:

Evacuees
Should Bring:

- Immunization Records
- Any Prescribed Medications
- One Blanket Per Person
- Proof of Citizenship

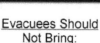

Evacuees Should Not Bring:

- Pets
- Weapons
- Baggage that weighs more than 50 lbs

Tune Your Radio to AM 640 For More Information

Figure I-3. Generic NEO Product (Poster)

Road sign to be placed along evacuation routes.

MILITARY CONVOY ROUTE
ROAD CLOSED
FROM 0700 - 1900
INFORMATION:
TUNE RADIO TO AM 640

Figure I-4. Generic NEO Product (Road Sign)

Poster to be placed near evacuation points.

U.S. Forces are providing security for the peaceful evacuation of American citizens. Do not interfere.

For more information tune your radio to AM 640.

Figure I-5. Generic NEO Product (Poster)

Poster to be displayed in the vicinity of departure points.

U.S. FORCES WILL NOT EVACUATE CITIZENS OF (HOST NATION) DO NOT ATTEMPT TO BOARD U.S. VEHICLES OR AIRCRAFT INFORMATION: TUNE TO AM 640

Figure I-6. Generic NEO Product (Poster)

PSYOP IN SUPPORT OF COUNTERDRUG OPERATIONS

I-8. PSYOP forces may be employed to support geographic combatant commanders and law enforcement agencies (LEAs) to detect, monitor, and counter the cultivation, production, trafficking, and use of illegal drugs and the infrastructure of drug-trafficking entities. PSYOP forces ensure clear communication of the goals and objectives as they support U.S. and HN efforts. PSYOP units conduct CD operations in support of CD agencies within the U.S. Country Team and with HN counterparts. PSYOP units use their cross-cultural communication skills, regional expertise, and language capabilities to train HN counterparts in developing CD programs. JP 3-07.4, *Joint Counterdrug Operations*, contains details of the CD threat, CD organizations, operations, planning, and execution.

COUNTERDRUG POLICY GUIDANCE

I-9.   The authority to conduct CD operations and legal aspects governing CD operations are contained within the following directives:

- *Presidential Decision Directive (PDD) 68, U.S. International Public Information (IPI).* PDD 68 ordered the creation of an IPI system designed to "influence foreign audiences" in support of U.S. foreign policy and to counteract propaganda by enemies of the United States. The intent is to "enhance U.S. security, bolster America's economic prosperity, and to promote democracy abroad." The group's charter states that IPI control over "international military information" is intended to "influence the emotions, motives, objective reasoning, and ultimately, the behavior of foreign governments, organizations, groups, and individuals." IPI is a mechanism that has been established to ensure agencies conducting international public diplomacy (USIA, State Department, and so on) work in a coordinated manner.

- *PDD 14, Counternarcotics.* PDD 14 provides a policy framework for U.S. international drug control efforts as part of the Administration's overall CD control policy. This directive concentrates the emphasis of international drug control efforts across three programs:

  - Assisting "source countries" in addressing the root causes of narcotics production and trafficking through assistance for sustainable development, strengthening democratic institutions, and cooperative programs to counter narcotics traffickers, money laundering, and supply of chemical precursors.

  - Combatting international narco-trafficking organizations.

  - Emphasizing more selective and flexible interdiction programs near the U.S. border, in the transit zone, and in source countries.

- *PDD 44, Heroin Control Policy.* This policy guides U.S. efforts against production and trafficking of heroin. Major tenets of this strategy include the following:

  - Boost international awareness and strengthen international cooperation against heroin traffickers. Use diplomatic and public channels to focus international awareness on the growing heroin threat.

  - Implement coordinated international law enforcement efforts aimed at disrupting and destroying heroin trafficking organizations.

  - Assist source and transit nations in developing comprehensive narcotics policies.

- *National Security Decision Directive (NSDD) 130, U.S. International Information Policy.* International information is an integral and vital part of U.S. national security policy and strategy, and is a key strategic instrument for shaping fundamental political and ideological trends. The fundamental purpose of U.S. international information programs is to affect foreign audiences in ways favorable to U.S. national interests. NSDD 130 directs DOD to participate in overt PSYOP programs in peacetime. The purpose is to employ PSYOP effectively and economically by establishing a set of national guidelines, a funding program, and defining roles and relationships of the agencies involved in these programs.

- *National Narcotics Leadership Act of 1988.* This act established the Office of National Drug Control Policy (ONDCP) as the primary agency within the Executive Branch responsible for developing and implementing the National Drug Control Strategy. This act unifies the efforts of the various federal and local agencies.

- *National Drug Control Strategy.* The strategy focuses on prevention, treatment, research, law enforcement, and protection of our borders, drug supply reduction, and international cooperation. The overriding objective of the drug control strategy is to keep Americans safe from the threats posed by illegal drugs. The National Drug Control Strategy has five goals, of which PSYOP supports two:

  - *Goal 4*: Shield America's air, land, and sea frontiers from the drug threat. PSYOP units focus on interdiction efforts to disrupt drug flow and increase the risk to traffickers, thus preventing significant quantities of drugs from reaching the United States. PSYOP units also assist the U.S. Country Team and HN to identify and dismantle drug trafficking organizations.

  - *Goal 5*: Break foreign and domestic drug sources of supply. PSYOP units focus on eliminating drug cultivation and production, encouraging alternate crop cultivation, and highlighting the hazards of drug use and production while protecting the country's natural resources.

- *DOD Instruction S-3321-1, (S) Overt Psychological Operations Conducted by the Military Services in Peacetime and in Contingencies Short of Declared War (U).* This directive is the legal basis and foundation for peacetime PSYOP activities. PSYOP forces conduct CD missions in support of a geographic commander's theater security cooperation plan (TSCP) under the auspices of peacetime PSYOP activities. PSYOP supports a combatant commander's TSCP by use of the following means:

  - International military information teams (IMITs) deployed to selected countries to train HN forces or agencies in the production of drug awareness programs.

  - Teams to provide information management for SOF joint combined exercises for training (JCETs).

  - Production of publications or pamphlets that provide information on drug awareness and CD operations.

  - Peacetime PSYOP activities or programs planning, coordination, and execution in peacetime and contingencies. PSYOP support promotes U.S. regional objectives, policies, and interests.

INTERAGENCY COORDINATION

I-10. CD activities have evolved from independent actions to a national effort of joint military and civilian cooperation. DOD has been tasked as the lead agency of the Federal Government for the detection and monitoring of illegal drug shipments into the United States in support of law enforcement agencies. PSYOP personnel supporting CD operations must work with numerous U.S. and HN state, local, and private authorities. Table I-1, pages I-8 and I-9, depicts federal lead and primary agencies and their responsibilities. Federal agencies that PSYOP units interact with include, but are not limited to, DOS, DOJ, DEA, U.S. Coast Guard, and the U.S. Customs Service. Interagency coordination forces the vital link between the military instrument of power and the economic, diplomatic, and informational entities of the USG, NGOs, and international organizations. Success in CD operations depends greatly on the ability to blend and synergize all elements of national power effectively. Thorough coordination ensures military operations are synchronized with those other agencies of the USG, as well as with foreign forces and regional and international organizations. JP 3-08, *Interagency Coordination During Joint Operations, Volumes I and II*, contains greater details on interagency coordination.

Table I-1. Federal Lead and Primary Agencies and Their Responsibilities

Lead and Primary Agencies	Responsibilities
Department of Defense	Detect and monitor aerial and maritime transit of illegal drugs in support of law enforcement agencies.
Drug Enforcement Administration	Enforce laws and regulations on drugs and controlled substances: • Investigate major interstate and international drug law violators. • Enforce regulations on legal manufacture and distribution of controlled substances. • Participate in drug intelligence sharing with other national agencies. • Coordinate DEA and international counterparts' efforts. • Provide operational support and conduct drug interdiction in concert with HN LEAs.
Federal Bureau of Investigation	Investigate violations of criminal laws (concurrent with DEA): • Target major multijurisdictional trafficking organizations. • Dismantle trafficking networks.
U.S. Attorneys	Prosecute criminals: • Prosecute violations of federal laws concerning controlled substances, money laundering, drug trafficking, tax evasion, and violent and organized crime. • Oversee Organized Crime Drug Enforcement Task Force (OCDETF) activities.

Table I-1. Federal Lead and Primary Agencies and Their Responsibilities (Continued)

Lead and Primary Agencies	Responsibilities
U.S. Border Patrol	Primary agency—Land interdiction between U.S. POEs.
Department of State—International Narcotics and Law Enforcement Affairs	Coordinate U.S. international supply reduction strategies.
U.S. Customs Service	Lead—Interdiction at land and sea U.S. POEs (with U.S. Border Patrol as primary agency between POEs and U.S. territorial waters). Co-Lead (with Coast Guard)—Air interdiction.
U.S. Coast Guard (see also DHS)	Lead—Maritime interdiction. Co-Lead (with Customs Service)—Air interdiction.
U.S. Department of Homeland Security (DHS)	The agencies slated to become part of the DHS will be housed in one of five major directorates: • Border and Transportation Security. • Emergency Preparedness and Response. • Science and Technology. • Information Analysis and Infrastructure Protection. • Management. Besides the five directorates of DHS, several other critical agencies are folding into the new department or being newly created: • United States Coast Guard. • United States Secret Service. • Bureau of Citizenship and Immigration Services. • Office of State and Local Government Coordination. • Office of Private Section Liaison. • Office of Inspector General.

HUMAN RIGHTS AND COUNTERDRUG OPERATIONS

I-11. The promotion of respect for human rights is a central goal of U.S. foreign policy. The United States understands that the existence of human rights helps secure the peace, deter aggression, promote the rule of law, combat crime and corruption, strengthen democracies, and prevent humanitarian crises. As the promotion of human rights is an important national interest, the United States seeks to—

- Hold governments accountable to their obligations under universal human rights norms.
- Promote greater respect for human rights.
- Promote the rule of law.
- Coordinate human rights activities with important allies and regional activities.

I-12. The Leahy Human Rights Law is another means used to support human rights around the world. This law seeks to hold members of foreign security forces who are implicated in human rights abuses accountable for their actions. The Leahy Amendment makes it mandatory to conduct human rights screening of those foreign organizations, agencies, and individuals PSYOP units will be working with or training. No assistance will be provided to any organization or individual for which there is credible evidence of human rights violations. The human rights vetting must be completed before deployment. Text of the Leahy Amendment includes the following:

None of the funds made available by this Act may be provided to any unit of the security forces of a foreign country if the Secretary of State has credible evidence that such unit has committed gross violations of human rights, unless the Secretary determines and reports to the Committees on Appropriations that the government of such country is taking effective measures to bring the responsible members of the security forces unit to justice: Provided, That nothing in this section shall be construed to withhold funds made available by this act from any unit of the security forces of a foreign country not credibly alleged to be involved in gross violation of human rights: Provided further, That in the event that funds are withheld from any unit pursuant to this section, the Secretary of State shall promptly inform the foreign government of the basis for such action and shall, to the maximum extent practicable, assist the foreign government in taking effective measures to bring the responsible members of the security forces to justice so funds to that unit may be resumed.

Counterdrug Organization

I-13. The organization of PSYOP forces supporting a CD operation is normally based on the geographic combatant commander's assessment. A regionally oriented team will deploy to the target country to conduct a predeployment site survey (PDSS) to evaluate general and PSYOP-relevant HN conditions, such as political sensitivities, social and cultural factors, and communications resources and force protection measures. Special mention must be made that no deployment occurs without a SecDef-approved CJCS deployment order. The PDSS conducts coordination with Embassy and HN personnel concerning deployment of main body and execution of the mission. PDSS teams are tailored to support each mission. Although there is no prescribed composition, the assessment team will, as a minimum, contain the requisite planners for PSYOP development, production, distribution, and dissemination. Depending on the mission profile, the assessment team may also contain communications, SSD analysts, and logistics planners. The PDSS develops a CONPLAN that addresses all aspects of the mission.

I-14. The main body, PSE, conducts CD operations to support the U.S. Embassy's CD efforts and enhance the HN's ability to participate in a sustained drug awareness program. The priority of effort for PSYOP objectives should mirror and support the U.S. Embassy's priority of effort and objectives. Key objectives of the mission are to provide training and support for CD operations, promote foreign military interaction, and support humanitarian and civic assistance projects.

I-15. Deployment of a posttest team follows mission execution. The posttest team compiles posttest data to reflect the MOEs of the mission's products and activities. Reporting these performance measurements are directed by the Government Performance and Results Act of 1993. The purpose of this act is to "initiate program performance reform with a series of pilot projects in setting program goals, measuring program performance against these goals, and reporting publicly on their progress." This act holds Federal agencies accountable for achieving program results.

Responsibilities

I-16. The responsibilities of the PSYOP forces are to train, mentor, and assist HN CD personnel in—

- Developing a multimedia national CD information plan.
- Developing a CD training program.
- Developing and producing products to support the campaign plan.
- Coordinating the dissemination of approved CD products.
- Coordinating with other government departments, as needed, to execute the CD campaign successfully.
- Coordinating with the UN and NGOs to ensure CD programs initiated by outside agencies are coordinated and integrated into the national drug awareness campaign.

Planning for CD operations follows the same planning process mentioned in Chapter 4.

PSYOP IN SUPPORT OF HUMANITARIAN MINE ACTION PROGRAMS

I-17. PSYOP offer unique capabilities to HMA efforts. PSYOP units execute the humanitarian mine awareness portion of HMA. PSYOP personnel are trained and experienced in developing mine awareness programs in different regions of the world. They possess key skills as subject matter experts, planners, and designers of public information strategies. U.S. PSYOP units coordinate all of their activities with the U.S. Embassy, international peacekeeping or relief organizations in-country, and other HN or contractor organizations involved in the overall demining operation. The desired end state of the mission is a self-sustaining capability to develop and execute national UXO and mine awareness programs and institutions.

I-18. The USG HMA program assists selected countries in relieving human suffering and in developing an indigenous demining capability while promoting U.S. interests. The program provides increased HMA assistance to countries suffering from the presence of land mines, which maim and kill innocents, obstruct emergency assistance activities, hamper economic development, and impede free movement of citizens.

I-19. Within DOS, the Office of HMA serves as the lead organization in coordinating U.S. humanitarian activities worldwide. The office develops and implements country-specific HMA programs and oversees the interagency strategic and planning development process supporting U.S. global demining activities.

I-20.   The USG HMA Strategic Plan provides the strategy and implementing methodology to develop a more effective and better integrated humanitarian demining program that helps selected countries relieve human suffering and develop indigenous capacity, while promoting U.S. political, security, and economic interests. The strategic plan is developed, coordinated, and approved by the geographical and functional policy coordination committees (PCCs). The PCC Subgroup on HMA is charged with identifying which countries receive U.S. demining assistance and managing U.S. resources committed to the program. To initiate consideration for a demining program in a given country, the PCC Subgroup on HMA must receive a request for demining assistance from the host country via the appropriate U.S. Embassy. The goals of the PCC Subgroup on HMA are to—

- Assist nations to alleviate the threat of land mines to innocents.

- Promote U.S. foreign policy and national security.

- Encourage international participation to eliminate the threat of land mines to civilians around the world by 2010.

I-21.   The desired end state of the HMA program is having a select country reach a point where HMA assistance is no longer necessary from either a humanitarian or foreign policy perspective. Normally, at end state the HN has a fully established, self-sustaining, humanitarian demining program or has eliminated the threat of land mines and UXO to the local populace, and made significant strides in returning land to economic productivity.

I-22.   The archive site for State Department information is www.state.gov/www/global/arms/pm/hdp. This site contains information on HMA policy.

HUMANITARIAN MINE ACTION POLICY GUIDANCE

I-23.   The associated legislation and assorted policies that govern CD operations also govern HMA. Special attention must be paid to humanitarian demining programs conducted pursuant to Title 10, USC, Section 401, which prohibits any member of the armed forces from engaging in the physical detection, lifting, or destroying of land mines. It is also the policy that this restriction shall apply to DOD civilian employees.

ROLE OF PSYOP

I-24.   PSYOP plays important roles in the following facets of demining missions, public awareness, and "train the trainer" programs. PSYOP focuses on assisting HNs to develop and execute UXO and mine awareness missions and training programs, and to develop and disseminate UXO and mine awareness products. PSYOP personnel—

- Execute mine awareness public information programs.

- Support train-the-trainer demining programs.

- Assist the HN in developing its own mine awareness process and institution.

The goal of these programs and missions is to minimize hazards to the populace through the achievement of selected behavioral objectives.

Mine Awareness Programs

I-25. The awareness component of demining can be a relatively complicated and demanding enterprise, politically, logistically, and operationally. The United States employs PSYOP specialists because of their ability to get programs started quickly. Any local program will be successful only if it enjoys the support of the host government, including a commitment to developing or designating an infrastructure to carry out these programs over the long term.

I-26. Mine awareness programs should be viewed as an integral part of the larger demining process and should not be performed in isolation from that process. Demining typically involves at least the following four components: locating, mapping, marking, and clearing. There is an informational element required in each of these undertakings. Public awareness, mine location, and mine mapping involve an exchange of information with the public, as well as an effort to persuade individuals to perform desired actions.

I-27. Mine marking and mine clearing also have information requirements, such as informing the public of the progress of minefield marking and clearing operations and persuading local populations not to interfere with personnel engaged in these activities. Marking and clearing also require coordination between local communities or public officials and military or contract mine and ordnance disposal units. This coordination can best be facilitated through an information program.

PSYOP Support Element

I-28. PSEs are resourced from regional PSYOP battalions and are focused on operational-level PSYOP. A PSE executes missions in support of a geographic combatant commander's theater security cooperation plan or non-DOD agencies, usually under the auspices of the peacetime PSYOP activities, and developed, coordinated, and overseen directly by the ASD[SO/LIC] as per DOD Directive 5111.10, *Assistant Secretary of Defense for Special Operations and Low-Intensity Conflict.* Within the geographic combatant commander's AORs, other terms are sometimes used by the U.S. Country Teams to refer to PSYDETs that directly support their demining programs, such as the military information support team (MIST) and mine awareness teams.

I-29. PSEs execute PSYOP mine awareness operations in support of humanitarian mine awareness agencies within the U.S. Country Team and its HN. Once the PSE is deployed, C2 of a PSE passes to the geographic combatant commander. The PSE operates under the day-to-day control of the DAO, senior military commander, or other representatives designated by the U.S. Ambassador. Product approval rests with the Ambassador or designated representative (as outlined in the JSCP), typically the deputy chief of mission (DCM) or the PAO. PSEs—

- Develop and execute multimedia national mine awareness information plans.

- Coordinate with local production sources, such as print plants and newspapers, for mass production of approved products.
- Coordinate the dissemination of approved products nationally.
- Coordinate with other sections within the national defense organization and with other ministries on matters dealing with mine awareness.
- Ensure all mine awareness programs originating from outside sources are coordinated and integrated as necessary in the national UXO and mine awareness mission.
- Ensure the HN's designated approval authority approves the national UXO and mine awareness program and subsequent products.

I-30.   PSEs are generally collocated with the mine awareness section. In addition, PSEs support national-level demining courses. Finally, PSYOP personnel support Special Forces operational detachments A (SFODAs) by providing appropriate products and coordinating publicity with media outlets for local support of "train the trainer" programs. Figure I-7 is an example of the Superman and Wonder Woman comic books used in Central America to teach mine awareness to children.

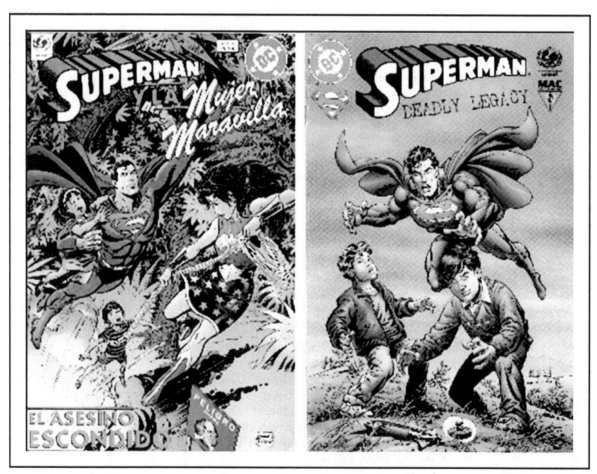

Figure I-7. Superman and Wonder Woman Mine Awareness Comic Books

Behavioral Objectives

I-31.   The PSE develops mine awareness information operations that have defined public behavioral objectives. Some typical behavioral objectives associated with demining, depending upon local circumstances, include—

- Recognition of common mine types: Educate local populace to be able to identify common types of mines or other UXO.

- Avoidance of mined areas: Persuade people to avoid mined sites and refrain from handling, defusing, or collecting mines or UXO; instill a sense of both the immediate danger and the long-term personal, family, or community consequences of handling mines, fuzes, and UXO.

- Basic first-aid procedures: Provide basic knowledge of field-expedient first-aid procedures for coping with mine-related injuries until proper medical attention can be provided.

- Hazards or illegality of possessing explosive ordnance.

- Persuasion of people to refrain from collecting or trafficking in explosive artifacts for either criminal or economic motives.

- Notification of authorities: Persuade the public to communicate information about the location of mines and other explosive artifacts to designated authorities charged with coordinating awareness, marking, and clearing activities.

- Noninterference: Persuade the public not to interfere with official personnel who may be entering an area to perform mapping, marking, and clearing activities.

- Status of mine marking and clearing: Inform local populace when and where it is safe to enter previously mined territory.

I-32.   PSYOP personnel design public awareness programs that provide step-by-step procedures for leaving a mined area without mishap. Some examples of these safety procedures include—

- Leaving a marker at the location of a mined area so that authorities can find the mined area upon being notified.

- Notifying local civil, military, or multilateral authorities of the location of the discovered minefield or mine.

- Administering first-aid procedures in instances of injury.

Figure I-8, page I-16, is an example of a public awareness product.

PROGRAM DEVELOPMENT

I-33.   Developing and implementing a comprehensive public awareness program usually requires three distinct steps—assessment, mine awareness plan integration, and operation planning and product development designed to educate and to fulfill the desired behavioral objectives.

Assessment

I-34.   The first stage of information operation development is a thorough assessment of the existing conditions that may affect implementation of the mine awareness program in the target area. The assessment focuses on political sensitivities, social and cultural factors, and available communications resources. The on-site assessment centers on eight primary areas:

- TAs.
- Production facilities.
- Communications infrastructure.
- Competing media.
- Available indigenous commercial and governmental information holders.
- Logistics support (U.S. military, as well as coalition and HN).
- Dissemination facilities.
- Tactical considerations (when required).

Figure I-8. Mine Awareness Product in Bosnia

I-35. An HMA assessment team should accompany the theater assessment team to evaluate general and PSYOP-relevant HN conditions. The assessment team also focuses on the capabilities, technology, and likely availability of HN resources. Priority of work is divided into two broad categories:

- Resolving mission, administrative, and logistical support issues.
- Identifying the who, what, when, where, and how of the U.S. mine awareness program.

I-36. HMA assessment teams are tailored to support each mission and the duration of the assessment varies. These teams normally consist of one officer, one NCO, and a civilian analyst (if possible) from one of the 4th POG(A)'s regionally oriented SSD. The civilian analyst can be a crucial member of the team. Analysts are particularly adept at discussing mission requirements with members of the UN or NGOs. The team develops a CONPLAN that addresses all aspects of the assessment. The CONPLAN should include a milestone chart for predeployment activities and a draft itinerary for the trip. Although each HMA is unique, many similarities exist, especially in planning considerations. Careful evaluation of these considerations results in an effective plan based on firsthand facts, not assumptions.

I-37. The following list, though not all-inclusive, serves as a road map to resolve issues and to identify physical requirements in support of the mission. The U.S. Country Team may provide most of the information required for HMA. Every attempt should be made to ensure no issues are left unresolved before deployment. The HMA assessment team cannot assume that anything will be provided or be available upon arrival. The HMA assessment team—

- Coordinates for a thorough security briefing by the U.S. Embassy regional security office (RSO). The team finds out the current security climate of the country and identifies hostile areas, off-limits areas, curfews, and terrorist threats. The team discusses how to contact the local police or military in case of emergency, and reads and becomes familiar with the country's emergency action plan (EAP).

- Assesses the local communication systems and determines its reliability. The team determines types of systems used by NGOs and UN personnel (cellular, FM, AM), any constraints on the use of U.S. Embassy equipment, and assets available for communication outside the country. The team determines organic communication equipment available, and access to and availability of secure data and voice systems.

- Meets with the U.S. Embassy finance and contracting officers to ensure they are prepared to support the team financially. The team determines what supplies are available locally and what may take longer to receive.

Mine Awareness Plan Integration

I-38. PSYOP HMA planners must be included at the earliest stages of any HMA planning process. Although U.S. PSYOP program planning depends on a thorough assessment, units maintain a number of prototype programs that are applicable in many situations and may be adapted to local conditions with relative ease. These programs, which articulate mission objectives and product concepts rather than fully developed product prototypes, provide the basis for selecting an approach that can best be adapted to meet local requirements.

I-39. PSYOP HMA planners follow these guidelines for the integration of mine awareness plans:

- Conduct assessment of UN, NGO, and HN mine awareness plans and programs.

- Identify the lead agency and determine the desired end state and general magnitude of the problem. If available, HMA planners request interagency assessments.

- Present mine awareness capabilities briefing to key agencies. HMA planners distribute sample products for review and possible pretest.

- Identify methods to conduct a pretest and means to conduct a posttest.

- Develop a product distribution and dissemination plan.

Product Development

I-40. PSYOP HMA planners must be included at the earliest stages of any HMA planning process. Although U.S. PSYOP program planning depends on a thorough assessment, units maintain a number of prototype programs that are applicable in many situations and may be adapted to local conditions with relative ease. These programs, which articulate campaign objectives and product concepts rather than fully-developed product prototypes, provide the basis for selecting an approach that can best be adapted to meet local requirements.

I-41. The PSYOP program development process is addressed in Chapter 6. A key consideration to remember in program planning, though, is that program objectives are achieved through sequence and execution of numerous individual PSYOP activities, each designed to achieve a measured response in a specific TA. Once the assessment has been completed and the initial program planning accomplished, prototype informational material is developed.

I-42. Products are geared to the local situation and support accomplishing the behavioral objectives. An effective mine awareness program normally requires the design of a variety of mine awareness materials and their production in audio, visual, and print media. Depending on local circumstances, any or all of the following types of products may be useful:

- Posters, pamphlets, and leaflets.

- Products aimed specifically at children (school supplies, coloring books, comic books, and games).

- Posters and booklets (first aid, minefield marking).

- Novelty items (T-shirts, caps, pencils).

- Publicity materials concerning dates and locations of demining team operations.

- Electronic media materials, such as radio scripts and videocassettes.

I-43. Producing the products locally in conjunction with the host country government and other organizations engaged in HMA enhances self-sustainment. By involving these organizations in the production process, they become an integral part of the mine awareness effort and enhance HN capability to prepare, produce, and disseminate mine awareness products and information.

PSYOP IN SUPPORT OF PEACE OPERATIONS

I-44. This section provides guidance for the planning and execution of PSYOP in support of peace operations. Peace operations are conducted under the authority of UN or other international organization mandates. These mandates assign responsibility for the planning and execution of the peace operation. Military forces from numerous nations will be participants in the peace operation and U.S. PSYOP forces may often be the only PSYOP forces present.

I-45. Peace operations are directed by the UN, international organizations, or other appropriate authority whereby military forces are introduced into a conflict to establish peace or to enforce existing peace accords. The JTF commander or peace operations force commander is the head official in the area responsible for the enforcement of peace operations mandates. During execution of a peace operation, DOD operates in support of the UN peace operation or task force commander. Peace operations are defined as a broad term that encompasses peacekeeping operations and peace enforcement operations in support of diplomatic efforts to establish and maintain peace.

PSYOP SUPPORT TO PEACE OPERATIONS

I-46. The operational environment is characterized by complex, ambiguous, and at times, uncertain situations that may have some or all of the following: asymmetrical threats, failed states, absence of rule of law, gross violations of human rights, collapse of civil infrastructure, or presence of displaced persons and refugees. Political objectives will dominate and political influence will extend down to tactical formations. In peace operations, actions at the tactical level can directly affect the strategic level.

I-47. Developments in telecommunications have created an emerging medium adversary that forces will use to shape the battlespace and influence public opinion. The ability to get the PSYOP message out to those in a conflict region has sometimes been perceived as ineffective, while adversary forces have been able to rapidly generate and disseminate propaganda and misinformation. PSYOP must be synchronized with public information, public affairs, OPSEC, and EW activities. The development of a sound PSYOP plan, in coordination with the IO plan, with input from national agencies, international organizations, NGOs, and troop-contributing nations, has the potential to greatly enhance the effectiveness of the peace operation.

I-48. The unique nature of peace operations will result in the migration of some support below doctrinally assigned echelon. PSYOP units normally assigned to higher echelons may find themselves operating in support of brigades, battalions, or even companies. PSYOP forces will be working with international, multinational, and NGOs.

I-49. PSYOP units support peace operations by assessing the psychological climate in the AO and determining the most effective application of PSYOP to influence TA. The peace operations commander uses PSYOP to influence the belligerents, warring factions, HN government, military, and the general populace to promote the peace. PSYOP forces also disseminate the ROE to the belligerents or warring factions. Execution of the PSYOP program may involve radio, television, loudspeaker, printed material, and leaflet operations. Execution of PSYOP during the earliest phases of the peace operation will minimize or decrease the potential for renewed hostilities. PSYOP forces will also conduct information programs directed at DFNs. These programs provide instructions and guidance to facilitate the conduct of the peace operation.

I-50. The decision to employ PSYOP in a peace operation should be coordinated with the JTF or peace operations force commander. The PSYOP officer or NCOIC should provide a capabilities brief and a concept brief to the commander. The PSYOP officer obtains the commander's approval for PSYOP products and execution of the PSYOP plan, while seeking to have approval delegated to the POTF commander. PSYOP activities are designed to promote peace, persuade TAs to comply with peace operation requests and directives, and facilitate the smooth transition to peace and enforcement of mandates.

I-51. The PSYOP area of interest is used to identify all outside influences on the operation, such as assessing the degree of influence of political groups, media, and other nations' support on the belligerents of the conflict. PSYOP specialists gather pertinent demographic data and discern economic and social issues that are associated with specific TAs. PSYOP specialists perform analyses of living conditions, religious beliefs, cultural distinctions, allocation of wealth, political grievances, social status, and political affiliations, as well as most of the remaining political-military factors. Specific questions related to TA analysis are—

- What are the root causes of the conflict from the perspective of all belligerents?
- What would cause each side to agree to peace?
- Are there any new issues that have increased tensions since peace was initiated?
- How committed is each belligerent group to keeping the peace? How much trust and faith do the belligerents have in each other to keep the peace?
- How capable is each belligerent of keeping the peace? Can the leadership, which negotiated the peace, enforce discipline throughout the belligerent parties?
- How likely is each belligerent group to obey the laws and provisions of treaty agreements?
- What is the political organization of each of the belligerent groups? Who are the key personnel that control the rank and file of each faction?

I-52. The PSYOP specialists, during the course of the IPB, must identify the following:

- All factions involved in the peacekeeping operation, including those that are likely to violate the peace.
- The reasons certain factions may violate the peace.
- The political ideologies that directly affect or influence the conduct of the belligerents.

- The religious beliefs that directly affect or influence the conduct of the belligerents.
- The level of local support and the specific sources of support to all belligerent parties.
- Possible actions of the belligerents to the peacekeeping mission, including consideration of acts of terrorism.

I-53.   The following are some examples of POs in support of peace operations:

- Establish the conditions for the entry of U.S. or multinational forces.
- Reduce civil interference with the peace operation.
- Discourage illegal migration.
- Facilitate civil order.
- Support CMO.
- Increase the effectiveness of the local police force.
- Prepare the community for elections.
- Inform the community of available services (water, medicine, food, and shelter).
- Reduce rumors and disinformation.
- Assist in the administration of DC camps.
- Establish exit conditions for the peace operations force.
- Build a favorable image of peace operations Soldiers.
- Promote mine awareness and education.
- Reinforce the peace operation's fundamentals of consent, impartiality, transparency, credibility, and freedom of movement.

Examples of PSYOP themes to stress include—

- Peace operations personnel are in the HN only to enforce the peace mandate or charter.
- Peace operations personnel will maintain resolve and successfully complete designated operations.
- Peace operations personnel will defend themselves if threatened.
- Peace operations personnel are operating under the provisions of international law.
- The HN population should continue their lawful activities throughout the mandate of the peace operation.
- Provision of opponent audiences' alternatives to continued conflict.
- Projection of a favorable image of UN or U.S. actions.

Examples of PSYOP themes to avoid include—

- Themes that appear to favor one faction over another.
- Themes that imply the peace operations force is establishing itself as a military government.
- Degradation of local ethnic, cultural, or religious values.

- Any actions by peace operations force personnel that convey a lack of resolve to complete the mission or the intent to use force in self-defense.

I-54. The psychological impact of a peace operation is enormous as it demonstrates UN or U.S. resolve to enforce the peace. PSYOP units facilitate the peace process by keeping the population informed, and influencing the local populace, HN military, police, and other potential belligerent groups through employment of appropriate media, the appropriate language, and appropriate themes. Judicious use of PSYOP can preclude escalation from peace to hostilities.

I-55. The following are examples of peace operation products or activities (Figures I-9 through I-11, pages I-22 and I-23).

LOUDSPEAKER SCRIPTS

ATTENTION! ATTENTION!
United Nations forces are here to assist in the international relief effort for the Somali people. We are prepared to use force to protect the relief operation and our Soldiers. We will not allow interference with food distribution or with our activities. We are here to help you.

Figure I-9. Example of Peace Operation Product

Figure I-10. Tactical PSYOP Teams Using Loudspeakers in Haiti

**Figure I-11. A Tactical PSYOP Soldier Distributes a
Pro-U.S. Forces Newspaper**

PSYOP SUPPORT TO CIVIL-MILITARY OPERATIONS

I-56. CMO are an inherent responsibility of the commander in support of the overall peace operations mission. PSYOP forces can provide essential support and information for CMO. PSYOP units can provide specific and tailored support to CA units by effectively integrating the following considerations into the PSYOP mission:

- Develop information for CA forces concerning the location, state of mind, and health of civilians, and the physical characteristics of the operational area.

- Disseminate information concerning the safety and welfare of the indigenous civilian population.

- Influence a civilian population's attitude toward UN or U.S. policy and prepare it for CA involvement in postconflict activities.

- Maximize CA activities in the area of HA by exploiting the goodwill created by the UN or U.S. efforts in the area of medical and veterinary aid, construction, and public facilities activities.

- During disaster-relief operations, PSYOP may foster international support for host governments and may assist the PAO to coordinate publicity for U.S. efforts, IAW approved peace operations.

- Conduct assessments before and after the operation to determine the most effective application of effort and document the results.

- Provide direct support to CA units conducting emergency relocation operations of DCs and for operation of the DC camps.

- When conducted within the framework of a viable CMO concept, CA activities can contribute significantly to the overall success of PSYOP activities (deeds versus words).

PSYOP in Support of Unconventional Warfare

PSYOP units are a vital part of UW operations. When properly employed, coordinated, and integrated, they can significantly enhance the combat power of resistance forces. PSYOP specialists augmenting the Special Forces operational detachments (SFODs) can deploy into any joint special operations area (JSOA) and plan the themes, messages, media, and methods to be used, based on TA analysis. PSYOP in contemporary and future UW become more critical as ideological and resistance struggles increase. It is critical to understand that a temporary tactical advantage may create a long-term psychological disadvantage. All actions must be reviewed based upon their local, regional, or even international impact.

To maintain a common frame of reference, PSYOP planners and forces must use the same terminology used by the forces that they support. FM 3-05.20, *Special Forces Operations*, defines UW as a broad spectrum of military and paramilitary operations, predominantly conducted through, with, or by indigenous or surrogate forces organized, trained, equipped, supported, and directed in varying degrees by an external source. UW includes, but is not limited to, guerrilla warfare, subversion, sabotage, intelligence activities, and unconventional assisted recovery (UAR).

UNCONVENTIONAL WARFARE ASPECTS

J-1. The intent of U.S. UW operations is to exploit a hostile power's political, military, economic, and psychological vulnerability by developing and sustaining resistance forces to accomplish U.S. strategic objectives. FM 3-05.201, *Special Forces Unconventional Warfare Operations*, contains more detailed information.

J-2. UW includes the following interrelated activities:

- Guerrilla warfare is the overt military aspect of an insurgency.

- Sabotage selectively disrupts, destroys, or neutralizes hostile capabilities with a minimum of manpower and material resources.

- Subversion is any action designed to undermine the military, economic, psychological, political strength, or morale of a regime.

- Intelligence activities assess areas of interest ranging from political and military personalities to the military capabilities of friendly and enemy forces.

- UAR is a subset of nonconventional assisted recovery (NAR) conducted by SOF. UW forces conduct UAR operations to seek out, contact, authenticate, and support military and other selected personnel as they move from an enemy-held, hostile, or sensitive area to areas under friendly control.

PHASES OF A U.S.-SPONSORED INSURGENCY

J-3. There are seven phases of a U.S.-sponsored insurgency (Figure J-1). Although each insurgency is unique, U.S. sponsorship of a resistance organization generally passes through the seven phases. Each phase is discussed below.

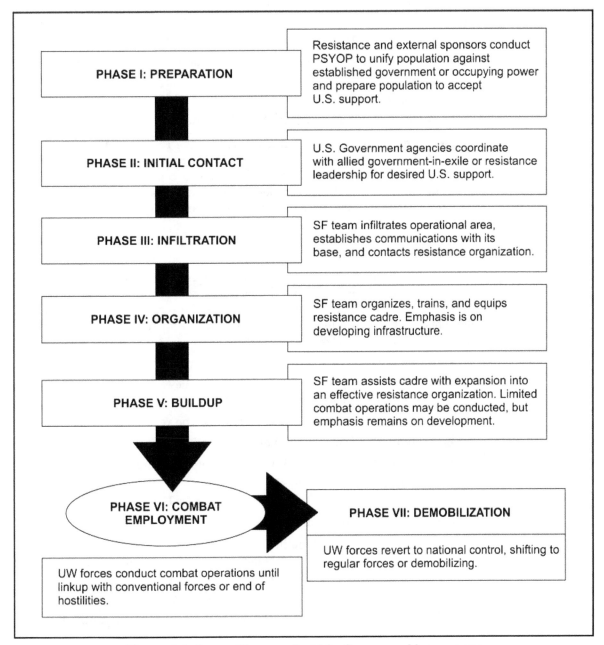

PHASE I: PREPARATION — Resistance and external sponsors conduct PSYOP to unify population against established government or occupying power and prepare population to accept U.S. support.

PHASE II: INITIAL CONTACT — U.S. Government agencies coordinate with allied government-in-exile or resistance leadership for desired U.S. support.

PHASE III: INFILTRATION — SF team infiltrates operational area, establishes communications with its base, and contacts resistance organization.

PHASE IV: ORGANIZATION — SF team organizes, trains, and equips resistance cadre. Emphasis is on developing infrastructure.

PHASE V: BUILDUP — SF team assists cadre with expansion into an effective resistance organization. Limited combat operations may be conducted, but emphasis remains on development.

PHASE VI: COMBAT EMPLOYMENT — UW forces conduct combat operations until linkup with conventional forces or end of hostilities.

PHASE VII: DEMOBILIZATION — UW forces revert to national control, shifting to regular forces or demobilizing.

Figure J-1. Seven Phases of a U.S.–Sponsored Insurgency

PHASE I: PREPARATION (FORMERLY CALLED PSYCHOLOGICAL PREPARATION)

J-4. The preparation phase includes PSYOP support. PSYOP units or other governmental organizations may prepare the resistance organization and civilians of a potential JSOA to accept U.S. sponsorship and the subsequent assistance of SFODs. The USG begins PSYOP as far in advance as possible and conducts PSYOP to unify the population against the established government or occupying power. PSYOP units prepare the resistance organization and the civilian population of a potential JSOA to accept U.S. sponsorship. Tasks to be accomplished include—

- Integration with OGAs and HN government leaders in exile.
- Development of a plan for the PSYOP mission.
- Coordination with OGAs and resistance movement on PSYOP messages and objectives.
- Production and approval of PSYOP programs.

J-5. During Phases II and III, it is critical for the PSYOP planner for the SF group to maintain constant communications with the PSE or POTF to ensure that critical information and staff work is being coordinated. This includes, but is not limited to, mission support for products, translation, requirements for SSD products, such as SPAs and SPSs, and requirements for Class A purchasing agents.

PHASE II: INITIAL CONTACT

J-6. Ideally, initial contact with the established or potential resistance movement should be made before committing SOF units. This procedure allows for an accurate assessment of the potential resistance in the JSOA and arranges for the reception and initial assistance of the infiltrated element. PSYOP objectives in a UW operation include—

- Creating popular support for the insurgency movement.
- Developing support of the populace to allow the insurgents to avoid detection and move freely.
- Promoting the recruitment of others into the resistance movement.
- Discrediting the existing government and its programs.
- Informing the international community of the goodwill and intent of the United States and insurgents.
- Gaining support of the indigenous populace for U.S. support and presence.
- Countering hostile propaganda.
- Training members of the indigenous population or force in PSYOP (TA analysis, local product development, targeting, dissemination, and analysis of impact indicators).
- Maintaining motivation among the insurgents.
- Passing information or instructions to the resistance organization or its subordinate elements.

- Providing a link between the resistance organization and foreign populations.
- Promoting reforms the insurgent organization will establish after the hostile government's overthrow.

J-7. Other USG agencies normally conduct the initial contact. During contact, SOF, including PSYOP personnel, assess the resistance potential in the AO and the compatibility of U.S. and resistance interests and objectives. This phase also allows assessment planners to make arrangements for the reception and initial assistance of the SFOD. The SOC should arrange to exfiltrate an asset from the AO to brief the staff and SFOD while in isolation. Under certain circumstances, a small, carefully selected "pilot team" composed of individuals possessing specialized skills may make initial contact. This team's mission is to assess designated areas to determine the feasibility of developing the resistance potential and to establish contact with indigenous leaders. Once the theater command or SOC has determined the feasibility of developing the area, additional SOF elements may be infiltrated. The pilot team may remain with the SFODs or be exfiltrated as directed.

J-8. During this phase, PSYOP units can select symbols and develop themes and programs that support the planned resistance operations. They can also prepare the local inhabitants to receive allied forces and actively assist in the UW mission to follow. PSYOP units begin targeting the enemy and resistance forces with the need to adhere to the law of war, highlighting enemy violations. PSYOP elements may begin establishing contact with indigenous leaders.

PHASE III: INFILTRATION

J-9. During the infiltration phase, the SFOD clandestinely or covertly infiltrates into the JSOA. After infiltration, the SFOD meets the resistance organization and moves to its secure area. Infiltration is not complete until the initial entry report is sent to the Special Forces operational base (SFOB) or forward operational base (FOB). The detachment submits the initial entry report as soon as possible upon infiltration. The report must be sent even if the SFOD does not contact the local resistance. Immediately upon infiltration, the SFOD begins a continuous area assessment to confirm or refute information received before infiltration. The detachment will continue to report all relevant operational information. If the mission warrants, selected PSYOP team members may infiltrate into the JSOA with the SF detachment. Otherwise, PSYOP team members support infiltration and subsequent phases as reachback assets from the SFOB or FOB.

PHASE IV: ORGANIZATION

J-10. The SFOD begins to establish rapport with the resistance leadership by showing an understanding of, confidence in, and concern for the resistance organization and its cause. The detachment explains its capabilities and limitations and begins to assist the resistance leadership with the development of the resistance organization. The SFOD must then prove its value in actual operations. Building rapport is a difficult and complicated process based on mutual trust, confidence, and understanding. It is not accomplished overnight.

J-11. Before a resistance organization can successfully engage in coordinated combat operations, the resistance leadership must organize an infrastructure that can sustain itself in combat and withstand the anticipated hostile reaction to armed resistance. During the organization phase, the resistance leadership develops a resistance cadre to serve as the organizational nucleus during the buildup phase. The SFOD assists the resistance leadership in conducting a cadre training program to prepare for the eventual buildup of the resistance organization.

J-12. The specifics of resistance organization depend on local conditions. UW requires centralized direction and decentralized execution under conditions that place great demands on the resistance organization and its leadership. Armed rebellion inherently creates an ambiguous and unstructured environment. No two resistance organizations need the same degree or level of organization. The SFOD commander should consider the following factors when advising the resistance leadership concerning organization:

- Effectiveness of existing resistance organization.
- Extent of cooperation between the resistance organization and the local populace.
- Hostile activity and security measures.
- Political boundaries, natural terrain features, potential targets, population density, and other characteristics of the JSOA.
- Religious, ethnic, political, and ideological differences among elements of the population and competing resistance organizations.
- Proposed type and scope of combat operations.
- Degree of U.S. influence with the resistance organization.

J-13. During the organization phase, PSYOP personnel can be used to promote the resistance movement's expansion and development by highlighting the enemy's weaknesses and countering the enemy's propaganda. PSYOP forces use themes to help the resistance organization influence attitudes and behavior to win the populace's support and promote recruitment. U.S. PSYOP elements can train the resistance in conducting basic, field-expedient PSYOP (graffiti). PSYOP programs can support damage control and assist the development of a sound infrastructure. Such programs contribute to the overall attainment of the resistance movement's goals. PSYOP programs can cover the resistance movement's political, economic, and social goals; the resistance movement cadre's ideological indoctrination; the practical impact of tactical operations on the population; and the significance of and need for the resistance member's proper personal conduct with the populace. PSYOP can assist CA team members when they assess the effect of the organization efforts on the political, economic, information (social and cultural), and humanitarian aspects of the JSOA.

PHASE V: BUILDUP

J-14. The buildup phase involves expanding the resistance elements and their activities. Their tasks include infiltration or procurement of equipment and supplies to support the expansion and subsequent combat operations. During the buildup phase, the resistance cadre expands into an effective organization that can conduct combat operations. Recruitment increases due to successful missions. Guerrilla force missions and tactics dictate a simple, mobile, and flexible organization capable of rapid dispersion and consolidation in response to the tactical situation. Each unit must be self-contained with its own intelligence, communications, and logistics systems.

J-15. In this phase, PSYOP units can be used to focus on the resistance movement's full expansion and development. PSYOP programs enhance the resistance leadership's legitimacy and effectiveness, emphasize the ROE, and identify targets whose destruction would impact adversely on the civilian populace. PSYOP programs highlight the government's actions taken against the population during its counterinsurgency campaign. PSYOP units can promote the uncommitted population's support for the insurgency and counter the enemy's propaganda. PSYOP units continue to capitalize, promote, and assure the success of the resistance movement and allied operations. They can assist the SFOD in training insurgent military forces in PSYOP activities. PSYOP units begin focusing on planning posthostilities transition operations, to include training potential members of the post-hostilities infrastructure separately and concurrently with the guerrilla force.

J-16. Although PSYOP teams can be infiltrated during Phase III with the SFODA teams, it is more realistic for the TPTs that are attached to the SFODB teams to go forward with the B teams once the FOB has been established in the AO.

PHASE VI: COMBAT EMPLOYMENT

J-17. Combat operations increase in scope and size to support the objectives of the area command. During the combat employment phase, the resistance organization conducts combat operations to achieve its strategic politico-military objectives. The SFOD ensures that resistance activities continue to support the goals of the area command. Interdiction is the basic UW combat activity. These operations can drain the hostile power's morale and resources, disrupt its administration, and maintain the civilian population's morale and will to resist. Each target should contribute to destroying or neutralizing an entire target system.

J-18. In this phase, PSYOP units can exploit successful combat operations to attract more recruits. They focus on themes and symbols of nationalism, success, and inevitability of complete victory. PSYOP units can also induce enemy defections or noncompliance with orders. They continue targeting the population to increase their support for the insurgency, the allied forces, and the eventual follow-on government. PSYOP units can assist in controlling or directing the DC flow to facilitate the movement of combat forces and to minimize casualties. They continue to counter the enemy's propaganda.

PHASE VII: DEMOBILIZATION

J-19. Demobilization is the last, most important, and most difficult phase of UW operations. Demobilization planning begins when the USG decides to sponsor a resistance organization and ends in the JSOA (start to end state). Civilian USG agencies, along with international organizations and agencies, such as the UN and the Organization of American States (OAS), normally conduct demobilization of the military groups. SF, PSYOP, and CA units help these agencies conduct demobilization using their knowledge of the terrain and the forces within the JSOA. The manner in which demobilization occurs will affect the postwar attitudes of the people and the government toward the United States. The greatest demobilization danger is the possibility that former resistance members may resort to subversion of the new government, factional disputes, or banditry. The new government brings arms and ammunition under its control to ensure public security and to return to a functional civil structure based on the rule of law. It helps resistance forces return to previous occupations and may integrate them into the new reconstituted national army. The new government must make every effort to reorient former resistance members into a peaceful society and gain their trust.

J-20. PSYOP units help explain the demobilization process and promote the insurgent's orderly transition to peaceful civilian life. Their primary aim is to prevent the formation of groups opposing the recognized government. Maintaining loyalty to the legitimate (newly established) government is the major concern. PSYOP units also conduct many direct and indirect activities that assist the new government's demobilization effort. These include—

- Helping to secure LOCs.
- Controlling rumors by publishing and broadcasting the news.
- Assisting the marshalling of available labor.
- Supporting the establishment of law and order.
- Continuing to assist controlling DCs by directing them to available assistance.

J-21. During this transition of operations from military to indigenous authority, as well as from former to new regime, PSYOP personnel can perform various roles in support to CA and civil administration. They support the conduct of DC operations.

J-22. The primary concern in any demobilization program is the guerrilla. His personal and political motives vary. The resistance organization can include peasants, laborers, bandits, criminals, merchants, and a few social and intellectual leaders. During the conflict, some guerrillas may have achieved status and leadership positions that they are now reluctant to relinquish. Others may have found adventure in combat that they would not now trade for peace or prosperity. Hostile groups may have clandestinely infiltrated the guerrilla force to continue their own personal or political agenda. They may take advantage of the demobilization program to organize paramilitary or political groups that will be in conflict with the new provisional government or U.S. authorities. It is imperative that demobilization programs and procedures be executed quickly and with major political support. The programs and procedures begun are a direct result of decisions made by high-level civilian and military authorities. Their successful implementation requires maximum effort and coordination among SF, CA, and PSYOP.

J-23. Traditionally, SOF will remain in their AO because of their knowledge and history of the guerrilla forces to assist in demobilization. This assistance will most likely include the PSYOP team with the SFOD. SFOD commanders and their supporting PSYOP elements ensure transfer of U.S. responsibility without loss of control, influence, or property accountability. The key to long-term strategic success in UW is planning and executing postmission responsibilities.

J-24. PSYOP elements can psychologically prepare the resistance organization to assume whatever roles the legal government wants it to play. These roles include, but are not limited to, their incorporation into the national army, paramilitary organizations, national police, or demobilization.

J-25. PSYOP programs explain the demobilization process. They promote the insurgents' orderly transition to peaceful civilian life. PSYOP personnel attempt to prevent the formation of quasi-military or political groups opposing the recognized government. Loyalty to the legitimate government is the major concern.

TARGET AUDIENCES

J-26. PSYOP usually involve several major TA categories in a JSOA. Each of these is discussed in the following paragraphs.

ENEMY FORCES

J-27. These elements may represent the government forces, an occupying power, or one assisting the hostile government and may be of the same nationality as the local populace. In any case, PSYOP personnel wage programs against the members of the enemy forces to make them feel isolated and improperly supported, doubtful of the outcome of their struggle, distrustful of each other, and unsure of the morality of their cause.

ENEMY SYMPATHIZERS

J-28. This TA consists of civilians in an operational area who are willing enemy collaborators, unwilling enemy collaborators (will collaborate under duress), and passive enemy sympathizers. The goal of a PSYOP program aimed at this group is to identify and discredit the enemy collaborators and to weaken their belief in the enemy's military strength and power.

THE UNCOMMITTED

J-29. These members of the general population are neutral during the initial stage of hostilities or resistance movements. They may fear the aims of the movement or are uncertain of its success. To win over the uncommitted, PSYOP personnel must stress that the resistance shares and fights for the political and social goals of the population. The United States and its allies, in backing the resistance movement, support these same goals to ensure the resistance movement will be successful.

RESISTANCE SYMPATHIZERS

J-30. This TA includes civilians and government, military, or paramilitary members who support the goals of the movement but who are not active members of the resistance force. PSYOP directed at this TA stress themes that encourage the populace to support actively (though generally covertly) or cooperate passively with the resistance force in achieving common goals.

These appeals ensure that the people, their sensitivities, culture, customs, and needs are respected. PSYOP advisors and the SFODs with whom they work exploit PSYOP opportunities. The PSYOP teams attached to the SFOD help convince the guerrillas to conduct operations that create popular support for the resistance movement, both in and out of the JSOA. Indigenous personnel are trained in the effective conduct of PSYOP and then integrated into the political infrastructure and guerrilla forces. These forces then conduct PSYOP in support of the needs of the area commander. Those needs should relate to the goals of the unified commander, specific situation, or UW mission. Through face-to-face meetings with local indigenous leaders, SFOD and PSYOP personnel strengthen mutual respect, confidence, and trust. They also gain valuable insight into the guerrilla force's problems and gain rapport by sharing the same living and fighting conditions.

OTHER SUPPORT MISSIONS

J-31. In UW, the auxiliary is that element of the resistance force established to provide the organized civilian support of the resistance movement. The auxiliary employs populace and resources control (PRC) measures to minimize or eliminate black marketing and profiteering and to demonstrate to the enemy the power of the guerrilla movement. The auxiliary may use subtle coercion or other stricter means to control collaborators. PRC consists of two distinct, but related, concepts—populace control and resources control.

POPULACE CONTROL

J-32. Populace controls provide security for the populace, mobilize human resources, deny personnel to the enemy, and detect and reduce the effectiveness of enemy agents. Populace control measures include curfews, movement restrictions, travel permits, registration cards, and resettlement of villagers. DC operations and NEO are two special categories of populace control that require extensive planning and coordination among various military and nonmilitary organizations.

RESOURCES CONTROL

J-33. Resources controls regulate the movement or consumption of materiel resources, mobilize materiel resources, and deny materiel to the enemy. Resources control measures include licensing, regulations or guidelines, checkpoints (for example, roadblocks), ration controls, amnesty programs, and inspection of facilities.

BASIC TRAINING

J-34. METT-TC determines the need for base camps within the JSOA. All guerrillas may receive basic training, including the area command. Each base camp may conduct its basic training in sectors independent of the other two, or it may conduct a part of basic training and rotate to another camp for more training. Either the SFOD and PSYOP personnel or guerrillas may rotate. Basic training contains subjects on small arms, first aid, land navigation, and political or PSYOP classes. The time allotted for training needs to be flexible—between 21 and 31 days, depending on the knowledge and abilities of the force.

LINKUP OPERATIONS

J-35. The JSOA commander plans and coordinates linkup operations if the JSOA is coming under the OPCON of a conventional force. A physical juncture is necessary between the conventional and guerrilla forces. The mission of the conventional force may require SF and guerrilla force personnel to support conventional combat operations. The conventional force commander, in coordination with the SFOB, prepares an OPLAN and synchronizes PSYOP programs to simplify the linkup of forces within the JSOA. The senior PSYOP commander at the conventional force HQ plans PSYOP activities and programs to support the linkup of the resistance movement with conventional operations.

PHYSICAL LINKUP

J-36. Normally, a joint or allied force uses a physical linkup when operating in the JSOA. A physical linkup is difficult to plan, conduct, and control. It requires detailed, centralized coordination and a planning conference between those involved. Commanders conduct physical linkups for the following reasons:

- Joint tactical operations.
- Resupply and logistic operations.
- Intelligence operations.
- Exfiltration of sick, wounded, and recovered U.S. and indigenous personnel.
- Exfiltration of very important persons and EPWs.
- Infiltration of U.S. and indigenous personnel.
- Transfer of guides and liaison personnel to the conventional forces.

NONPHYSICAL LINKUP

J-37. Forces must establish a nonphysical linkup when operations are conducted in a JSOA and a physical linkup is not required or desirable. A nonphysical linkup also requires coordination between the linkup forces. Commanders must state procedures before operations begin and when joint communications are established. Commanders use nonphysical linkups when the conventional force conducts a deep raid and guerrillas conduct security missions. They also use these linkups when the conventional force attacks and guerrillas—

- Serve as a blocking force.
- Screen flanks and block threats.
- Conduct deception operations.
- Conduct reconnaissance or surveillance.

PSYOP personnel can assist by—

- Supporting defector programs.
- Preparing the civilian population to cooperate fully with the conventional tactical forces.

- Briefing the resistance organization's leaders on the importance of cooperating with the tactical force commanders and accepting the conventional force leadership during linkup.
- Urging the civilian population to remain in place and not hinder operations.

Leaflet Operations

This appendix describes leaflet dissemination operations and calculations from air platforms. Included are techniques for leaflet packing, calculations, plotting, and mission planning requirements for actual and training missions with dissemination aircraft.

GENERAL

K-1. Leaflet dissemination planning must be done after target analysis. The target analysis will determine the suitability of leaflet drops, the appropriate density on the ground, and the frequency of delivery. For example, a target analysis determined that there are few literate people in a town being targeted. The social structure is such that there are fewer than ten key communicators who make up the leadership. In this situation, only a few leaflets would be necessary. Leaflet density per 100 square meters would be appropriate at the minimum of 10 because the inhabitants of the village would take them to the leadership or to the few members who could read.

K-2. In preparation, the best size and weight for the leaflets should be determined. The content has no effect on the dissemination, but the size and weight are critical elements in determining the leaflets' ballistic data. If the mission dictates a leaflet characteristic that is not listed, personnel should choose the closest size and weight.

K-3. Successful leaflet-drop missions depend on an understanding of the behavior of leaflets falling through the air. Once released, leaflets are subject to drift and diffusion. Drift is the movement of the center of the leaflet cloud. Diffusion is the spread of the leaflets caused by wind turbulence and the ballistic characteristic of the leaflet. Identical leaflets do not fall at an identical rate. Individual differences between the leaflets and variations in the air cause identical leaflets to fall at slightly different rates. This creates a cloud that is taller than it is wide making an oblong pattern on the ground (Figure K-1, page K-2). Plotting the ground pattern is essential to ensure that the target area is completely covered. Multiple release points may be required.

K-4. Leaflets can be dropped from several different platforms, such as the C-130, F-16, and A-10. All three aircraft are certified to drop leaflets. The USAF and USN have a variety of airdrop aircraft capable of performing M129/PDU-5/B leaflet bomb missions. The new leaflet bomb (PDU-5/B) (steel-shell canister type) can be dropped by fast movers; M129 leaflet bombs (fiberglass type) may break apart during high-speed turns of fast movers. The C-130 uses the static-line-box drop method to disseminate leaflets.

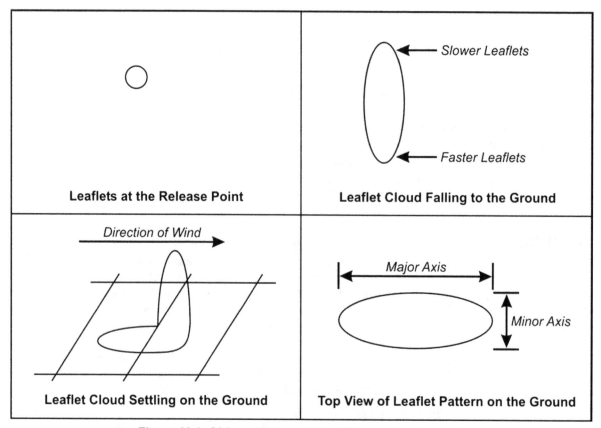

Figure K-1. Oblong Pattern of Leaflets on the Ground

MISSION PLANNING FACTORS

K-5. The following information must be known before any of the calculations are done, to aid the planner in determining the release point, proper dissemination pattern, and leaflet density:

- Density desired (10 to 30 leaflets per 100 square meters, depending on terrain and population of target area).
- Size and weight of the leaflet being used (needed for the appropriate descent and spread factors).
- Type of platform.
- Location of the target.
- Size of the target.
- Wind speed and azimuth around the target area in 1,000-foot increments below 10,000 feet and 2,000-foot increments above 10,000 feet.

K-6. At least 48 hours prior to dissemination, coordination must be effected through a mission planning meeting with the aircrews flying the mission. On the day of the mission, the mission planner from the POTF or PSE must meet with the aircrews to go over last minute data.

PLOTTING

K-7. The following items are needed:

- Pencil.
- Protractor (a navigation plotter works well for this and as a scale ruler).
- Map (preferably 1/100,000).
- Leaflet calculation worksheet.
- Tables with rates of descent, leaflet spread factors, and descent time factors.
- Calculator.
- Scale ruler.
- Overlay paper or acetate.
- Current weather data from the staff weather officer (SWO).

Step 1

K-8. The first step in the leaflet drop calculation is to determine the size of the leaflet and the weight of the paper being used, which have a direct influence on how the leaflets will fly. Personnel fill in the information on the top of the leaflet work sheet (Figure K-2, pages K-3 and K-4).

1. Mission Data:
   a. Mission number _____   d. Release coordinates _____
   b. Product number _____   e. Target altitude _____
   c. Release altitude _____ f. Target coordinates _____

2. Leaflet Data:
   a. Size _____   e. Spread factor _____
   b. Paper weight _____ f. Leaflets per pound _____
   c. Autorotator? yes no   g. Number of pounds _____
   d. Rate of descent _____ h. Number in mission _____
                              (multiply f. by g.)

3. Descent Data:

Altitude (k = 1000)	Descent Time Factor	x	Wind Speed (in Knots [kt])	=	Drift Distance (in Nautical Miles [NM])	@	Wind Azimuth (in Grid)
25k	_____	x	_____	=	_____	@	_____
23k	_____	x	_____	=	_____	@	_____
20k	_____	x	_____	=	_____	@	_____
18k	_____	x	_____	=	_____	@	_____
16k	_____	x	_____	=	_____	@	_____
14k	_____	x	_____	=	_____	@	_____

Figure K-2. Example of Leaflet Calculation Work Sheet

Altitude (k = 1000)	Descent Time Factor	x	Wind Speed (in kt)	=	Drift Distance (in NM)	@	Wind Azimuth (in Grid)
12k	_____	x	_____	=	_____	@	_____
10k	_____	x	_____	=	_____	@	_____
9k	_____	x	_____	=	_____	@	_____
8k	_____	x	_____	=	_____	@	_____
7k	_____	x	_____	=	_____	@	_____
6k	_____	x	_____	=	_____	@	_____
5k	_____	x	_____	=	_____	@	_____
4k	_____	x	_____	=	_____	@	_____
3k	_____	x	_____	=	_____	@	_____
2k	_____	x	_____	=	_____	@	_____
1k	_____	x	_____	=	_____	@	_____
Surface	_____	x	_____	=	_____	@	_____

4. Total Drift Distance _____ NM

   sum of Drift Distance column

5. Maximum Deviation _____ NM

   furthest distance from the net drift azimuth

6. Major Axis _____ NM

   .5 x release altitude / 6076.115 + total drift x spread factor = NM

7. Minor Axis _____ NM

   .5 x release altitude / 6076.115 + maximum deviation x spread factor = NM

8. Area in Square (sq) NM _____ sq NM

   .785 x minor axis x major axis = sq NM

9. Mean Density per sq NM _____

   number of leaflets (item 2.h) / sq NM (item 8.) = mean density

10. Density per 100 Meters Square _____

Figure K-2. Example of Leaflet Calculation Work Sheet (Continued)

Step 2

K-9. Personnel determine the rate of descent and spread factor from Table K-1, page K-5, based on the size and weight of the leaflet. They fill in the information at the top of the work sheet.

Example: Using a 6- x 3-inch leaflet of 20-pound paper, the rate of descent is 2.5, the spread factor is 1.11, and the leaflet autorotates.

Step 3

K-10. Using the leaflet descent time factor tables (Tables K-1 through K-4, pages K-5 through K-7), personnel write the time factors for each altitude from the surface to the projected release point making sure to use the autorotating or non-autorotating table as appropriate. Using the wind data that the SWO provided, personnel write the wind speeds (in knots) in the wind speed column of the work sheet so they coincide with the altitudes that are in the first column. Personnel must change the wind directions provided by the SWO from magnetic to grid azimuths and place them in the azimuth (AZ) column of the work sheet.

Table K-1. Standard Leaflet Rates of Descent and Spread Factor

Paper Size (in Inches)	Paper Weight (in Pounds)				
	9	13	16	20	60
8.5 x 8.5	2.9 0.24	2.5 0.31	2.7 0.26	2.8 0.35	
8.5 x 4.25	2.7 0.20	3.4 0.25	3.8 0.68	5.2 0.71	
8.5 x 3.09	3.0 0.15	3.2 0.15	3.6 0.65	1.9 0.42	
7.5 x 3				1.8 0.51	
6 x 4	2.3 0.26	2.7 0.37	3.3 0.63	4.0 0.46	
6 x 3	3.1 0.48	3.6 0.89	4.7 1.04	2.5 1.11	1.8 0.54
6 x 2	2.3 0.67	1.3 0.59	1.6 0.36	1.7 0.22	
6 x 1.5	1.8 0.30	1.5 0.09	2.1 0.17	2.1 0.22	
4 x 4	2.0 0.31	2.2 0.12	2.4 0.20	2.6 0.19	
4 x 3.2	2.2 0.18	2.4 0.12	2.6 0.11	3.0 0.16	
4 x 2.67	2.2 0.30	2.6 0.13	2.8 0.20	3.1 0.16	
4 x 2	2.1 0.13	1.8 0.27	1.5 0.05	1.7 0.05	
4 x 1.6	1.3 0.56	1.3 0.16	1.4 0.23	1.7 0.05	
4 x 1.23	1.3 0.24	1.5 0.34	1.6 0.28	1.6 0.65	
4x1	1.3 0.18	1.6 0.50	1.9 0.63	2.1 0.54	

NOTES: 1. The first number is the rate of descent; the second number is the spread factor.

2. Underlined numbers are leaflets that autorotate.

Table K-2. Standard Leaflets per Pound

Paper Size (in Inches)	Paper Weight (in Pounds)				
	9	13	16	20	60
8.5 x 8.5	288	199	162	129	
8.5 x 4.25	575	398	324	259	
8.5 x 3.09	791	548	445	356	
7.5 x 3				416	
6 x 4	866	599	487	390	
6 x 3	1,154	799	649	519	440
6 x 2	1,731	1,199	974	779	
6 x 1.5	2,309	1,598	1,299	1,039	
4 x 4	1,299	899	730	584	
4x3.2	1,623	1,124	913	730	
4x2.67	1,948	1,349	1,096	877	
4x2	2,597	1,798	1,461	1,169	
4x1.6	3,247	2,248	1,826	1,461	
4x1.23	4,220	2,922	2,374	1,899	
4x1	5,194	3,596	2,922	2,338	

NOTE: Underlined numbers are leaflets that autorotate.

Table K-3. Autorotating Leaflet Descent Time Factors

Autorotating Descent Rate	Thousands of Feet																	
	Surface	1	2	3	4	5	6	7	8	9	10	12	14	16	18	20	23	25
1.3	.11	.21	.21	.21	.21	.20	.20	.20	.20	.19	.28	.37	.35	.34	.33	.39	.37	.48
1.4	.10	.20	.20	.19	.19	.19	.19	.18	.18	.18	.26	.34	.33	.32	.30	.36	.34	
1.5	.09	.18	.18	.18	.18	.18	.17	.17	.17	.17	.24	.32	.31	.29	.28	.34	.32	.42
1.6	.09	.17	.17	.17	.17	.17	.16	.16	.16	.16	.23	.30	.29	.28	.27	.32	.30	.40
1.7	.08	.16	.16	.16	.16	.16	.15	.15	.15	.15	.21	.28	.27	.26	.25	.30	.28	.37
1.8	.08	.15	.15	.15	.15	.15	.14	.14	.14	.14	.20	.26	.25	.25	.24	.28	.27	.35
1.9	.07	.15	.14	.14	.14	.14	.14	.14	.13	.13	.19	.25	.24	.23	.22	.27	.25	.33
2.1	.07	.13	.13	.13	.13	.12	.12	.12	.12	.12	.17	.23	.22	.21	.20	.24	.23	.30
2.3	.06	.12	.12	.12	.12	.12	.11	.11	.11	.11	.16	.21	.20	.19	.18	.22	.21	.27
2.5	.06	.11	.11	.11	.11	.11	.10	.10	.10	.10	.10	.15	.19	.18	.18	.17	.20	.19
2.0	.05	.14	.14	.14	.14	.13	.13	.13	.13	.13	.19	.25	.24	.23	.22	.26	.24	.31
2.1	.05	.13	.13	.13	.13	.13	.13	.13	.12	.12	.18	.24	.23	.22	.21	.25	.23	.30
2.2	.04	.13	.12	.12	.12	.12	.12	.12	.12	.12	.10	.22	.22	.21	.20	.24	.22	.28
2.3	.04	.12	.12	.12	.12	.12	.12	.11	.11	.11	.17	.21	.21	.20	.19	.23	.21	.27
2.4	.04	.12	.11	.11	.11	.11	.11	.11	.11	.11	.16	.21	.20	.19	.18	.22	.20	.26
2.5	.04	.11	.11	.11	.11	.11	.11	.11	.10	.10	.15	.20	.19	.18	.18	.21	.19	.25
2.6	.04	.11	.11	.11	.10	.10	.10	.10	.10	.10	.15	.19	.18	.18	.17	.20	.19	.24
2.7	.04	.10	.10	.10	.10	.10	.10	.10	.10	.10	.14	.18	.18	.17	.16	.19	.18	.23
2.8	.03	.10	.10	.10	.10	.10	.10	.09	.09	.09	.14	.18	.17	.16	.16	.19	.17	.22
2.9	.03	.10	.09	.09	.09	.09	.09	.09	.09	.09	.13	.17	.16	.16	.15	.18	.17	.22

Table K-4. Non-Autorotating Leaflet Descent Time Factors

Non-Autorotating Descent Rate	Thousands of Feet																			
	Surface	1	2	3	4	5	6	7	8	9	10	12	14	16	18	20	23	25
3.0	.03	.09	.09	.09	.09	.09	.09	.09	.09	.09	.13	.16	.16	.15	.15	.17	.16	.21
3.1	.03	.09	.09	.09	.09	.09	.09	.09	.08	.08	.12	.16	.15	.15	.14	.17	.16	.20
3.2	.03	.09	.09	.09	.09	.08	.08	.08	.08	.08	.12	.15	.15	.14	.14	.16	.15	.20
3.3	.03	.08	.08	.08	.08	.08	.08	.08	.08	.08	.12	.15	.14	.14	.13	.16	.15	.19
3.4	.03	.08	.08	.08	.08	.08	.08	.08	.08	.08	.11	.15	.14	.13	.13	.15	.14	.18
3.6	.03	.08	.08	.08	.08	.07	.07	.07	.07	.07	.11	.14	.13	.13	.12	.14	.14	.17
3.8	.03	.07	.07	.07	.07	.07	.07	.07	.07	.07	.10	.13	.13	.12	.12	.14	.13	.16
4.0	.02	.07	.07	.07	.07	.07	.07	.07	.07	.06	.10	.12	.12	.11	.11	.13	.12	.16
4.7	.02	.06	.06	.06	.06	.06	.06	.06	.05	.08	.11	.10	.10	.09	.11	.10	.13	.17
5.2	Data not available																	

Step 4

K-11. To determine the drift in nautical miles, personnel should multiply the descent time factor by the wind speed at each altitude. The drift identifies how far the leaflets will move laterally through that altitude.

Example: (This information is used for all following examples.)

Altitude	Descent Time Factor	Wind Speed	Drift (NM)	at	AZ (degrees)
Surface	.06	5 kt	.30	at	180
1,000 feet	.11	7 kt	.77	at	196
2,000 feet	.11	10 kt	1.1	at	210

Total drift = 2.17

Step 5

K-12. Personnel start at the center of the target on a map. The USAF provides wind azimuths for the direction the wind is coming from, so when plotting from the surface up, it is not necessary to calculate back azimuths. Using the example, personnel start with the surface drift distance (.30) and azimuth (180). Using the protractor or plotter, personnel mark a 180-degree line from their starting point. They use the scale ruler or plotter and mark a point .30 nautical miles away from the center point along the 180-degree azimuth. Next, they mark a 196-degree line from the last point they marked. Personnel measure .77 nautical miles along this azimuth, and plot the 2,000-foot drift distance. The path of the leaflet cloud is shown in the example in Figure K-3, page K-8.

Step 6

K-13. The maximum deviation is the greatest distance between the net drift line and the actual flight pattern of the leaflets. The maximum deviation line shows how far the leaflets will stray from the net drift line and is used to determine the minor axis of the ground pattern. In the example (Figure K-3), the maximum deviation is 1.02 nautical miles.

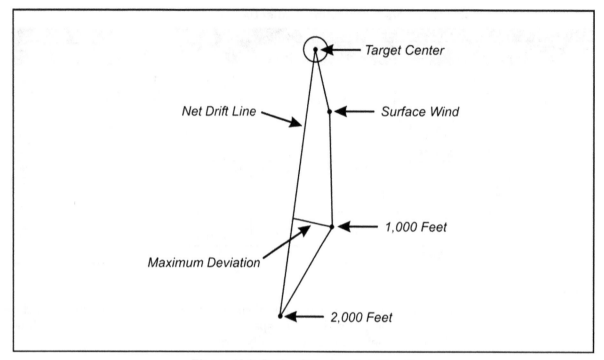

Figure K-3. Path of the Leaflet Cloud

Step 7

K-14. Personnel determine the major axis. The major axis is the long axis that follows the leaflet path. It is calculated by using this formula: .5 (release altitude) / 6076.115 + (total drift) spread factor = NM. The total drift distance for this example is 2.17 NM; 6076.115 is used to convert feet to nautical miles.

Example:

Release Altitude	+	(Total Drift) Spread Factor	=	NM
.5 (2000) / 6076.115	+	(.3 + .77 + 1.1) 1.11	=	2.565
1000 / 6076.115	+	(.3 + .77 + 1.1) 1.11	=	2.565
0.165	+	(.3 + .77 + 1.1) 1.11	=	2.565
0.165	+	**(2.17)** 1.11	=	2.565
0.165	+	**2.4**	=	2.565 NM

Step 8

K-15. Personnel determine the minor axis. The minor axis is the greatest width of the short axis of the leaflet pattern. It is calculated similarly to the major axis. The only difference is that the maximum deviation distance is substituted for the total drift distance. The minor axis is calculated by using this formula: .5 (release altitude) / 6076.115 + (maximum deviation) spread factor = NM. It is plotted by taking the total from the formula and plotting it perpendicular to the major axis and over the target area. The maximum deviation for this example is 1.02 NM. Figure K-4 shows the final pattern in which 90 percent of the leaflets will land.

Example:

Release Altitude	+	(Maximum Deviation) Spread Factor	=	NM
.5 (2000) / 6076.115	+	(1.02) 1.11	=	1.297
1000 / 6076.115	+	(1.02) 1.11	=	1.297
0.165	+	(1.02) 1.11	=	1.297
0.165	+	1.132	=	1.297

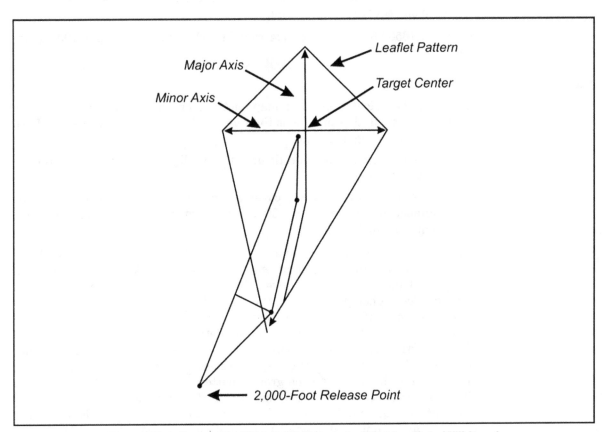

Figure K-4. Pattern in Which 90 Percent of the Leaflets Will Land

Step 9

K-16. The final steps show if the leaflet density coincides with the commander's intent of 10 to 30 leaflets per 100 square meters. First, personnel determine the area of the leaflet pattern on the ground. The formula to determine the area is .785 (major axis) minor axis = NM; .785 is used to calculate an ellipse and is π (pi, or 3.14) divided by 4.

Example: .785 (2.565) 1.297 = 2.612 NM

Step 10

K-17. Personnel determine the mean density per square nautical mile. For this formula, the area of the pattern (2.612) must be used. The formula is number of leaflets / area = leaflets per nautical mile.

Example: 20,000 / 2.612 = 7656.968 leaflets per NM

Step 11

K-18. Personnel determine the density per 100 square meters. This portion tells the commander if the 10 to 30 leaflet requirements are met. Using the mean density (7656.968), the formula is mean density / 343 = leaflets per 100 square meters. Personnel should note that there are 343 units of 100 square meters in one square nautical mile.

Example: 7656.968 / 343 = 22.324 rounded off to 22 leaflets per 100 square meters

Step 12

K-19. All the calculations and map plotting are now completed. The key point in the calculation process is the release altitude. The plotter should ask himself the following questions:

- Does the release altitude fit in with the flight requirements of the air platform being used?
- Does the ground pattern cover the desired target area and does the number of leaflets per 100 square meters meet the commander's requirements?

K-20. If these questions are answered with a "yes," the mission should be successful. If not, there are some ways to meet the mission requirements. If the ground pattern does not cover the target, personnel should go up in altitude. The higher the altitude, the larger the area covered. If the number of leaflets per 100 square meters is not enough, two things can be considered—increase the number of leaflets being dropped or lower the altitude of the drop. If the leaflets per 100 square meters are over the limit, personnel should stay with the original release point using fewer leaflets or go up in altitude and make the ground pattern larger. Before the altitude is changed, personnel must ensure that the air planners and pilots are informed and that they agree to the change in altitude. Figure K-2, pages K-3 and K-4, provides an example of a leaflet calculation work sheet used for leaflet dissemination planning.

K-21. Attention must be paid to the possibility of violating sovereign international boundaries during leaflet operations. Notification and coordination must be made whenever there is potential that either aircraft or leaflets may cross into or land in a third country.

AIRCRAFT

K-22. Most DOD fixed- and rotary-wing platforms can be used to disseminate leaflets. Leaflets can be disseminated by hand, trash bag, leaflet box, and leaflet bomb, depending on the aircraft type and tactical situation.

K-23. The C-130 is used when there is minimal threat in the area and the airplane can fly at low altitudes. This is beneficial because the lower the drop, the less effect wind gusts will have on the flight of the leaflet. The C-130 has the ability to carry well over 1 million leaflets in 20 boxes. When dropping leaflets out of a C-130, a PSYOP NCO or officer should be on board in case the winds shift in flight and last minute calculations are needed to determine a new release point. 81Ls may also be required to help the loadmaster in the responsibilities of hooking and kicking the boxes out of the airplane. The airplane should fly at about 190 knots when the leaflets are kicked out. Anything faster causes the leaflets to get sucked back into the airplane. The aircraft commander determines the speed, so he should be made aware of speed requirements. The release altitude on a C-130 drop is always left up to the pilots flying the mission. They know the safety issues of the aircraft and the current intelligence and air threat from the target area. In the meeting 48 hours out, the OIC/NCOIC of the leaflet mission should discuss what the optimum altitude should be with the navigator. They should determine a "no higher than" and a "no lower than" limit. Once these altitudes are determined, they can be used for planning purposes. The actual altitude will not be known until the winds are determined for the actual day of the drop. On the mission day, the altitude that suits the required leaflet coverage is used.

K-24. Aircraft, such as the F-16, A-10, and F/A-18, will be used when the target is in a higher threat area and the airplanes must fly at higher altitudes to avoid air defenses. This does not affect the leaflet planning directly because these aircraft drop either the M129 or PDU-5/B leaflet bombs. This means the aircraft can fly at any altitude desired to avoid the threat, and the leaflet bomb can be detonated at any altitude that the leaflet OIC and aircraft commander determine will give the proper target coverage. In planning the F-16, A-10, or F/A-18 drop, an important fact to know is that the leaflet bombs can be stored after they have been packed, and the fuse does not have to be set until it is loaded onto the airplane. This is helpful to the leaflet OIC and the 81Ls involved in the mission. The personnel can pack the bomb as soon as the leaflets are printed and do not have to wait until the day of the mission, as long as they mark the bomb with paint using the leaflet number, the target desired, and the number of leaflets packed. Once the fuse is set and the airplanes are off the ground, the fuse cannot be reset—if the winds change in flight, the distance the bomb travels before detonation cannot be changed. For example, if the pilot flies 10 nautical miles away from the detonation point, then the release point must remain 10 nautical miles away. The release point needs to move either to a higher altitude that is closer, or to that lower altitude that is farther away. The leaflet OIC must be at the flight squadron's HQ so that the pilots can radio back current wind data and the OIC can recalculate, if necessary.

K-25. Rotary-wing aircraft, such as the CH-47, UH-60, and others, can be used to disseminate leaflets. Leaflet boxes, trash bags, and simply tossing leaflets out by hand are some common dissemination methods used. In some cases, the aircrew will not allow static-line leaflet boxes to be used because of the risk of the boxes (after deployment) being sucked up into the rotors due to the rotor wash. Personnel should check with the aircrew or liaison prior to mission execution. Trash bags are a very effective means of dissemination.

This method alleviates the risk of anything attached to the aircraft coming into contact with the rotors. To use this method, personnel should—

- Untie the opening of the trash bag.
- With one hand on the opening, push forward with the other hand from the bottom toward the opening, turning the trash bag inside out.
- Once emptied, secure the trash bag out of the way and continue.

PDU-5/B LEAFLET DELIVERY SYSTEM

K-26. The PDU-5/B leaflet bomb (SUU-76C/B without leaflet payload) is a demilitarized Mk-7 munitions dispenser canister with tail cone. It is 95 inches long and weighs approximately 140 pounds, with an interior diameter of 11 inches and a maximum carrying capacity of 152 pounds.

Procedures for Making Leaflet Rolls

K-27. Before making leaflet rolls, personnel ensure that they inspect all equipment for serviceability:

- 1 x packing ring (11 inches in diameter, 4 inches tall).
- 3 x steel banding rings (1 x 29 inches, 1 x 18 inches, 1 x 15 inches).

Personnel ensure that the packing ring is free from any major dents and still holds a circular shape when placed on a flat surface. Also, personnel ensure that steel banding rings are not warped and bent. They should be rigid enough to hold leaflets in place, but not so stiff that they cannot be deflected (Figure K-5).

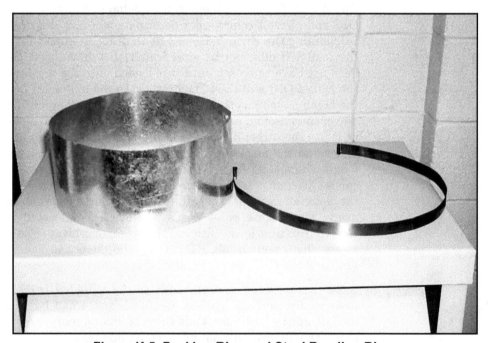

Figure K-5. Packing Ring and Steel Banding Ring

K-28. Other equipment needed includes the following:

- 3-Inch brown box tape.

- Any type of adhesive tape.

- Scale.

NOTE: The PSYOP dissemination team on-site should already have the packing rings and steel banding rings. If personnel are deploying to a place without a dissemination team already in place, they must be sure to bring these items with them. If this is not possible, they should follow the instructions below on how to create the packing ring and steel banding rings.

K-29. A packing ring can be made using any material that is sturdy enough not to collapse in on itself when stood up. Sheet metal is the preferred material; however, stiff plastic or other materials can also be used. Its dimensions should be cut so that when formed into a circle, the circle's diameter is 11 inches, and it stands anywhere from 3 to 4 inches tall. The securing of the metal band to itself can be done using any means available, so long as it does not interfere with the rolling of leaflets in the inside of the ring. The ideal dimensions of the ring will be 11 inches in diameter, 4 inches tall, and made of 1/16 (.063 inches thick) sheet metal.

K-30. Banding rings need to be sufficiently rigid to hold leaflets in place, but not so stiff that they cannot be deflected. Rings made of steel box banding (.75 inches wide x .031 inches thick) have worked well in the past. Rings that are made too stiff will not uniformly contact the leaflets inside the packing ring. To reduce the tearing of leaflets, personnel should roll the ends of the banding rings onto themselves. There should be three banding rings measuring 29 inches, 18 inches, and 15 inches long.

K-31. Personnel follow the steps listed below to make leaflet rolls:

- *Step 1.* Line the inside of the packing ring with the 3-inch brown box tape. Personnel use adhesive tape to secure the two ends of the brown box tape together.

- *Step 2.* Place the 29-inch steel banding ring inside the packing ring.

- *Step 3.* Take a small stack of leaflets and fan them so that each leaflet has an exposed edge (leaflets should have a "stair step" effect); place the leaflets into the packing ring, between the brown box tape and the steel banding ring (Figure K-6, page K-14).

- *Step 4.* Continue fanning stacks of leaflets and inserting them into the packing ring. This procedure should be done in a continuous circle. Personnel must ensure that the fanned ends of each new stack interlock with the fanned ends of the previous stack.

NOTE: As the circle gets tighter, personnel will have to switch out banding rings to allow for the smaller area. After they remove the shortest banding ring, they will begin to pack the leaflets by hand. Personnel should always try to pack the leaflet rolls as tightly as possible. There should be little to no opening left in the center of the roll when it is finished.

- *Step 5*. After the center of the roll has been tightly packed, lift the packing ring three-fourths of the way off of the leaflet roll. Then locate the seam where the two ends of the brown box tape overlap, and secure the outer part of the brown packing tape to itself using adhesive tape.

- *Step 6*. Weigh the roll to ensure that it is 7.5 pounds.

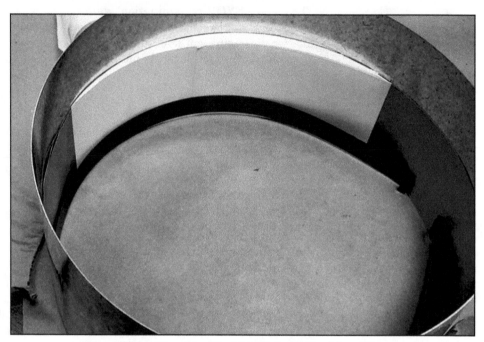

Figure K-6. Placement of Leaflets in Packing Ring

Procedures for Loading the PDU-5/B LDS

K-32. These procedures are for the most common size leaflet (3 x 6 inches). All rolls will be 11 inches in diameter regardless of the leaflet size. Table K-5 provides information on using different-sized leaflets.

Table K-5. Leaflet Sizes and Weights

Leaflet Size (in Inches)	Rolls Needed	Individual Roll Weight (in Pounds)
3 x 4	20	7.5
3 x 6	20	7.5
4 x 4	15	10
6 x 6	10	15

K-33. Before loading the PDU-5/B, personnel ensure that they inspect all equipment for serviceability:

- 1 x Cardboard tube (cut into half lengthwise).
- 2 x Cardboard end caps.

- 4 x Foam spacers (3 thick and 1 thin).
- 1 x PDU-5/B.

Personnel ensure that the equipment is free from cuts, dents, tears, water damage, or anything else that may impair the function of the equipment. They also ensure the inside of the PDU-5/B is empty.

K-34. Other equipment needed includes the following:

- Cutting utensil.
- Masking tape.
- Grease pencil.

NOTE: All items for the PDU-5/B are stored inside of the bomb section. If the tail section has not already been removed before beginning, personnel should notify an authorized bomb technician to remove the tail section.

K-35. Personnel follow the steps listed below to load the PDU-5/B LDS:

- *Step 1*. Load 20 leaflet rolls into cardboard tube half; ensure that the weight of the tube does not exceed 152 pounds (Figure K-7).

NOTE: When loading the leaflet rolls into the cardboard tube, personnel will be almost out of room at roll number 19. To get roll number 20 loaded, personnel should have one Soldier brace one of the sides of the tube and have another Soldier forcefully push the leaflet rolls into the tube until they all fit. There may be a slight protrusion from either end of the cardboard tube.

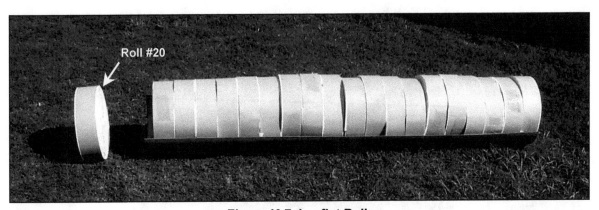

Roll #20

Figure K-7. Leaflet Rolls

- *Step 2*. Cut the brown protective tape on each roll two-thirds the width of the roll (the roll should be 3 inches wide; the cut should be 2 inches) (Figure K-8, page K-16).

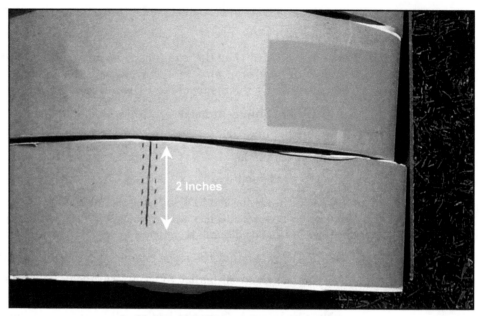

Figure K-8. Brown Protective Tape

- *Step 3.* Place the other half of the cardboard tube on top of the first half; use masking tape to secure the two halves together—use five pieces of tape on both sides, spreading out equally along the length of the seam of the two halves (Figure K-9).

NOTE: When the top half of the tube is put on, it does not necessarily have to be flush with the other half of the tube.

Figure K-9. Cardboard Tube Placement

- *Step 4.* Place the two cardboard end caps on both sides of the cardboard tube; secure the end caps to the tube using masking tape (Figure K-10).
- *Step 5.* Using the grease pencil, write the product number of the leaflets in the tube on the top of the cardboard tube and on both end caps (Figure K-10).

Figure K-10. Cardboard End Cap

- *Step 6.* Using two Soldiers, load the cardboard tube into the PDU-5/B; ensure cardboard tube is as far forward in the body of the bomb as possible (Figure K-11, page K-18).
- *Step 7.* While the cardboard tube is inside the bomb, observe the product number written on the cardboard end cap; using the grease pencil, write the product number on the side of the PDU-5/B.
- *Step 8.* Load the foam spacers into the bomb; load the three thick spacers first, then the thin spacer.
- *Step 9.* Notify bomb technician that the tail section is ready to be attached.
- *Step 10.* Observe the product number written on the side of the PDU-5/B; using the grease pencil, write the product number on the top fin of the tail.

NOTE: Tail section will be attached to bomb body when the product number is written on fin.

Figure K-11. Loading the Cardboard Tube Into the PDU-5/B

Procedures for Unloading the PDU-5/B LDS

K-36. Personnel follow the steps listed below to unload the PDU-5/B LDS:

- *Step 1.* Notify bomb technician that the tail section is ready to be removed.
- *Step 2.* Remove foam spacers from the body of the bomb.
- *Step 3.* Remove cardboard tube containing the leaflet rolls.

NOTE: To get the tube out of the bomb, the bomb technician will have to lift the nose of the bomb.

- *Step 4.* Remove cardboard end caps and the top half of the cardboard tube; use masking tape to repair the cuts made on the brown protective paper of the leaflet rolls.
- *Step 5.* Remove leaflet rolls from the cardboard tube; label each roll with the product number so that it can be easily identified for future use.
- *Step 6.* Return cardboard tube, cardboard end caps, and foam spacers to the bomb.
- *Step 7.* Notify authorized bomb technician to return tail section to bomb.

STATIC-LINE BOX

K-37. At high altitudes, the use of leaflet bundles or boxes opened by a static line has proven effective. Through use of rollers on the deck of the aircraft, boxes weighing up to 49.90 kilograms can be ejected with minimum exertion. The box is rolled out of the aircraft, and as the container comes to the end of the static line, the sides of the box split (Figure K-12). In effect, the box is turned inside out, and the leaflets fall away from the empty box. The steps required to prepare boxes for high-altitude, static-line dissemination are shown in Figure K-13, page K-20.

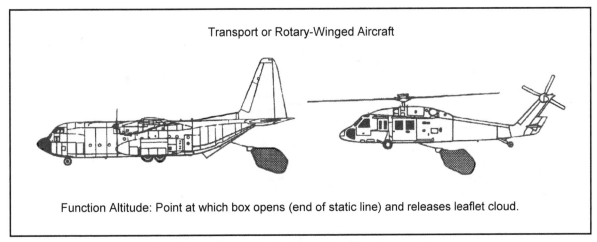

Transport or Rotary-Winged Aircraft

Function Altitude: Point at which box opens (end of static line) and releases leaflet cloud.

Figure K-12. Static-Line Box Employment

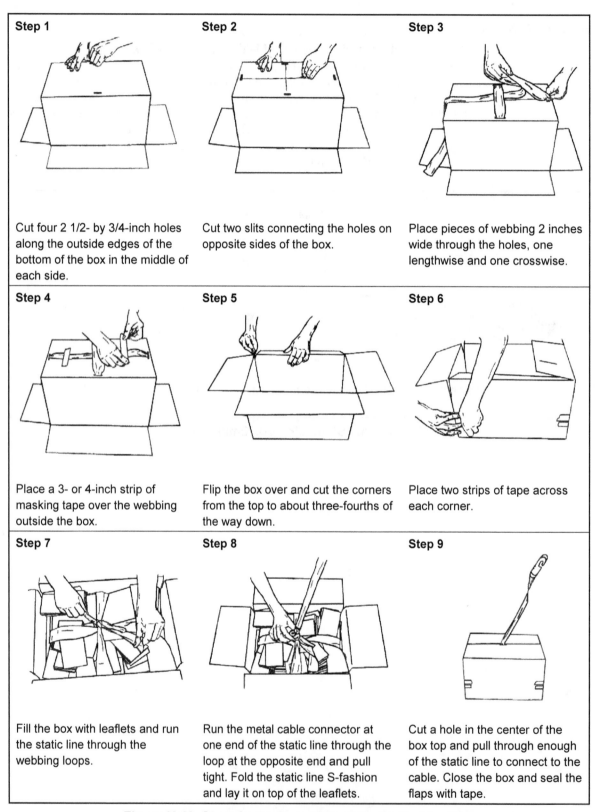

Step 1

Cut four 2 1/2- by 3/4-inch holes along the outside edges of the bottom of the box in the middle of each side.

Step 2

Cut two slits connecting the holes on opposite sides of the box.

Step 3

Place pieces of webbing 2 inches wide through the holes, one lengthwise and one crosswise.

Step 4

Place a 3- or 4-inch strip of masking tape over the webbing outside the box.

Step 5

Flip the box over and cut the corners from the top to about three-fourths of the way down.

Step 6

Place two strips of tape across each corner.

Step 7

Fill the box with leaflets and run the static line through the webbing loops.

Step 8

Run the metal cable connector at one end of the static line through the loop at the opposite end and pull tight. Fold the static line S-fashion and lay it on top of the leaflets.

Step 9

Cut a hole in the center of the box top and pull through enough of the static line to connect to the cable. Close the box and seal the flaps with tape.

Figure K-13. Steps in the Assembly of the Static-Line Box

Appendix L

Weights, Measures, and Conversion Tables

Tables L-1 through L-5, pages L-1 and L-2, show metric units and their U.S. equivalents. Tables L-6 through L-15, pages L-2 through L-5, are conversion tables.

Table L-1. Linear Measure

Unit	Other Metric Equivalent	U.S. Equivalent
1 centimeter	10 millimeters	0.39 inch
1 decimeter	10 centimeters	3.94 inches
1 meter	10 decimeters	39.37 inches
1 decameter	10 meters	32.8 feet
1 hectometer	10 decameters	328.08 feet
1 kilometer	10 hectometers	3,280.8 feet

Table L-2. Liquid Measure

Unit	Other Metric Equivalent	U.S. Equivalent
1 centiliter	10 milliliters	0.34 fluid ounce
1 deciliter	10 centiliters	3.38 fluid ounces
1 liter	10 deciliters	33.81 fluid ounces
1 decaliter	10 liters	2.64 gallons
1 hectoliter	10 deciliters	26.42 gallons
1 kiloliter	10 hectoliters	264.18 gallons

Table L-3. Weight

Unit	Other Metric Equivalent	U.S. Equivalent
1 centigram	10 milligrams	0.15 grain
1 decigram	10 centigrams	1.54 grains
1 gram	10 decigrams	0.035 ounce
1 decagram	10 grams	0.35 ounce
1 hectogram	10 decigrams	3.52 ounces
1 kilogram	10 hectograms	2.2 pounds
1 quintal	100 kilograms	220.46 pounds
1 metric ton	10 quintals	1.1 short tons

Table L-4. Square Measure

Unit	Other Metric Equivalent	U.S. Equivalent
1 square centimeter	100 square millimeters	0.155 square inch
1 square decimeter	100 square centimeters	15.5 square inches
1 square meter (centaur)	100 square decimeters	10.76 square feet
1 square decameter (are)	100 square meters	1,076.4 square feet
1 square hectometer (hectare)	100 square decameters	2.47 acres
1 square kilometer	100 square hectometers	0.386 square mile

Table L-5. Cubic Measure

Unit	Other Metric Equivalent	U.S. Equivalent
1 cubic centimeter	1,000 cubic millimeters	0.06 cubic inch
1 cubic decimeter	1,000 cubic centimeters	61.02 cubic inches
1 cubic meter	1,000 cubic decimeters	35.31 cubic feet

Table L-6. Temperature

Convert From	Convert To
Fahrenheit	Celsius Subtract 32, multiply by 5, and divide by 9
Celsius	Fahrenheit Multiply by 9, divide by 5, and add 32

Table L-7. Approximate Conversion Factors

To Change	To	Multiply By	To Change	To	Multiply By
Inches	Centimeters	2.540	Ounce-inches	Newton-meters	0.007062
Feet	Meters	0.305	Centimeters	Inches	3.94
Yards	Meters	0.914	Meters	Feet	3.280
Miles	Kilometers	1.609	Meters	Yards	1.094
Square inches	Square centimeters	6.451	Kilometers	Miles	0.621
Square feet	Square meters	0.093	Square centimeters	Square inches	0.155
Square yards	Square meters	0.836	Square meters	Square feet	10.76
Square miles	Square kilometers	2.590	Square meters	Square yards	1.196
Acres	Square hectometers	0.405	Square kilometers	Square miles	0.386
Cubic feet	Cubic meters	0.028	Square hectometers	Acres	2.471

Table L-7. Approximate Conversion Factors (Continued)

To Change	To	Multiply By	To Change	To	Multiply By
Cubic yards	Cubic meters	0.765	Cubic meters	Cubic feet	35.315
Fluid ounces	Millimeters	29.573	Cubic meters	Cubic yards	1.308
Pints	Liters	0.473	Millimeters	Fluid ounces	0.034
Quarts	Liters	0.946	Liters	Pints	2.113
Gallons	Liters	3.785	Liters	Quarts	1.057
Ounces	Grams	28.349	Liters	Gallons	0.264
Pounds	Kilograms	0.454	Grams	Ounces	0.035
Short tons	Metric tons	0.907	Kilograms	Pounds	2.205
Pounds-feet	Newton-meters	1.356	Metric tons	Short tons	1.102
Pounds-inches	Newton-meters	0.11296	Nautical Miles	Kilometers	1.852

Table L-8. Area

To Change	To	Multiply By	To Change	To	Multiply By
Square millimeters	Square inches	0.00155	Square inches	Square millimeters	645.16
Square centimeters	Square inches	9.155	Square inches	Square centimeters	6.452
Square meters	Square inches	1,550	Square inches	Square meters	0.00065
Square meters	Square feet	10.764	Square feet	Square meters	0.093
Square meters	Square yards	1.196	Square yards	Square meters	0.836
Square kilometers	Square miles	0.386	Square miles	Square kilometers	2.59

Table L-9. Volume

To Change	To	Multiply By	To Change	To	Multiply By
Cubic centimeters	Cubic inches	0.061	Cubic inches	Cubic centimeters	16.39
Cubic meters	Cubic feet	35.31	Cubic feet	Cubic meters	0.028
Cubic meters	Cubic yards	1.308	Cubic yards	Cubic meters	0.765
Liters	Cubic inches	61.02	Cubic inches	Liters	0.016
Liters	Cubic feet	0.035	Cubic feet	Liters	28.32

Table L-10. Capacity

To Change	To	Multiply By	To Change	To	Multiply By
Milliliters	Fluid drams	0.271	Fluid drams	Milliliters	3.697
Milliliters	Fluid ounces	0.034	Fluid ounces	Milliliters	29.57
Liters	Fluid ounces	33.81	Fluid ounces	Liters	0.030
Liters	Pints	2.113	Pints	Liters	0.473
Liters	Quarts	1.057	Quarts	Liters	0.946
Liters	Gallons	0.264	Liters	Gallons	3.785

Table L-11. Statute Miles to Kilometers and Nautical Miles

Statute Miles	Kilometers	Nautical Miles	Statute Miles	Kilometers	Nautical Miles
1	1.61	0.86	60	96.60	52.14
2	3.22	1.74	70	112.70	60.83
3	4.83	2.61	80	128.80	69.52
4	6.44	3.48	90	144.90	78.21
5	8.05	4.35	100	161.00	86.92
6	9.66	5.21	200	322.00	173.80
7	11.27	6.08	300	483.00	260.70
8	12.88	6.95	400	644.00	347.60
9	14.49	7.82	500	805.00	434.50
10	16.10	8.69	600	966.00	521.40
20	32.20	17.38	700	1127.00	608.30
30	48.30	26.07	800	1288.00	695.20
40	64.40	34.76	900	1449.00	782.10
50	80.50	43.45	1000	1610.00	869.00

Table L-12. Nautical Miles to Kilometers and Statute Miles

Nautical Miles	Kilometers	Statute Miles	Nautical Miles	Kilometers	Statute Miles
1	1.85	1.15	60	111.00	69.00
2	3.70	2.30	70	129.50	80.50
3	5.55	3.45	80	148.00	92.00
4	7.40	4.60	90	166.50	103.50
5	9.25	5.75	100	185.00	115.00
6	11.10	6.90	200	370.00	230.00
7	12.95	8.05	300	555.00	345.00
8	14.80	9.20	400	740.00	460.00
9	16.65	10.35	500	925.00	575.00
10	18.50	11.50	600	1110.00	690.00
20	37.00	23.00	700	1295.00	805.00
30	55.50	34.50	800	1480.00	920.00
40	74.00	46.00	900	1665.00	1033.00
50	92.50	57.50	1000	1850.00	1150.00

Table L-13. Kilometers to Statute and Nautical Miles

Kilometers	Statute Miles	Nautical Miles	Kilometers	Statute Miles	Nautical Miles
1	0.62	0.54	60	37.28	32.38
2	1.24	1.08	70	43.50	37.77
3	1.86	1.62	80	49.71	43.17
4	2.49	2.16	90	55.93	48.56
5	3.11	2.70	100	62.14	53.96

Table L-13. Kilometers to Statute and Nautical Miles (Continued)

Kilometers	Statute Miles	Nautical Miles	Kilometers	Statute Miles	Nautical Miles
6	3.73	3.24	200	124.28	107.92
7	4.35	3.78	300	186.42	161.88
8	4.97	4.32	400	248.56	215.84
9	5.59	4.86	500	310.70	269.80
10	6.21	5.40	600	372.84	323.76
20	12.43	10.79	700	434.98	377.72
30	18.64	16.19	800	497.12	431.68
40	24.86	21.58	900	559.26	485.64
50	31.07	26.98	1000	621.40	539.60

Table L-14. Yards to Meters

Yards	Meters	Yards	Meters	Yards	Meters
100	91	1000	914	1900	1737
200	183	1100	1006	2000	1828
300	274	1200	1097	3000	2742
400	366	1300	1189	4000	3656
500	457	1400	1280	5000	4570
600	549	1500	1372	6000	5484
700	640	1600	1463	7000	6398
800	732	1700	1554	8000	7212
900	823	1800	1646	9000	8226

Table L-15. Meters to Yards

Meters	Yards	Meters	Yards	Meters	Yards
100	109	1000	1094	1900	2078
200	219	1100	1203	2000	2188
300	328	1200	1312	3000	3282
400	437	1300	1422	4000	4376
500	547	1400	1531	5000	5470
600	656	1500	1640	6000	6564
700	766	1600	1750	7000	7658
800	875	1700	1860	8000	8752
900	984	1800	1969	9000	9846

Glossary

AAR	after action report
ABCS	Army Battle Command System
ACO	airspace control order
ADA	air defense artillery
A/DACG	arrival/departure airfield control group
adversary	Anyone who contends with, opposes, or acts against one's interest. An adversary is not necessarily an enemy.
ADVON	advanced echelon
AFATDS	Advanced Field Artillery Tactical Data System
AFFOR	Air Force forces
AFN	Armed Forces Network
AFSOC	Air Force Special Operations Command
AGL	above ground level
AGM	attack guidance matrix
AI	area of interest
AIA	Air Intelligence Agency
AIDS	Acquired Immune Deficiency Syndrome
AJP	allied joint publication
ALD	available-to-load date
ALLOREQ	allocation request
ALS	airborne loudspeaker system
AM	amplitude modulation
AMC	Air Mobility Command
AMCIT	American citizen
AMD	air and missile defense
AMDPCS	Air and Missile Defense Planning and Control System
AMDWS	Air and Missile Defense Workstation
AO	area of operations
AOR	**area of responsibility**—The geographical area associated with a combatant command within which a combatant commander has authority to plan and conduct operations. (JP 1-02)

APF	afloat pre-positioning force
APOD	aerial port of debarkation
APOE	aerial port of embarkation
AR	Army regulation
ARFOR	Army forces
ARNG	Army National Guard
ARPERCEN	United States Army Reserve Personnel Center
ARSOF	Army special operations forces
ARSOLL	Automated Repository for Special Operations Lessons Learned
ASAS	All-Source Analysis System
ASCC	Air Standardization Coordinating Committee
ASD(SO/LIC)	Assistant Secretary of Defense (Special Operations and Low Intensity Conflict)
ASI	additional skill identifier
ASIP	Advanced System Improvement Program
ASL	authorized stockage list
asset (intelligence)	Any resource—person, group, relationship, instrument, installation, or supply—at the disposition of an intelligence organization for use in an operational or support role. Often used with a qualifying term such as agent asset or propaganda asset. (JP 1-02)
assign	To detail individuals to specific duties or functions where such duties or functions are primary and/or relatively permanent. (JP 1-02)
AT	annual training
ATCCS	Army Tactical Command and Control System
ATL	assistant team leader
ATO	air tasking order
attach	The detailing of individuals to specific functions where such functions are secondary or relatively temporary, e.g., attached for quarters and rations; attached for flying duty. (JP 1-02)
AUEL	automated unit equipment list
AWIS	Army WWMCS Information System
AZ	azimuth
BAS	Battlefield Automated System
BBC	British Broadcasting Corporation
BC	battle command

BC2A	Bosnia command and control augmentation
BDA	**battle damage assessment**—The timely and accurate estimate of damage resulting from the application of military force, either lethal or non-lethal, against a predetermined objective. Battle damage assessment can be applied to the employment of all types of weapon systems (air, ground, naval, and special forces weapon systems) throughout the range of military operations. Battle damage assessment is primarily an intelligence responsibility with required inputs and coordination from the operators. Battle damage assessment is composed of physical damage assessment, functional damage assessment, and target system assessment. (JP 1-02)
BE	basic entry
Bi-SC	of the two strategic commands
BMNT	beginning morning nautical twilight
BPS	**basic Psychological Operations study**—A document that describes succinctly the characteristics of a country, geographical area, or region which are most pertinent to psychological operations, and which can serve as an immediate reference for the planning and conduct of psychological operations. (JP 1-02)
C	combined
C2	command and control
C3	command, control, and communications
C4	command, control, communications, and computers
C4I	command, control, communications, computers, and intelligence
CA	**Civil Affairs**—Designated Active and Reserve component forces and units organized, trained, and equipped specifically to conduct civil affairs activities and to support civil-military operations. (JP 1-02)
campaign	A series of related military operations aimed at accomplishing a strategic or operational objective within a given time and space. (JP 1-02)
campaign plan	A plan for a series of related military operations aimed at accomplishing a strategic or operational objective within a given time and space. (JP 1-02)
CAO	Civil Affairs operations
CAP	civic action program
capability	The ability to execute a specified course of action. (A capability may or may not be accompanied by an intention.)
CAR	Chief of the Army Reserve
CCIR	commander's critical information requirements

CD	counterdrug; compact disc
CDC	continental United States demobilization center
CDR	commander
chain of command	The succession of commanding officers from a superior to a subordinate through which command is exercised. Also called command channel. (JP 1-02)
CI	civilian internee
CIA	Central Intelligence Agency
CISO	counterintelligence support officer
civil affairs activities	Activities performed or supported by civil affairs that (1) enhance the relationship between military forces and civil authorities in areas where military forces are present; and (2) involve application of civil affairs functional specialty skills, in areas normally the responsibility of civil government, to enhance conduct of civil-military operations. (JP 1-02)
CJCS	Chairman of the Joint Chiefs of Staff
CJCSI	Chairman of the Joint Chiefs of Staff Instruction
CJTF	commander of the joint task force
CLS	combat lifesaver
CND	computer network defense
CNN	Cable News Network
COA	course of action
coalition	An ad hoc arrangement between two or more nations for common action. (JP 1-02)
COCOM	combatant command (command authority)
COE	common operating environment
combatant command	A unified or specified command with a broad continuing mission under a single commander established and so designated by the President, through the Secretary of Defense and with the advice and assistance of the Chairman of the Joint Chiefs of Staff. Combatant commands typically have geographic or functional responsibilities. (JP 1-02)
COMJTF	commander, joint task force
COMMZ	communications zone
COMSEC	communications security
conditions	Those external elements that affect a target audience but over which they have little or no control. Conditions may be man-made or environmental in nature.
CONEX	container express

CONOPS	concept of operations
CONPLAN	concept plan; operation plan in concept format
contingency	An emergency involving military forces caused by natural disasters, terrorists, subversives, or by required military operations. Due to the uncertainty of the situation, contingencies require plans, rapid response, and special procedures to ensure the safety and readiness of personnel, installations, and equipment. (JP 1-02)
CONUS	continental United States
conventional forces	Those forces capable of conducting operations using nonnuclear weapons. (JP 1-02)
COP	common operational picture
COS	chief of staff
counterinsurgency	Those military, paramilitary, political, economic, psychological, and civic actions taken by a government to defeat insurgency. (JP 1-02)
counterpropaganda	Programs of products and actions designed to nullify propaganda or mitigate its effects.
CP	counterproliferation
CPIC	Coalition Press Information Center
CPT	captain
CPX	command post exercise
CRAF	civil reserve air fleet
CRC	continental United States replacement center
CRD	commander's required date
crisis	An incident or situation involving a threat to the United States, its territories, citizens, military forces, possessions, or vital interests that develops rapidly and creates a condition of such diplomatic, economic, political, or military importance that commitment of U.S. military forces and resources is contemplated in order to achieve national objectives. (JP 1-02)
critical information	Specific facts about friendly intentions, capabilities, and activities vitally needed by adversaries for them to plan and act effectively so as to guarantee failure or unacceptable consequences for friendly mission accomplishment.
CS	combat support
CSA	Chief of Staff, United States Army
CSM	command sergeant major
CSS	combat service support
CSSCS	Combat Service Support Control System

CT	counterterrorism
DA	Department of the Army; direct action
DAO	defense attaché officer
data	Representation of facts, concepts, or instructions in a formalized manner suitable for communication, interpretation, or processing by humans or by automatic means. Any representations, such as characters or analog quantities, to which meaning is or might be assigned.
DC	dislocated civilian; direct current
DCM	deputy chief of mission
DCS	deputy chief of staff
DCSLOG	Deputy Chief of Staff for Logistics
DCSOPS	Deputy Chief of Staff for Operations and Plans
DD	Department of Defense (for example, DD Form)
DDIO	Deputy Director for Information Operations
DEA	Drug Enforcement Agency
deception	Those measures designed to mislead the enemy by manipulation, distortion, or falsification of evidence to induce the enemy to react in a manner prejudicial to the enemy's interests.
DEL	deployment equipment list
DET	detachment
DFN	designated foreign national
DII	defense information infrastructure
diversion	The act of drawing the attention and forces of an enemy from the point of the principal operation; an attack, alarm, or feint that diverts attention. (JP 1-02)
DJS	Director, Joint Staff
DJTFAC	deployable joint task force augmentation cell
DLA	Defense Logistics Agency
DMS	demobilization station
DOD	Department of Defense
DODI	Department of Defense instruction
DOJ	Department of Justice
DOS	Department of State; disk operating system
DPPC	Deployable Print Production Center
DS	direct support
DSN	Defense Switched Network

DSVT	digital subscriber voice terminal
DTG	date-time group
DVD	digital video disc
DVR	digital voice recorder
DZ	drop zone
EAC	echelons above corps
EAP	emergency action plan
ECC	effects coordination cell
EEFI	essential elements of friendly information
EENT	ending evening nautical twilight
Encl	enclosure
ENG	electronic news gathering
ENSIT	enemy situation
EPW	enemy prisoner of war
EW	electronic warfare
EWO	electronic warfare officer
executive order	Order issued by the President by virtue of the authority vested in him by the Constitution or by an act of Congress. It has the force of law. (AR 310-25)
FABS	Flyaway Broadcast System
FAX	facsimile
FBCB2	Force XXI Battle Command, Brigade and Below
FBIS	Foreign Broadcast Information Service
FDO	flexible deterrent option
FID	**foreign internal defense**—Participation by civilian and military agencies of a government in any of the action programs taken by another government to free and protect its society from subversion, lawlessness, and insurgency. (JP 1-02)
FIPS	Federal Information Processing Standard
FIWC	fleet information warfare center
FM	field manual; frequency modulation
FMC	fully mission capable
FO	force operations
FOB	forward operational base
FOL	family of loudspeakers

force multiplier	A capability that, when added to and employed by a combat force, significantly increases the combat potential of that force and thus enhances the probability of successful mission accomplishment. (JP 1-02)
force protection	Security program designed to protect Service members, civilian employees, family members, facilities, and equipment, in all locations and situations, accomplished through planned and integrated application of combatting terrorism, physical security, operations security, and personal protective services, and supported by intelligence, counterintelligence, and other security programs. (JP 1-02)
FORMDEPS	United States Army Forces Command Mobilization and Deployment Planning System
FORSCOM	United States Army Forces Command
FPC	final planning conference
FRAGORD	fragmentary order
FS	fire support
FSCL	fire support coordination line
FSCOORD	fire support coordinator
FSS	fast sealift ships
FT	force tracking; foot/feet
FTP	File Transfer Protocol
FTX	field training exercise
functional component command	A command normally, but not necessarily, composed of forces of two or more military departments that may be established across the range of military operations to perform particular operational missions that may be of short duration or may extend over a period of time. (JP 1-02)
G-1	Deputy Chief of Staff for Personnel
G-2	Deputy Chief of Staff for Intelligence
G-3	Deputy Chief of Staff for Operations and Plans
G-4	Deputy Chief of Staff for Logistics
G-6	Chief Information Officer/Director, Information Systems for Command, Control, Communications, and Computers
G-7	Deputy Chief of Staff for Information Operations
GCCS	Global Command and Control System
GCCS-A	Global Command and Control System-Army
GCSS-A	Global Combat Support System-Army
GOS	Government of Snoring

GOT	Government of Terrifica
GPS	global positioning system
GRM	graduated response measure
GS	general support
GSA	General Services Administration
GSR	general support reinforcing
HA	humanitarian assistance
HF	high frequency
HFAC	Human Factors Analysis Center
HFM	high frequency module
HMA	humanitarian mine action
HMMWV	high mobility multipurpose wheeled vehicle
HN	**host nation**—A nation that receives the forces and/or supplies of allied nations, coalition partners, and/or NATO organizations to be located on, to operate in, or to transit through its territory. (JP 1-02)
HNS	host-nation support
HPF	Heavy Print Facility
HPT	high-payoff target
HQ	headquarters
HQDA	Headquarters, Department of the Army
HS	home station
HUMINT	**human intelligence**—A category of intelligence derived from information collected and provided by human sources. (JP 1-02)
HVT	high-value target
Hz	hertz
IAW	in accordance with
IBM	International Business Machines
ICC	information coordinating committee
ICRC	International Committee of the Red Cross
IDP	internally displaced persons
IET	initial entry training
IEW	intelligence and electronic warfare
IFOR	Implementation Force
IMA	individual mobilization augmentee

IMIT	international military information team
info	information
INMARSAT	international maritime satellite
INSCOM	United States Army Intelligence and Security Command
insurgency	An organized movement aimed at the overthrow of a constituted government through use of subversion and armed conflict. (JP 1-02)
INTELINK	intelligence link
INTELINK-S	intelligence link-Secret
INTSUM	intelligence summary
IO	information operations
IPB	intelligence preparation of the battlespace
IPTF	International Police Task Force
I/R	internment/resettlement
IR	information requirement
IRR	Individual Ready Reserve
ISR	intelligence, surveillance, and reconnaissance
ITO	installation transportation officer
ITV	in-transit visibility
J2T	J-2 Targets
J-1	Manpower and Personnel Directorate
J-2	Intelligence Directorate
J-3	Operations Directorate
J-4	Logistics Directorate
J-5	Plans Directorate of a joint staff
J-6	Command, Control, Communications, and Computer Systems Directorate
J-7	Operational Plans and Joint Force Development Directorate, Joint Staff
JC2WC	Joint Command and Control Warfare Center
JCCC	joint combat camera center
JCDB	Joint Common Database
JCEOI	joint communications-electronics operating instructions
JCET	joint combined exercise for training
JCEWS	joint force commander's electronic warfare staff

JCS	Joint Chiefs of Staff
J/CTF	joint or combined task force
JFACC	joint force air component commander
JFC	joint force commander
JFE	joint fires element
JFSC	Joint Forces Staff College
JGAT	joint guidance, apportionment, and targeting
JIF	joint interrogation facility
JIOC	Joint Information Operations Center
JIPTL	joint integrated prioritized target list
JMCIS	joint maritime command information system
JOA	joint operations area
JOC	joint operations center
joint	Connotes activities, operations, organizations, etc., in which elements of two or more military departments participate. (JP 1-02)
joint doctrine	Fundamental principles that guide the employment of forces of two or more military departments in coordinated action toward a common objective. It is authoritative; as such, joint doctrine will be followed except when, in the judgment of the commander, exceptional circumstances dictate otherwise. It will be promulgated by or for the Chairman of the Joint Chiefs of Staff, in coordination with the combatant commands and Services. (JP 1-02)
joint force	A general term applied to a force composed of significant elements, assigned or attached, of two or more military departments operating under a single joint force commander. (JP 1-02)
joint operations	A general term to describe military actions conducted by joint forces or by Service forces in relationships (e.g., support, coordinating authority) which, of themselves, do not create joint forces. (JP 1-02)
JOPES	Joint Operation Planning and Execution System
JP	joint publication
JPEC	joint planning and execution community
JPOTF	**joint Psychological Operations task force**—A joint special operations task force composed of headquarters and operational assets. It assists the joint force commander in developing strategic, operational, and tactical psychological operation plans for a theater campaign or other operations. Mission requirements will determine its composition and assigned or attached units to support the joint task force commander. (JP 1-02)

JRFL	joint restricted frequency list
JSC	Joint Spectrum Center
JSCP	Joint Strategic Capabilities Plan
JSOA	joint special operations area
JSOTF	joint special operations task force
JTCB	joint targeting coordination board
JTF	**joint task force**—A joint force that is constituted and so designated by the Secretary of Defense, a combatant commander, a subunified commander, or an existing joint task force commander. (JP 1-02)
JULLS	Joint Universal Lessons Learned System
JUMPS/JSS	Joint Uniform Military Pay System/Joint Service Software
JWAC	Joint Warfare Analysis Center
KIA	killed in action
kt	knot(s) (nautical miles per hour)
LAD	latest arrival date
LAN	local area network
lb	pound(s)
LBE	load-bearing equipment
LC	legal council
LDS	leaflet delivery system
LEA	law enforcement agency
LF	low frequency
LFM	low-frequency module
LNO	liaison officer
LOC	logistics operations center
LOGCAP	logistics civilian augmentation program
LOP	**line of persuasion**—An argument used to obtain a desired behavior or attitude from the target audience.
LOS	line of sight
LZ	landing zone
MAAP	master air attack plan
MACOM	major command
MAJ	major
MARFOR	Marine Corps forces

MAVS	Mobile Audiovisual System
MB	megabyte
MBITR	Multiband Intra-Team Radio
MC	Military Committee
MCS	Maneuver Control System
MDMP	military decision-making process
MDRD	mobilization, deployment, redeployment, and demobilization
MEDCAP	medical civic action program
media	Transmitters of information and psychological products. (FM 3-05.30)
METT-TC	mission, enemy, terrain and weather, troops and support available—time available, and civil considerations
MI	military intelligence
MIA	missing in action
MICON	mission concept
MIPR	military interdepartmental purchase request
MISREP	mission report
MIST	military information support team
MITASK	mission tasking
MMC	Materiel Management Center
MND-N	Multinational Division North
MOA	memorandum of agreement
MOC	media operations complex
MOE	**measure of effectiveness**—A tool used to measure results achieved in the overall mission and execution of assigned tasks. Measures of effectiveness are a prerequisite to the performance of combat assessment. (JP 1-02)
MOOTW	military operations other than war
MOS	military occupational specialty
MOU	memorandum of understanding
MP	military police
MPAD	mobile public affairs detachment
mpg	miles per gallon
MPLS	manpack loudspeaker system
MPS	Modular Printing System
MRE	meal, ready to eat

MS	mobilization station
MSE	mobile subscriber equipment
MSR	mission support request
MTMC	Military Traffic Management Command
multinational joint Psychological Operations task force	A task force composed of Psychological Operations units from one or more foreign countries formed to carry out a specific psychological operation or prosecute Psychological Operations in support of a theater campaign or other operations. The multinational joint Psychological Operations task force may have conventional non-Psychological Operations units assigned or attached to support the conduct of specific missions.
multinational operations	A collective term to describe military actions conducted by forces of two or more nations, usually undertaken within the structure of a coalition or alliance. (JP 1-02)
NAR	nonconventional assisted recovery
national objectives	The aims, derived from national goals and interests, toward which a national policy or strategy is directed and efforts and resources of the nation are applied. (JP 1-02)
NATO	North Atlantic Treaty Organization
NAVFOR	Navy forces
NAVSECGRU	Naval Security Group
NAWCAD	Naval Air Warfare Center, Aircraft Division
NBC	nuclear, biological, and chemical
NC	North Carolina
NCO	noncommissioned officer
NCOER	noncommissioned officer evaluation report
NCOIC	noncommissioned officer in charge
NEO	noncombatant evacuation operation
NFA	no-fire area
NGO	**nongovernmental organization**—Transnational organizations of private citizens that maintain a consultative status with the Economic and Social Council of the United Nations. Nongovernmental organizations may be professional associations, foundations, multinational businesses, or simply groups with a common interest in humanitarian assistance activities (development and relief). "Nongovernmental organizations" is a term normally used by non-United States organizations. (JP 1-02)
NIMA	National Imagery and Mapping Agency
NIPRNET	Nonsecure Internet Protocol Router Network
NLT	not later than

NM	nautical miles
NMC	nonmission capable
NRP	non-unit-related personnel
NSC	National Security Council
NSDD	National Security Decision Directive
NSN	National Stock Number
NTSC	A type of video output, established by the National Television Standards Committee of America, in which picture information is delivered as a single electronic signal. (**NOTE:** NTSC and PAL **are not** compatible or interchangeable.)
OAE	operational area evaluation
OAS	Organization of American States
OASD	Office of the Assistant Secretary of Defense
OCDETF	Organized Crime Drug Enforcement Task Force
OCONUS	outside the continental United States
OD	other detainee
OER	officer evaluation report
OGA	other government agency
O/H	on hand
OIC	officer in charge
ONDCP	Office of National Drug Control Policy
OPCON	**operational control**—Transferable command authority that may be exercised by commanders at any echelon at or below the level of combatant command. Operational control is inherent in combatant command (command authority). Operational control may be delegated and is the authority to perform those functions of command over subordinate forces involving organizing and employing commands and forces, assigning tasks, designating objectives, and giving authoritative direction necessary to accomplish the mission. Operational control includes authoritative direction over all aspects of military operations and joint training necessary to accomplish missions assigned to the command. Operational control should be exercised through the commanders of subordinate organizations. Normally this authority is exercised through subordinate joint force commanders and Service and/or functional component commands. Operational control normally provides full authority to organize commands and forces and to employ those forces as the commander in operational control considers necessary to accomplish assigned missions. Operational control does not, in and of itself, include authoritative direction for logistics or

matters of administration, discipline, internal organization, or unit training. (JP 1-02)

OPLAN — operation plan

OPORD — operation order

opponent — An antagonistic force or organization that counters mission accomplishment by military means.

OPR — office of primary responsibility

OPSEC — **operations security**—A process of identifying critical information and subsequently analyzing friendly actions attendant to military operations and other activities to: a. identify those actions that can be observed by adversary intelligence systems; b. determine indicators that hostile intelligence systems might obtain that could be interpreted or pieced together to derive critical information in time to be useful to adversaries; and c. select and execute measures that eliminate or reduce to an acceptable level the vulnerabilities of friendly actions to adversary exploitation. (JP 1-02)

OPSUM — operations summary

OSD — Office of the Secretary of Defense

PA — public affairs

PACE — primary, alternate, contingency, and emergency

PAL — **phase alternating line**—A type of video output used OCONUS, established to meet European television standards, in which picture information is delivered. (**NOTE:** NTSC and PAL **are not** compatible or interchangeable.)

PAO — Public Affairs Office

PAW — product/action work sheet

PCC — policy coordination committee

PCI — precombat inspection

PDB — Psychological Operations dissemination battalion

PDC — **Psychological Operations development center**—A regional PSYOP unit that designs informational products and programs and makes recommendations to the JFC through the JTCB for other joint forces to conduct psychological actions in support of military and national objectives. The PDC is the central core of a POTF. The PDC consists of a target audience analysis detachment, a plans and programs detachment, a product development detachment, and a test and evaluation detachment. (FM 100-25)

PDD — Psychological Operations development detachment; Presidential Decision Directive

PDS — Psychological Operations Distribution System

PDSS	predeployment site survey
PDT	Psychological Operations development team
PDW	Product Development Workstation
PDW-L	Product Development Workstation-Light
peacekeeping	Military operations undertaken with the consent of all major parties to a dispute, designed to monitor and facilitate implementation of an agreement (ceasefire, truce, or other such agreement) and support diplomatic efforts to reach a long-term political settlement. (JP 1-02)
peacemaking	The process of diplomacy, mediation, negotiation, or other forms of peaceful settlements that arranges an end to a dispute and resolves issues that led to it. (JP 1-02)
peace operations	A broad term that encompasses peacekeeping operations and peace enforcement operations conducted in support of diplomatic efforts to establish and maintain peace. (JP 1-02)
PERSCOM	personnel command
PFC	private first class
Ph.D.	doctor of philosophy
PIFWC	person(s) indicted for war crimes
PIR	**priority intelligence requirements**—Those intelligence requirements for which a commander has an anticipated and stated priority in the task of planning and decisionmaking. (JP 1-02)
PLA	plain language address
PLL	prescribed load list
PM	provost marshal
PMCS	preventive maintenance checks and services
PO	**Psychological Operations objective**—A statement of a measurable response that reflects the desired attitude or behavior change of a selected foreign target audience as a result of Psychological Operations.
POAS	Psychological Operations automated system
POAT	**Psychological Operations assessment team**—A small, tailored team (approximately four to twelve personnel) that consists of Psychological Operations planners and product distribution/dissemination and logistics specialists. The team is deployed to theater at the request of the combatant commander to assess the situation, develop Psychological Operations objectives, and recommend the appropriate level of support to accomplish the mission.
POB	Psychological Operations battalion

POC	point of contact
POD	port of debarkation
POE	port of embarkation; port of entry
POG(A)	Psychological Operations group (airborne)
POI	program of instruction
POL	petroleum, oils, and lubricants
POLAD	political advisor
POM	preparation for overseas movement
POTF	**Psychological Operations task force**—A task force composed of Psychological Operations units formed to carry out a specific psychological operation or prosecute Psychological Operations in support of a theater campaign or other operations. The Psychological Operations task force may have conventional non-Psychological Operations units assigned or attached to support the conduct of specific missions. The Psychological Operations task force commander is usually a joint task force component commander.
PPD	plans and programs detachment
PPT	plans and programs team
PRB	product review board
PRC	populace and resources control
PRCA	Presidential Reserve Call-Up Authority
PSA	port support activity
PSE	**Psychological Operations support element**—A tailored element that can provide limited Psychological Operations support. Psychological Operations support elements do not contain organic command and control capability; therefore, command relationships must be clearly defined. The size, composition, and capability of the Psychological Operations support element are determined by the requirements of the supported commander. A Psychological Operations support element is not designed to provide full-spectrum Psychological Operations capability; reachback is critical for its mission success.
PSYACT	**Psychological Operations action**—Action or activity planned primarily for its psychological impact.
psychological consolidation activities	Planned psychological activities across the range of military operations directed at the civilian population located in areas under friendly control in order to achieve a desired behavior that supports the military objectives and the operational freedom of the supported commanders.
PSYOP	**Psychological Operations**—Planned operations to convey selected information and indicators to foreign audiences to

influence their emotions, motives, objective reasoning, and ultimately the behavior of foreign governments, organizations, groups, and individuals. The purpose of psychological operations is to induce or reinforce foreign attitudes and behavior favorable to the originator's objectives. (JP 1-02)

PSYOP enabling action Action required of non-Psychological Operations units or non-DOD agencies to facilitate or enable execution of a Psychological Operations plan developed to support a commander, joint task force, a commander-in-chief, or other non-DOD agency.

PSYOP impact indicator An observable event or a discernible subjectively determined behavioral change that represents an effect of a Psychological Operations activity on the intended foreign target audience at a particular point in time. It is measured evidence, ascertained during the analytical phase of the Psychological Operations development process, to evaluate the degree to which the Psychological Operations objective is achieved.

PSYOP plan A series of Psychological Operations programs conducted at the theater level to achieve short- and mid-term objectives in support of a geographic combatant commander's goals.

PSYOP program A sequential, coordinated presentation of a series of actions and/or products to achieve a specific Psychological Operations objective.

1. Action program. A sequential, coordinated presentation of a series of actions to achieve a specific Psychological Operations objective.

2. Product program. A sequential, coordinated presentation of a series of products to achieve a specific Psychological Operations objective.

PTAL potential target audience list

PTS Product Tracking Sheet

pub publication

PW prisoner of war

PWRS pre-positioned war reserve stock

QRF quick-reaction force

R reinforcing

RA regular Army

RAA redeployment assembly area

RC Reserve Component

refugee A civilian who, by reason of real or imagined danger, has left home to seek safety elsewhere. (JP 1-02)

rep representative

RFA	restrictive fire area
RFI	**request for information**—Any specific time-sensitive ad hoc requirement for intelligence information or products to support an ongoing crisis or operation not necessarily related to standing requirements or scheduled intelligence production. (JP 1-02)
RFO	request for orders
RI	routing indicator
RLD	ready-to-load date
ROE	rules of engagement
ROTC	Reserve Officer Training Corps
RP	retained person
RPV	remotely piloted vehicle
RRF	Ready Reserve Force
RSO	regional security office
RWS	remote workstation
S-2	intelligence officer
S-3	operations and training officer
S-4	logistics officer
S-6	signal officer
SAW	squad automatic weapon
SCAME	source, content, audience, media, and effects
SCI	sensitive compartmented information
SCIF	sensitive compartmented information facility
SCW	series concept work sheet
SDW	series dissemination work sheet
SECARMY	Secretary of the Army
SecDef	Secretary of Defense
series	All actions and products developed in support of a single supporting objective and single target audience combination.
Service component command	A command consisting of the Service component commander and all those Service forces, such as individuals, units, detachments, organizations, and installations under that command, including the support forces that have been assigned to a combatant command or further assigned to a subordinate unified command or joint task force. (JP 1-02)
SFC	sergeant first class
SFOB	Special Forces operational base

SFOD	Special Forces operational detachment
SFODA	Special Forces operational detachment A
SFODB	Special Forces operational detachment B
SFOR	Stabilization Force
SGT	sergeant
SINCGARS	single-channel ground and airborne radio system
SIO	senior intelligence officer
SIPRNET	Secret Internet Protocol Router Network
SITREP	situation report
SITTEMP	situation template
SJA	Staff Judge Advocate
SO	special operations
SOC	special operations command
SOF	special operations forces
SOI	signal of interest
SOMS-B	Special Operations Media System-B
SOP	standing operating procedure
SOR	statement of requirement
SORTIEALOT	sortie allotment message
SORTS	Status of Resources and Training System
SOSCOM	Special Operations Support Command
SOTSE	special operations theater support element
SOW	special operations wing
SPA	**special Psychological Operations assessment**—A Psychological Operations intelligence document which focuses on any of a variety of different subjects pertinent to Psychological Operations, such as a particular target group, significant social institution, or media analysis. It can serve as an immediate reference for the planning and conduct of Psychological Operations.
SPC	specialist
SPINS	special instructions
SPO	supporting Psychological Operations objective
SPOD	seaport of debarkation
SPOE	seaport of embarkation
SPS	special Psychological Operations study

sq	square
SRP	Soldier Readiness Processing
SSD	strategic studies detachment
SSG	staff sergeant
STAMMIS	standard Army multicommand management information system
STANAG	standardization agreement
STCCS	Strategic Theater Command and Control System
STO	special technical operations
STU-III	secure telephone unit III
supported commander	The commander having primary responsibility for all aspects of a task assigned by the Joint Strategic Capabilities Plan or other joint operation planning authority. In the context of joint operation planning, this term refers to the commander who prepares operation plans or operation orders in response to requirements of the Chairman of the Joint Chiefs of Staff. (JP 1-02)
supporting commander	A commander who provides augmentation forces or other support to a supported commander or who develops a supporting plan. Includes the designated combatant commands and Defense agencies as appropriate. (JP 1-02)
supporting PSYOP program	All actions and products developed in support of a single program supporting objective.
SW	short wave
SWO	staff weather officer
symbol	A visual, audio, or audiovisual means, having cultural or contextual significance to the target audience, used to convey a line of persuasion.
TA	target audience
TAA	target audience analysis
TAACOM	Theater Army Area Command
TAAD	target audience analysis detachment
TAAP	target audience analysis process
TAAT	target audience analysis team
TAAW	target audience analysis work sheet
TACC	theater Army component command
TACON	**tactical control**—Command authority over assigned or attached forces or commands, or military capability or forces made available for tasking, that is limited to the detailed, and usually, local direction and control of movements or maneuvers necessary

to accomplish missions or tasks assigned. Tactical control is inherent in operational control. Tactical control may be delegated to, and exercised at any level at or below the level of combatant command. (JP 1-02)

TACP   tactical air control party

TACSAT   tactical satellite

TALO   theater airlift liaison officer

TAMCA   theater Army movement control agency

TBMCS   theater battle management core system

TC   track commander

TC-ACCIS   Transportation Coordinator's Automated Command and Control Information System

TCP/IP   transmission control protocol/Internet protocol

TED   testing and evaluation detachment

terrorism   The calculated use of unlawful violence or threat of unlawful violence to inculcate fear; intended to coerce or to intimidate governments or societies in the pursuit of goals that are generally political, religious, or ideological. (JP 1-02)

theme   An overarching subject, topic, or idea. (FM 3-05.30)

threat   The ability of an enemy to limit, neutralize, or destroy the effectiveness of a current or projected mission organization or item of equipment. (TRADOC Regulation 381-1)

TI   Tactical Internet

TL   team leader

TM   technical manual

TMPC   Theater Media Production Center

TOC   tactical operations center

TPB   **tactical Psychological Operations battalion**—Psychological Operations unit that normally provides tactical- and operational-level Psychological Operations support to an Army corps, a Marine expeditionary unit, or a Navy fleet, although it could also provide support at an Army or equivalent headquarters.

TPC   **tactical Psychological Operations company**—Psychological Operations unit that normally provides tactical-level Psychological Operations support to a division- or equivalent-sized element.

TPD   tactical Psychological Operations detachment

TPDD   tactical Psychological Operations development detachment

TPFDD   time-phased force and deployment data

TPT	**tactical Psychological Operations team**—Psychological Operations unit that normally provides tactical-level Psychological Operations support to a brigade- or equivalent-sized element to include a marine expeditionary unit, a Special Forces group, an armored cavalry regiment, a separate infantry regiment, or a brigade.
TRADOC	United States Army Training and Doctrine Command
TSCP	theater security cooperation plan
TSS	target selection standards
TV	television
UAR	unconventional assisted recovery
UAV	unmanned aerial vehicle
UAV-P	unmanned aerial vehicle-payloads
UCC	unified combatant command
UCMJ	Uniform Code of Military Justice
UCP	**Unified Command Plan**—The document, approved by the President, that sets forth basic guidance to all unified combatant commanders; establishes their missions, responsibilities, and force structure; delineates the general geographical area of responsibility for geographic combatant commanders; and specifies functional responsibilities for functional combatant commanders. (JP 1-02)
ULN	unit line number
UMD	unit movement data
UN	United Nations
UNHCR	United Nations High Commissioner for Refugees
unified command	A command with a broad continuing mission under a single commander and composed of significant assigned components of two or more military departments, that is established and so designated by the President through the Secretary of Defense with the advice and assistance of the Chairman of the Joint Chiefs of Staff. (JP 1-02)
U.S.	United States
USA	United States Army
USACAPOC	United States Army Civil Affairs and Psychological Operations Command
USAF	United States Air Force
USAID	United States Agency for International Development
USAJFKSWCS	United States Army John F. Kennedy Special Warfare Center and School

USAR	United States Army Reserve
USARC	United States Army Reserve Command
USASOC	United States Army Special Operations Command
USD(P)	Under Secretary of Defense for Policy
USG	United States Government
USIA	United States Information Agency
USIS	United States Information Service
USMC	United States Marine Corps
USN	United States Navy
USSOCOM	United States Special Operations Command
USSPACECOM	United States Space Command
USSTRATCOM	United States Strategic Command
USTRANSCOM	United States Transportation Command
UTM	universal transverse mercator
UW	**unconventional warfare**—A broad spectrum of military and paramilitary operations, normally of long duration, predominantly conducted by indigenous or surrogate forces who are organized, trained, equipped, supported, and directed in varying degrees by an external source. It includes guerrilla warfare and other direct offensive, low visibility, covert, or clandestine operations, as well as the indirect activities of subversion, sabotage, intelligence activities, and evasion and escape. (JP 3-05.5)
UXO	unexploded ordnance
VCD	video compact disc
VCR	videocassette recorder
VHS	**video home system**—Trade name for a commercial videotape format using half-inch-wide videotape housed in a cassette, normally used for distribution.
VTR	videotape recording
WARNORD	warning order
WIA	wounded in action
WIN	Warfighter Information Network
WIN-T	Warfighter Information Network-Tactical
WMD	weapons of mass destruction
WWMCS	Worldwide Military Command and Control System
XO	executive officer

Bibliography

AR 190-8. *Enemy Prisoners of War, Retained Personnel, Civilian Internees and Other Detainees*. 1 October 1997.

Axtell, Roger E. *Do's and Taboos Around the World*. Parker Pen Company, February 1993.

CJCS Instruction 3110.05C, *Joint Psychological Operations Supplement to the Joint Strategic Capabilities Plan FY 2002 (CJCSI 3110.01 Series)*. 18 July 2003.

CJCS Instruction 3210.01A. *(S) Joint Information Operations Policy (U)*. 6 November 1998.

CJCS Manual 3122.03A. *Joint Operation Planning and Execution System, Volume II: Planning Formats and Guidance*. 31 December 1999, with Change 1, 6 September 2000.

DOD Directive 5111.10. *Assistant Secretary of Defense for Special Operations and Low-Intensity Conflict (ASD[SO/LIC])*. 22 March 1995.

DOD Directive S-3600.1. *(S) Information Operations (IO) (U)*. 9 December 1996.

DOD Instruction S-3321-1. *(S) Overt Psychological Operations Conducted by the Military Services in Peacetime and in Contingencies Short of Declared War (U)*. 26 July 1984.

FM 3-0. *Operations*. 14 June 2001.

FM 3-05.20. *Special Forces Operations*. 26 June 2001.

FM 3-05.30. *Psychological Operations*. 19 June 2000.

FM 3-05.102. *Army Special Operations Forces Intelligence*. 31 August 2001.

FM 3-05.201. *Special Forces Unconventional Warfare Operations*. 30 April 2003.

FM 3-07. *Stability Operations and Support Operations*. 20 February 2003.

FM 3-13. *Information Operations: Doctrine, Tactics, Techniques, and Procedures*. 28 November 2003.

FM 3-19.40. *Military Police Internment/Resettlement Operations*. 1 August 2001.

FM 3-25.26. *Map Reading and Land Navigation*. 20 July 2001.

FM 6-0. *Mission Command: Command and Control of Army Forces*. 11 August 2003.

FM 27-10. *The Law of Land Warfare*. 18 July 1956, with Change 1, 15 July 1976.

FM 34-1. *Intelligence and Electronic Warfare Operations*. 27 September 1994.

FM 34-81/AFM 105-4. *Weather Support for Army Tactical Operations*. 31 August 1989.

FM 34-130. *Intelligence Preparation of the Battlefield*. 8 July 1994.

FM 41-10. *Civil Affairs Operations*. 14 February 2000.

FM 100-7. *Decisive Force: The Army in Theater Operations.* 31 May 1995.

FM 100-8. *The Army in Multinational Operations.* 24 November 1997.

FM 100-25. *Doctrine for Army Special Operations Forces.* 1 August 1999.

FM 101-5. *Staff Organization and Operations.* 31 May 1997.

FORSCOM Regulation 55-1. *Unit Movement Planning.* 1 March 2000.

JFSC Pub 1. *The Joint Staff Officer's Guide 2000.*

JP 0-2. *Unified Action Armed Forces (UNAAF).* 10 July 2001.

JP 1-02. *Department of Defense Dictionary of Military and Associated Terms.* 12 April 2001.

JP 2-0. *Doctrine for Intelligence Support to Joint Operations.* 9 March 2000.

JP 3-0. *Doctrine for Joint Operations.* 10 September 2001.

JP 3-05. *Doctrine for Joint Special Operations.* 17 April 1998.

JP 3-05.1. *Joint Tactics, Techniques, and Procedures for Joint Special Operations Task Force Operations.* 19 December 2001.

JP 3-05.2. *Joint Tactics, Techniques, and Procedures for Special Operations Targeting and Mission Planning.* 21 May 2003.

JP 3-07. *Joint Doctrine for Military Operations Other Than War.* 16 June 1995.

JP 3-07.4. *Joint Counterdrug Operations.* 17 February 1998.

JP 3-08. *Interagency Coordination During Joint Operations, Volumes I and II.* 9 October 1996.

JP 3-13. *Joint Doctrine for Information Operations.* 9 October 1998.

JP 3-53. *Doctrine for Joint Psychological Operations.* 5 September 2003.

JP 3-57. *Joint Doctrine for Civil-Military Operations.* 8 February 2001.

JP 3-58. *Joint Doctrine for Military Deception.* 31 May 1996.

JP 5-0. *Doctrine for Planning Joint Operations.* 13 April 1995.

JP 5-00.1. *Joint Doctrine for Campaign Planning.* 25 January 2002.

JP 5-00.2. *Joint Task Force Planning Guidance and Procedures.* 13 January 1999.

NSDD 130. *U.S. International Information Policy.* 6 March 1984.

PDD 14. *Counternarcotics.* 2 November 1993.

PDD 44. *Heroin Control Policy.* November 1995.

PDD 56. *Managing Complex Contingency Operations.* May 1997.

PDD 68. *U.S. International Public Information (IPI).* 30 April 1999.

USAJFKSWCS Pub 525-5-14. *Unconventional Assisted Recovery*. January 1999.

USAJFKSWCS Pub 525-5-15. *Psychological Operations: Capabilities and Employment.* January 1999.

USAJFKSWCS Pub 525-5-16. *Psychological Operations: Equipment Types, Specifications, and Capabilities*. May 2001.

Index

★ WE STRIVE ★

...*To bring you*
THE BEST
HOW-TO BOOKS
★ IN THE WORLD ★

Printed in the USA
CPSIA information can be obtained
at www.ICGtesting.com
LVHW081650131123
763835LV00045B/611